OKANAGAN COLLEGE LIBRARY

03684511

D1738354

Ireland

OKANAGAN COLLEGE
LIBRARY
BRITISH COLUMBIA

Ireland

Contested Ideas of Nationalism and History

Hugh F. Kearney

New York University Press

NEW YORK AND LONDON

NEW YORK UNIVERSITY PRESS
New York and London
www.nyupress.org

© 2007 by New York University
All rights reserved

Library of Congress Cataloging-in-Publication Data

Kearney, Hugh F.
Ireland : contested ideas of nationalism and history / Hugh F. Kearney.
p. cm.
Includes bibliographical references and index.
ISBN-13: 978-0-8147-4800-8 (alk. paper)
ISBN-10: 0-8147-4800-7 (alk. paper)
1. Nationalism—Ireland.   2. Nationalism—Ireland—History.
3. Ireland—History.   I. Title.
DA913.K43   2007
320.5409415—dc22   2006047034

New York University Press books are printed on acid-free paper,
and their binding materials are chosen for strength and durability.

Manufactured in the United States of America

10 9 8 7 6 5 4 3 2 1

For Kate as a Golden Wedding present

Contents

Acknowledgments

I wish to thank Joe Lee for his encouragement and advice in connection with this volume. I also wish to thank Dr. Proinsias O Drisceoill for inviting me to speak at Kilkenny under the auspices of the Arts Education Programme of the County Kilkenny Vocational Educational Committee. I also am grateful to Edna Longley for inviting me to the John Hewitt Summer School and Patrick Crotty for an invitation to the Merriman Summer School, both most pleasant occasions. I also owe a debt to the organizers of conferences at Wicklow, Sussex, York, and Oxford at which I spoke. I wish also to thank my colleagues Evelyn Rawski and Irina Liveseanu, who shared the seminar on "Comparative Nationalism" at the University of Pittsburgh.

Permission to reproduce copyrighted material is acknowledged from:

Cultures of Ireland for "Language and Politics: Teanga agus Polaitiocht," *Language and Politics* (Dublin 2001): 7–1.

Studies: An Irish Quarterly Review for "The Great Famine: Legend and Reality," *Studies* (Summer 1957): 184–92.

Oxford University Press for "The Irish and Their History," *History Workshop* 31 (1991): 149–55.

University of Notre Dame Press for "1875: Faith or Fatherland: The Contested Symbolism of Irish Nationalism," Stewart J. Brown and David W. Miller, eds., *Piety and Power in Ireland, 1760–1960: Essays in Honour of Emmet Larkin* (Notre Dame, Indiana: University of Notre Dame Press, 2000): 65–80.

———. "Faith and Fatherland Revisited," *Bullán: An Irish Studies Journal* 4 (Winter 1999/Spring 2000): 145–57.

Cambridge University Press for "Ecclesiastical Politics and the Counter-Reformation in Ireland, 1618–1648," *Journal of Ecclesiastical History* 11 (October 1960): 202–12.

Blackwell Publishing Ltd. for "Four Nations or One?" Bernard Crick, ed., *National Identities: The Constitution of the United Kingdom* (Oxford: Blackwell Publishers, 1991): 1–6.

. "The Importance of Being British," *The Political Quarterly* 71 (January March 2000): 15–25.

————. "The Political Background to English Mercantilism," *Economic History Review*, second series 11 (1959): 484–96.

Palgrave Macmillan for "Four Nations History in Perspective," Helen Brocklehurst and Robert Phillips, eds., *History, Nationhood and the Question of Britain* (Basingstoke and New York: Palgrave Macmillan, 2004): 10–19.

Cork University Press for "Contested Ideas of Nationhood, 1800–1995," *The Irish Review* 20 (Winter/Spring 1997): 1–22.

————. "Visions and Revisions: Views of Irish History," *The Irish Review* 27 (Summer 2001): 113–20.

————. "Canny sets the Agenda," *The Irish Review* 29 (Autumn 2002): 105–13.

I am particularly grateful to John Fuller for permission to quote from his father Roy Fuller's poem in memory of the historian W. H. Chaloner.

I am also conscious of the fact that in reprinting papers and lectures written over many years it is impossible to avoid some measure of repetition. For this I must apologise to my readers.

Preface

On Being a Historian in Four Countries

In 1942 I had the good fortune to win a state scholarship worth £250 a year. It also covered university fees. Without the state scholarship I might have gone to Liverpool University; with it I was able to apply for admission to Cambridge University. Cambridge, like Oxford, was a collegiate university and in becoming an undergraduate I also had to choose a college. Quite by chance I became a member of Peterhouse, mainly because my history teacher Frank Grace had been a research student there in the 1920s. Peterhouse was also well known as the college of Herbert Butterfield, a former grammar schoolboy, whose book *The Whig Interpretation of History* (1931) challenged the assumptions of the orthodox nationalist interpretation of English history. I had come across it at my own grammar school. Peterhouse had earned a reputation as a college in which history had been taken seriously since the days of Adolphus Ward, master of the College from 1900 to 1924. One of the editors of the *Cambridge Modern History*, Harold Temperley, a leading diplomatic historian, had been a fellow. It was thus not surprising that it should be my choice of college.

History teaching at Cambridge revolved around lectures organized on a university basis and tutorials centered on the college. We attended most lectures out of a sense of duty but there are some which I still recall with pleasure, in particular those by Michael Oakeshott on political thought and by Michael Postan on economic history. Helen Cam's course of lectures on medieval constitutional history was also an impressive performance. She was a great admirer of Stubbs but she also introduced us to the works of Maitland and we were made very much aware that there was a good deal of debate about such issues as the Magna Carta and the role of parliament. We also read Stubbs's *Charters* as well as parts of his *History*.

Oakeshott's lectures were intellectually exciting but it was in Postan's lectures that we were made aware of what today we would call history

1

from the "bottom up," contrasting with the "top down" approach of most other lecturers. In his lectures on medieval economic history Postan emphasized the importance of such factors as population growth, price movements, and labor supply. It was in his lectures that I first heard Marc Bloch's *Feudal Society* mentioned and George Homan's *Villagers of the Thirteenth Century*, both of which I came to appreciate only after I had left Cambridge. Postan's approach derived from his European background, his training as an economist, and his work as a graduate student at the London School of Economics where history was studied in the context of social science. Here he had been a junior colleague of R. H. Tawney and of Eileen Power (who became his wife). Curiously enough the London School of Economics was billeted at Peterhouse during the war but there was little contact between the two institutions. I did, however, hear a talk given by Tawney at Peterhouse after he had been made an honorary fellow of the College.

I also recall lectures given by J. H. Parry, later a professor at Harvard as part of a course on the Expansion of Europe. Parry was fascinated by such details as the "lateen" rig used by Muslim traders in the Indian Empire and the "fore and aft" rig of European vessels. He was also, more importantly, the author of *The Spanish Theory of Empire* and it was through this that I was introduced to the ideas of Las Casas, Victoria, and Sepulveda and the assumptions which lay behind Castilian imperialism. In contrast, other lectures on European history by Butterfield, Sir George Clark, the Regius Professor, and others seemed more commonplace. (It was said of Clark that he reduced the Scientific Revolution to the influence of a watchmaker in Leyden.) Needless to say it was assumed that English history was in no sense "European." England had taken its own "sonderweg."

It was possible to attend lectures in other disciplines and I took advantage of the opportunity to hear F. R. Leavis lecturing on poetry and on the novel. What I remember about the poetry lectures was his handing out sheets on which poems were printed without being attributed to an author. He then invited our comments about which we thought superior in terms of originality or use of language. This was my first contact with Cambridge "Practical Criticism" and it made a lasting impression. Leavis was an unpopular figure in some Cambridge academic circles but he took his role as a social and literary critic seriously and saw himself, along with his wife, as the spokesman of the true Cambridge tradition stretching back to Henry Sidgwick in the late nineteenth century. It was only later, after I had left Cambridge, that I had the chance to read Leavis's journal *Scrutiny* at my leisure.

Lectures by and large were very much a passive form of education. It was in the collegiate supervisions based upon the presentation of a weekly essay that the student took on a more active role. My own supervisors were Brian Wormald, David Knowles, and Leonard Henry, a former housemaster at Harrow. Wormald, the college chaplain, was a somewhat withdrawn figure but it was thanks to him that I was encouraged to read articles in learned journals, such as those by Kosminsky in the *Economic History Review* and Postan himself in the *Transactions of the Royal Historical Society*. The tutorial essay gave me the opportunity to read current views on a particular topic and then to consider "revisionist" alternatives. Under Wormald's guidance I read R. H. Tawney's *The Agrarian Problem of the Sixteenth Century* and the works of George Unwin and Eileen Power. When I asked for a general reading list he recommended the works of A. D. Lindsay on modern democracy, G. H. Gooch on Nineteenth-century historians, Jacques Maritain's *True Humanism*, and R. H. Tawney's *Equality*—reflecting his own wide range of interests. He also brought Etienne Gilson's book *The Unity of Philosophical Experience* to my attention. The tutorial system thus made it possible for students to discuss their work and wider matters with an established scholar.

My supervisor during my second year was Dom David Knowles, a former Benedictine monk and a very distinguished historian, whose book *The Monastic Order in England* was an outstanding contribution to medieval history. However, such scholars do not always make good teachers and my memory of Knowles is that he was more interested in his own work than in discussing my weekly essays. He had originally read classics and was not as familiar with the requirements of the History Tripos as Wormald had been. I do not recall him recommending specific articles in the historical journals, as Wormald had done.

During my third year I was supervised by a former history teacher at Harrow School, L. W. Henry, one of a number of additional supervisors recruited by the college to cope with the flood of ex-servicemen returning after 1945. Henry, a man in his sixties, was the most successful of my supervisors largely because of the fact that he showed great, (or apparently great) interest in my essays, taking notes as I read and raising points of criticism later. He also insisted that I read chapters from books in French, including as I recall Henri Hauser's *La Preponderance Espagnol*. Under Henry's guidance, I also read *The Netherlands Divided* by the Dutch historian Peter Geyl, and works on the French wars of religion, the Counter-reformation, and the controversies between the Jesuits and the Jansenists. I also recall reading Paul Hazard's study of the early enlightenment, *La Crise de la Conscience Européenne*. It is thanks to Henry that I realized what a tutorial system can offer a committed student. In my later experience, however, seminars can work just as well and are of course much less costly in terms of manpower.

It remains to mention the Special Subject which was a key feature of the Historical Tripos. Third-year students were asked to choose a small number of topics which were offered by university lecturers. The key feature of such "special subjects" was the requirement that one read the "sources" and discuss them in one or two examination papers. In my third year the special subjects included a Tudor topic presented by Norman Sykes, professor of ecclesiastical history, and an eighteenth-century topic offered by Jack Plumb. My own choice was "St. Francis and the Franciscan Order," which was given by David Knowles. This proved to be a most rewarding experience. The problems raised by the sources for the life of St. Francis paralleled those for the life of Christ and other religious figures in that the historian faced the challenge of recovering the original vision of Francis from material written at a later period.

The history of the Franciscan Order also showed how the founder's idealism gave way to bureaucratic organization during a second generation. Knowles showed how architecture reflected these changes, for example, in the way in which Francis's little chapel, the Portiuncula, was incorporated within the vast church of St. Maria del Angeli in Assisi. The grandiose building program of Brother Elias reflected in the Upper Church of Assisi illustrated a similar transition. Finally, there was the tension within the order between those who wished to recover the vision of the founder and those who sought accommodation with the world at large. Thus a key issue for Franciscans was their attitude to money. Francis himself refused to handle money but a later generation came to believe that it was lawful to have financial dealings through an "interposed person" (*per interpositam personam*). Still later, the order was bitterly divided over the millenarian ideas of Joachim of Flore. Knowles's treatment of these topics was masterly in the way he brought out the lessons of more general history from the particularities of the Franciscan experience. I was also lucky enough later to receive a travel grant from the college to visit the sites about which we had read in the course.

Undergraduates at Cambridge were fortunate individuals. Most colleges were wealthy institutions and as a scholar of the college (from December 1942) I lived for two years in a comfortable set of rooms which were kept clean by a college servant (my "gyp") and a female "bedmaker." All meals were provided in the medieval college hall. Like other colleges, Peterhouse had its own library from which books could be borrowed and which in my recollection was open day and night. In addition there was a University History Library (the Seeley) and the University Library. There was thus every encouragement for bookish individuals such as myself to make good use of their time.

A student who had the advantage of using such facilities and the chance of hearing such lecturers as Oakeshott, Postan, Knowles, and Butterfield had little reason to complain. Looking back, however, I have often been struck by the limitations of some of the intellectual fare which we were offered. The Cambridge emphasis upon English constitutional history rested upon an evolutionary model which played down the role of conflict in history. It was also very much concerned with administrative institutions such as "the medieval sheriff." From this approach specific individuals and local politics were missing. The approach was very much "top down." It also failed to consider the role of class or the history of women. Above all, the uniqueness of English historical experience was emphasized, with the consequence that students were not encouraged to make comparisons. Ireland, Scotland, and Wales were almost totally ignored. Differences between various parts of England were also lost sight of. In a word, the Whig Interpretation of History which Butterfield had criticized in 1931 was still very much alive. Indeed Butterfield himself in his wartime book *The Englishman and His History* (1944) had shown sympathy with Whig views.

Though I did not realize it in the 1940s, the History Tripos still bore the imprint of the founding fathers. History at Cambridge was a relatively new subject. The Historical Tripos was set up as recently as 1873 partly in response to the challenge posed by Oxford where the School of Modern History was already attracting about two hundred undergraduates a year. But what was the attraction of history? Part of the answer lay in the possibilities which it opened up for success in examinations for the Home and Indian Civil Service, as well as entry into other professions such as law or the established church. History soon came to rival Classics in popularity, although in the early years it was regarded as something of a soft option.

Sir John Seeley, who was Regius Professor when the Tripos was set up, looked upon history as a "school of statesmanship," which should be linked with such disciplines as political philosophy, jurisprudence, and political economy. For him, as for Freeman, his Oxford counterpart, "History was past politics and politics past history." The aim of history, in Seeley's view, was to educate the political elite of the nation, an idea which had its origins in the belief of Samuel Taylor Coleridge and Thomas Arnold, that the destinies of the nation should be in the hands of a highly educated "clerisy."

But what was the nation? In a series of lectures published as a book, *The Expansion of England* (1884), Seeley expounded his view that the English nation was a "greater" England which included its English-speaking colonial possessions overseas. Seeley also regarded as English the Irish, the Scots, and the Welsh on the grounds that they shared the same language and religion (or so he thought). It was not surprising that Seeley should have opposed Irish Home Rule. In due course he became a leading figure within the circles of liberal imperialism. His statesmanship, far from being detached, was anti-Gladstone and anti-Parnell. Seeley's concerns were very much with the relevance of history to the present day and for this reason he wished to maintain a place for political economy and international law in the History Tripos.

The Expansion of England may well have been published in response to those historians, led by George Prothero, who were pressing the case for English constitutional history in the Tripos. It was this group which first modified and then undermined the Seeley approach. Seeley himself thought that "history has to do with the State" and he criticized those historians who made "too much of mere parliamentary wrangle and the agitation about liberty" during the seventeenth and eighteenth centuries. Within the internal politics of the History Tripos, however, Seeley was defeated and victory went to those who wished to give English constitutional history a more prominent place. This created what J. B. Bury, the then Regius Professor, described in 1908 as "a very unfortunate boom" in English history, giving "a certain note of insularity to the Tripos which was much to be deplored." For their part the constitutionalists argued that "the subject was extremely valuable from the educational point of view because it represented a long historical evolution on the one hand and yet on the other was based upon charters and original documents so that students acquired some knowledge of the ways in which history was made."

In taking this line the constitutionalists turned their backs upon the influence of a colleague who was generally recognized as a historian of genius —Frederick William Maitland. Maitland's vision was, in his own words, "to produce, after due consideration of the undigested and scattered materials, a scientific and philosophical history of English law from the earliest times in all its bearings upon the economic, political, constitutional, social and religious life of the English people." He included women's history within the scope of history. He was also well aware of the need to compare English developments with those in Western Europe. In 1897 when the Tripos was reformed Maitland thought the program was "much too miscellaneous." Later generations of Cambridge historians always referred to Maitland with reverence as their founding father, but in fact it was the influence of Prothero and his associate J. R. Tanner which counted in the long run.

Looking back I would now argue that the Seeley and Prothero schools of thought each offered nationalist interpretations of English history, although they had differing views as to what constituted the English nation. Seeley's brand of imperialism has now passed into history, although his *Expansion of England* is a remarkable piece of work, still worth reading. For all his insistence on the need to analyze the contemporary political scene, however, he failed to appreciate the power of Irish nationalism and its impact upon the empire. In contrast, Prothero's equally nationalist emphasis upon uniqueness of English constitutional development proved to be longer lasting, at least in the Cambridge context.

Needless to say, undergraduates like myself were quite unaware of the prehistory of the History Tripos. Our historical awareness might have been alerted by being informed that the first chapter of Stubbs's *Constitutional History* was no longer required reading. This was the chapter in which Stubbs traced the origins of English freedom to its origins in the German forests. We might have been asked to consider why a key assumption of Stubbs had been quietly jettisoned. However, we were merely grateful for the fact that our reading load had been reduced.

In his autobiography *Interesting Times* (2002), Eric Hobsbawn dismissed the Cambridge of his undergraduate years as "a finishing school." I think this is too harsh a judgment. There is no doubt that history teaching at Cambridge as well as at Oxford was seen as a modern equivalent of the classical Greats in the sense of providing an appropriate higher education for products of those public schools who in due course would form part of an English ruling elite.[1] Those who reacted against it, apart from Eric Hobsbawm, included Victor Kiernan, author of *The Lords of Human Kind*, and Edward Thompson the brilliant historian of the English working class, both of them Cambridge graduates in the thirties.

In the contest between two nationalist versions of English history, victory by and large went to Prothero. In the 1940s the only relic of Seeley's influence was a compulsory course on the history of political thought in

Part I of the Tripos and an optional course on "the Modern State" in Part II. In contrast, the Prothero school's emphasis on the use of documents was still strongly represented in the prominent place accorded to constitutional history in Part I and the Special Subject with its two papers in Part II. The place of constitutional history was to be reinforced when Geoffrey Elton arrived in Cambridge in the 1960s.

During my last year at Cambridge I was lucky enough to be awarded a French government scholarship to study medieval thought in Paris, sitting, I ventured to hope, at the feet of the well-known historian of ideas Etienne Gilson. I considered myself a medievalist and even had a topic related to the twelfth-century Renaissance. But job opportunities were few and far between. Knowles backed me for a research assistantship to Fritz Saxl of the Warburg Institute in London but Saxl died suddenly and I decided instead to apply for the post of assistant secretary at Manchester University Press. Like many other arts students, I had always thought of publishing as a possible career and had spent some weeks at Cambridge University Press during a summer vacation. When the job was offered to me I accepted it with alacrity. It was this which brought me to Manchester in August 1948.

Manchester University was a very different institution from Cambridge. Cambridge was a national university. Manchester prided itself on its local roots. Cambridge still had strong links with the established church. Dissenters, and other outsiders such as Jews and Catholics, were few and far between on its teaching body. It also drew heavily upon the foremost public (sc. private) schools for its undergraduates. Manchester had been founded in 1850 as Owens College, an institution like University College, London, open to all irrespective of belief, and its students by and large came from local grammar schools. Cambridge was situated in what was then a small market town whereas Manchester was a city which prided itself for its role in the Industrial Revolution. Manchester had given its name to the "Manchester School" of Free Trade, and it could boast a world famous newspaper, *The Manchester Guardian*, and a renowned orchestra, the Hallé, conducted by Sir John Barbarolli. Manchester was thus "no mean city" and its university and university press reflected this confidence, despite the depressing industrial surroundings.

The School of History at Manchester saw itself as fully the equal of Oxford or Cambridge. Adolphus Ward, who was familiar with modern German scholarship, had been professor there before coming to Peterhouse. In the person of Maurice Powicke Manchester had provided Oxford with its Regius Professor, and in L. B. Namier it boasted a leading historian whom many expected in due course to become Regius Professor. Since the days of T. F. Tout, a student of Stubbs and professor at Manchester from 1890 to 1925, the medievalists had close links with Oxford. Ernest Jacob was now Chichele Professor there, and C. R. Cheney, professor of medieval history at Manchester, had been a fellow of Magdalen College, Oxford. A. J. P. Taylor, then at Oxford, had been a lecturer at Manchester. Manchester historians regarded themselves as educating their students on more professional lines than was the case at Oxford or Cambridge, requiring honors students in history to write dissertations. An M.A. degree at Oxford and Cambridge could be bought for a fee three years after graduation as a B.A, whereas the M.A. at Manchester required a dissertation.

Namier's influence in the History Department was striking. He had been professor there since 1931 and the younger historians in the department followed his lead in their "Namierite" approach to the history of parliament. John Roskell specialized in the membership of the later medieval parliament and Eric Robson in the role of parliament during the American Revolution. Donald Pennington wrote a Namierite study of the Long Parliament. Namier himself rejected "ideas" in history and regarded Edmund Burke as little more than a "gentleman's gentleman" in the service of the Rockingham Whigs. This anti-ideas prejudice led to departmental antagonism toward Butterfield. When Butterfield published his *George III, Lord North and the People* in 1950, Namier encouraged his junior colleague Eric Robson to write a highly critical review, unsigned, in the *Times Literary Supplement.*

As well as enjoying a reputation for a "Namierite" approach to history and for excellence in medieval studies, the Manchester History Department had also made its mark in economic history. In particular it had pioneered the study of the Industrial Revolution, thanks especially to the work of T. S. Ashton. It could also claim as a founding father the historian George Unwin, whose work on the economic and social history of the later Middle Ages was recognized as being highly innovative. Mark Hovell, author of a classic study of the Chartist movement, had also been at Manchester. The History Department had also developed an interest in the local history of the Industrial Revolution and in later years one of its members, W. H. Chaloner, wrote a serious history of "fish and chips," surely a symbol of history "from the bottom up." Roy Fuller commemorated this in a poem

I.m. W.H. Chaloner ob.25.v.1987

Professor Chaloner linked the history
Of fish and chips to the cotton industry
My native town of Oldham especially.

This in the legendary final section
Of the work entitled *Trends in Fish Consumption*
Reached by students with sudden stupefaction.

Moreover, lived and died in that damp place,
Among green moors and roseate factories;
By then the deafening spindles more or less

Mere things historical, even (perhaps
According to his thesis) fish and chips,
Among vile dens of hamburgers and kebabs.

The Spectator, 25 June 1988

I was not a history student at Manchester, nor was I a member of the History Department. But in my role at the University Press I soon came to know most members of the History Department, although I only knew Namier by sight. As a result of these contacts I was asked to give a series of extramural classes on the Industrial Revolution, since the nominal tutor of the course was unwilling to venture "outside his period." The Industrial Revolution was outside my period too but I was anxious to gain experience in university teaching and as a consequence found myself giving a small class at Weaverham, thirty miles from Manchester (a journey which involved catching a train home at midnight after waiting in a signalman's cabin). At this time, I also wrote a review article discussing Herbert Butterfield's *Christianity and History* (1950) which was published in *The Downside Review*. I sent him a copy of it partly to remind him of my existence. It may have been my casting my bread upon the waters in this manner which led to a surprise invitation to enter for a post at University College, Dublin.

While at Peterhouse I had got to know a research student named Desmond Williams who was reputed to know everybody and everything. His presence there was due to Herbert Butterfield who had been external examiner to the National University of Ireland, where he had met Williams and recognized his remarkable intellectual powers. As a consequence,

Williams came over to Peterhouse as his research student in 1946 and eventually in 1949, with Butterfield's backing, he was appointed, at the age of twenty-eight, to the newly vacant professorship of modern history at University College, Dublin. Williams had the support of Michael Tierney, the president of U.C.D., and with this behind him was in a position to expand the History Department by appointing assistant lecturers. The key proviso was that they should be Catholic, even though U.C.D. was in principle a secular institution. It was as a result of these informal comings and goings that I was asked to go for an interview in Dublin.

In September 1950 I became a member of the academic staff as an "assistant" in the History Department. I was without tenure and on a yearly contract but my superiors assured me that nobody was ever dismissed (this turned out to be not quite true, as John Whyte, an assistant in the Politics Department later found out to his cost). The institution I was joining was in many ways the equivalent of the University of Manchester in the sense that both were founded to cater for the needs of a group hitherto lacking full access to higher education. Manchester traced its origins back to Owens College in 1850. U.C.D. looked back to the Catholic University founded in the same year by John Henry Newman with the backing of the Catholic episcopate. At the time of their foundation both colleges were marginalized and impoverished institutions serving in the shadow of richer, well-established competitors—Oxford and Cambridge in the case of Manchester and Trinity College, Dublin in the case of U.C.D.

During the nineteenth century Trinity College had been very much an organ of the Anglo-Irish Ascendancy. Catholics (and Presbyterians) could attend the college but the dominant ethos of the fellows remained Anglican and Unionist. By 1950, however, times had changed. The Irish Revolution of 1916–21 led to the overthrow of the Ascendancy and Trinity became the institution of an embattled minority. It was now the National University, of which U.C.D. was much the largest college, which spoke for the newly dominant Catholic majority. Paradoxically, the National University was a secular institution, its eventual foundation in 1908 having come about as a result of tortuous political negotiations between the Liberal government and the Catholic hierarchy. The hierarchy still met once a year to maintain the formal existence of Newman's university. But in practice the only Catholic institution of university standing, in a formal sense, was St. Patrick's College at Maynooth.

University College, Dublin was the most influential academic institution within the new Irish State. Perhaps inevitably, it was also a heavily politicized institution. It was in fact a stronghold of the Fine Gael party, which looked back for its origins to those who had accepted the Anglo-Irish Treaty of 1921. The president of the college, Michael Tierney, a Fine Gael stalwart, had been a member of the (quasi-fascist) Blue Shirt movement in the 1930s. Two former historians within the college, Eoin Mac-Neill and John Marcus O'Sullivan, were also strongly Fine Gael (Tierney was in fact MacNeill's son-in-law). The bitter divisions of the Irish Civil War left their mark upon the college. So also did the political history of the 1930s, when Fine Gael which had been in power during the 1920s was defeated at the polls by De Valera's Fianna Fail party in 1932. In 1950 the college was in large measure an academic outpost of Fine Gael. Of the two parties Fianna Fail was supposedly more independent of the church, but a Dublin wit commented that whereas Fianna Fail genuflected in the presence of a Catholic bishop, Fine Gael prostrated themselves.

This complex situation in Ireland was made even more complicated by the fact that from 1920 to 1922 Ireland was partitioned between a twenty-six-county Irish Free State (from 1949 termed "the Republic of Ireland") and a six-county unit of "Northern Ireland" which remained part of the United Kingdom. The practical effect of Partition in the south was to make the new state 90 percent Catholic. In the north the protestant majority saw itself as a besieged group within a largely Catholic island and as a consequence Queen's University, Belfast, in theory secular, remained strongly Protestant and unionist in outlook.

Needless to say all this was as yet unknown to the young Englishman (as he saw himself) who arrived in Dublin in 1950. Indeed his anglocentric historical education at Cambridge acted as a barrier to understanding. Within the evolutionary framework of the English "Whig interpretation of History" there was no place for the revolutions and paradoxes of Irish history. Seeley's alternative imperial view of English history might have provided a basis for a colonial interpretation of Anglo-Irish relations. Seeley himself referred to the treatment of French Canada in 1867 as a success for English policy, but the parallels between this and the Irish situation escaped him.

As a Fine Gael-dominated institution the college could expect no favors from the Fianna Fail party and when in power De Valera (1932–48, 1951–54, 1957–59) was rumored to favour Trinity. In the eyes of the History Department, however, the chief threat to their independence came not from the politicians but from the Catholic Church. Within the new state the Church was wholly dominant in the sphere of primary and secondary education (except for Protestant schools). It was also extremely influential within the National University. At University College, Galway, the local bishop, Michael Browne, was a controlling figure. At University College, Cork, Alfred O'Rahilly, polymath and Catholic zealot, was president. At University College, Dublin, however, Michael Tierney, though in some ways an ultra-Catholic, managed to keep the archbishop, John Charles McQuaid, at arm's length, in one instance resisting his attempts to have crucifixes placed on the walls of the lecture rooms. Nevertheless the clergy exercised considerable influence, thanks to the fact that certain "sensitive" departments, those of ethics, politics, metaphysics, and psychology, were regarded as falling within the Church's sphere. History was also a possible candidate for inclusion under this rubric and in fact of the four history professors two were Jesuit priests. One of them, Fr. John Ryan S. J., who held the chair of early Irish history, chose to remain outside the History Department. The two lay professors could count on the general support of Fr. Aubrey Gwynn, S.J., professor of medieval history, but in a crisis he could hardly be expected to resist strong pressure from the Archbishop's House. (As an indication of the tone of these years it may be mentioned that Fr. Gwynn was unable to attend his own father's funeral on the grounds that it was a Protestant service!)

The influence of the Church partly rested on the fact that within the archdiocese of Dublin there were a number of seminaries whose students attended courses at University College. The largest of these was the diocesan seminary at Clonliffe, north of the Liffey, whose students used to march in crocodile formation wearing bowler hats through the streets of north Dublin on their way to Earlsfort Terrace. Other seminaries included those of the Vincentians, the Marists, and the Jesuits. The archbishop himself was a member of the Holy Ghost Order, whose seminary was at Kimmage, a suburb of south Dublin, where students were exposed to the lectures of a certain Fr. Fahey. Fahey's book *Christ in the Modern World* blamed Freemasons for the spread of immorality and unbelief and thus equipped Holy Ghost students with their order's own interpretation of history if and when they became history students at U.C.D. The "Holy Ghost" interpretation of modern history in fact reflected the experience of the order during the French Third Republic when they and other orders faced the threat of anticlericalism. The French Revolution itself was seen as a Masonic conspiracy aiming to undermine the Church, a view which enjoyed papal backing. History essays produced by Holy Ghost students at U.C.D. regularly reproduced such monocausal views, presenting the

History Department with a challenge as to what should be the appropriate response.

The Church also gave its backing to what in some ways was the equivalent of the Whig interpretation of history with an Irish twist. On this view the Church represented the Irish nation in its struggle through centuries of persecution. The period of the penal laws in the eighteenth century was seen as one in which the alliance between priest and people was forged in a spirit of "Faith and Fatherland," leading in the nineteenth century to a resurgence by the Church under the leadership of such figures as Daniel O'Connell and Cardinal Cullen.

But the Church was not the only source of anxiety. Another challenge to the History Department was that provided by the "Fenian" view of history, with which the Fianna Fail party sympathized. From this standpoint the true Irish political tradition was that exemplified by the revolutionary outlook of Wolfe Tone, Robert Emmet, Thomas Davis, John Mitchel, and Patrick Pearse. There was no Fenian equivalent of the Catholic seminaries, but within the National (that is, primary) schools, *Notes for Teachers: History* (1933) formed the basis of a Fenian-style curriculum. On this view of Irish history "the Irish people" were seen as resisting their English conquerors in every generation. The Christian Brothers in their secondary schools also sponsored this interpretation. The majority of history students entering University College had thus been exposed to nationalist interpretations of one form or another and the newly established History Department saw its role as that of engaging them in critical debate.

The History Department itself was something of a broad church, covering various political viewpoints. Desmond Williams himself, professor of modern European history, had strong Fine Gael connections. Conservative politically, he had got to know Michael Oakeshott well while at Cambridge and had actually helped to establish *The Cambridge Journal* which Oakeshott edited. As a Catholic his sympathies were liberal. One of his historical interests was the figure of Cardinal Morone who had shown himself to be supportive of compromise with the Lutherans during the Council of Trent. Desmond also admired Lord Acton and seems to have sympathized with his dilemmas during the Vatican Council of 1870. (I remember Desmond once discussing the decree concerning papal infallibility and explaining its ambiguity.)

Aubrey Gwynn, professor of medieval history, was also an interesting figure. Smith O'Brien, the aristocratic rebel of 1848, was his grandfather. His father was Stephen Gwynn, a well-known writer and journalist and

Home Rule party M.P. The Gwynns, a Protestant family, had long-standing links with Trinity College but Aubrey had converted to Catholicism at the age of twelve and as a Jesuit novice had gone to the Royal University, precursor of U.C.D. Michael Tierney, later to be professor of Greek, was a fellow student of his, who never forgot coming second to Aubrey in the final exams.

The third member of the triumvirate, Robin Dudley Edwards, professor of modern Irish history, came from a very different background. Son of an English father, he had attended Patrick Pearse's school, St. Enda's, possibly at the urging of his maternal grandmother, who had strong republican views. "Dudley" had good friends on the Fianna Fail side of the political divide and shared with them a certain anticlericalism. He was always suspicious of Aubrey Gwynn. "Dudley" also knew Irish well, a fact which helped to placate those who thought the History Department was too anglophile.

Despite the contrast in their personalities and their differing views on many matters, Williams, Gwynn, and Edwards had come together in a united History Department to advance the cause of what they saw as a more "critical" view of Irish history. They were the advocates of a liberalism "which dared not speak its name" in a narrow world dominated by the certainties of orthodox nationalism, whether clerical or lay. Herbert Butterfield was an important influence on them. He had been external examiner to the National University during the war years and remained a frequent visitor during the 1950s. As the academic mentor of Desmond Williams he also helped to establish a link between Peterhouse and University College which lasted for thirty years.

Another link with Cambridge during the 1950s was provided by the presence of Michael Oakeshott as external examiner. In English terms Oakeshott was not a liberal but he was opposed to dogmatism and his brand of skepticism proved very welcome to the History Department. Dudley Edwards in particular was very fond of quoting Oakeshott's dictum that "History is what the evidence obliges us to believe." It was this approach which lay behind what was later to be attacked as "revisionism." Butterfield regularly referred to "putting on a new thinking cap" and "picking up the stick at the other end," both aphorisms which implied the need for historians to be critical of current historical orthodoxies. It was a skeptical attitude which he had first exposed in his book *The Whig Interpretation of History*.

Though we did not use the term, "revisionism" was central to the approach of the History Department. Desmond Williams published a "revisionist" article on the origins of the Second World War, which later influenced A. J. P. Taylor. He also gave a public lecture on the Irish Civil War in which he tried to make sense of the attitudes of both sides. But the most productive scholar writing on "revisionist" lines was Maureen Wall, a young Irish speaker from Co. Donegal. Maureen Wall had trained as a teacher and came late to history as a result of taking an evening degree at U.C.D. With Dudley Edwards's encouragement she began to work on eighteenth-century Ireland, focusing on the hidden world of Catholicism. Her work soon took on a "revisionist" stance. In an article for *Irish Historical Studies* on the apparently abstruse topic of "Quarterage" she was able to show that Catholic merchants were able to maintain their place in the trading guilds as "quarter" members despite being legally excluded. This insight led her to demonstrate that there was a substantial Catholic middle class in eighteenth-century Ireland, a major "revisionism" of the orthodox view that in penal Ireland all Irish Catholics were "hewers of wood and drawers of water." She was further able to show that by the eighteenth century the British authorities in Ireland had come to depend upon loans from Catholic merchants such as John Keogh. Maureen Wall's "revisionist" approach, backed by original scholarship, led her to write a brilliant essay on the Penal Laws which won the N. U. I. prize for the best work on Irish history in 1961. During these years she challenged current orthodoxies more than any other Irish historian. Not surprisingly the English historian she most admired was that persistent "gadfly of the establishment, A. J. P. Taylor." She particularly admired his book *The Troublemakers*, a study of radical critics of British foreign policy. She was also interested in the work of William Carleton, whose *Tales and Stories of the Irish Peasantry* she urged me to read. Carleton, together with the Whiteboys and the Ribbonmen, offered insights into Irish history "from the bottom up."

Maureen Wall's work has been of lasting importance. Another revisionist contribution produced under the auspices of the U.C.D. History Department, *The Irish Famine*, proved to be more controversial. The editors, Williams and Edwards, intended to produce a scholarly reassessment of the Famine. In the event they were seen to have sponsored a volume in which the tragic aspects of those years were played down. A version of the Famine more acceptable to nationalist opinion was brought out by Cecil Woodham Smith, a gifted amateur scholar, who, using local archives, brought out the horrors of the Famine. Today the pendulum has swung very much against the revisionist view and in the United States the Famine has come to be seen in some circles as the Irish version of the Jewish holocaust, with the British playing the role of the Nazis. In academic circles, however, debate continues and perhaps no final judgment is possible about ultimate responsibility.

During these years there were also a number of institutions which helped to maintain the academic independence of Irish historians. The most important of these was the Irish Historical Society, situated in Dublin, and its counterpart in Northern Ireland, the Ulster Society for Irish Historical Studies. These bodies were interdenominational and non-sectarian, and the Irish Historical Society in Dublin took pains to elect chairmen alternatively from U.C.D. and Trinity College. Another nonsectarian institution was the Irish Committee of Historical Sciences, which, thanks to the initiative of Desmond Williams, established a series of biennial Irish Conferences of Historians held in turn at university institutions throughout Ireland. Visiting speakers at the conferences included Herbert Butterfield, Hugh Trevor-Roper, Alfred Cobban, and Geoffrey Barraclough. It was at one of them that Michael Oakeshott read his skeptical paper, "The Activity of Being a Historian."

Dudley Edwards's contribution during these years was to set up the Catholic Historical Committee, the aim of which was to open up diocesan archives throughout Ireland and thus make available evidence relating to the still-neglected world of Irish Catholicism. Dudley's poor eyesight made writing difficult for him but he put his prodigious energy to good use in perambulations throughout Ireland, persuading individual bishops to open up their archives and even to subsidize the publication of historical journals, in one of which Maureen Wall published an important article on the Dublin middle class.

During the 1950s the U.C.D. History Department represented what may be seen as the voice of liberal Catholic views on Irish history. In adopting a liberal standpoint they looked for support to such figures as T. W. Moody of Trinity College, J. C. Beckett at Queen's, and David Quinn at Liverpool. Quinn represented a viewpoint which stressed the colonial aspect of Anglo-Irish relations, an interpretation which later assumed central importance, though his influence at this time remained marginal. Kenneth Connell at Queen's Belfast, as the author of the classic work *The Population of Ireland* (1950), was an original scholar whose social science emphasis deriving from his education at the London School of Economics was still unusual in Ireland. Connell's insistence on using the concept "peasant" in an Irish context aroused antagonism in some circles. Other productive scholars during these years included John Whyte of the U.C.D. Politics Department and the Welsh scholar Thomas Jones Hughes of the Geography Department, whose work gave rise to an influential school of Irish historical geography. As far as the History Department was concerned, however, both Whyte and Jones Hughes were very much outsiders, their value unappreciated and their future importance unforeseen. One other institution should also be mentioned, namely, the Institute of Advanced Studies, founded by De Valera in 1940. Apart from science, the Institute provided substantial backing for distinguished scholars in the field of Celtic studies, among them T. F. O'Rahilly and Daniel Binchy, both of whom were strong "revisionists" in our modern sense.

I had come to Ireland as a medievalist. Almost immediately, however, I found myself conscripted into lecturing on early modern English history and on modern European history upto the outbreak of the First World War. I had as yet no interest in Irish history, but the topic of the Irish career of Thomas Wentworth, earl of Strafford, lord deputy from 1633 to 1641, was suggested to me by Brian Wormald, and I soon came to see the attractions of working on something which straddled both sides of the Irish Sea. Dudley Edwards was my supervisor and it was thanks to him that I began to make some progress in Irish history. He recommended Daniel Corkery's *The Hidden Ireland* was a work which would give me some insight into Gaelic Ireland, though I regret now that he did not urge me to study Irish. In 1956 I completed my doctorate and in 1959 published *Strafford in Ireland* which was noticed favorably and later won a prize for Irish history. Ironically one English reviewer referred to me as writing more clearly than my fellow countrymen, a comment which caused amusement at U.C.D.

It remains to mention the history curriculum at U.C.D. There was a sharp distinction between pass students and honors students, the former being examined in June and the latter in September. History could be studied on its own or in a joint honors degree, along with English, Irish, or Economics. Desmond Williams had introduced a tutorial system on the Cambridge model whereby a small group of students met members of the staff or graduate students to discuss a weekly essay. Under the previous professor of Modern history, John Marcus O Sullivan, the history course had concentrated on Luther, the French Revolution, and the Origins of the First World War, a curriculum that had the great virtue of coherence. I am not sure that those who succeeded him provided a superior alternative.

Desmond Williams introduced "Pan-Slavism" as a topic for First Year Honors but this was too complex for them to understand. He also introduced a special subject for Third Years on the Council of Trent, which was more successful. I myself gave first-year lectures on early modern Europe. I also gave a seminar-style class on the history of political thought.

University College had the resources of a provincial university in England or Wales but in fact its role was the education of a national elite, clerical and lay. The Economics Department under George O'Brien produced Garrett Fitzgerald, later Taoiseach, and Patrick Lynch, an important figure in the Irish establishment. The History Department tended to produce lawyers, several of whom became judges of the high court. My first seminar class included a student who went on to become Lord Chief Justice. Other graduates of University College included Charles Haughey, the future Taoiseach, and Tony O'Reilly, the entrepreneur. Others went on to careers in the Irish diplomatic service. For politicians and others the "L and H," the Literary and Historical Society, was a valuable training ground, comparable to a less formal Oxford Union.

The fact remains, however, that liberalism even of the palest hue was very much on the defensive in an Ireland where education was dominated by a fundamentalist Church. In my first year I was asked to give a course of lectures on modern history and I used R. H. Tawney's *Religion and the Rise of Capitalism* as a convenient text, available in paperback. I was not invited again. I also recall ordering Henry James's novel *Portrait of a Lady* from an Oxford bookshop. When it arrived, I was summoned to the Customs Office and asked to open the parcel in the presence of customs officials. When I offered a course on the history of ideas, a clerical professor brought pressure to bear to ensure that orthodox views on "Natural law" were represented on the examination paper. More serious, however, was the fate of John Whyte, assistant in the Politics Department, who was eased out of the department for going ahead with his own research on the role of the Church in contemporary Ireland. Whyte, a devout Catholic of Ulster background, moved to Queen's and eventually brought out a magisterial work, *Church and State in Modern Ireland 1923–79* (1980). In an ironic turn of events he was appointed professor of politics at University College in 1984, an indication of how times had changed.

Change was slow in coming to Ireland but when it did come it arrived suddenly in the wake of the election of Pope John XXIII in 1958 and the succession of Sean Lemass as Taoiseach to Eamon De Valera in 1959. The 1960s proved to have a radical effect in Ireland both north and south of the border. Soon the Church, at least in the Irish Republic, found itself on the defensive.

I did not remain in Ireland long enough to witness the full extent of the changes which were to come, as in 1962 my own fortunes and those of my family changed drastically. Our younger son was found to be suffering from phenylketonuria, a serious metabolic disorder, which if not treated leads to severe brain damage. It was essential for us to move to Britain and its National Health Service, and I was fortunate enough to be offered a lectureship at the newly established University of Sussex. My views about the role of a historian, shaped by twelve years in Ireland, were about to be transformed.

I arrived in Sussex in September 1962 and soon discovered that history there was a very different discipline from that which I knew at Cambridge or Dublin. At Cambridge history was still in the main "past politics," with social and economic history playing a relatively minor role. The same was true of University College, Dublin, with the accent on national history. At Sussex, however, political history was relegated to a secondary position. Instead, social history and to a lesser extent the history of ideas took pride of place in the Sussex curriculum.

The key figure in setting the tone of history at Sussex was Asa Briggs, a leading historian of Victorian England. In his publications he had shown himself to be sympathetic to the rise of social history. But what happened at Sussex was part of a more general "social turn" in historical studies due in part perhaps to a widespread reaction against Namierite concerns with "high politics." The work of the French *Annales* school was also becoming more widely recognized, thanks to the advocacy of Michael Postan. In particular Fernand Braudel's book *The Mediterranean World in the Reign of Phillip II* soon became recognized as a classic. In it Braudel stressed the importance of geography and of the perspective of the "longue durée," relegating the role of politics and Philip II to a relatively minor position. In France the *Annales* school, writing under the influence of Durkheim, steered clear of Marxism although the study of the French Revolution was still dominated by social historians such as Lefebvre and Albert Soboul, writing from a Marxist perspective.

In England the "social history turn" had been led by R. H. Tawney at the London School of Economics. Tawney was a Christian Socialist whose writings had constantly challenged the optimism of the Whig interpretation of history and whose version of English social history was very different from that which Trevelyan had produced in his best-selling volume

English Social History (1944). Tawney's efforts were followed in the 1950s by a more specifically Marxist contribution led by Christopher Hill of Balliol College, Oxford, thanks to whom the concept of an "English Revolution" came to challenge that of a "Puritan Revolution." So successful was Hill that a Marxist model based upon the decline of a feudal ancien regime and the rise of a middle class showed signs of becoming a new orthodoxy. Indeed Hill's textbook *The Century of Revolution* (1959) offered a clear-cut alternative to the Whig interpretation offered by G. M. Trevelyan in his *England under the Stuarts* (1904.) Other Marxist scholars also made the running. In 1963, for example, Edward Thompson's book *The Making of the English Working Class* made an extraordinary impact and it was eventually mentioned by the *Arts and Humanities Citations Index* (1976–83) as one of the most cited of twentieth-century works.

But not all social historians were Marxist. Tawney himself was a socialist but non-Marxist. At Oxford there were prominent non-Marxist social historians such as Lawrence Stone who was a great admirer of Tawney. Hugh Trevor-Roper, a bitter critic of Tawney, Hill, and Stone was an admirer of Braudel. Asa Briggs was unsympathetic toward Marxism and within the ranks of the Marxist historians themselves bitter divisions developed after the Soviet suppression of the Hungarian uprising in 1956. A crucial event in the rise of social history was the decision of Marxist historians in 1959 to "liberalize" the editorial board of the journal *Past and Present* and to jettison the subtitle "a journal of scientific history." Non-Marxist historians such as Laurence Stone and John Elliott now felt able to join the editorial board of *Past and Present*, which was soon recognized as being on a par with *Annales* as a leading journal of social history.

Anthropology was another discipline whose approach seemed relevant for social historians. E. R. Dodds in his brilliant book *The Greeks and the Irrational* (1957) showed how Greeks could be seen as moving from a "shame" culture to a "guilt" culture. Edward Thompson in his essay on "The Moral Economy" reflected approvingly on Durkheim and Malinowski. Keith Thomas benefited from discussions with the Oxford anthropologist Evans-Pritchard when writing his magisterial study *Religion and the Decline of Magic* (1971).

It was thus not surprising that historians at the University of Sussex should seek to associate themselves with the newly fashionable mode of social history. I myself took the plunge with an article for *Past and Present* entitled "Puritanism, Capitalism and the Rise of Science" in which I criticized Christopher Hill and as a result became embroiled in controversy. I also published a book *Scholars and Gentlemen* in 1970 which was subtitled "Universities and Society in Pre-Industrial Britain 1500–1700." In this I attempted to place university curricula in a social history context, using the concept of "social function" as the basis of my argument. In the Sussex environment of the 1960s the "social history turn" seemed irresistible. Peter Burke, a younger colleague of mine and former student of Keith Thomas, wrote for *Annales*. Evans-Pritchard came to give us a series of lectures; Edward Thompson spoke on "Moral Economy," David Riesman, the American sociologist, visiting professor for a term, lectured among other things on Thorsten Veblen, inventor of the concept "conspicuous consumption."

Elsewhere in England, however, historians were not for turning. The *English Historical Review*, rooted in Oxford, stood firm against the new fashion. In Cambridge, Geoffrey Elton denounced the distortions of social history. Alfred Cobban of University College, London, in his "revisionist" Wiles lectures, *The Social Interpretation of the French Revolution* (1964), criticized the views of Lefebvre and Soboul on the French Revolution. Herbert Butterfield defended the flexibility of narrative against what he regarded as the rigidity of sociological interpretation. Other younger historians such as Richard Cobb and Theo Zeldin moved away from the generalizations of social history toward a mode of history which emphasized the lives and choices of individuals.

At Sussex, social history did not have all its own way. In particular the history of ideas provided an alternative focus of interest. A lecture course entitled "The Modern European Mind," given by a variety of speakers, proved to be very popular, attracting audiences of both faculty and students. Seminars such as "Politics and Literature in the Age of Pascal," and "Poetry, Science and Religion in Seventeenth-Century England," combined interdisciplinary discussion of literature with the history of ideas. John Cruikshank edited a series of volumes on "French History and Literature," recruiting Sussex faculty as his team of authors. Another series, *Problems and Perspectives*, edited by myself and published by Longmans, took "The Renaissance," "The Scientific Revolution," "The Enlightenment," "Romanticism," and "The Modern European Mind" as the basis for a series analyzing various interpretations of key movements in the history of ideas. A unit centred on the history of ideas was eventually formed, led by Donald Winch, John Burrows, Peter Burke, and Stefan Collini—a formidable quartet of scholars.

But the 1960s were the heyday of a Marxist approach in which ideas were discussed in their social context. In his Ford lectures published as

The Intellectual Origins of the English Revolution (1965) Christopher Hill made an ambitious attempt to interpret such figures as Francis Bacon in Marxist terms. The Marxist critic Lucien Goldman in *The Hidden God* (1964) provided a Marxist view of Jansenism, arguing that it was the ideology of a class of alienated office holders. The 1960s was also a decade when the Marxist literary critic George Lukacs enjoyed a great deal of influence. At Sussex, some younger faculty members pressed for the recruitment of such Marxist historians as Eric Hobsbawm and Isaac Deutscher.

At the beginning in 1962 it was assumed that an interdisciplinary approach was to be the norm at Sussex. All students in their first year were required to take two courses, "Introduction to History" and "Introduction to Philosophy." History involved either Tawney, *Religion and the Rise of Capitalism* or Burckhardt, *Civilisation of the Renaissance in Italy*, a choice which implied a distinction between "social history" or "history of ideas" approaches. What was also of interest was the way in which from the start students were to be encouraged to consider differing interpretations, the use of concepts, and the weighing of evidence. Studying Tawney led naturally to discussions of capitalism, Marx, and Weber, and the validity of Tawney's own attempt to connect religion and economic change. Reading Burckhardt encouraged students to consider his concept of "Renaissance," his use of such sources as Petrarch, and his critical attitude to German state-centered historiography. Later, Turner's essay *The Frontier in American History* provided a third choice for students. I found these tutorial-centred courses very stimulating indeed.

In my last year in Dublin I had become involved with my colleague Denis Donoghue, an as-yet-unknown literary critic, in a course linking "Literature and History in the Seventeenth Century." I still recall his analysis of poems by George Herbert and Andrew Marvell and I am grateful to him for introducing me to modern literary criticism. The interdisciplinary approach of Sussex was thus very welcome to me and I took part in joint seminars on "Politics and Religion in the Age of Pascal" and "Poetry, Science, and Religion in Seventeenth-Century England." Somewhat later after hearing David Daiches lecture on Joyce and Yeats in the lecture course "The Modern European Mind," I suggested an interdisciplinary course, "Politics and Literature in the Age of Joyce and Yeats," with Matthew Hodgart, an expert on Joyce, as my literary colleague. I was not a specialist in modern Ireland but I welcomed the chance to introduce Irish history into the curriculum in its own right and not merely as "the Irish problem."

The Yeats-Joyce seminar proved to be very popular with students. For me also it was an extraordinarily enlightening experience. The seminars involved close readings of a selection of Yeats's poems, of "Ivy Day," "Grace," and "The Dead" in Joyce's *Dubliners, A Portrait of the Artist*, and the Cyclops episode in *Ulysses*. We were also led on naturally to read Somerville and Ross, John Millington Synge and Seán O'Casey. History was inextricably involved with the literature and we could not avoid discussing such figures as Charles Stewart Parnell, or the Rising of 1916. The historiography was not as plentiful as it is now, but work by Conor Cruise O'Brien, F. S. L. Lyons, and Tim Pat Coogan helped to enlighten us. A newly published edition of *Intelligence Notes*, printing police reports on the activities of Sinn Fein during 1912–15, was also a valuable source of evidence for discussion.

With the backing of David Daiches we were also able to invite visiting speakers to address the seminar. Among these were F. S. L. Lyons, Denis Donoghue, T. W. Moody, Kenneth Connell, the anthropologist Rosemary Harris, Leon O Broin and a young economic historian, Joe Lee. E. R. Dodds, who had known such figures as the writer George Russell (A. E.), came to speak about his recollections of Dublin before 1916. This was a moment before the outbreak of "the Troubles" of 1969 in Northern Ireland, when it seemed possible that the rapprochement between Sean Lemass and Terence O'Neill would bear lasting fruit. We did not take seriously such events as the blowing up of Nelson's Pillar in Dublin in 1966 or the "No Popery" campaigns of a young revivalist preacher named Ian Paisley.

Sussex seemed remote from such unrest. In hindsight, however, it was not surprising that the Paris student revolt of 1968 should have had an impact on Sussex. In 1969 a pot of paint was hurled at an American embassy official visiting the campus, an incident which led to several months of student unrest in the university. Student groups occupied administrative offices, meetings were held to assert student rights to sit on faculty appointment committees, and Asa Briggs, the vice-chancellor, was regularly denounced as "Briggs" in student mass meetings. At a public lecture given by him in 1970 as a commemoration of the 1870 Education Act, he was howled down by a minority within the audience and could hardly complete the lecture. Perhaps it was true after all that history was past politics and politics past history.

The events at Sussex proved to be a storm in a teacup. Northern Ireland, however, was a problem which grew in intensity. It was also one which we had failed to foresee. Our *Annales* emphasis on the "longue durée" had blinded us to the importance of short-term "events." One of the speakers to the Yeats-Joyce seminar, Leon O Broin, had written a short but brilliant book *Dublin Castle and the Rising of 1916* in which he demonstrated how the British administration in Ireland failed to take the Sinn Fein manoeuvres seriously until it was too late. Joyce's *Dubliners* had also indicated that to the characters in "The Dead" the idea of a rebellion seemed utterly remote. In our enthusiasm for the long-term social dimension at Sussex we perhaps went too far in playing down the significance of the short term. As Harold Wilson declared in a different context, "a week is a long time in politics."

At a more mundane level, my own career also changed course unexpectedly when in 1970 I moved to Edinburgh University as Richard Pares Professor of History. I was very flattered to be offered the job. The university enjoyed a great deal of prestige, as did its History Department. My chair in fact took its name from the brilliant Oxford historian who had been professor at Edinburgh after the Second World War before dying early of an incurable disease. My future colleagues were three highly respected historians, Denys Hay, an expert in Italian history, "Sam" Shepperson, a major scholar in British imperial history, and Geoffrey Best, who had made his reputation in modern British history. I had some hesitation about leaving Sussex and had in fact turned down the offer of a chair at Kent but the attraction of moving to a well-established university in a beautiful city which housed the National Library of Scotland seemed too good to miss.

The reputation of the Edinburgh History Department was well founded. What I was unprepared for was the internal division within the department into different "spheres of influence" jealously guarded by individual professors. Each professor, it seemed, enjoyed a paternalistic role, looking after the welfare of the junior colleagues entrusted to his care. In some cases this "care" extended beyond the confines of work to social occasions. A junior colleague of one professor was reprimanded for attending football matches with another professor (namely, myself). Professors enjoyed considerable prestige. They sat in the University Senate ex officio. It was only recently that assistant lectureships had come to be regarded as more than temporary three-year appointments, a situation which meant that professors ruled the roost without question, on lines made familiar by Kingsley Amis in *Lucky Jim*.

There were other departments distinct from the History Department proper. These were Scottish History and Economic History, each of which guarded their own independence from their much larger rival. The History Department in contrast had a strong tradition of English political history going back to the days of George Prothero, who had been professor in the 1890s. The strongly unionist history professors viewed with alarm the rising tide of Scottish nationalism which became manifest in the 1960s. There was little contact with the small Scottish History Department or the School of Scottish Studies.

After the loose interdisciplinary structure of Sussex organized around schools rather than departments, the strongly departmental culture of Edinburgh came as a disappointment. It did have some compensations, however. In particular Sam Shepperson had recruited younger scholars with an interest in imperial history. Edinburgh thus had a cluster of historians who could offer courses on African history and Indian history, and in due course he succeeded in establishing a chair of Canadian history. Thanks to such figures as David Livingstone, imperial history had a place in Scottish culture which it did not have in Ireland and Shepperson had made the most of this. I had hoped to introduce courses of "literature and history" but departmental boundaries made this impossible. I did, however, manage to set up an internal "interdisciplinary" course within the History Department entitled "The Atlantic Community." This was an attempt to examine the interaction between England and its American colonies on lines outlined by the American historian Edward Eggleston in his book *The Transit of Civilization.* The course was run by myself together with Alan Day, a young scholar in Shepperson's group, and Nicholas Phillipson, who specialized in the history of the Scottish Enlightenment. This venture led to the holding of a successful conference on similar lines, which was attended by such figures as Christopher Hill and Peter Laslett from English history, and Richard Dunn and Jack Green on the colonial history side. On the downside, however, a proposal about a course on world history making use of the talents of my colleagues in imperial history was dismissed out of hand. I also found that administrative chores were seriously depleting my energies and eating into the time available for research and developing new courses.

Added to this, I found that I missed the interdisciplinary atmosphere of Sussex more than I had anticipated. The course that I missed most was "Politics and Literature in the Age of Yeats and Joyce." I found that my research interests were now more focused on Irish history than upon "Universities and Society." I had published my book *Scholars and Gentlemen* in 1970 and felt that I had had my say on that topic. My new project was to write an *Annales*-style study of social history using sources available in the Northern Ireland Record Office. I gave an inaugural lecture entitled "Godly Landlords" which took the outlook of a group of evangelical landlords in nineteenth-century Ulster as its theme. My enthusiasm also led me to take Irish language courses under Professor Kenneth Jackson, the great Celtic scholar.

It was at this point that the chance arose of moving to the University of Pittsburgh as Amundson Professor of British History. I had come to know "Pitt" well after a year as visiting professor in 1966–67, followed by two years of teaching summer school there. I had enjoyed the experience and my wife and family liked the United States, but when an earlier offer had been made I turned it down. When it was renewed in 1974 I decided to accept. Family reasons played their part but there was also the fact that I would have no administrative responsibilities, a burden which I found increasingly irksome at Edinburgh. I would also enjoy a great deal of freedom in teaching. The thought that I could once again design innovative courses was irresistible. So it was that in the summer my wife and two of our children left for the United States.

The University of Pittsburgh looked back to its foundation as a "log cabin" in the 1780s. In fact the university which I joined in 1975 was very much a new foundation which had been transformed in the 1960s thanks to the largesse of the Mellon family, which had Pittsburgh roots. The Mellons brought in as the new chancellor Edward Litchfield, a successful businessman. Hitherto the university had been very much a "streetcar" college, catering to the needs of the local community. In this role it had been relatively successful and the various departments had been brought together in a skyscraper-style building known as "The Cathedral of Learning," though during the depression of the 1930s it remained unfinished. Chancellor Litchfield, with the backing of the Mellons, planned to change "Pitt" into a "Harvard of the Alleghenies." With this aim in view he imported the whole of the very distinguished Yale Anthropology Department. He also believed that a "real" university should have a Philosophy Department and in a short time took steps to put this into effect with the appointment of Adolph Grunbaum, under whose leadership it rapidly assumed a leading position in the United States. Litchfield also provided funding for a good Classics Department. To lead a revamped History Department Litchfield chose a young scholar from Iowa, Samuel P. Hays, a graduate of Swarthmore and Harvard. During the ancien regime the department had been no more than adequate. Hays, very much the new broom, got rid of some younger historians, not without recrimination, and began to introduce his own choices.

His aim was to build up a department which would establish a reputation in social history and he brought in young scholars who were beginning to establish themselves. They included David Montgomery, Seymour Drescher, William Stanton, and Murdo McLeod, all of whom made their mark as distinguished scholars. Hays also established two journals: *Peasant Studies* and the *Historical Methods Newsletter*. The History Department also, among other leading departments in the Faculty of Arts, acquired a Mellon Chair. These highly paid professorships were designed to attract leading scholars in the field who would set an appropriate intellectual tone. In the case of history, the first Mellon Professor was Carter Goodrich, a highly regarded scholar in American social history. Other departments appointed such scholars as Ronald Syme of Oxford (Classics) and L. C. Knights of Cambridge (English) as visiting Mellon professors. The whole scene seemed very promising and Litchfield looked forward to a second, even more grandiose, stage of development.

In 1964, however, the vision collapsed. Litchfield quarreled with his Mellon patrons and lost their confidence. He was forced to resign and the university itself went bankrupt and was forced to seek state aid. Hitherto an independent foundation, it now became a "state-related" institution, dependent for one-third of its income from the State of Pennsylvania. All this happened in the mid-1960s. By the mid-1970s, however, the university was back again on an even keel, complete with a new university library and a soon to be completed Arts Building.

Surprisingly, Samuel Hays was able to continue his plans of building up the History Department. By the time I arrived he had brought in groups of young scholars in Asian studies, Russian studies, and Latin American studies, alongside historians in American history and European history. He had set up a very impressive department with a world history focus which I was proud to join in 1975. It was also an egalitarian department very different in ethos from the Edinburgh which I had just left. All of us were expected to vote on the filling of appointments. Discussions about promotion to tenure (that is, from assistant professor to associate professor) were also made by the appropriate groups. Statements of opinion on sensitive issues were expected from all members of the department at such meetings, although on tenure questions there was a secret ballot.

There was also freedom to set up new interdisciplinary courses and I soon found myself teaching a literature-history graduate seminar on

"Shakespeare and Society" with a critic from the English department. In later years I joined a drama specialist in running a successful seminar on "Shakespeare's Histories" for honors students. This also proved to be very popular and for me a most enlightening experience. As with Sussex we were able to invite outside speakers. I regret, however, that Pitt was unable to establish a link with the Folger Library in Washington, D.C.

A further development was the setting up, in alliance with our neighboring university Carnegie Mellon, of a Center for Social History. This proved to be a fruitful interdisciplinary venture, encouraging historians to work together with anthropologists. Hitherto at Pitt the departments of anthropology and history, although next door to each other, had rarely communicated. Now there was regular contact.

Looking back at the Pittsburgh History Department, there was a clear divide between those social historians who accepted "modernization" as a paradigm and those who looked to a Marxist model. Samuel Hays himself took modernization as a guide to social change. His original major as an undergraduate at Swarthmore had been psychology and despite moving to history for his doctorate he retained an interest in "perception" and "response" as valuable concepts for historians. His first book *The Response to Industrialism*, which was well reviewed, showed him carrying out this approach. As time went on Hays turned to the sociologist Tonnies, whose distinction between community (*gemeinschaft*) and association (*gesellshaft*), he found illuminating as a way of discussing the experience of immigrants to the United States. An important article, "Modernising Values in the History of the United States" (1977), showed him examining the impact of social changes such as immigration or urbanization upon religion, education, and the family. Hays used the term "modernisation" as a short-hand description of these changes but as the article makes clear he was well aware of the complexities involved.

In general Hays assumed that the impact of "modernization" was on the whole beneficial. David Montgomery, like Hays a product of Swarthmore, who had been brought into the History Department at its refoundation in 1961, took a very different view. Montgomery had actual experience of industry on the shop floor as a trade union organizer and was a great admirer of Jimmy Hoffa. After coming to Pittsburgh he soon established close links with groups among local steel workers at a time when their future was under threat. (Once the steel capital of the United States, Pittsburgh no longer produces steel.) Montgomery's research interest was in what he saw as the malign impact of "modernisation," in particular the effect of "scientific management" upon workers' standard of living. It was not surprising that he should find inspiration in the work of Edward Thompson, whom he persuaded to take up the post of Visiting Mellon Professor in the fall semester of 1975. Montgomery in his turn spent a year at the newly established Institute of Social History, headed by Thompson, at the University of Warwick. At Pittsburgh, the tension between Hays and Montgomery was put to fruitful use in the graduate seminars which they ran jointly. Montgomery was eventually to leave the History Department, but not before having successfully established a focus on labor history. The red flag of radicalism continued to be flown in subsequent decades.

For his part, Samuel Hays looked upon the city of Pittsburgh as an opportunity to explore the history of immigration and ethnicity and his research seminar attracted a regular supply of graduate students. Hays wanted to examine the influence of the immigrant experience on those who had been "pulled" to the United States rather than "pushed." He regarded immigration to America as an example of "modernization" in practice. I also recall him recommending a book on the Middle East, Daniel Lerner's *The Passing of Traditional Society* (1962), which took modernization as its theme. In this case his prognostications proved to be very wrong. Hays also encouraged his students to take Ireland as a case study with a view to distinguishing between differing types of immigrant. It was thanks to him that I became acquainted with a wide range of studies dealing with the experiences of immigrants from different parts of Europe. His own work, whose focus eventually shifted to environmental studies, made his name known beyond Pittsburgh and he was visiting professor at Oxford for a year.

The tradition of social history begun by Samuel Hays was carried on in subsequent decades by younger scholars. One of these was Peter Karsten, whose book *The Naval Aristocracy* was a brilliant analysis of the officer class of the U.S. navy, a task which he as a former naval officer was well qualified to carry out. Another was Seymour Drescher, who became an acknowledged expert on slavery. Important contributions on Asian history were made by Evelyn Rawski and Richard Smethurst. In English history Janelle Greenberg produced a major reassessment of "the Ancient Constitution" in her book *The Radical Face of the Ancient Constitution* (2001). It is also worth pointing out that women made up a substantial proportion of the history faculty, and that women's history figured prominently in the curriculum, a development of which Eileen Power would have approved.

This was an intellectual environment in which a multidisciplinary approach was taken for granted. It was further enriched in due course by the appointment of Fritz Ringer as Mellon Professor. Ringer was the author of *The German Mandarins*, a study of the German professoriate before and under the Nazis. Apart from his interest in the history of education, Ringer also offered a seminar on historical methodology, which I attended. In it he introduced history graduate students to the writings of David Hume and Wittgenstein and to Winch's *Idea of Social Science* and thanks to him we learned to be more critical of our use of the concept of "cause." Ringer enjoyed a close interdisciplinary link with the History and Philosophy of Science departments. I must also mention William Stanton, who as a historian of ideas offered a contrast to the general social history stance of the department.

I think that I have said enough to indicate that I found the History Department a stimulating place to be. It was there that I was able to move beyond an anglocentric approach to British history and eventually to write *The British Isles: A History of Four Nations* (1989). At Pittsburgh I was also encouraged to develop a seminar on nationalism using recent work by Anderson, Hobsbawm, and Gellner but also calling on the mixture of ethnicities represented among graduate students at the university. In later years I ran this seminar with a younger colleague, Irina Liviseanu, who produced a major study of Romanian nationalism. It was thanks to her that I was able to attend a conference in Bucharest, my first experience of Eastern Europe.

During my final years at Pittsburgh, I developed an interest in Irish nationalism seen in a comparative context. It is the work written during those years and later which provide the major part of the collection printed in this volume. However, as I hope this memoir has shown, my interest in the questions involved goes back to my days at Dublin and Sussex. In dealing with nationalism, I have come to see that the sociological approaches of Anderson, Hobsbawm, and Gellner leave out the role played by individual decision making.

The opportunity to look back over my five decades as a historian in so many different environments has been most illuminating. I can see that my working life has been one of continuous education in several distinctive cultures. In this I consider myself very fortunate. To have the leisure to teach, think, read, and write has been a source of great enjoyment. I have found helpful and stimulating colleagues in all my universities. My Cambridge experience was obviously formative but my decision to take a chance in 1950 and move to Ireland was a crucial one. It was there that I had the opportunity to develop as a historian in another culture and to learn about my trade from my gifted though wayward colleagues, Dudley Edwards and Desmond Williams, amid the pub culture of Hartigans on Leeson Street. I also joined the archeological society and made a good friend of Sean P. O Riordan, professor of archeology. Journeys through Ireland with "Sean P." gave me further understanding of its complexities. It was at University College that I met my wife who as a Northerner brought me into contact with yet another hidden Ireland. I should also mention James Carney, a distinguished Celtic scholar who became a good friend of mine. When I returned to England I was a very different person. At Sussex, however, my education as a historian continued and I was introduced to new worlds of literary criticism and of social science. At my next port of call, Edinburgh, I had the good fortune to have two years learning something of the Irish language as a student of the great scholar Kenneth Jackson. Finally, at Pittsburgh I enjoyed twenty-five more years of "further education" in social history at the hands of Samuel Hays and my other colleagues. I still enjoy my history and in the past few weeks have particularly enjoyed two works which break new ground in Irish history, Joep Leersen's *Hidden Ireland: Public Sphere (2002)* and Tom Dunne, *Rebellions: Memoir, Memory and Rebellion 1798* (2003), both of them pieces of history which have a general relevance beyond Ireland. There is no end, apparently, to debate in history, not least in Irish history.

NOTES

1. See Reba Soffer's excellent article, "Nation, Duty, Character and Confidence: History at Oxford 1850–1914," in *The Historical Journal*, 30, 1 (1987), pp. 77–104 and the ensuing discussion. Ibid. pp. 933–42, and 31, 4 (1988) pp. 933–46. In 1994, she published a substantial book, *Discipline and Power: The University and the Making of an English Elite (Stanford University Press, 1994)*.

Nationalism

The Case of Ireland—An Introduction

> At the dawn of the twentieth century, in the twilight of
> the continental empires, Europe's subject peoples dreamt
> of forming "nation states," territorial homelands where
> Poles, Czechs, Serbs and others might live free, makers of
> their own fate. When the Hapsburgs and Romanov em-
> pires collapsed after the First World War their leaders
> seized the opportunity.
>
> A flurry of new states emerged and the first thing
> they did was to set about privileging their national "eth-
> nic" majority—defined by language or religion or antiq-
> uity or all three—at the expense of inconvenient local
> minorities, who were consigned to second-class states.[1]

In these comments on the emergence of Europe's "subject peoples" Tony
Judt does not mention Ireland. Yet Ireland provides a striking example of
the power of nationalism. The British Empire, unlike the Hapsburg,
Romanov, and Hohenzollern regimes, did not collapse after 1918 but the
British government, during "the Troubles" of 1916–22 was unable to control the rising tide of Irish nationalism, backed as it was by powerful lob-
bies among the Irish Diaspora, in the United States and Australia. The
Irish situation was no doubt unique in many ways but as an example of
the political power of nationalism it provides an illuminating case study
for students of the modern world.

The vision of a free and territorial homeland provided inspiration for
all nationalists during the First World War. Unfortunately, for Irish nationalists, as for Poles, Czechs, Hungarians and Romanians, and other
"subject peoples," their homelands were contested territories. The concept
of "nation" itself was contested and it was unclear how membership
should be defined. Was it by religion, ethnicity or language or was the

nation a civic unit? In the case of Ireland, much of the North-East as well as parts of Munster had been colonized during the Reformation period by Scottish and English settlers, many of whom were committed Protestants. Urban areas such as Dublin and Cork as well as Belfast had substantial and wealthy Protestant minorities. The distinctive character of the North East had been reinforced by the spread of industrialization in the Lagan Valley. When the rest of Ireland was hard hit by the Great Famine of 1845–48 the North East remained relatively, though not totally, unscathed and bitter memories of the Famine did not fuel resentment here as they did elsewhere in Ireland and among the Catholic Irish Diaspora in the United States. Despite Presbyterian involvement in the rebellion of 1798, and the prominence of such individuals as W. B. Yeats in nationalist circles, Irish nationalism did not take root in the North among Protestant sections of the population. Indeed, as Home Rule became dominant in the South during the 1880s, a British-centered counternationalism developed in the North. By 1912 Ireland seemed on the brink of civil war.

The outbreak of war in Europe postponed this crisis but not indefinitely. At Easter 1916 a small group of committed nationalists with the backing of Germany and some Irish-American groups, seized control of the Post Office in central Dublin and in the name of the Irish people, declared an Irish Republic. In doing so, however, they inevitably aroused the bitter antagonism of the Ulster Protestant population, whose relatives were in France on the Western Front, the eve of the Battle of the Somme (1 June 1916). The Rising of 1916 thus polarized opinion between North and South even more bitterly than had been the case hitherto.

In the rhetoric of the 1916 Proclamation there was little hint that such divisions existed. The self-proclaimed leaders of the rising, Patrick Pearse and his followers, addressed all Irishmen and Irishwomen in the name of an unproblematic Ireland.

> In the name of God and of the dead generations from which she receives her old tradition of nationhood, Ireland, through us, summons her children to her flag and strikes for her freedom.

Pearse also referred to an apparently undivided "Irish people," declaring that

> In every generation the Irish people have asserted their right to national freedom and sovereignty; six times during the past three hundred years they have asserted it in arms.

Pearse went on to proclaim the Irish republic as a sovereign independent state and to pledge "our lives and those of our comrades-in-arms to the cause of its freedom, of its welfare and of its exaltation among nations." In a reference to divisions within Ireland the insurgents played down "the differences carefully fostered by an alien government, which have divided a minority from the majority in the past." In their conclusion, the insurgent leaders placed the cause of the Irish Republic "under the protection of the Most High God."

If we attempt to see this document in comparative terms, "ethnic" or "civic," there is no doubt that the Declaration of 1916 is an example of "civic nationalism."

> The Irish Republic is entitled to, and hereby claims, the allegiance of every Irishman and Irishwoman. The republic guarantees religious and civil liberty, equal rights and opportunities to all its citizens and declares its resolve to pursue the happiness and prosperity of the whole nation and all its parts, cherishing all the children of the nation equally, and oblivious of the differences carefully fostered by an alien government, which have divided a minority from the majority in the past.

The insurgents clearly attempted to include all the inhabitants of Ireland within their definition of "the Irish people." The reference to "the Most High God" is undoctrinal and is in sharp contrast with the appeal to the Trinity in the 1937 Constitution. Historians have drawn attention to the staunch Catholicism of most of the insurgent leaders, although the socialist James Connelly was a man without strong religious convictions, as was Tom Clarke, and all of them accepted Catholic ministrations before death. The fact remains, however, that the Proclamation of 1916 is an example of "civic nationalism" and as such was consciously in a nonsectarian tradition stretching back to the freethinker Wolfe Tone and including the Protestant Thomas Davis and Presbyterian John Mitchel.[2] As we will see below, however, the Rising of 1916 had unintended consequences not least in that it led to a political division between a largely Catholic South and a Protestant-dominated North. The Irish Free State which came into existence in 1922 became increasingly Catholic in its orientation, a trend reinforced by the 1937 Constitution. In Northern Ireland the state became ever more Protestant. "Ethno-religious" nationalism thus replaced the "civic" ideals of Pearse and Connolly. Nation-building in both North and South almost inevitably took a sectarian turn.

These tensions between civic and ethno-religious nationalism were paralleled in other parts of Europe, most notably in Czecho-Slovakia, Romania, and Poland. In Czecho-Slovakia, for example, the civic nationalism of Tomas Masaryk faced a challenge from "ethnic" Germans and his fellow Slavs, the Slovaks. A tragic denouement eventually followed with the ethnic cleansing of the Sudeten Germans after 1945. In due course Slovakia broke away and became an independent state. Thus Masaryk's imagined civic community collapsed in the face of ethnic realities.[3] The new states of Poland and Romania also faced similar problems and similar far-reaching consequences.[4] Ireland thus was far from being a unique case, and the history of Irish nationalism inevitably invites a comparative context.

What was the Irish nation? Who was included in it? Pearse spoke of "the Irish people" as an unproblematic entity, but the troubled history of Ireland cannot be ignored so easily. The impact of the Norman invasions, of the Reformation and Counter-Reformation, of colonization, and not least the French Revolution left "the Irish people" deeply divided. These divisions emerged most clearly in the early seventeenth century when, in 1641, scores, possibly hundreds of settlers were killed by a resentful section of the Irish Catholic population. The myth that over a hundred thousand were killed swiftly became accepted as fact.[5] On the Catholic side, long-standing divisions between "Gaelic Irish" and "Old English" were accentuated after the 1641 rebellion by differences about the future role of the Catholic Church. In 1646 the papal envoy, Archbishop Rinuccini, excommunicated those members of the Confederate Supreme Council who had sought a compromise settlement with Ormond, Charles I's representative in Ireland. The history of Ireland during this period cannot be treated as an unproblematic tale of the resistance of the people of Ireland to an alien government. Rather the Confederates had risen in the name of God, the King, and the Fatherland (Pro Deo, pro Rege, et pro Patria). Indeed, during the seventeenth and eighteenth centuries, the Stuart monarchy was able to count upon Irish Catholic support because of its Gaelic origins, stretching, so its historians maintained, back into the mists of time.[6]

But were the Irish a Catholic nation or could Protestants such as James Butler, Duke of Ormond, or Morrogh O'Brien, earl of Inchiquin, claim to be Irish? Some commentators, such as the Jesuit Conor Mahony writing in exile in the early seventeenth century, had no difficulty in equating Irishness and Catholicism, and on the basis of the Jewish example in Exodus XXXII advocated the expulsion of those not willing to accept Catholicism. He even congratulated the insurgents of 1641 in having killed 150,000 heretics.[7] Mahony, however, was very much in a minority. Catholics in general accepted the legitimacy of the rule of the Protestant Stuart kings, although bitter debates continued over the extent to which Catholicism was the basis of Irish nationhood. The troops of Owen Roe O'Neill proclaimed themselves the army of the Pope and the papal envoy Rinuccini found considerable support for his condemnation of the First Ormond Peace (1646). In contrast John Lynch backed the Protestant Ormond and distinguished in his writings between Puritans and Protestants, the latter being acceptable fellow subjects.[8] Others, such as Confederate spokesmen, in 1644 openly defended the idea of a comprehensive Irish nation, declaring:

> For he that is born in Ireland, though his parents and all his ancestors were aliens, nay if his parents are Indian[9] or Turks, is converted to Christianity, is an Irishman as fully as if his ancestors were born here for thousands of years. And by the laws of England, as capable of the Liberties of a subject.

Thus the distinction between ethnic-religious and civic concepts of nationhood was clearly not unknown during the period of Reformation and Counter-Reformation. It was not until the French Revolution, however, that the concept of citizenship took hold. France now came to provide the example of a nation in which the status of being a citizen overrode religious or ethnic differences. For many this symbolized liberation. In Ireland during the 1790s the United Irishmen saw the French model as pointing the way to a future Irish nation which would include Dissenters and Catholics alike. As the freethinker Wolfe Tone put it:

> To unite the whole people of Ireland, to abolish the memory of all past dissensions and to substitute the common name of Irishman in place of the denominations of Protestant, Catholic and Dissenter—these were my means. (1796)

It was this "imagined community" which inspired the rebellion of 1798 (itself preceded by an abortive French landing at Bantry Bay in 1796). For many, a civic, inclusive Irish nation seemed a real possibility. For others, however, including Catholic clergy alienated by the French civil constitution of 1792, France represented impiety and sacrilege. Thus in 1798 "the Irish people" were divided and the defeat of the rebels and the subsequent executions left bitter memories for some sections of the population.

Suppression of the Rebellion of 1798 paved the way for the passing of the Act of Union with Britain, a measure which, as envisaged by its sponsor William Pitt, was to allow Catholics into the British Parliament. In the eyes of George III, however, such an Act of Union would have undermined the religious basis of the British monarchy, and hence, the concept of Britain as an ethno-religious unit. The conflict between ethnic and civic conceptions of the future United Kingdom could hardly have been clearer. It was a struggle from which George III emerged the victor. The Protestant Ascendancy in Ireland which had been under siege in the 1790s also emerged with its privileged position in place.

For the whole of the subsequent century and beyond, the Union remained a central issue and with it the question as to whether the Irish nation was an ethno-religious or a civic entity. This issue lay behind the political struggle between Daniel O'Connell's party, "Old Ireland," and the Young Irelanders led by the Protestant Thomas Davis. O'Connell himself changed his own political rhetoric from time to time, appealing on some occasions to a wider "civic" Irish nation, and on others to a Catholic nation which had suffered on such occasions as Mullaghmast (1577)[10] or been victorious, as at Clontarf (1014).

At a local level, the type of support upon which O'Connell could rely is illustrated in an appeal printed at Clonmel, Co. Tipperary in the 1820s. Leaders of the area urged local factions to show loyalty to O Connel's Catholic nation:

> The Catholic Association, which had been the means under Providence, of calling Catholic People into existence, as a Nation—which has taught the humblest Individual in the community to appreciate his Rights—the Catholic Association of Ireland, virtually representing the feelings, the opinions, and the interests of the duty they owe to you, to address the brave, the intelligent, and the docile People of Tipperary, on an occasion which they deem of great public importance, not only to the Inhabitants of Munster, but to the Catholic cause itself.[11]

It was this Catholic nationalism which became increasingly influential in the course of the nineteenth century, achieving an important political victory in 1869 with the disestablishment of the Church of Ireland. For Church leaders such as Paul Cullen, archbishop of Dublin, the Irish were indeed a Catholic nation. Those who held a more civic view found Protestant leaders in such figures as Isaac Butt or Charles Stewart Parnell. In the United States, Catholic bishops played a key role in supporting Cullen, but there was also the Fenian movement advocating an Irish Republic with its implication of a more inclusive, civic polity.

To see Irish politics solely in terms of a clash between civic and ethno-religious ideas of nationhood, however, is to run the risk of oversimplification. As Professor Theo Hoppen has shown, local issues were often the key to parliamentary elections. The rise of the Home Rule movement, first under Butt and then Parnell, showed that civic-minded leaders could exercise considerable power. After the fall of Parnell in 1891, however, there was bitter division between ethnic and civic nationalists. The great divide between North and South also widened.

Civic nationalism survived and in the early twentieth century, John Redmond, leader of the united Irish Parliamentary Party, attempted to meet the criticism that "Home Rule means Rome Rule" by denying that the party was essentially Catholic. In doing so he—a man who had taken Parnell's side in the Divorce Scandal of 1890—was following in the Parnellite tradition. He declared in a speech of September 1908:

> We are told that the Irish people of Great Britain owe a divided duty; they owe a duty, no doubt, to their country's freedom; but that alongside there is another duty which occasionally may be held, rightly, to override the first, a duty due to the Catholic religion and the Catholic Church. I say that THIS NATIONAL MOVEMENT IS NOT A CATHOLIC MOVEMENT. It is a National movement. It is not in conflict with the interests of the Catholic religion—God forbid—that is the religion of the overwhelming majority of our people. But the national movement is a National movement embracing within its folds men of all religions, and those who would seek to turn this National movement simply into a Catholic movement would be repudiating some of the brightest pages of our National history and forgetting the memory of some of the greatest of our national heroes who PROFESSED THE NEWER AND NOT THE OLDER CREED OF OUR COUNTRY.[12]

It is clear from these quotations that the question of the criterion of Irish nationhood remained contentious. Who was to be included? Was the criterion to be religious or linguistic or was it to be a civic commitment to the cause of Home Rule? How was the question to be decided? On these and other issues Ireland remained deeply divided in the decades before 1916. For a time, in the 1880s it seemed a possibility that the great majority would unite under the Protestant Parnell in a nonsectarian Home Rule Party. After the Divorce Scandal of 1890, however, bitter divisions appeared between clerical and anticlerical groupings. In addition, Protestant Ulster came to fear the establishment of a Catholic Ascendancy, their fears intensified after the publication of a Papal decree, *Ne Temere* (1904), imposing restrictive conditions upon mixed marriages. At the same time

Catholics had cause to feel that they were excluded from a just share of influential posts. The words of Eoin MacNeill, a Catholic northerner of great natural abilities, express this resentment:

> I entered the Accountant-General's Office (in Dublin) in 1887. I was then the only Catholic on the permanent staff of the office. The Accountant-General, the Chief Clerk, the senior clerk and all the junior clerks but myself were appointed before the competition law came into effect. They were all patronage men and they were all Episcopalian Protestants and garrison men![13]

The situation improved in some respects as a consequence of competitive examinations replacing patronage for entry into government service, but progress was slow. Attention-seeking journalists such D. P. Moran, editor of *The Leader*, were also able to capitalize on the still widespread sense of relative deprivation among Catholics in trade and industry where it was felt Freemasons were unduly favored. The religious divide in Ireland around 1900, with a substantial Protestant minority amounting to a quarter of the population, was clearly a problem facing the future nation-state. If Catholicism was the hallmark of Irishness in a future "Irish-Ireland," Protestants faced an uncertain future, much as Jews did in Romania and German-speakers in a Czech-dominated Czech republic. In the pages of *The Leader* D. P. Moran ceaselessly expounded the view that Irishness was synonymous with Irish Catholicism. In Moran's view the Protestant nationalism of Grattan, Tone, Davis, and Parnell had led Ireland in the wrong direction, toward accepting "the great canker of English ideas, ideals and manners." "The next few years will decide for all time whether the Gael is to lift up the Irish race once more, or whether the Pale is to complete its effacement."[14] Moran's ideal of an Irish-Ireland was a Catholic Ireland. Small wonder then if a Protestant Ulster was unwilling to commit its political future to a Home Rule Parliament.

The question as to what constituted Irish identity became more complex with the rise of cultural movements such as the Gaelic Athletic Association and the Gaelic League. For members of these movements the test of "Irishness" was willingness to play Gaelic games and to speak or at least learn Irish. In 1903, for example, Arthur Griffith attacked the idea of inviting a Soccer Association to help with the fund-raising of a Christian Brothers bazaar. His editorial warned that "it would not be tolerated that the Christian Brothers should throw in their lot with the alien and all that he represents." The executive of Cumann na nGaedhal also spoke out in the strongest terms, deploring "the action of the Christian Brothers in allowing their bazaar to be associated with the deadly Anglicising element connected with Association football playing."[15] The advocates of this policy were not a lunatic fringe but a group who saw themselves as the leaders of the Irish people. Griffith himself was a complex figure. He edited a popular edition of John Mitchel's *Jail Journal*, an action which suggests a sympathy with civic nationalism. He was also associated with anti-Semitism. Sinn Fein, the political party which he founded, was Catholic in its orientation and drew upon the support within the network of Christian Brothers' schools, a powerful and growing force in Irish secondary education. Thanks to such organizations as Sinn Fein, the exclusivist ethnic nationalism of what came to be called Irish-Ireland took root. In such an Ireland the Protestants of the North had no place.

In explaining the rise of anti-English sentiment during these years, some account must be taken of the rise of ethnic nationalism in England itself, not least during the period of the Boer War of 1899–1901. In their important book *Englishness: Politics and Culture 1880–1920* (1986), Robert Colls and Philip Dodd argued that it was during these decades that the modern sense of English identity took root when England became a "Land of Hope and Glory." One of their key points was that "the Celts" were seen by the popular English mind as a distinctive and inferior "race." Matthew Arnold's controversial view on the volatile and childlike temperament of the Celts help to fuel these attitudes, and not surprisingly there was a reaction in Ireland, leading in its turn to the idea of a Celtic Renaissance. Patrick Pearse's own idealization of the role of the Celtic warrior Cuchulain emerged from such crosscurrents.

Thus in the early years of the twentieth century there were several movements competing for a decisive say in what constituted Irishness and Irish identity in contemporary Ireland. John Redmond, as we have seen, spoke out for a civic conception of Irishness. In contrast, the Catholic clergy saw the Irish as a Catholic nation. For others, "ethnicity," that is, that the Irish were a distinct Gaelic race, was the key to national identity. The Gaelic League stressed the key role of language. Yet others such as Sir Horace Plunkett pressed for economic cooperation at the local level for Protestant and Catholic alike. The radical labor leaders, James Larkin and James Connolly, hoped to unite the Irish working class despite sectarian divisions. The vision of Yeats and the Abbey Theatre was of a nonsectarian Ireland.

A political shift to a more sectarian future, however, occurred in 1912 with the formation of the Ulster Volunteers, an organization formed to defeat Home Rule. The Ulster Covenant, a key symbol, drew upon the covenanting traditions of seventeenth-century Scotland for its inspiration. In reaction to this the National Volunteers formed in the South. For a time Redmond's authority was challenged but he managed to regain control. However, a breakaway group formed, calling itself the Irish Volunteers, within which there was a secret organization, the Irish Republican Brotherhood. After the outbreak of war, the IRB planned a rising against the British government. Early in 1916 it was by no means clear which of these various currents of opinion, civic or ethnic or ethno-religious, would prevail. In 1914 Redmond's vision of an inclusive Ireland was still a possibility.[16] After 1916, however, thanks in large measure to the miscalculations of the British government in executing the rebel leaders, his party began to lose ground. The Catholic episcopate, at first opposed to the rising, came increasingly to give its support to the cause of the insurgents. By 1918 all was "changed, changed utterly," in Yeats's words, but the new political reality both North and South lay with ethno-religious nationalism, in which such figures as W. B. Yeats found themselves increasingly marginalized.

The years following the Rising of 1916 witnessed a drastic shift in public opinion within Ireland. Perhaps most importantly, the gap between the mainly Catholic South and the Protestant population of the North widened to an apparently unbridgeable gulf. Secondly, within Catholic Ireland John Redmond's inclusivist civic nationalism lost ground to Sinn Fein, a party which the Catholic episcopate came to support for what it saw as the long-term interest of the Church. A common hostility toward the possible introduction of conscription in 1918 was another factor helping to link the Catholic clergy and the more "advanced" nationalists. By 1918 "Sinn Fein" was a Catholic party in all but name. An ethno-religious nationalist movement was now in control of much of Ireland.

The civic Proclamation of 1916 was a dead letter. In 1921 after the British acceptance of de facto independence for an Irish Free State (excluding six counties in Ulster), a peaceful future seemed possible. In fact, however, a civil war in the South broke out almost at once between those who accepted the compromises of the Anglo-Irish Treaty and those who held out for the full independence of a republic. At the same time what amounted to a second civil war broke out between the North and South. In the subsequent turmoil within the Irish Free State, Catholic churchmen in the main supported the pro-Treaty groups, and in the polity which emerged after the civil war their influence was dominant in the spheres of education and public morality. Nation-building took an increasingly Catholic tone. In 1925 divorce was in essence ruled out within the new state and in 1929 a Censorship of Publications Act was passed. Perhaps most importantly of all, the role of the Church in primary and secondary education was fully recognized by the state. During these years also, as Peter Hart has shown,[17] what is now termed "ethnic cleansing" took place at the expense of Protestants in the South and in the border counties. Yeats himself was moved to protest about the plight of the Protestant community.

In February 1932 Eamonn De Valera's Fianna Fail party came to power after winning the general election but there was no shift toward a more inclusive sense of Irish identity. The new government took full advantage of the holding of a Eurcharistic Congress in 1932 to emphasize its Catholic credentials. In 1936 the sale and importation of contraceptives was made illegal. De Valera was more resolutely anti-English in his policies than his predecessor W. T. Cosgrave, but he was no less Catholic. The Fianna Fail newspaper, *The Irish Press*, showed itself as resolutely pro-Franco as its Fine Gael counterpart, *The Irish Independent*. In the new constitution which De Valera drew up for approval in 1937, the government followed the advice of John Charles McQuaid, a prominent figure in the Holy Ghost Order who in due course was appointed Archbishop of Dublin, not least because of De Valera's backing. The new constitution did not declare "Eire"[18] a Catholic state but it recognized the dominant position of the Catholic Church, it appealed to the Holy Trinity in the preamble, and it followed Catholic teaching in relation to the family and the role of women.

The key role of the Church was reinforced during the war years 1939–45 when "Eire" remained neutral. On 18 August 1940 (after the fall of France) special trains brought many to the Marian shrine of Knock Co., Mayo, in what was termed "a National Pilgrimage." The war was described as the "inevitable consequence of universal sin and infidelity" and the official preacher declared that

> A nation united stands at the "Ready" for Homes and Altars free, a nation *faithful*—who never bent the knee to gods however false—nor willed to taste forbidden flesh pots however sweet is represented here today to pray to God through Mary Immaculate to save us from impending peril.

It was clear that the nation referred to was indubitably Catholic.

The preacher Fr. John Power also spoke of Knock in terms of the rural ideal which inspired the official image of the new state. To Fr. Power, "those thatched roofs, those simple Irish countryside houses, the smell of turf as one watched the blue smoke rising from the cottage chimneys, carried one's mind back to the scenes we associate with Mary, the Lourdes of Bernadette's day."[19] "Here in this lush hillside we had everything that the Catholic mind associates with the name and character of Mary—the rural beauty, innocence, simplicity and deep lasting love of God."[20]

In August 1945 Fr. Angelus, a retired Capuchin friar, spoke of the "fervent rosaries recited by the vast throng of pilgrims." For him this was an image of the Irish nation. "It was the nation on its knees, praying for peace, praying to Mary, the Queen of Peace, Mary the Queen of Ireland." The preacher ignored the impact which the war had made in the North-East. He was quite clear that it was a punishment for the world "for its wickedness and sin." He also spoke of the island as if the industrial world of the Lagan Valley did not exist and that Belfast had remained untouched by German bombing. "All through its unspeakable horrors our little island home was sacred, our cities were untouched, our simple country homesteads were unharmed and our people in the enjoyment of peace continued to lead their innocent lives serving God and Mary his mother."[21] It was this note which De Valera had struck in his broadcast message of 1943 when he referred to

> A land whose countryside would be bright with cosy homesteads, whose fields and villages would be joyous with the sounds of industry, with the romping of sturdy children, the contents of athletic youths and the laughter of comely maidens, whose friends would be forums for the wisdom of serene old age. It would, in a word, be the home of a people living the life that God desires that a nation should live.[22]

The message of Faith and Fatherland was a powerful one during these years though it is well to remember that in thousands of Irish pubs throughout the land there was a less overtly religious tone to the conversation. In Ireland, as in Wales, there was a contrast between the cultures of the chapel and the pub and we may well ask: Which more realistically symbolized the nation? (Were the pubs the basis of another "Hidden Ireland"?)

In 1940 a German victory had seemed likely and with it an end to partition,[23] but as the years went by the main role of De Valera's government was the maintenance of neutrality. A strict censorship prevented the direct reporting of war news in the newspapers although there was no way in which radios could be jammed. After the war, the Irish language remained a key issue. For example, during the years of the coalition government (1948–51), the minister for education Richard Mulcahy still saw language as the key to national identity.

> The aim is to have all know Irish and to let the nationalising and assimilating influence of the language and all it opens up work on all. It is stupid and shortsighted of the Protestants to be trying to segregate themselves from their fellow countrymen in this matter. More and more language is coming to be regarded as the badge of nationality. The Protestants must decide whether they wish to be thought English or Irish. Up to the present they appear to prefer to be thought English and their senseless opposition to Irish will in the end discredit them in the eyes of other countries. They are definitely cutting off their noses to spite their faces.
> [Memo from Dept. of Education to Richard Mulcahy, Minister of Education, 1948–51][24]

In the 1960s, however, change did come. A key shift occurred in 1959 with the retirement of Eamonn De Valera from the government. His successor as Taoiseach, Sean Lemass, was a man very different in character, much less religious and less committed to the cause of the Irish language than his predecessor. A Dubliner by birth, Lemass showed little interest in the rural and religious view of Irish identity which had inspired De Valera. Coincidently the 1960s in "Ireland" were marked by a rapid growth in urbanization, which led to a marked shift in the urban-rural balance in "Irish" society. Lemass was also behind the decision to encourage the Irish tourist industry, one which was to have far-reaching consequences for the Irish economy. The most important decision of Lemass's relatively short period of office was to plan for economic growth in alliance with a gifted civil servant, T. K. Whitaker. Lemass also took a conscious decision to improve relations with Northern Ireland and in 1965 paid a formal visit to Northern Ireland where he met the new prime minister of Northern Ireland, Terence O'Neill. This was a "New Departure" which, it was hoped, would lead to an amelioration of the position of the Catholic community in the North. In itself it was an episode which indicates the importance of the role of the state in the formation of national idenity.

To the influence of the political and economic decisions was added that of an extraordinary and totally unexpected religious event—the election of Pope John XXIII, "Pope John" as he came to be known in the world at large, was elected as a stopgap appointment to the papacy. In fact during his short pontificate, by calling a General Council of the Church (Vatican 2) and by encouraging a better relationship with the other Christian churches, he inaugurated what turned out to be a revolution, not least so far as Ireland was concerned. During the 1950s John Charles McQuaid had routinely issued a Lenten pastoral letter condemning the evils of the modern world, including the admission of Catholic students to that hotbed of unbelief, Trinity College, Dublin. After the election of Pope John, John Charles McQuaid found himself in the position of having to take active steps to encourage good relations with the Protestant archbishop of Dublin. A more inclusive Christian policy now gradually replaced the exclusive Catholicism of the years since 1922.[25]

The conditions were now in place for the rise of a more "civic," more inclusive sense of Irish identity as a challenge to the established ethnic "Faith and Fatherland" image. Change was slow but it was occurring nonetheless. One of the first major signs of this was the gradual liberalization, from 1957 onward, of the system of literary censorship which had been set up in 1929. In 1967 a ban on over five thousand books was removed. The official teaching of the Catholic Church outlawed the practice of contraception (this is still the case in 2004), but it proved impossible to stem the flow of contraceptive information, especially after the invention of "the Pill."[26] A dramatic encounter took place in 1971 when a woman's group returning from Northern Ireland carrying contraceptives about their persons successfully defied the customs authorities. As late as the 1990s, however, contraception was still a hot potato for the Taoiseach, Charles Haughey, who eventually handed over responsibility for the sale and distribution of condoms to regional health boards,[27] "an Irish solution to an Irish problem," as he whimsically remarked.

A battle was taking place between traditional and modern concepts of Irish identity over sexual morality, an area in which the Catholic Church since 1922 had exercised authority. Divorce had been outlawed in the Free State in 1925 and the official Catholic view of the indissolubility of marriage had been enshrined in De Valera's Constitution of 1937. It was not until the mid-1980s, however, that politicians such as Garrett Fitzgerald felt able to press for the removal of the ban. In the event a referendum held on the divorce issue in 1986 resulted in a defeat of the reformers by almost two to one.

The Irish Republic was far from being a secular state, a fact underlined with particular force during the 1979 visit of John Paul II, a pope with a particular devotion to the Virgin Mary for whom a pilgrimage to the Marian Shrine at Knock was of special significance. In the 1980s, however, a number of scandals seriously dented the image of the Church and led to a marked decline in its influence. The first case involved the popular bishop of Galway who was shown to have concealed the existence of his illegitimate child. More significant were the apparently endless series of cases indicating that serious sexual abuse had taken place in orphanages run by the Christian Brothers and other religious orders. It had been accepted almost without question that it was the role of the Church to run such institutions. Now it was shown that abuse had taken place on a massive scale, to which the Church authorities turned a blind eye. (This was still a live issue in 2004.)

This spate of scandals created an undercurrent of anticlericalism within the Republic and did nothing to prevent the decline of religious vocations and of attendance at mass in urban areas. In 2002, however, the display of relics of St. Theresa of Lisieux in cathedrals throughout Ireland was an enormous popular success, with the state providing a ceremonial military escort. Clearly it was premature to say "Goodbye to Catholic Ireland." The tension between ethnic and civic conceptions of nationhood remained.

In the 1990s, however, with the rise of the "Celtic Tiger" and unprecedented economic growth it became apparent that De Valera's image of Ireland as a simple rural society had passed into history. In 1995 a referendum permitted the legalization of divorce. On the basis of a booming tourist industry, a well-educated work force, and a committed class of entrepreneurs, the republic has enjoyed remarkable economic success. New problems—those of drug abuse, soaring house prices, and racialism—replaced the old.

The course of events proved to be very different in the North. Since 1920 Ireland had been partitioned into two political units, the Irish Free State which was politically independent and Northern Ireland, a six-county statelet which enjoyed Home Rule status within the United Kingdom.[28] As we have seen, the Free State was almost wholly Catholic, a state of affairs which had been intensified by the loss of a third of its Protestant population as a consequence of what is now termed "ethnic cleansing."[29] In the North, however, a two-thirds Protestant majority was confronted by a Catholic minority of roughly one-third. In this ministate (pop. 1.5 m.) religion was regarded as the basis of identity and the opening gambit of any conversation with a stranger almost inevitably involved discovering "what foot he dug with," not by a direct question but by ascertaining what the person's name was and which school he went to. "The North" was in essence based upon the coexistence of two ethno-religious communities, one of which controlled the machinery of government. In towns such as Derry/Londonderry (the very name is a matter of debate) a system of gerrymandering ensured that despite then being a minority of the urban population, there was a built-in Protestant minority on the city council. Lord Craigavon's slogan, "A Protestant parliament for a Protestant people," provided the counterpart to the Southern politicians' assumption that the Irish were a Catholic people. In this situation the Catholic minority in Northern Ireland seemed to have little choice but to aim at survival. More so even than in the South the Catholic clergy provided leadership, a role strengthened by their influence in the schools and the teachers' training colleges. The Catholic Church also encouraged pupils to play Gaelic games, hurling, and Gaelic football, rather than what were seen as the English games of cricket, soccer, and rugby which were played in Protestant schools. Thus there was in effect a system of cultural apartheid accepted by both sides as a means of preserving their respective ethnic identities.

In the North, radical change was almost impossible to conceive. Sporadic attempts by the IRA to arouse resistance among the Catholic population, the latest being in 1962, had little effect. Nevertheless the 1960s proved to be a decade of political movement. Rising expectations within the Catholic community arose in part as a consequence of the impact of the 1948 Education Act, which had made possible the growth of a small but active, university-educated Catholic middle class. Practices which had once been tolerated now seemed to be unacceptable abuses. A new political radicalism appeared within the Catholic community, inspired in part by the civil rights movement in the United States and a new generation of political leaders replaced the old-style "machine" politicians. The new leaders attempted to cross the sectarian divide and to seek support among the liberally minded Protestants. For a time indeed it seemed as if a Social Democratic and Labour Party founded in 1971 might develop along nonsectarian "civic" lines. Optimism was encouraged by the attitude of the new premier of Northern Ireland, Terence O'Neill, who appeared more liberal than his "hard-line" predecessors.

Thus in the mid-1960s there was a certain "civic" optimism in the air. It was hoped, for example, that a new university would be established in Derry/Londonderry on the lines of similar "new" universities in England and catering for the needs of the largely Catholic population of that area. In the event, however, these hopes were dashed despite jointly run demonstrations by Catholics and Protestants and the new university was established in 1968 in the largely Protestant town of Coleraine. Similar hopes of a fresh start raised by plans for a new town established on English lines were ruled out by the choice of the name "Craigavon." A further blow to liberal hopes occurred in 1969 when a peaceful civil rights demonstration in Derry met with water cannon, used by the police with the backing of the hard-line minister of home affairs, William Craig. Police baton charges also broke up the crowd. The message being given to the reformers was the traditionally ethnic one of "No Surrender." The Catholic community, however, was in no mood to accept a return to a pre-civil rights situation and further incidents later in 1969 led to the arrival of a peacekeeping force of British troops in August of that year. The Labour government pressed for political reform in Northern Ireland, but the election of a Conservative government in 1970 brought about a political shift more favorable to the Unionists.

A detailed analysis of the course of events during the next thirty years lies beyond the scope of this brief overview. Mention must be made, however, of the botched attempt to introduce internment without trial in August 1971 and the fatal shooting of thirteen civilians by the British army on "Bloody Sunday" in January 1972. Official-backed terror now met with unofficial terror at the hands of the Provisional IRA, an organization run on traditionally ethnic lines, which had ousted its civic competitor, the Official IRA.

Unionist attempts to impose "normal" methods of repression which had worked in earlier decades now failed totally. Their only result was to create a determined spirit of resistance among large sections of the Catholic population. Official British policy over the years wavered between conciliation (as during the short period of the Sunningdale Agreement in 1973–74) and hard-line suppression (during the early Thatcher administration after 1979). An important turning point came in May 1981 when the IRA activist Bobby Sands died while on hunger strike. This was an event which may be seen in retrospect as the equivalent in Northern Ireland of 1916. Sands's death and his subsequent enshrinement in Sinn Fein mythology might well have been avoided, but the intransigence of Mrs. Thatcher paralleled that of her predecessors in 1916, despite the pleas of John Hume, the leader of the S.D.L.P. Within the Irish diaspora in the United States the IRA received renewed widespread support, although senior politicians such as Edward Kennedy pressed for compromise. On both the Republican and Unionist sides, however, bitterness increased with each incident of terrorism and counterterrorism. It was only in the late 1990s after nearly thirty years of civil war and a number of false starts that, political compromise seemed to be a real possibility, with the signing of the Good Friday Agreement in April 1998. At the time of writing (2004), however, the Agreement has been suspended and it is likely that hopes for a lasting constitutional solution to the problems of Northern Ireland will once again be dashed.

With relation to the main issue discussed in this introduction, namely the contrast between civic and ethnic nationalism, it seems clear that the fortunes of nationalism have been very different south and north of the border. In the South there has been a distinct shift away from the romantic, ethnic, Catholic nationalism of the De Valera period to a situation in which it is challenged by civic secular attitudes to Irish nationality. With the abolition of censorship, the legalization of divorce and contraception, and the acceptance of abortion, the Irish Republic faces a situation in which there is no single, unproblematic sense of Irish identity. The flow of Irish emigrants to England in the postwar years has led to the creation of multiethnic Irish-English identities explored by John Walsh in his book *The Falling Angels*. Irish interest in "English" sports such as soccer and rugby has vastly increased and the years when such involvement would lead to individuals being banned from Gaelic sports seem to belong to prehistory. The role of women is now increasingly recognized and here again the traditionalist role assigned to women in the Irish constitution is becoming a dead letter. Television programmes such as "The Late Late Show" opened up discussions on topics which had been taboo. Above all, massive immigration from Europe and elsewhere transformed the character of Iron society with extraordinary speed. The Republic like Britain now faced the challenge of multi-culturalism.

The Republic is not a secular state. The influence of the Church, though declining, is still important. Mass attendance, though now much lower than in the De Valera period, is still relatively high by European standards. It is still possible for scholars to argue that the basis of a "normal" sense of nationality is "religion, language, and race,"[30] but this view, though universally accepted in the first half of the century, is now under challenge. The new civic emphasis was clear in a speech in 1981 by the then Taoiseach Garrett Fitzgerald when he declared, "The fact is our laws and our Constitution, our practices, our attitudes reflect those of a majority ethos and are not acceptable to Protestants in Northern Ireland."[31]

All the changes which have been explored imaginatively by such novelists as John McGahern and Roddy Doyle, are in marked contrast with the

situation north of the border. In the 1960s a young Ian Paisley was regarded as a maverick fundamentalist. Over the decades, however, his
influence has grown within Unionist circles to such an extent that his
brand of ethno-religious British nationalism attracts wide support on the
Unionist side, and his party, the Democratic Unionist Party, is now in
2004 the largest party in Northern Ireland. On the Catholic side, the moderate Social Democratic and Labour Party has lost ground to the strongly
republican Sinn Fein, whose opponents see it as the political wing of the
IRA. In 2004 Northern Ireland is thus as polarized on ethno-religious lines
as it has ever been.

The hopes raised in the 1960s for a politics based on civic identities
have been disappointed. In his rhetoric the Sinn Fein leader Gerry Adams
refers to Wolfe Tone but in practice it is the image of a Catholic nationalism which he puts to constant use. In the United States he refers to the
way in which the British government created the Great Hunger and
robbed "us" of our language.[32] Sinn Fein has hopes of making political
gains within the Irish Republic but it will need to shift to a more class-
based rhetoric if it is to appeal to a new urban proletariat. In the world of
the Celtic Tiger, with its innumerable financial scandals, traditional nationalist rhetoric carries less weight than it does north of the border.

In the interview which he gave in October 1999 Seamus Heaney spoke
of his experience as "a Catholic kid" in rural Derry putting on *Macbeth* or
The Tempest.[33]

> On the one hand you can do the reading that says you were force-fed colo-
> nial matter and that you became a good little subject of the English lan-
> guage by acknowledging Shakespeare and that he was part of the cultural
> clinching of the power situation.
>
> That's one truth all right. But there is another truth, which is that there's
> some form of transformation or radiance. Admittedly he's a cultural icon
> and part of the hegemony and so on. But there is also the extra-ness that
> comes just from going into a school play and seeing yourself and your com-
> panions all for the moment carried away. There was an element of enlight-
> enment bringing light into your life. So, is Shakespeare an imposition and a
> steady political Infiltration or is he a radiant transformer? Surely both.[34]

Heaney's multiethnic detachment is exceptional. In the political world of
Northern Ireland the shift has been toward the creation of two ever more
distant ethno-religious communities.

Postscript

To what extent does the history of Ireland in the twentieth century throw light upon the general phenomenon of nationalism? As a case study its significance surely cannot be denied. The fortunes of Irish nationalism offer clear parallels with those of similar political movements in Spain, Belgium, former Czecho-Slovakia, and Romania, not to mention other areas such as the Tyrol. The episodes of "1916" and of Bobby Sands are no doubt unique but the history of Irish nationalism raises general questions about the causes and course of such movements. In the 1980s there was a surge of interest in nationalism led by such studies as Ernest Gellner, *Nations and Nationalism* (1983), Benedict Anderson, *Imagined Communities* (1983), and Eric Hobsbawm, *Nations and Nationalism since 1780* (published in 1990 but based on lectures given in 1985). Before these works appeared nationalism had been largely neglected as a topic for serious historical analysis. Rather, class and class conflict had been a central focus of interest for historians. What these authors offered were new explanations for the rise of nationalism. Gellner linked nationalism with the rise of industrialization and its concomitant social changes. Anderson introduced the concept of an "imagined community." Hobsbawm analyzed nationalism from a Marxist standpoint, emphasizing its link with class. All three authors rejected the belief that nations owed their origins to some god-given principle. All stressed the "modernity" of nationalism.

So far as Irish nationalism is concerned it would seem that Anderson's concept of an "imagined community" has particular relevance. Such figures as Wolfe Tone, Thomas Davis, and Patrick Pearse envisioned a future Ireland which would be free from dependence upon Britain. This was the basis of their "imagined community." But one man's imagined community was not necessarily shared by all his fellowcountrymen. Such differences could lead to civil war between nationalist groups, as occurred in 1921 and again in Belfast in 1970.

What does not seem to work in the case of Ireland is Gellner's hypothesis linking nationalism and industrialism. On the contrary, Irish nationalism seems to have taken hold in rural areas. Hobsbawm's stress upon the importance of the French Revolution is somewhat undermined by his assumption that there was a Dual Revolution linking the French Revolution and the English Industrial Revolution. If nationalism did appear in Ireland it was in areas affected by deindustrialization.

Isaiah Berlin's brief essay on nationalism throws a good deal of light upon the case of Ireland.[35] Berlin argued that a group's experience of a "wound" creates a sense of deprivation. What he had in mind was the "stab in the back" theory as an explanation for the rise of German nationalism. A similar sense of relative deprivation in respect of the Great Famine took hold among the Irish diaspora in the United States. As we have seen, there was a sense of relative deprivation among lower-middle-class Catholics in Ireland around 1900. Among Catholics in Northern Ireland in the 1960s and 1970s the rise of nationalism was also fueled by the experience of discrimination.

Such general "causes," however, are not in themselves sufficient. What was needed was particular leadership or a particular course of events to create a vigorous political movement. This was as true of the rise of Hitler's brand of German nationalism in the 1920s as it was of Irish nationalism. For political success what needed to be called into being was a sense of national consciousness, and this depended upon a number of variables. Had the British authorities reacted more promptly to the threat of a rising in 1916 or had they behaved with greater circumspection afterward, the course of events might have been very different. An argument might be made on similar lines in the case of Zionism.

What is lost sight of in the work of Gellner, Anderson, and Hobsbawm is the extent to which all nationalisms are political movements which aim at gaining or retaining power. All such movements raise questions of leadership, political rhetoric, commitment by dedicated minority groups, the impact of changing circumstances, and the role of violence. In the case of nationalism the key issues of what constitutes nationhood, language, religion, or race (sc., ethnicity or the implied membership of a descent group) all play their role.

In this introduction and in the pages which follow I have obviously made considerable use of the distinction between "ethnic" and "civic" nationalism, discussed so brilliantly by Rogers Brubaker in *Citizenship and Nationhood in France and Germany* (Harvard University Press, 1992).[36] This raises the key issue of who is included within the nation and who is excluded and at what cost. Nationalism also raises the issue of what is termed "the tyranny of the majority." Finally there is the key question as to why nationalist rhetoric should often be more successful in the polls than political argument based upon economic or class consideration.

On all these issues, Irish nationalism may be seen as a significant case study. The problems faced after independence by successive Irish governments were unique to Ireland. From a more general point of view, however, the experience of Ireland in relation to the membership of the nation, the role of history in nation building, the balance between "civic" and "ethnic" considerations, the roles of religion, language, and ethnicity, runs parallel to that of other nations and other nationalist movements. Even England, which long considered itself to be above such considerations, is now being forced to concern itself with issues of ethnicity, Englishness, and Britishness.

NOTES

1. Tony Judt, "Israel: The Undivided Solution," in *The Sunday Times*, 26 October 2003.

2. Graham Walker, "Irish Nationalism and the Uses of History," in *Past and Present*, no. 126, pp. 208–14.

3. Derek Sayer, *The Coasts of Bohemia: A Czech History* (Princeton University Press: 1998).

4. Norman Davies, *The Heart of Europe: A Short History of Poland* (Oxford University Press: 1984); Irena Livezeanu, *Cultural Politics in Greater Romania* (Cornell University Press: 1995).

5. See N. Canny, *Making Ireland British* (Oxford University Press: 2001).

6. See Bernadette Cunningham's brilliant book, *The World of Geoffrey Keating: History, Myth, and Religion in Seventeenth-Century Ireland* (Dublin: Four Courts Press, 2000), especially chapter 6.

7. See Tadhg Ó hAnnracháin, *Catholic Reformation in Ireland: The Mission of Rinuccini 1645–1649* (Oxford: Oxford University Press, 2002).

8. Tadhg Ó hAnnracháin, "Political Ideology and Catholicism in Ireland," in Jane Ohlmeyer, ed., *Political Thought in Seventeenth-Century Ireland: Kingdom or Colony* (Cambridge: Cambridge University Press, 2000), p. 159.

9. Ibid., p. 168.

10. O'Connell held one of his monster outdoor meetings of Mullaghmast, Co. Leix, the site of a massacre in 1577. Clontarf, Dublin, was the scene of Brian Boru's victory over the Vikings in 1014.

11. Provided by Mr. William Corbett, ref. PRO London Home Office Papers HO-100-223. See also Clonmel Museum.

12. *The Irish Catholic*, 26 Sept. 1908, quoted in David W. Miller, *Church, State and Nation in Ireland 1898–1921* (Dublin: Gill and Macmillan, 1973), pp. 227–28.

13. Willard Potts, *Joyce and the Two Irelands* (Austin: University of Texas Press, 2000), p. 11.

14. Potts, Joyce and the *Two Irelands*, p. 33. See also Patrick Maume, *D. P. Moran* (Dublin: Dundalgan Press, 1995).

15. Barry M. Coldry, *Faith and Fatherland: The Christian Brothers and the Development of Irish Nationalism 1838–1921* (Dublin: Gill and Macmillan, 1988), p. 243.

16. See Senia Paseta, *Before the Revolution: Nationalism, Social Change and Ireland's Catholic Elite 1879–1922* (Cork: Cork University Press, 1999).

17. P. Hart, *The IRA and Its Enemies: Violence and Community in Cork 1916–1923* (Oxford: Oxford University Press, 1998).

18. The term "Eire" is often misused. For De Valera it referred to a unified Ireland, a future prospect in 1937. But often it was employed as equivalent to "The Irish Free State." The term "Ireland" itself is also misleading if used to mean "the Republic of Ireland" (of twenty-six counties).

19. Liam ua Cathain, *Cnoc Muire (Knock Shrine) in Picture and Story* (Galway: 1945). Fifth impression 1949, pp. 318–19.·

20. Ibid, p. 327.

21. Ibid, p. 338.

22. T. P. Coogan, *Ireland in the Twentieth Century* (London: Palgrave Macmillan, 2003), p. 274.

23. The impending British defeat raised hopes in some Irish circles that Germany might unify Ireland.

24. Quoted in Gabriel Doherty, "National Identity and the Study of Irish History," *English Historical Review* (April: 1996), p. 340.

25. Progress slowed, however, after the election of a new Pope, Paul VI, in 1963. See John Cooney, *John Charles McQuaid: Ruler of Catholic Ireland* (Dublin: O'Brien Press 1999), chapter 24.

26. There was a marked contrast with the situation in Britain where doctors' waiting rooms carried advertisements with such slogans as "There was an old woman who lived in a shoe, She had so many children because she did not know what to do."

27. Coogan, p. 623.

28. The Free State had a population of 2.9 million, Northern Ireland one of 1.5 million. See Dermot Keogh, *Twentieth Century Ireland: Nation and State* (Dublin: Gill and Macmillan, 1994), p. 88.

29. Peter Hart, "The Protestant Experience of Revolution in Southern Ireland," in Richard English and Graham Walker, eds., *Unionism in Modern Ireland: New Perspectives on Politics and Culture* (London: Gill and Macmillan, 1996), p. 81.

30. In his influential and brilliant book, *Ireland 1912–1985: Politics and Society* (Cambridge: Cambridge University Press, 1989), p. 661, Professor Lee declares of religion, language, and race that "It is the defining characteristic of normal European states and normal European peoples."

31. Coogan, p. 591.

32. In 1998, when political leaders from Northern Ireland visited Pittsburgh, David Trimble and Seamus Mallon spoke at the nonsectarian University of

Pittsburgh whereas Gerry Adams chose to speak at the Catholic University of Duquesne.

33. *The Irish Times*, 30 Oct. 1999.

34. *The Irish Times*, 30 Oct. 1999.

35. Isaiah Berlin, "Nationalism, Past Neglect and Present Power," in *Against the Current: Essays in the History of Ideas* (New York: Viking, 1980) pp. 333–55.

36. See also his *Nationalism Reframed: Nationhood and the National Question in the New Europe* (Cambridge: University Press, 1996).

Part I

Contested Ideas of Nationhood

In this section I have brought together essays on issues involving nationalism in Ireland, Britain, and to some extent Europe. A work which had considerable impact on me and other historians working in this field is *Citizenship and Nationhood in France and Germany* by Rogers Brubaker (1992) which raises key issues of civic and ethnic nationalism. In his comparison of France and Germany, the French emphasis on "civic" identity comes off best. Now, however (2004), the legal ban on Muslim women wearing headscarves (the hijab) in French state schools presents civic nationalism with a challenge. The official identity of the state is secular and the hijab with its religious implications is raising problems of assimilation which are proving difficult to deal with.

In an Irish context, the Cyclops episode in *Ulysses* illustrates a similar situation. Leopold Bloom, a Jew, claimed to be Irish ("I was born here") but "the Citizen" representing an ethnic nationalist outlook indignantly rejected this. Within liberal states it would seem that tensions between ethnic and civic attitudes to identity cannot be avoided. Today, for example, the United Kingdom advocates a multiethnic approach toward such problems but here also there seems to be no simple solution to the task of making new immigrants feel "British." Is the possession of a passport enough or should immigrants be required to learn English and acquire some knowledge of politics, history, and the constitution? In the Irish Republic, so far as recent decades are concerned, emigration—not immigration—was the main problem faced by successive governments. Today, however, the arrival of asylum seekers and economic migrants is creating a situation which, though apparently novel, raises familiar issues of national identity, as the essays presented in this section suggest. The Republic is now a full member of the European Community and in this context the old slogan of "Sinn Fein" (Ourselves Alone) does not have the same resonance.

Chapter One

Contested Ideas of Nationhood, 1800–1995

(1997)

In a recent book *Citizenship and Nationhood in France and Germany* Rogers Brubaker contrasts the way in which the French define citizenship (*ius soli*—the law of the soil) according to which those born on French territory are regarded as French, with the German definition which demands familial descent (*ius sanguinis*—the law of blood). Brubaker sees French citizenship as civic, German nationhood as tribal. The distinction is not merely an academic one since it affects the legal status of immigrants. French national identity encourages acculturation, so that, for example, M. Balladur born of Romanian parents, could be accepted as completely French and able to aspire to the Presidency of France. In contrast German national identity, with its emphasis upon German blood, makes it difficult if not impossible for third- or fourth-generation Turkish immigrants fully fluent in the German language to become German citizens, whereas ethnic Germans, emigrating from Russia and non-German speaking, run into no such difficulties.[1]

However, the contrast between France and Germany is not perhaps as sharp as Brubaker makes out. There are many in France who wish to define French national identity in religious terms. For these, Frenchness and Catholicism are inextricably intertwined. It is to this sense of religious identity that M. Le Pen appeals when he points to the dangers, as he sees them, presented by North African immigrants. Le Pen's sense of French national identity may not be based upon *ius sanguinis* in a literal sense but it clearly appeals to a sense of ethno-cultural exclusiveness.

This tension between civic and ethnic concepts of national identity in France is not merely a contemporary phenomenon. To take the most notorious example, the Dreyfus case at the end of the nineteenth century revealed how bitterly France was divided upon the issue of anti-Semitism. The key question put by Action-Française was whether French Jews could ever be fully French. During those years the political nation split over whether Frenchness was civic or ethnic, and even within each category there was no agreement as to the necessary criteria (were the French a Celtic nation, for example?). The case for reclaiming German-speaking Alsace-Lorraine rested of course upon the assumption that French identity was civic not ethnic in character. But civic national identity also has its problems. In Brittany, for example, the use of Celtic first names is forbidden by law. In France generally, Muslim schoolgirls are forbidden by the state to cover their heads. French civic identity, in the eyes of the religiously committed, can appear aggressively secularist.

Where have we, the inhabitants of these islands, stood in all this? In a famous article, "Nationality and Liberty," Sir Lewis Namier argued that British national identity was unproblematic. He stated confidently

> The British and Swiss concepts of nationality are primarily territorial: it is the State which created nationality not vice versa... Liberty and self government have moulded the territorial nation of Britain and given content to its communal nationality. The political life of the British island community centres in its Parliament at Westminster, which represents men rooted in British soil. This is a territorial and not a tribal assembly.[2]

Namier, a Jewish immigrant from Poland, understandably stressed the civic character of British identity. More recently, however, Liah Greenfeld in *Nationalism: Five Roads to Modernity* and Linda Colley in *Britons: The Forging of a Nation*[3] have stressed the importance of religion as the essential component of English/British national identity. From this point of view English/British national identity is *ethno-cultural* not *territorial* in character. In terms of a contrast between tribal and civic identity, their view suggests that England approximates more to a Le Pen French model than a French civic model. As with France and Germany there is more at stake here than terminology. After the end of World War II, the United Kingdom received a massive influx of immigrants from India, Bangladesh, Pakistan, the West Indies and not least the Republic of Ireland. It matters a great deal to the children of these newcomers in Bradford or Kilburn, what the basis of their nationality is to be, civic or ethnic or a workable compromise. Norman Tebbit's view is ethnic. "The cricket test—which side do they cheer for? Are you still looking back to where you came from or where you are?"[4]

The contrast between these two concepts of nationhood goes back at least to the French Revolution. It was Edmund Burke in his *Reflections on the French Revolution* who put the case for a historic, hereditary concept of a nation stretching back over time: "As the ends of such a partnership cannot be obtained in many generations it becomes a partnership not only between those who are living but between those who are living, those who are dead and those who are to be born." He declared that "the majority of the people of England, far from thinking a religious national establishment unlawful, hardly think it lawful to be without one!"

> This principle runs through the whole system of their polity. ... Church and state are ideas inseparable in their minds and scarcely is the one ever mentioned without mentioning the other. ... Our education is so formed as to confirm and fix this impression. Our education is in this manner solely in the hands of ecclesiastics and in all stages from infancy to manhood. By this connection we conceive that we attach our gentlemen to the church; and we liberalise the church by an intercourse with the leading characters of the country.[5]

From Burke's point of view the key symbols of the nation were the monarchy, the Church, and the aristocracy. The monarchy and the House of Lords represented the hereditary element in the constitution, but within the House of Commons itself a *quasi*-hereditary element was also to be found in the persons of the younger sons of the peerage. The established Church itself was also closely linked with the nobility. The bishops sat in the House of Lords by right, but in any case in 1815 eleven of them were of noble birth. In the Church of Ireland, as Halevy tells us, three archbishops and eight bishops came from influential backgrounds.[6] Three members of the Beresford family were bishops! The Universities of Oxford and Cambridge were also key institutions of the established Church. The Protestant Constitution survived the challenge of the French Revolution, unscathed, even strengthened. The implications of all this for citizenship were far-reaching, since it meant that only those who belonged to the established Church were full members of this ethno-cultural state.

There was, however, an alternative view of the English nation which was civic, not ethno-cultural in character. Recent studies have drawn attention to the role of the French Revolution in creating the concept of citizenship. The new French nation which emerged in 1789 was a civic nation replacing the ethno-cultural Catholic nation of the *ancien régime*. Protestants and Jews could now be full citizens. However, the simplicity of the early vision soon became more complex. Divisions appeared among the revolutionaries, some stressing, as did Robespierre, "liberty, equality and fraternity"; others, like Danton, the importance of "natural frontiers" and the destiny of *La Grande Nation*. Often indeed French civic nationalism was largely lost to sight amid the political turmoil of the nineteenth century until it re-emerged during the Third Republic.

It was the United States, rather than France, which took the first decisive steps toward a civic national identity (though even here many groups were at first excluded, among them women, blacks, and Indians). Tom Paine's *Rights of Man* put the case for civic identity. But Paine was a controversial figure in England. Professor Jim Epstein, in a recent book, mentions how during the 1790s Manchester taverns displayed boards inscribed "No Jacobins admitted here." Copies of the *Rights of Man* and effigies of Tom Paine were burned. Peterloo in 1819 was followed by repression when radicalism went into decline.[7] (Even as late as the Second World War, a statue erected in his birth place at Thetford was tarred and feathered.)

More significant as a spokesman for civic nationhood in an English context was Jeremy Bentham, to whose name may be added that of his intellectual disciple, John Stuart Mill. In 1776 Bentham had provided arguments for use against the American rebels. By 1789, however, in his *Introduction to the Principles of Morals*, he referred to the United States as "that newly created nation, one of the most enlightened if not the most enlightened at this day in the globe." By 1809 he supported the full radical demand for universal suffrage, secret ballots, annual parliaments, and equal electoral districts. In 1817 he published a *Catechism on Reform* in which he urged his readers to "look to America." In his *Plan for Parliamentary Reform* he spoke of America as the best government that is or ever has been. In America, there was no established Church, no hereditary aristocracy, and no standing army. He attacked the ritual which surrounded monarchy as a "delusion"—a "factitious dignity" designed to mystify the people. America was a "never-to-be expunged reproach to our Matchless Constitution—matchless in rotten boroughs and sinecures."[8]

Bentham's hostile attitude toward the existing regime was followed by James Mill and above all by John Stuart Mill, whose work on *Representative Government* (1861) devoted a long chapter to the issue of nationality. In this chapter, with its emphasis upon consent, we find a more inclusive conception of national identity. Mill stated that, though the Irish had been treated abominably in the past, he believed that recent reforms had led them to accept the benefits of being fellow citizens of "one of the freest as well as the most civilised and powerful nations on earth."

At the level of general debate, there was perhaps little to choose between the voices of Burke and Coleridge on the one hand and Bentham and Mill on the other. In terms of institutions and political power, however, the balance was heavily weighted in favor of the ethnic identity defended by Burke and against the civic identity espoused by Bentham. The British monarchy successfully repulsed the challenge of the French Revolution. The hereditary character of the Constitution survived in the monarchy and the House of Lords and in other key institutions of Church and State. In the aftermath of Waterloo, the ethno-cultural basis of the British state seemed secure. Fifteen years before Waterloo, however, an event had occurred which had long-lasting unforeseen consequences—the passing in 1800 of the Act of Union between Great Britain and Ireland. A new British state had been brought into existence. It was this which makes nonsense of Namier's view that British nationality was unproblematic. Historians might write of Britain and the British but, as a political unit, Britain had ceased to exist. "Our Island Story" now became "The Story of these Islands." The simple view that British identity was ethnic was to be subjected to a series of challenges which operated on the assumption that U.K. citizenship was "civic." The terms "ethnic" and "civic" are modern but the issues raised go back to the period of the American and French Revolutions and they were of course exemplified in the hopes and dreams of the United Irishmen.

In Pitt's view, the creation of a new British state in 1800 by the Act of Union made good economic sense, uniting as it did the ten million-strong population of Britain with the four million people of Ireland. In wartime, in the aftermath of the 1798 Rebellion, there were also sound strategic reasons for Britain to take a stronger grip on Ireland. Leaders of the Catholic majority in Ireland were in favor of the Union. Many Irish Catholics who had seen the penal laws against them gradually relaxed since the 1770s as a result of British governmental pressure on the Protestant Ascendancy were willing to accept the Union. Irish Catholics who had been granted the vote in 1793, on the basis of the 40/- freehold franchise, hoped for further concessions. The failure of the 1798 rebellion also strengthened the hand of the conservative Catholics. The Catholic hierarchy in 1799, with only one or two opposing, agreed to accept state payment of the clergy together with a government veto as to "the loyalty of the person appointed." In the Newry by-election of 1799 Archbishop Troy encouraged Catholic voters to support the pro-Union candidate. Edward Dillon, archbishop of Tuam, braved possible charges of being "an Orange bishop" and came out in favor of the Union. Leaders of the Catholic majority in Ireland were thus in favor of the Union.[9]

There was opposition to Pitt's Act of Union but it came from members of the Ascendancy and especially from the Orangemen of certain northern counties. Thomas Goold declared:

> The Great Creator of the world has given unto our beloved country the gigantic outlines of a Kingdom and not the pigmy features of a province. God and nature, I say, never intended that Ireland shall be a province and by God, she never shall.[10]

The ethnic nationalism expressed in these debates was by and large that of the Protestant Ascendancy, which had enjoyed autonomy since 1782 and now saw its freedom threatened by absorption into a wider union dominated by Great Britain. George Ogle spoke of "our happy Constitution in Church and State ... founded at the Glorious Revolution: and I will add the Protestant Ascendancy. We have only acted, [he declared] on the defensive in support of the constitution handed down by our Ancestors."[11] This ethnic nationalism was very different from the civic nationalism which had been advocated by Wolfe Tone and others in the United Irishmen movement founded in 1792. As William Drennan put it, "the full and free enjoyment of our rights is absolutely necessary to the performance of our duties ... the freedom of the public must necessarily be connected with their *virtue* as well as their happiness." As recent research has shown, Paine's *Rights of Man* sold more widely in Ireland than it did in Britain. The *Northern Star* promoted Paine's ideas. It was reported that at a United Irish dinner in Dublin in 1793 "Tom Paine's health was drunk with the greatest fervency and enthusiasm."[12]

The United Irishmen also attempted to politicize fairs, patterns, and other local venues, so much so that the Catholic bishop James Caulfield warned his flock against "all unnecessary meetings, associations, places of pilgrimage or patrons, of diversions and dissipation which can tend to no good."[13] In areas such as South Armagh this kind of warning fell on deaf ears, and the United Irishmen were able to recruit from the Catholic "Defender" movement. The 1790s in Ireland, as in England, were marked by a contest between civic and ethnic nationalism, which culminated in the rebellion of 1798, the subsequent defeat of which set back civic nationalism for several generations. Ethnic nationalism in the shape of the Orange Order, founded in 1795, was triumphant.

In Scotland, events took a somewhat different turn. During the 1790s the United Irishmen urged the Scots to follow the example of earlier heroes, such as William Wallace, George Buchanan, and Fletcher of Saltoun. But British unionism proved to be stronger than Scottish nationalism.[14] Scots radicals set up a British Convention and called themselves the "United Britains," not the "United Scotsmen." But civic nationalism in Scotland, as in Ireland, was defeated. Its leader Thomas Muir fled to France where he clashed with Wolfe Tone in competing for French military assistance. It is interesting to note in all this that civic nationalism made little or no headway in the Gaelic-speaking areas of either Ireland or Scotland. Civic nationalism implied literacy in English, as its counterpart in France demanded literacy in French. As the work of Brendan O Buachalla has shown, Jacobitism was extraordinarily strong in Gaelic-speaking Ireland during the eighteenth century. As a consequence, civic nationalism had little foundation on which to build in such areas.

In Ireland during the 1790s, the religious leaders of the Catholic majority showed no enthusiasm for the civic nationalism of the United Irishmen. However, when the Act of Union was proposed by the British government, the Catholic bishops saw it as a means of achieving full citizenship within the new state which the Act of Union would create. Archbishop Troy of Dublin placed his influence at the disposal of the government.

When the Act of Union passed, however, the expectations of the Catholics about admittance to Parliament were disappointed. George III stood firm on what he considered to be the terms of his Coronation Oath. The Protestant Constitution remained intact. A new state had been created, but within it a substantial minority of Irish Catholics, possessing the vote, were excluded from the benefits of full political representation, in particular the right to sit in Parliament. Fundamental change was difficult to avoid, however. The implications of a substantial Irish presence within the new state proved to be a powerful solvent. The unforeseen consequences of the Act of Union were to place a continuous strain upon the apparently secure Protestant Constitution. Those who supported a civic national identity were able to use Irish issues as a weapon against the Establishment. Defenders of the status quo, for their part, used traditional cries of "No Popery" to preserve the traditional ethno-cultural national identity. We tend to think of the rise of Irish nationalism as a central feature of nineteenth-century British history. It is perhaps more appropriate to stress *the rise of English ethno-cultural nationalism*, mobilized from the top down in defense of the institutions of the ancient ethno-cultural constitution. Benthamites and other radicals pressed for a civic identity throughout the United Kingdom. Against such challenges, ethnic nationalists tried, whenever possible, to preserve the traditional (that is, Protestant) institutions of Church and State. If the Irish Question was at the center of so many political storms, it was because it raised the fundamental issue of English national identity. It can also be argued that significant reforms for the English state were postponed or diverted by the influence of Ireland. The French historian Halevy looked for reasons why there was no revolution in industrial England. The Irish Question, rather than Methodism, should perhaps be at the center of an alternative explanation, since it kept English nationalism in ferment and diverted support away from radical reforms.

The first decisive battle in the prolonged war between civic and ethno-cultural nationalism took place in 1829 over Catholic Emancipation. The issue could no longer be avoided in the face of Daniel O'Connell's successful agitation in Ireland. Nevertheless the Protestant establishment fought hard in defense of the Constitution. In speaking against Catholic Emancipation in 1829, the Archbishop of Canterbury, Dr. Howley, declared that the "constitution was essentially Protestant, and that the present measure threatened an innovation, which would entirely alter the character of the constitution (hear, hear). Did he therefore say that the Constitution would be popish? He said no such thing: but he did say that the character of the country would be no longer Protestant, as it now was."[15] In one of his finest flights, Dr. Howley proclaimed:

> It was possible that a person of religious mind, looking at the position which England occupied—at the extensive colonies which she possessed in the east, in the west, the north and the south—might believe that she was ordained to be instrumental in the hands of Providence in extending true religion to the remotest corners of the globe.[16]

In this speech by the Archbishop we hear the tones of an authentic ethno-cultural nationalism, appealing to English history and to a religious identity at a moment which he perceived to be one of supreme crisis. The Catholic Relief Bill passed, but the nationalism which Howley's speech exemplified remained intact for many years to come.

In the 1830s the role of the established Church in education was challenged by the Whigs. The victory of the Whigs in 1830 had led to a remarkable educational experiment in Ireland which can be seen as encouraging the rise of a civic identity in that country. The state agreed to grant funding directly to so-called national schools from which religious teaching was formally excluded. National schools made possible the growth of "mixed education" in areas with different religious groups. The system was supported by liberal members of the Catholic hierarchy in the east of Ireland, in particular James Doyle, Bishop of Kildare, and Leighlin (J. K. L.) and Daniel Murray, Archbishop of Dublin. J. K. L. wrote in its favor:

> I do not see how any man, wishing well to the public peace, and who looks to Ireland as his country, can think that peace can ever be permanently established, or the prosperity of the country, ever well secured, if children are separated at the commencement of life, on account of their religious opinions. I do not know any measures which would prepare the way for a better feeling in Ireland than uniting children at an early age and bringing them up in the same school, leading them to commune with one another and to form those little intimacies and friendships which often subsist through life.[17]

(One of the major drawbacks of these changes from the viewpoint of later ethno-cultural nationalists was that the use of the Irish language was discouraged.)

The Whig Home Secretary Lord John Russell attempted to introduce a similar scheme in England, but his plan met with strong resistance from the Tories speaking as defenders of the national tradition. Among those who spoke was the young Benjamin Disraeli, who argued that the proposed change "must have a vast and incalculable influence on the character of the people." He opposed the state grant for education on the grounds that it would "interfere with the habit of self government by the people of England." He appealed to past history, arguing that the age which produced "truly English spirits" such as Pym and Hampden had changed during the Commonwealth "into the most degraded and most ignoble Tyranny which ever sported with the destinies of a great country." He said: "The national spirit had been destroyed: a great system of central organisation was established in the realm: the people had free institutions but their rights as subjects were destroyed." He foresaw "the rise of a new race of fifth monarchy men," and "the fury and violence of contending sects as in the time of the Commonwealth!" He asked the House to consider the achievement of those who had built their colleges, churches, and cathedrals. "Let them look abroad on England and witness the result. Where would they find a country more elevated in the social scale? Where a people more distinguished for all that was excellent in the human character? The time would come, if they persisted in their present course, they would find that they had revolutionised the English character and when that was effected then they could no longer expect English achievements." For these reasons, "he believed that the system of education which the noble Lord wants to establish was alien to the habits and contrary to the genius of this country." He asked the House of Commons not to scorn "the learning, the experience, the information and the patriotism of the House of Lords."[18]

The Archbishop of Canterbury argued that "this was a matter which affected the true foundation, not only of the church, but of religion itself."

> It was a question as to the manner in which the people should be educated—whether they should receive their education on the sound principles of the Church or whether the door should be open to the instillation of principles of every sect, however wild or extravagant.[19]

He criticized those "who wished to introduce a system of education which would entirely overthrow the National Church." He noted that "Religious instruction was to be considered as general and special," but did not understand what was meant by "general instruction in the truths of revealed religion." In fact, "there was no such thing as instruction in Christianity without instruction in those peculiar truths." In a final appeal he added:

> considering the connection of the Church with the State, they would also be acting with the greatest impolity with respect to the true interests of the people. ... If the Church does not teach the true doctrines of our holy religion—if it does not inculcate the purest morals—if it does not insist on obedience to the laws and the authorities of the country—upon which depend loyalty to the Sovereign and the performance of every Christian duty—I say, my lords, it is utterly unworthy of your support.
>
> In the distribution of the public money for the encouragement of religion, their first object ought to be to maintain and extend the religion of the State: that religion, which, by the instruction it imparts, combines the great majority of the people with the vast establishment which is responsible to the State for the proper performance of its duties.[20]

Tory ethno-cultural nationalism was victorious. Russell's educational proposals were defeated. What the Archbishop of Canterbury and Benjamin Disraeli were objecting to was the same plan which had been introduced into Ireland in 1831 and which aimed at including churches of all denominations with the active cooperation of the clergy of all denominations. As Thomas Wyse of Waterford asked: "If the adoption of a mixed system of education was right in Ireland, it was equally right and proper in England and he could not understand why it had been rejected or repudiated by the noble Lord."[21] Wyse pointed out how similar systems had been adopted in Greece, Naples, Tuscany, and Switzerland, in France by the law of 1834 and in every state in Germany from 1834, in Russia, Sweden, Holland, and even in the United States. The Church of England was not the Church of "the entire nation" and hence "had no right over those who had no sort of communion with her." The Irish Catholic bishops, Murray and Doyle, and the majority of their colleagues had shown themselves willing to accept a *civic nationalism* within the United Kingdom at a time when the Church of England stood firm in its role as defender of *ethno-cultural nationalism*.

The vehemence of the debate was extraordinary, and understandably so, since what was at stake was an essential element in the process of creating and maintaining a national identity. In his excellent study of France, *Peasants into Frenchmen*, Eugene Weber pointed to the importance of the schools and the army in propagating a sense of Frenchness. French state schools throughout much of the nineteenth century had the aim of inculcating a *civic* identity. French Church schools, in contrast, saw themselves as attempting to preserve an *ethno-cultural* identity in a political environment which was normally hostile to religion. In England the boot was on the other foot. There the considerable resources of the state Church, backed by the wealth and prestige of clerical universities, supported schools dedicated to preserving an ethno-cultural identity. The paradox was that in another part of the state, government policy was directed toward subsidizing an educational system of "National Schools" which had something approaching a civic national identity in view. It was a view which Daniel O'Connell supported, at least in 1839. He considered it a disgrace that "of all countries in Europe, England alone should have no system of national education." He criticized those who had attacked "any system of national education which was not founded on the principles of the Established Church."

The note of English nationalism which Howley had sounded in 1829 continued to be heard in succeeding decades. It reappeared in 1844 when Sir Robert Peel, the Tory Prime Minister, proposed to increase the government grant for the Irish Catholic seminary at Maynooth. This minor issue in economic terms aroused extraordinary emotion on the Tory benches, which led to a permanent split within the party in the following year. English national feeling was again aroused in 1851 in the so-called "Papal

Aggression agitation" which followed upon a decision by the papacy to establish territorial dioceses in England. Astonishingly, it was Lord John Russell, the erstwhile champion of "civic" education who raised the "no popery" issue for his own political reasons.

The Earl of Winchelsea, speaking in the House of Lords, declared:

> no man could place his finger upon any point in English history in which the political horizon presented so dark a prospect, or in which England stood in so humiliating and degrading a position. ... Great and imminent as were the dangers which had threatened this country throughout that long and eventful war in which the contest had been for national liberty, in his opinion these dangers sunk [*sic*] into perfect insignificance when compared with the domestic calamities which were now impending.

He predicted that if the government acted upon grounds of expediency:

> a great struggle must speedily take place between the Protestant feeling of this country and the Church of Rome and against the victim of her power, which would never be effected without first involving England in the horrors of a civil war.[22]

Disraeli took a more detached view, but his ironic comments give some impression of the "genie" which Russell had released from the bottle. He poked fun at the relatively innocuous proposals which Russell eventually put forward:

> Was it for this (that is, the government bill) that the Lord High Chancellor of England trampled on a Cardinal's hat—amidst the patriotic acclamations of the metropolitan municipality? Was it for this that the First Minister, with more reserve, delicately hinted to the assembled guests that there had been occasions when the shadow of the Armada darkened the seas of England? Was it for this that all the counties and corporations of England met? Was it for this that all our learned and religious societies assembled, at a period the most inconvenient, in order, as they thought to respond to the appeal of their Sovereign, and to lose no time in assuring Her Majesty of their determination to guard Her authority and Her supremacy?[23]

After the debacle of the Papal Aggression issue, the power of ethno-cultural nationalism in England showed signs of abating during the first half of the nineteenth century. During the Crimean War Tennyson's poem "The Charge of the Light Brigade" provided eloquent expression for the national mood. After the war was over, in 1856 signs of political change began to appear. Gladstone moved slowly to the left. John Bright, scourge of the

Tory establishment, returned to favor. And toward the end of the decade, Liberalism found a spokesman for a civic identity in John Stuart Mill whose treatise on *Representative Government* was published in 1861.

Though couched in general terms, this work was in fact as much an attack upon the Burkean view of the English Constitution as the work of Paine and Bentham had been earlier in the century. In Mill's treatise we hear the argument for civic identity:

> It is a great discouragement to an individual and a still greater one to a class, to be left out of the constitution: to be reduced to plead from outside the door to the arbiters of their destiny, not to be taken into the constitution within. The maximum of the invigorating effect of freedom upon the character is only obtained when the person acted on either is, or is looking forward to become, a citizen as fully privileged as any other.

In theory, within the British Constitution, sovereignty was invested in three coordinate members, but in practice the preponderance of power lay with the popular element in the Constitution. Unlike the Tories, Mill played down the constitutional roles of the monarchy and the House of Lords. "The British government is thus a representative government in the correct sense of the term; and the powers which it leaves in the hands not directly accountable to the people can only be considered as precautions which the ruling power is willing should be taken against its own errors." Mill was optimistic about the future prospects of the United Kingdom:

> No Irishman is now less free than an Anglo-Saxon nor has a less share of every benefit either to his country or to his individual fortunes than if he were sprung from any other portion of the British dominions. The only remaining real grievance of Ireland, that of a State Church, is one which half, or nearly half of the people of the larger island have in common with them. There is now next to nothing, except the memory of the past, and the difference in the predominant religion, to keep apart two races perhaps the most fitted of any two in the world to be the completing counterpart of one another.

Mill argued that the Irish were no longer "foreigners" but "fellow-citizens."[24] Mill had good reason to feel optimistic about the prospects of incorporating the two nations, England and Ireland, within a wider civic identity. A new party, the Liberal Party, had been founded which brought together the various groups opposed to the dominance of the Anglican Establishment. But the first real test of Liberalism—the disestablishment of the Church of Ireland—ran into fierce and bitter opposition. Gladstone regarded the measure as "the first of our great experiments in the work of pacifying and satisfying Ireland." Opponents of the bill saw it as the first step toward disestablishing the Church of England. One member (Whalley) "thought that the general feeling of the country was that this was not an Irish question but an English question and a Church of England question—an attempt to put all religions on the basis of equality."[25] In the House of Lords the Protestant Bishop of Tuam entered his protest "against every part and every enactment of this shameful bill." He declared to its supporters:

> Victory, if you gain it, will be victory, not over your enemies, but over your best friends. Victory, if you gain it, will be victory over the friends of order, of loyalty, of British connection. Victory, if you gain it, will be victory by forcing a breach in the strongest bulwark of our Constitution, through which anarchy and democracy may rush in. ... Our struggle then is for the truth of God—for that righteousness which embodied in the State exalts a nation.[26]

Lord Derby declared that

> the question [of disestablishment] involves a complete revolution in the constitution of this country. ... When I speak of a revolution, I speak of a bloodless revolution—of an entire social revolution. I speak of a revolution that will make an entire change in the feelings and habits of the people.[27]

After bitter and prolonged debate in Parliament in 1868–69 the Irish Church Disestablishment Bill became law. It had the effect of meeting the grievances of dissenters such as John Bright and of those Irish Catholic groups, especially the Catholic hierarchy, whose support Gladstone was seeking in his policies of Liberal reform. For us, however, the significance of the episode lies in the light which it throws upon the appeal of a Protestant ethno-cultural national identity faced with the challenge of a civic national identity. Faced with the challenge of new circumstances in the wake of the Act of Union, this traditional ethno-cultural identity proved to be remarkably resilient. Its symbols were a Protestant monarchy, a House of Lords based upon a hereditary peerage, an established Church whose bishops sat in the Lords, two ancient universities closely linked with the established Church, and an army whose most prestigious regiments enjoyed a close relationship with the monarchy and the aristocracy. The conflict between an ethno-cultural identity and a civic identity within the United Kingdom was never fully resolved. Nor, it may be said, was it resolved in France. The difference between the two cases lay in the fact that from 1870 in France onward the power of the state tilted sharply in favor of a civic identity. In contrast, within the United Kingdom, the conservative party enjoyed political power over a long period. The party defended symbols and used a political rhetoric which implied the supremacy of an ethno-cultural rather than a civic identity within the United Kingdom.

In the second half of the century, two developments occurred which added to the obstacles in the way of creating a civic British identity. The first of these was a shift toward a fully blown Catholic ethno-cultural iden-tity in Ireland. As we have seen, leaders of the Catholic community had shown themselves willing to support a national system of "mixed educa-tion." Even Daniel O'Connell, though often stereotyped as a Catholic na-tionalist, in fact pressed throughout much of his career for what we can recognize as a civic identity for Ireland. O'Connell died in 1847. Before then, he had however clashed with the Young Irelanders over the issue of "mixed education" at university level. More important than O'Connell's death, was the arrival in Ireland of the ultramontane cleric, Paul Cullen, later to become primate. Under Cullen's leadership the Catholic Church in Ireland set its face firmly against "mixed education." At the synod of Thurles in 1850, Cullen clashed with Murray over the acceptability of the Queen's Colleges and won by a narrow vote. Thus ethno-culturalists in Ireland followed the example of their counterparts in England.

Spokesmen for a civic nationalism, however, were still to be found among Republicans both in Ireland and the United States and among Liberal Presbyterians.[28] In 1865 John Elliot Cairnes, a professor at Queen's College, Galway, and friend of Mill, put the anti-Cullen case: "What can be better fitted to qualify the virus of bigotry and engender feelings of mutual consideration and respect, what better preparation for the duties of citi-zenship in a country of mixed religious faith can be imagined than a system of education which furnishes to the youths of all denominations neutral ground on which they may meet and cultivate in common, without refer-ence to the causes which divide them, those pursuits in which they have a common interest."[29] In general, however, the tide had turned toward an ethno-cultural identity. Schools, as always in the creation of a national identity, were a crucial issue. Cullen was a strong supporter of Christian Brothers' schools whose brand of "Faith and Fatherland" nationalism spread widely throughout Ireland. Jesuit schools, in contrast, were much cooler toward nationalism; in part because they were an international order, in part because many of their students looked toward a career in the existing framework of the United Kingdom or the British Empire.

The O'Connell centenary celebrations held in Dublin in August 1875 and marked by the erection of a statue in his memory, provide an illuminating example of the tensions which existed in Ireland during the second half of the nineteenth century.[30] The conflict between ethnic and civic nationalism was sharply focused in the contest between Cullen and the Protestant politician Isaac Butt over O'Connell's historical significance. For Cardinal Cullen and his allies O'Connell symbolized the struggle for Catholic Emancipation. For Cullen's opponents, who included the redoubtable John MacHale, Catholic archbishop of Tuam, O'Connell was a champion of Repeal. In the long run the ethnic nationalists established a monopoly over the memory of O'Connell the Catholic Liberator. The civic nationalists found an alternative symbol in Charles Stewart Parnell whose statue stands at the opposite end of O'Connell Street. Nelson's Pillar, symbol of a beleaguered British ethnic identity, stood between the two for a century before being blown up by the IRA in 1966. But the fundamental issues still remain as part of the contemporary Irish scene.

Parnell may be classified as a civic nationalist. Politician that he was, however, he came to an understanding with the forces of Catholic nationalism led by Archbishop Croke. This alliance broke down in 1890 when the party split over the O'Shea divorce case. It was then that Parnell appealed to "the hillsiders," that is, those who supported the anticlerical Fenians. At this moment his commitment to a civic nationalism became clear.

Parnell knew no Irish and was largely indifferent to the details of Irish history. He died in 1891, but had he lived on he would have had to face the challenge of the Gaelic Revival and the Irish-Ireland Movement. The first of these, led by Douglas Hyde, pressed for the deanglicization of Ireland, an objective which had obvious implications for the English-speaking (or Scots-speaking) North. The Irish-Ireland movement, with D. P. Moran as its propagandist, looked forward to the victory of a Catholic and "Gaelic" ethno-cultural nationalism. For the moment, however, until 1916 the largely civic nationalism of John Redmond, who inherited the mantle of Parnell and had succeeded in uniting the Home Rule Party, held its own. Redmond found himself fighting a war on two fronts, between the ethno-culturalism of Protestant Ulster and that of Irish-Ireland. In 1918 his party went down to defeat.

I have confined my comments to England and Ireland. A similar analysis could be made, however, in relation to Wales and Scotland. In Wales the symbol of national identity for the majority was membership of one or other of the nonconformist churches. "Welshness" for these was as much an ethno-cultural construct as "Irishness" was for substantial numbers in Ireland. In Scotland the situation was made more complex by "the Disruption" of 1843—the split which divided the established Presbyterian Church of Scotland. For a great majority, however, Scottishness was an ethno-cultural identity of which Presbyterianism was a key element. By this criterion Catholics of Irish descent could never be fully Scottish, even though in the decades following the Great Famine they became a substantial minority. Indeed in 1923 the General Assembly formally approved a report entitled *The Menace of the Irish Race to Our Scottish Nationality.* Throughout the 1920s and 1930s the "Church and Nation" committee of the General Assembly reported on the threat to the "nation." In 1934, for example, statistics were quoted to show that "the population of Scotland is every year becoming less Scottish in blood, tradition and religious attachment." The Church of Scotland saw itself as the mouthpiece of the Scottish people. In 1927, for example, it was declared that:

> The church of Scotland, whose interests have been in the past so intimately involved with the Scottish people has clearly an obligation to defend Scottish nationality such as no other institution or organisation has against a kind of peril which was "the gravest which the Scottish people have ever confronted."[31]

Such nationalism was as ethno-cultural as that of Howley or Cullen. Modern Scottish nationalism may be more civic in character, but the issues raised by Rangers and Celtic are not moribund.[32]

My main point in this essay is to draw attention to the conflict between two concepts of national identity within the United Kingdom. If the argument is well founded, it makes possible a comparison between the United Kingdom and other European states, including also, perhaps, the United States and Canada. By confining their attention to Britain, historians have managed to make British nationhood seem unproblematic.

"Britain" is not the state, though it may sometimes be used as shorthand for it. "The state" is the United Kingdom, which even today, and even more during the nineteenth century, includes territory beyond "the British island." One of the main tests which the United Kingdom faced was to devise or create an identity for the inhabitants of the state, inhabitants who were divided by history, religion, and ethnicity. The United Kingdom thus confronted problems which were similar to those faced by Prussia when, at the Congress of Vienna, it acquired Catholic provinces in the Rhineland in addition to Polish provinces it already possessed in the East. Another parallel is the new kingdom of the Netherlands created by uniting Protestant Holland and Catholic Belgium. This united kingdom split into constituent parts in 1830. It lasted fifteen years. The U.K. of Great Britain and Ireland broke up in 1921 after a century of often troubled existence.

The second crucial development which took place from mid-century was the rise of racial stereotyping. The image arose of a superior Anglo-Saxon race and of an inferior Celtic race. In his excellent study *Anglo-Saxons and Celts* Perry Curtis has shown how widespread such stereotypes became. What is significant, however, and this is lost sight of in his book, is how such ethnic nationalism was largely confined to the Tory party. It was in Tory periodicals that Anglo-Saxon racial prejudice found its main spokesmen. Full consideration of the implications of this ethnic nationalism would take us beyond the confines of our topic. Clearly, however, ethnic nationalism combined with a revival of imperialism provided a potent mix. It proved too much for Gladstone in his second ministry from 1880 to 1886. Gladstone's solution for Ireland was Home Rule, by which was meant not independence but autonomy within a United Kingdom political framework. It rested on the assumption of a common U.K. civic identity exemplified in the political reforms of 1884–85 which for the first time included Ireland within a common U.K. framework. The challenge proved too much for the Liberal Party. In particular Joseph Chamberlain, who in the first half of his political career was a fierce opponent of the establishment, a republican sympathizer and a critic of the peerage, and who on balance seemed to have favored a civic identity, shifted his ground. By 1887 while touring Ulster he spoke of a community connected by ties of "race and religion and sympathy with the greater nation of which it is proud to form a part." His conversion from civic to ethnic nationalism was complete.[33] This Anglo-Saxon racialism had the paradoxical effect of stimulating the rise of a Celtic racialism exemplified in the writings of D. P. Moran and other Irish-Ireland enthusiasts.

It is not the rise of Irish nationalism which has been my main topic but the continued struggle within the United Kingdom between two concepts of national identity—ethno-cultural and civic. The balance of political power favored ethno-cultural identity. It was only with the rise of liberalism during Gladstone's first ministry in 1868–74 that inroads began to be made upon the power of the ethno-cultural establishment. The crux came in 1886 with the Home Rule crisis. Gladstone's solution was not Irish independence but a form of autonomy, which could have included Wales and Scotland, and which would have left the United Kingdom intact. An Irish ethnic identity (or identities) would have been possible within a general "civic" framework. In the contest which followed, Joseph Chamberlain, who in the first part of his career can be classified as a civic nationalist, moved toward an ethno-cultural position. Gladstone, who began life as an ethno-cultural nationalist, moved gradually toward a civic position. In the contest between them it was Chamberlain who was victorious.

Today, within the United Kingdom, the tensions between ethno-cultural and civic identities persist. There is still a monarchy based upon Protestant succession. In England there is still an established Church. There are still strongly established, ethno-cultural identities in all four units of the United Kingdom. The problems of Northern Ireland pose the difficulty in acute form. In addition, since the end of World War II, the arrival of new immigrants from India, Pakistan, East Africa, the West Indies, and of course the Republic of Ireland has added a new urgency. The symbols of a multiethnic multinational United Kingdom are still in many ways those of an ethno-cultural nation formed in 1688. This situation has led, and still leads, to extraordinary confusion about the nature of British identity.

These tensions are no less acute within Ireland. In the Republic a struggle seems to be going on between civic and ethno-cultural nationalism. Traditional stereotypes of "faith and fatherland" are being undermined. In Co. Clare a Muslim doctor defeated a member of the de Valera family in the last election—a result almost as revolutionary as O'Connell's election in 1828. The constitutional position of the Catholic Church is being slowly modified, though it still remains dominant in the field of primary and secondary education.

In Northern Ireland, the situation is more complex. Here an ethno-cultural state was in power for half a century. Only in the 1960s did concepts of civil rights and civil identity begin to make headway, but in 1995 it is still difficult to say where events are tending. Sinn Féin claims the heritage of the United Irishmen but in practice seems to resemble more the Catholic "Defenders" of the late eighteenth century. The revival of the Irish language also has symbolic political overtones, as the cry "Tiocfaidh ár lá" (our day will come) implies. The SDLP is still described as "mainly catholic." The marching season of July and August annually illustrates the strength of ethno-religious loyalties within the Protestant community.

Within England, and perhaps also Wales and Scotland, however, the traditional symbolism of Church and State is on the defensive. As yet, ethno-cultural nationalists have failed to seize control of the Conservative party. The face of English ethnic nationalism is seen only among a minority of football supporters on occasions such as the international match at Lansdowne Road in 1995. For the moment, a *quasi*-civic nationalism seems to be dominant in England in the face of the challenge of the European Community. Ethnic nationalism seems to be strongest in the so-called "Celtic Fringe." (Why "Celtic" when religious rather than racial animosities are uppermost?)

The tensions between civic and ethnic identity are part of our modern world. They arose in the wake of the American and French Revolutions and have remained as elements of our political vocabulary since then. There is no simple solution, as the case of Bosnia shows. To deny the pull of ethnic identity is to deny history. To allow it full play is to deny choice.

One final question may be raised. How far should we think that civic equals good and ethnic equals bad? The historian, as a scholar attempting a detached analysis, is surely not obliged to answer this question. The challenge lies elsewhere. It is to explain, in the light of available evidence, why civic nationalism made such little headway within the United Kingdom during a specific period. What was there about the views of Paine, Bentham, Mill, and others which seemed unpalatable to certain groups? Was there an aggressive secularism or anglocentricity? Did Mill's views on the rights of women run into an almost instinctive, centuries-old, reaction?

In the abstract the question civic equals good/ethnic equals bad? is unanswerable. Historical circumstances inevitably color the issue.[34]

NOTES

1. Brubaker, op. cit. (1992), p. 1. See also R. Gildea, *The Past in French History* (1994).

2. L. B. Namier, "Nationality and Liberty," in *Avenues of History* (1952), p. 21.

3. Liah Greenfeld, *Nationalism: Five Roads to Modernity* (1992); Linda Colley, *Britons: The Forging of a Nation* (1992).

4. See *Concise Oxford Dictionary of Quotations* (1994), under "Tebbit."

5. Edmund Burke, *Reflections on the French Revolution* (1993), pp. 96, 99–100. See also J. C. D. Clarke, *English Society 1688–1832* (1985).

6. E. Halevy, *History of the English People in 1815* (English trans. 1949), p. 393.

7. James A. Epstein, *Radical Expression: Political Language, Ritual and Symbol in England 1790–1850* (1995).

8. See J. R. Dinwiddy, *Radicalism and Reform in Britain 1780–1850* (1992), ch. 15. pp. 273–80.

9. See Daire Keogh, "Archbishop Troy, the Catholic Church and Irish Radicalism:

1791–3," in *The United Irishmen: Republicanism, Radicalism and Rebellion*, David Dickson, Daire Keogh, and Kevin Whelan, eds. (1993), pp. 124–34.

10. G. C. Bolton, *The Passing of the Irish Act of Union* (1966), p. 79.

11. *A Report of the Debate of the House of Commons of Ireland on the subject of the Union* (1799), p. 54.

12. See David Dickson, "Paine and Ireland," in Dickson, Keogh, and Whelan, op. cit., pp. 135–50.

13. See Kevin Whelan, "The United Irishmen, the Enlightenment and Popular Culture," ibid., p. 295.

14. See John Brims, "Scottish Radicalism and the United Irishmen," ibid., p. 79.

15. *Hansard* (Lords), Vol. xxi, 2 April 1828, p. 60. Debate on Catholic Relief Bill.

16. Ibid. p. 65.

17. Quoted in D. Akenson, *The Irish Educational Experiment* (1970), p. 92.

18. *Hansard* (Commons), Vol. xlviii, 20 June 1839, p. 583.

19. *Hansard* (Commons), Vol. xlviii, 20 June 1839, pp. 581, 583, 587.

20. Ibid., p. 1252.

21. Ibid., 19 June 1839, p. 532.

22. *Hansard* (Commons), Vol. cviv, 4 Feb. 1851, pp. 33–34.

23. Ibid., 7 Feb. 1851, p. 256.

24. John Stuart Mill, *Considerations on Representative Government*, chapter XVI, "Of Nationality" (1880), p. 123.

25. *Hansard* (Lords), Vol. cxcvii, 15 July 1869, p. 1984.

26. *Hansard* (Lords), Vol. cxcvii, 17 July 1869, pp. 112, 113.

27. Ibid., p. 19.

28. See Bruce L. Kinzer, "John Stuart Mill and the Irish University Question," in *Victorian Studies* (Autumn 1987), p. 61.

29. Ibid., p. 67.

30. For a fuller discussion of the issues involved in the centenary celebrations, see H. F. Kearney, "Faith or Fatherland," in *Essays presented to Professor Emmet Larkin* (1997).

31. *Church of Scotland*, General Assembly Reports (Committee of Church and Nation) 1924, p. 639.

32. See the references to the behavior of the English footballer Paul Gascoigne at a Glasgow Rangers match on 30 July 1995. *The Guardian*, 4 August 1995.

33. See James Loughlin, "Joseph Chamberlain, English Nationalism and the Ulster Question," *History* (June 1992), pp. 202–19.

34. A good example of this is provided by Professor David Eastwood in his article on "Robert Southey and the Intellectual Origins of Romantic Conservatism," *English Historical Review*, April 1989, pp. 308–31. Eastwood shows how the ethno-cultural English nationalist Southey wrote numerous articles in the *Quarterly Review* opposing Catholic Emancipation and supporting the Protestant Ascendancy. At the same time, however, he can be seen as being concerned, like

Cobbett, with improving the conditions of the poor, with providing, like Whitbread, a national education system or, like Robert Owen, with humanizing the world of industry (p. 311). Eastwood reminds us that national identity, whether civic or ethnic, does not stand on its own but is linked with many other issues. Irish ethno-cultural nationalism in the 1890s can also be seen as rejecting features of "modernity."

Chapter Two

1875: Faith or Fatherland?

The Contested Symbolism of Irish Nationalism

(2000)

Emmet Larkin was the first historian to draw attention to the significance of the Roman Catholic church in "the making of modern Ireland." His massive multivolume history is now recognized as an essential starting point for future scholars.[1] Thanks to his formidable researches, it is now necessary to place Paul Cullen, archbishop of Dublin, John MacHale, archbishop of Tuam, Thomas Croke, archbishop of Cashel, and W. J. Walsh, archbishop of Dublin, alongside the figures of Peel, O'Connell, Gladstone, Parnell, and Balfour. These bishops were able men of considerable political power with whom successive British governments had to deal in the second half of the nineteenth century and the early decades of the twentieth. Indeed, the Catholic hierarchy saw themselves as leaders of the Irish nation, as much as, if not more than, politicians like Parnell, Redmond, and Dillon. In making sense of Irish nationalism, it is necessary to follow Larkin's lead and keep the Catholic hierarchy at the center of the picture.

Larkin's work may be said to have introduced a new dimension into the study of Irish nationalism. However, it is not the only source of innovation. We may mention in particular a new level of sophistication in the study of nationalism associated with the work of Eric Hobsbawm, Terence Ranger, Ernest Gellner, and many others.[2] It is now possible to place Irish nationalism in a comparative context. For these scholars the main concern is uncovering the problematic aspects of the concept "nation." In contrast nationalists, and nationalist historians, look upon their own nation and nationhood as in some sense "God-given" or "natural." They see their national identity as resting upon "language" or "race" or "religion" or "territory" on a primordial basis. For them such signs of national identity are not the accidental product of historical change but part of a deeper providential pattern. In contrast, the new generation of scholars use such terms as "the invention of tradition" or "an imagined community" as the key to understanding the phenomenon of nationalism.

An article by Ashutosh Varshney, "Contested Meanings: India's National Identity, Hindu Nationalism and the Politics of Anxiety" provides a good example of this approach.[3] Varshney shows how a formerly dominant Indian secular nationalism, the creation of Gandhi and Nehru, is today being challenged by an increasingly powerful Hindu nationalism. Allowing for obvious differences of scale, there are illuminating parallels here with Ireland. Throughout the nineteenth and much of the twentieth century there was continuous tension within Ireland between two images of the Irish nation, a secular image looking back to Wolfe Tone, Robert Emmet, and the French Revolution, and a religious image deriving from the experience of a persecuted people during the Reformation and the post-Reformation period. The situation was complicated further by the incorporation of Ireland within the United Kingdom in 1800 by the Act of Union and by the later rise of a powerful "Orange" ethnic consciousness within the province of Ulster (the Irish equivalent of Kashmir or the Punjab).

In the wake of new interpretations, historians and anthropologists have become increasingly aware of the ambiguities and tensions which lie at the heart of most, perhaps one should say all, nationalist movements. Since it is impossible to define "nation" in such a way as to make it immediately and self-evidently acceptable to all possible members of a specific nation, disputes inevitably arise as to what constitutes the essential signs of the nation. "Contested symbols" thus seem to form part of the histories of various nationalist movements, not least Irish nationalism.

This essay is concerned with the commemoration of the centenary of O'Connell's birth, which was celebrated over three days (5–7 August) in Dublin during the summer of 1875. As such it is clearly limited in scope. In my view, however, following Varshney's lead, it illustrates long-lasting divisions among Irish political activists about the meaning of the "nation." A struggle took place during the centenary celebrations of O'Connell's birth about interpretation of a national symbol—in this case, the figure of Daniel O'Connell himself. The question at issue was whether O'Connell was to be seen primarily as a figure sponsoring Catholic emancipation or as an advocate of the repeal of the Union. What was at stake was the nature of Irish identity. Was it religious or secular? The symbolism of O'Connell's memory became a critical issue as each side sought to annex it for its own purposes.

But O'Connell, while alive, had been an ambiguous figure and after his death did not become less so. Before 1829 O'Connell had successfully played the role of the liberator in the campaign for Catholic emancipation. During the 1830s he oscillated between Repeal and a policy of pragmatic alliance with the Whigs. After his death, the memory of O'Connell assumed great importance as a symbol of nonviolent political agitation, particularly in reaction to the rise of the fenian movement in the 1860s. O'Connell's commitment to peaceful methods was undoubted. Where ambiguity arose was about the nature of his political aims. Was he prepared to accept the place of Ireland within the United Kingdom or was Repeal his long-term objective? It was this issue which divided the forces of constitutional nationalism during the early 1870s.[4] What was also at stake was the meaning of "nation" and "nationalism." Was Ireland a Catholic nation as popular preachers such as Tom Burke believed, or was it a nation defined by its historic territorial basis? The question had implications beyond the Irish Sea for Britain, the dominions of Canada, Australia, and New Zealand, and not least for the United States.

Fr. Tom Burke had declared in 1872: "Take an average Irishman—I don't care where you find him—and you will find that the very first principle in his mind is 'I am not an Englishman because I am a Catholic.' Take an Irishman wherever he is found all over the earth and any casual observer will at once come to the conclusion 'Oh he is an Irishman, he is a Catholic. The two go together.'"[5] The non-sectarian Home Rule League challenged this assumption head on. The three days of the O'Connell centenary thus became a contest between the two nationalist political groupings over the nature of Irish national identity.

The contest was focused largely upon two men, the Catholic prelate Paul Cullen and the Protestant lawyer Isaac Butt. In the preceding decade, Paul Cullen, archbishop of Dublin from 1850 and the most powerful prelate in Ireland, saw his role as that of combating Fenianism and by implication what Fenian success might bring with it, socialism and secularism. Cullen's answer to Fenianism was to encourage the development of a religious-based nationalism which could concentrate its aims upon the disestablishment of the Church of Ireland and the reform of higher education in the interests of the Catholics, with land reform as a third issue.[6]

In the election of 1874, however, Cullen's religious nationalism lost ground dramatically to the newly founded Home Rule League led by Isaac

Butt, who had shown sympathy for Fenianism to the extent of defending them in court. Butt was a secular nationalist for whom the Irish nation rested upon the uniting of Catholic and Protestant. Butt saw his aim as the restoration of the historic Irish nation of 1782, under the British crown, but with its own lords and commons. He was not a Republican, but he showed himself willing to use the issue of "amnesty" for Fenian prisoners as a means of increasing popular support for home rule. Cullen, in contrast, was bitterly opposed to home rule. In 1873 he wrote, "my opinion is that if we had a little parliament here, half Protestant or more than half and perhaps less than half Catholic, the MPs in order to give themselves something to do, would begin to make laws for priests and bishops and to fetter the action of the Church." It seems more than likely that in the aftermath of electoral defeat in 1874, Cullen and his political allies, led by Peter Paul McSwiney, lord mayor of Dublin, seized upon the forthcoming centenary of O'Connell's birth (6 August 1875) as a way of restoring their fortunes. The religious card was to be played as a response to the challenge of Butt's secular nationalism.

The first day of the centenary celebration began with the celebration of high mass in the Catholic cathedral, followed in the evening by a formal dinner given at the Mansion House by the lord mayor, Peter Paul McSwiney.[7] On both occasions the tone was that of an embattled but confident catholicism. Representatives were present from the Catholic hierarchies throughout the British Empire as well as France and Germany. The "Kulturkampf" was a major theme of the speeches, with references being made to Bismarckian persecution in Poland and the Catholic Rhineland. The organizers of the celebrations claimed that their aims were nonsectarian. The tone of the speeches, however, was unmistakably Catholic. Indeed, later comments were made in the press about the ultramontane tone of the celebrations.

The high point of the celebrations in the cathedral was the sermon by Thomas Croke, the newly appointed archbishop of Cashel.[8] Croke's theme was O'Connell's role as a great Catholic. He left consideration of O'Connell "the statesman" to "an Irish nobleman of ancient lineage and well established fame, glowing Irish genius, instinct with Irish feeling" by whom he meant Thomas O'Hagan, lord chancellor of Ireland under Gladstone. There was no hint here that O'Hagan was a controversial figure in the eyes of the home rule party, as a man who had taken office in a British government.

Croke drew a sharp contrast between English and Irish views of history. He expected an Englishman to speak of King Alfred, of the tyrant John and "the struggle for the Charter of British freedom" and of the battles of Crecy, Agincourt, and Poitiers. An Irishman, however, would refer to Ireland's "once famous schools and Universities" and to Brian's defeat of the Danes, and to "how the fruitful mother of so many saints and scholars was made to suffer for many a long and dreary age." Ireland "always held on to the faith of Patrick and was prepared to die in its defence." "If I say," Croke declared, "such themes as these are touched on, I recognise forthwith in the speaker an Irishman born, or one in heart and sympathy and affection." In this opening speech of the centenary celebration, Croke thus stressed the interlinkage of catholicism and Irish identity.

But what was "the faith of Patrick"? Croke stated that a true Catholic should "accept with a ready and unwavering assent every doctrine decree and decision that emanates from the Holy See." He stressed that education should be under the control "of the commissioned teachers and guardians of the Faith." He praised France where, after the vicissitudes of the French Revolution, "a new and bright educational era" had just begun thanks to the efforts of Felix Dupanloup, bishop of Orleans.[9] "Thus you see, brethren," Croke declared, "when France was infidel education was irreligious; and as it became Christian education became Christian also!" Croke went on to state that in Ireland, to be a Catholic was no longer contemptible. "In rank and station, in intelligence not less than in integrity, in commercial enterprise and professional skill, in all the virtues that create social respectability or tend to ennoble it—I had almost said in wealth— we are equal to, as in numbers we immeasurably surpass any and all other denominations of Christians in our country."

Croke praised O'Connell's character and career. O'Connell "was thoroughly convinced of the necessity of having education for Catholic children and I believe he was one of the first who applied the term 'Godless' to those Colleges which the late Sir Robert Peel founded for us in 1845." Had O'Connell not been a devout Catholic—"he could never have acquired that magic influence over his religious countrymen without which all his efforts would have been available: the great work of National regeneration, now so largely associated with his name could never have been achieved by him."

Croke then went on to refer to O'Connell's criticism of violence in politics. "He [O'Connell] thought much over and appreciated properly the very peculiar and indeed inflammable character of the materials with which he had to deal He knew and no man knew it better that the Irish Celt is from nature ardent and excitable, highly sympathetic, daring devoted and generous!" In O'Connell, "there was the righteous instinct of the just and religious man warning him to beware and suggesting to him, the awful responsibility of those who unite a struggling people to throw away the scabbard and to seek by the naked sword what in time they are sure to get by conciliation!" O'Connell was "the father of the salutary doctrine that there is no amount of national liberty that a people cannot win from their rulers without the shedding of one drop of blood or the desolation of one solitary hearth!" Moving toward his final peroration, Croke appealed to his audience "as Irishmen and as Catholics." "We are fast working ourselves into that position of equality and independence under the protection of what I am not afraid to designate as the best balanced constitution in the world! ... As Catholics we have every reason to be proud! ... For all this social, civic and ecclesiastical progress," Croke concluded, "we have every reason to be thankful." He looked forward to acquiring by peaceful means "our full complement of constitutional freedom."

In the course of this speech Croke was highly critical of "the Heathen Maxims" of the French Revolution and of "the evil influence of the Encyclopedists!" He attacked in particular the republican view that religion should be excluded from the schools. For Croke, O'Connell was a symbol of "the great work of national regeneration" in a peaceful manner, opposing those who sought to win "by naked sword what in time they are sure to get by conciliation." Surprisingly, in view of Croke's later reputation as an extreme nationalist, he seemed largely content with the position of the church. "While persecution rages elsewhere, the sky is serene over our heads here and we can meet in Synod, and in every other way, advance the interest of our Church without let or hindrance, without State licence or State control!" Croke saw O'Connell as the source of these "sound principles of political action." Whether or not O'Connell was as unswervingly orthodox on educational issues as Croke implied is open to question. What is clear is the attempt by religious nationalists to seize upon O'Connell as a symbol of policies. From this point of view O'Connell the Liberator, advocate of Catholic emancipation, was the "real O'Connell." O'Connell the advocate of Repeal was to be tacitly ignored or played down. Within the confines of the cathedral this was easy enough. Once the organizers moved into a less controlled environment, however, difficulties began to arise.

After the celebration of high mass in the cathedral, the next event was the lord mayor's banquet in the Mansion House.[10] After a splendid dinner, Lord Mayor McSwiney proposed the first toast to "His Holiness the Pope." He referred to the support of the Irish nation, the Catholics of England,

Scotland, France, Germany, and Italy and two hundred million Catholics who looked to the Holy Father as the infallible expounder of the word of God. McSwiney thus followed Croke's lead earlier in the day in stressing the Catholic identity of the Irish nation.

He followed this toast with toasts first to the Queen, then the Prince and Princess of Wales, and other members of the royal family. The lord lieutenant of Ireland was toasted next. McSwiney praised the lord lieutenant for pointing out "the advantages of ... a resident proprietary in contradistinction to the disadvantages of absenteeism." There was no hint here of the attack on "landlordism" which was to characterize the Land League only three years later.

The moment now arrived which Cullen and McSwiney were probably dreading, the speech by John MacHale, archbishop of Tuam. Throughout the middle decades of the century MacHale and Cullen had been at odds, with MacHale consistently supporting a more nationalist line. For MacHale, O'Connell the Repealer took precedence over O'Connell the liberator. In his short speech he did not disappoint his supporters, referring to "presages of the approaching autonomy exercising the right of self government which no people ever lost, to any extent, without being in a corresponding degree treated as slaves."

He praised O'Connell's heroic exertions to realize the blessings of self-government. He referred to "the Irish people," "the Irish nation," and "exalted patriotism." He deplored "the disastrous Famine" but expressed his hopes for the people's prosperity when the goal of legislative autonomy was reached.

McSwiney's and Cullen's response was once more to stress the role of the church. McSwiney in proposing the toast of "the Cardinal Archbishop of Dublin and the hierarchy of Ireland" pointed to the leadership of the hierarchy under whose fostering care "innumerable churches, educational establishments, hospitals and asylums have everywhere sprung up and been erected without State aid," and he also referred directly to the three aims of the National Association—religious equality, tenant compensation, and denominational education—of which two had been achieved.

In his reply to this toast, Cullen spoke of O'Connell as a "second Moses." He outlined what he saw as O'Connell's doctrines—"his determination to obey the law, his determination to maintain the authority of the Church and State, and his hatred of bloody revolution." He stressed O'Connell's loyalty to the pope and his influence outside Ireland. Cullen's O'Connell was clearly an anti-Fenian symbol.

There was thus a clear difference of emphasis in the speeches of MacHale on the one hand and those of McSwiney and Cullen on the other. MacHale's theme was self-government and his hopes of raising up a "host of young men animated with ardent desire of treading in [O'Connell's] footsteps." He argued that Ireland in seeking self-government was merely following England's example in asserting "the uncontrolled expression of her native insular freedom." In contrast, McSwiney and Cullen stressed what had been achieved under the leadership of the hierarchy. MacHale had ignored the hierarchy in his appeal for "a succession of genuine and sterling patriotism." For McSwiney and Cullen, the hierarchy were the natural leaders of the Irish people, under the leadership of the pope (unmentioned by MacHale). In McSwiney's final speech, however, there was a surprising shift, when he announced that "the salvation of Ireland demanded nothing less than the Repeal of the Union." The dinner at the Mansion House revealed what observers of Irish politics already knew—that Cullen and MacHale differed radically in their view of the Irish nation and its future. On the whole these tensions had been kept within bounds. On the following day, however, Cullen's opponents were able to mount a more open challenge.

The second day, Friday 6 August, "the hundredth birthday of O'Connell" began with the marshalling of the procession at 10 A.M.[11] The starting point was the south-west corner of St. Stephen's Green where middle-class catholicism had begun to make its mark. In this area were the Catholic University at 85–86 Stephen's Green, St. Vincent's Hospital, the Loreto Convent, and the Jesuit House of Studies at 35 Lower Leeson Street. The procession itself required a great deal of organizing, made more difficult by the vast crowds, including many from Glasgow, Liverpool, and Manchester. The organizers had given a great deal of thought to the route, which was largely based upon key sites connected with O'Connell's career—his house in Merrion Square, his role at City Hall as lord mayor, his imprisonment at Richmond Gaol, his early emancipation meetings in Capel Street, and finally the site of his still unfinished statue at the south end of Sackville Street (now O'Connell Street).

The procession was headed by contingents of over forty different groups representing the skilled and unskilled workmen of Dublin. The largest group were the bakers (1,000) and the grocers' assistants (1,500). Others included various groups associated with metal working, wood working, leather, shipbuilding, barrel making, silk weaving, boot and shoe-making, printing, hairdressing, chimney sweeping, and various food trades. There was some "modern" industry, represented by the United Machine Workers, but Dublin was clearly a preindustrial city, contrasting in its structure with the factories of Belfast and the Lagan Valley. It was the traditional laboring orders of Dublin who were most threatened by the industrial changes of the nineteenth century.

But the nationalism revealed by the banners of the trades groups were largely cultural in character. The symbols of Erin (a female figure), a harp, a wolfhound, a round tower, and shamrocks were most common. Banners with explicit political references were exceptional. The horseshoe workers referred to Grattan, Emmet, and Fitzgerald along with O'Connell. The Dublin Mariners, 600 in number, carried a banner with the names of Emmet, Hugh O'Neill, and Brian Boru as well as that of O'Connell. The banners of hairdressers and bakers referred to "amnesty," that is, the demand for clemency for Fenian prisoners. In contrast, the stationary engine drivers carried a banner with medallion portraits of Stephenson and Watts, along with the slogan "Encourage Irish manufacturers." The United Machine Workers had borrowed their banner from Manchester. On this the names of the British engineers Sir Joseph Whitworth and Sir William Fairbairn were displayed. The Skinners' banner included the rose and thistle, along with the shamrock. Thus, although the tone of the trades procession was "national," it can hardly be termed "nationalist" in the sense of aiming at "Repeal." Indeed the banner of the foresters, who marched later in the procession, illustrated Robin Hood's last shot along with the figure of little John, symbols from English, not Irish, folklore.

The remaining part of the procession, which was numerically much stronger, stressed the religious identity of the Irish. The sodalities of the Sacred Heart alone numbered 6,000 men. The contingents were organized on the basis of their parishes, led by their spiritual directors. National symbols such as the wolfhound and the shamrock appeared on the banners together with references to O'Connell and slogans such as "God save Ireland" but in general the overall effect was religious in character. Among the most common motifs were the Sacred Heart, our Lady of Lourdes, St. Joseph and "the infant Saviour." St. Patrick and St. Bridget appeared on some banners but not all. "The devotional revolution" of mid century had clearly left its mark.[12]

The organizers of the centenary had clearly aimed to present a united Catholic front, in alliance with groups from Liverpool, Manchester, and Glasgow. So far they had been largely successful. The unity of the proceedings, however, was deliberately challenged by a procession organized by the

Home Rule League with the aim of arousing support for "amnesty." This procession began from a different starting point, the Customs House, and had its own black banner with the words "Amnesty Association" on one side and "Remember the prisoners still in chains" and "God save Ireland" on the other. From another banneret were suspended a pair of prison anklets and chains. This rhetoric was Fenian in tone, clearly designed to recall "the Manchester Martyrs" of 1867 as well as Fenian activists still imprisoned.[13]

In the procession were delegates from a large number of towns in England and Scotland, as well as from Ireland. The Liverpool home rulers in particular were strongly represented. Among the political leaders present were Isaac Butt and John O'Leary, who drove up in a carriage, and a number of home rule MPs in a two-horse brake. Their object was to hijack the leadership of the grand procession by moving ahead of it at a convenient point, Kingsbridge station. But the manoeuver did not succeed. For the moment Amnesty men had to be content with joining the main procession at a point some way from the leading marchers.

The two processions illustrated the profound division which lay at the center of Irish nationalism. The organizers of the main procession stressed the progress which Catholics had made since O'Connell's death. The official account of the proceedings drew attention to the fact that "the great majority of the Judges of the Superior Courts, several of the Privy Councillors and many of the Judges of the County Courts" were Catholic. It also referred to the prominent place of Catholics among the high sheriffs and magistrates and the municipal governments of three of the provinces, and to the fact that fifty of the 103 Irish MPs were Catholics. Stress was also laid upon the advances which Catholics had made in the professions, in the possession of landed property, and in legislatures of the leading British colonies. There was a clear middle-class thrust to this rhetoric together with a strongly ethno-cultural dimension, in the sense that the emphasis was upon Catholic advancement.

Thomas O'Hagan, first baron O'Hagan (1812–85), the organizers' choice as keynote speaker, appropriately symbolized this point of view. After studying at the King's Inns, Dublin, and Gray's Inn, London, he was summoned to the Irish bar in 1835. He became a supporter of O'Connell, but drew back over Repeal. In 1861 he was appointed solicitor-general in Palmerston's government and in 1863 was returned as member for Tralee despite opposition from conservatives and nationalists. In 1868, on the formation of Gladstone's first ministry he was appointed lord chancellor of Ireland, the first Catholic to hold that office since the revolution of 1688.

O'Hagan was an enthusiastic advocate of the national system of education in Ireland and was also actively involved in plans to make university education more accessible to Catholics. He was thus a symbol of the success of constitutional gradualist reform in Ireland. Though an opponent of Repeal, he was in favor of the establishment of a local Irish legislature for local purposes. For the Home Rule Association, however, O'Hagan represented a system which they were determined to attack.[14]

Isaac Butt (1813–79), leader president of the Amnesty Association (1869) and founder of Home Government Association (1870), was a more ambiguous figure.[15] Originally a Tory, a committed Orangeman, and an opponent of O'Connell over Repeal, he later defended Fenians in court (1865–68). His political career was thus marked by extraordinary shifts. At this period, however, there is little doubt that he espoused a civic national identity for Ireland which would include Protestants as well as Catholics. His home rule party included MPs from varied religious backgrounds. Thus, where Cullen's National Association pointed to the election of fifty Catholic MPs as evidence of Catholic progress, the home rulers played down religious affiliation. Another difference between the two parties lay in the home rulers' demand for the extension of the franchise.

The first O'Connell dinner, on Thursday 5 August, had been a "private" event given by personal invitation of the lord mayor, at his own expense. The second dinner on Friday 6 August was a much larger affair, held by invitation in the vast exhibition hall in Earlsfort Terrace, near the Catholic University.[16] One hundred distinguished guests sat at a dais at one end while several hundred more were accommodated at four tables stretching the length of the hall. (Ladies had a separate area in the galleries.) As it was a Friday the cardinal archbishop issued a dispensation from the obligation of avoiding flesh meat, thus earning "the gratitude of the Irish race at home and abroad." (As with Croke's sermon earlier, it was assumed that the "Irish race" was Catholic.) Members of the hierarchy headed by the Catholic archbishop of Armagh, and members of parliament, including Isaac Butt, constituted the majority of guests at the high table. At the lower tables the clergy were strongly represented.

The proceedings began with a toast to Queen Victoria, described by McSwiney as "one of the best sovereigns." McSwiney then proposed a toast to "the memory of O'Connell" whose name he declared "symbolized Ireland." Sir Colman O'Loghlen, Bart, QC, MP, a friend of O'Connell, spoke to the toast, claiming that when O'Connell "sought to open the portals of the constitution to Catholics, when he sought for them the privilege of citizens, he did so in no sectarian spirit." O'Loghlen associated himself with MacHale in claiming that O'Connell was not simply "the Liberator of Catholics." "We should regard him," he declared, "as the greatest patriot Ireland ever saw" though "there may be men in this room who do not agree in the plan he adopted in the latter course of his life." O'Loghlen thus again brought into the open the division among the admirers of O'Connell between the "Liberator" and the "Repealer" groups, a division which corresponded to a large extent to that between "ethnic" and "civic" nationalism. The next toast was to "the French nation," which McSwiney described as "the land of the Montalemberts, the McMahons, and the Dupanloups!" A note of religious nationalism had been sounded, which was taken further by the bishop of Nantes who declared that "if a country is great, it is by religion that greatness is acquired." "In the religious order and in the political order," he added, "France and Ireland had grouped hands" (a reference to the French president Marshall McMahon). A letter from Dupanloup was now read out praising O'Connell as the "indefatigable champion of Emancipation." The Viscount O'Neill De Tyrone, subprefect of the Seine, also spoke at length.

The toasts were beginning to take a European course, linking Ireland with Catholic Europe. This direction was continued with the next toast, "Our foreign Guests," to which Prince Radziwill, member of the German Reichstag and representative of the imprisoned Cardinal Ledóchiwski, responded. He lamented the lack in Poland of a man like O'Connell and then went on to condemn revolutionary methods.

The lord mayor now proposed the toast of "Legislative Independence," coupling with it the name of Sir Charles Gavan Duffy. Duffy was the first editor of *The Nation* and had been imprisoned along with O'Connell in 1844. It was, however, as the official representative of Victoria, the Australian state to which he had emigrated in 1855, that he was called upon to speak. As a former prime minister of Victoria in 1871–72, who had been knighted in 1873, Duffy symbolized the possibility of Irish progress within the Empire. At this point, however, cries of "Butt" were heard throughout the hall from those who had demonstrated at the platform in Sackville Street earlier in the day. Duffy could not make himself heard and when Butt rose to address the company, the lord mayor condemned the proceedings for being "irregular and disorderly." He withdrew from the chair, and the gaslights were lowered, about midnight.

Thus, the O'Connell centenary did not go entirely as its organizers hoped. They had demonstrated the emotional power of Irish catholicism and, despite their assertions of nonsectarianism, had underlined a link between Irish national and religious identity. But the organizers had not succeeded in dominating secular nationalism by sheer force of numbers. The supporters of Butt had been able to make their presence felt during the centenary procession, at the platform in Sackville Street and at the conclusion of the Earlsfort Terrace dinner. More significantly, they also controlled the proceedings at the trades grand banquet held north of the river Liffey at the Rotunda.[17] Five hundred representatives of "the different operative classes" were present, many of them wearing the home rule medal. The two main guests were the pro-Fenian John O'Leary, who had been imprisoned from 1865 to 1874, and T. D. Sullivan, brother of A. M. Sullivan, editor of *The Nation*. Once the toasts had begun, it was clear that the tone of the Rotunda dinner was to be very different from that of Earlsfort Terrace. The first toast was not to "the Queen" but to "The Queen, Lords and Commons of Ireland"—for the reason, the chairman explained, "that the Irish people claimed to be a nation." The nationalist note was continued by T. D. Sullivan, who in fact referred in the toast to "Ireland a Nation." Sullivan spoke of the noble bearing of working men of Dublin and Ireland. He then went on to call for the restitution of the rights and powers of a nation to Ireland. In words echoing those of Robert Emmet, he spoke of "the determination to elevate Ireland to her right place in the full radiance of independence and freedom among the nations of the earth."

The next toast was "The People, the legitimate Source of Power." The speaker was Thomas Mooney, who referred to O'Connell's demand for Repeal of the Union and to MacHale's support for Repeal on the previous night. John O'Leary followed, with the toast of "the Restoration of Irish Independence." A new note was struck by the next speaker, Charles Dawson, who proposed a toast to "The Memory of Daniel O'Connell, the Man of the Irish People." Dawson called for the removal of "the shameful inequalities of the Parliamentary Franchise in Ireland and in England." He claimed that "the political rights of the middle and upper classes were won after many a struggle. … To complete the idea of O'Connell, we have yet to win for the working men of Ireland in field and factory, their political rights and for the country at large its political independence. This is our work. This is the legacy of O'Connell."

In contrast to the Earlsfort Terrace banquet, that held in the Rotunda was working class in character. The toasts made no mention of Catholic emancipation. On the contrary the emphasis throughout was on Repeal. There was clearly a whiff of popular radicalism about the proceedings.

The nationalist rhetoric of O'Leary and Sullivan was consciously nonsectarian. Their emphasis was on "the Irish people" not Irish Catholics. Sullivan referred to "the long night of slavery and suffering," not to Catholic progress within the Union which had been the theme of Croke's sermon and of McSwiney's speech at the Mansion House on the previous day. It remains to mention the third day, Saturday 7 August, which because of bad weather was something of an anticlimax when judged by the vast throngs of Friday. A relatively small crowd assembled at Glasnevin cemetery near the O'Connell monument to hear a speech by Butt calling for "the same franchise for Ireland that the English people enjoy."

This final meeting was not the end of the affair. Throughout the next few weeks, articles and letters in *The Nation* complained that Butt and the home rule party had been badly treated. One letter for example declared that "the man who leads the national party was either not to speak at all or to be shunted to the small hours of the morning!" O'Neill Daunt, the veteran home ruler, argued that it was "enormously wrong" to restrict public recognition of O'Connell to his services in the cause of Catholic emancipation. Daunt stated that O'Connell "repeatedly expressed his desire that if Repeal were not carried in his lifetime it might be recorded on his tomb that he died a Repealer!" A committee of enquiry under the Amnesty Association was presided over by Charles Stewart Parnell, MP, as yet a relatively minor figure, but a future leader who would unite at least temporarily the forces of civic and religious nationalism.

The split within Irish nationalism, exposed by the O'Connell centenary celebrations, was between two groups of activists for control of a powerful political symbol. In his own lifetime O'Connell's political position had shifted remarkably from time to time. At one period, that of the "Lichfield House Compact" he had worked openly with the Whig government of the day. On other occasions he openly espoused Repeal as an issue which would best unite Catholics and Liberal Protestants.[18] The groups who fought over his memory in the 1870s were thus guilty of trying to use the past for their own purposes. O'Connell, who read Gibbon avidly in his youth and was a close friend of Bentham, was clearly not a single-minded ultramontane. What he would have made of the Syllabus of Errors must be a matter of speculation.

In 1862 when plans for a national monument to O'Connell were first proposed, under the auspices of the *Freeman's Journal*, the image of O'Connell the liberator was dominant. John MacHale protested at that time about "honouring the Emancipator only and ignoring the Repealer."

By 1882, however, when the O'Connell monument was unveiled, the Home Rule Party dominated the proceedings and the main theme of the speeches by Parnell and Charles Dawson, who was now lord mayor of Dublin, was "O'Connell the Repealer." The political pendulum had swung considerably since the centenary commemoration in 1872. It was to swing back toward the church during the Parnellite split of 1890–91. In the long run the church succeeded in establishing a firm grip on the memory of O'Connell. It was O'Connell the liberator, the Catholic nationalist, not O'Connell the Repealer, the civic nationalist, which became the dominant image. Two statues now dominate O'Connell Street, those of O'Connell and Parnell.[19] They may be seen as representing two traditions of Irish nationalism, civic and religious. They also illustrate tensions which at the end of the twentieth century remained to be resolved.

NOTES

1. Emmet Larkin, *R. C. Ch. 1850–60, R. C. Ch. 1860–70, R. C. Ch. 1870–74, R. C. Ch. 1878–86, R. C. Ch. 1886–88, R. C. Ch. 1888–91*. Professor Larkin's own account of the O'Connell celebrations is now available in his recent published volume, *R. C. Ch. 1874–78*, pp. 401–20.

2. Ernest Gellner, *Nations and Nationalism* (Oxford, 1983). Benedict Anderson, *Imagined Communities: Reflections on the Origin and Spread of Nationalism* (London, 1983). Eric Hobsbawm, *Nations and Nationalism since 1780: Programme, Myth, Reality* (Cambridge, 1990). Eric Hobsbawm and Terence Ranger (ed.), *The Invention of Tradition* (Cambridge, 1983). Peter Alter's article "Symbols of Irish Nationalism" in Alan O'Day (ed.), *Reactions to Irish Nationalism 1865–1914* (London, 1987) provides an excellent introduction to the topic discussed in this essay. See especially his comments on the Manchester Martyrs and on the O'Connell Monument, pp. 9–12. Recent literature making use of processions and commemorations as means by which communities define themselves includes Mona Ozouf, *La fête révolutionnaire, 1789–1799* (Paris, 1976), translated by Alan Sheridan as *Festivals and the French Revolution* (Cambridge, MA, 1988), and George Mosse, *The Nationalization of the Masses: Political Symbolism and Mass Movements in Germany from the Napoleonic Wars through the Third Reich* (New York, 1975). See also Jonathan Sperber's excellent article "Festivals of National Unity in the German Revolution of 1848–1849" in *Past and Present*, no. 136 (Aug. 1992), pp. 114–38; Timothy O'Keeffe, "The 1898 Efforts to Celebrate the United Irishmen: The '98 Centennial" in *Eire-Ireland*, xxiii, no. 2 (Summer 1988), pp. 51–73, and "Who Fears to Speak of '98? The Rhetoric and Rituals of the United Irishmen Centennial, 1898" ibid., xxvii, no. 3 (Fall 1992), pp. 67–91.

3. *Daedalus*, cxxii, no. 3 (Summer 1993), pp. 227–62.

4. L. J. McCaffrey, *Irish Federalism in the 1870s: A Study in Conservative Nationalism* (Philadelphia, 1962). David Thornley, *Isaac Butt and Home Rule* (London, 1964). P. J. Corish, "Political Problems, 1860–1878" in P. J. Corish (ed.), *A History of Irish Catholicism* (Dublin, 1967).

5. Quoted in Hugh Kearney, *The British Isles: A History of Four Nations* (Cambridge, 1989), p. 184.

6. See Emmet Larkin, *R. C. Ch. 1870–74*, pp. 192–99.

7. My main source is *O'Connell Centenary Record 1875* (Dublin, 1878). A less laudatory account is provided in the pages of pro-Butt periodical *The Nation* (Aug.–Sept., 1875), which is discussed by R. W. Warden in "The Interaction of Protestants and Catholics in the Home Rule League, as Portrayed in the Pages of *The Nation* during the O'Connell Centenary of 1875" (unpublished paper produced for the seminar on Nationalism, Department of History, University of Pittsburgh, Oct. 1994).

8. *Centenary Record*, pp. 96–102.

9. Felix Dupanloup (1802–78), bishop of Orleans from 1849, was involved in the passing of the Falloux Law of 1850, which removed discrimination against church schools. He was a defender of the temporal power of the papacy but openly protested, like MacHale, against the doctrine of papal infallibility at Vatican I (1870), though he accepted it once promulgated. The references to Dupanloup in Croke's speech raise questions about the extent to which the French was seen as a model for Ireland in such areas as education. The "devotional revolution" itself needs to be placed in a European context.

10. *Centenary Record*, pp. 103–15. The menu is printed on p. 107.

11. Ibid., pp. 143 ff.

12. One of Emmet Larkin's most fruitful concepts has been that of "the devotional revolution." See *A.H.R.*, lxxvii, no. 3 (June 1972) pp. 625–52.

13. *Centenary Record*, p. 173.

14. The text of O'Hagan's speech was printed later in ibid., pp. 362–72.

15. For the text of Butt's speech see *The Nation* (21 Aug. 1875).

16. *O'Connell Cent. Rec.*, pp. 375 ff.

17. *The Nation* (18 Sept. 1875).

18. Jacqueline Hill, "The Response to Repeal: The Case of the Dublin Working Class," in Lyons & Hawkins, *Ireland*, pp. 35–68.

19. Oliver MacDonagh, *The Hereditary Bondsman: Daniel O'Connell, 1775–1829* (London, 1988), and MacDonagh, *Emancipist*, constitute the standard modern work, but W. E. H. Lecky's analysis in *Leaders of Public Opinion in Ireland* (new ed., London, 1903), vol. ii, is still well worth reading. On Parnell, see Frank Callanan, *The Parnell Split, 1890–91* (Cork, 1992), C. J. Woods, "The General Election of 1892: The Catholic Clergy and the Defeat of the Parnellites," in Lyons & Hawkins, *Ireland*, pp. 289–319.

Chapter Three

Faith and Fatherland Revisited

(2000)

The life and death of certain memorable inhabitants of the far off Atlantic archipelago that the Iceland-bound voyager sometimes beholds as "a wonderful vision in changing mist."[1]

In 1997 Mary Kenny published her controversial book *Goodbye to Catholic Ireland*. If Brendan Bradshaw's recent historical work is any guide, however, "Catholic Ireland" is still very much alive, at least within the confines of Irish historiography. In two of the volumes under review,[2] Dr. Bradshaw has contributed two substantial pieces, "The English Reformation and Identity Formation in Ireland and Wales," and "The Tudor Reformation and Revolution in Wales and Ireland: The origins of the British Problem." These essays taken together with an accompanying chapter by Marc Caball, "Faith, Culture and Sovereignty; Irish Nationality and Its Development 1588–1625," contribute a powerful restatement of Bradshaw's "Faith and Fatherland" view of Irish history and identity. It seems appropriate therefore to devote the first section of this review to discussing them.

These essays will be of great interest to those following current debates about Irish history and identity. Bradshaw himself takes to task those with different views whom he calls "revisionists," professors Nicholas Canny and Steven Ellis in particular. But the issues which these essays raise have a larger significance in the sense that Bradshaw's stress upon "a common faith and a common fatherland" finds obvious parallels in the history of European and indeed global nationalism. In Spain, for example, Catholicism has been seen by such historians as Mendendez y Pelayo as providing the key to Spanish identity. In Poland, Catholicism has been viewed by many as the essential basis of Polish national identity. In her recent book *Britons: Forging a National Identity*, Linda Colley has stressed the role of Protestantism in creating a sense of Britishness from the mid-eighteenth century onward. In the Republic of India, the party now in power (1999) stresses the role of Hinduism. Thus the interpretation of Irish history and identity that Brendan Bradshaw offers may be seen, not unreasonably, as exemplifying a specific type of religious nationalism.[3]

In all these cases, however, nationalist ideologies based upon a linkage of faith and fatherland have been faced with challenges based upon different assumptions about what constitutes national identity. In the case of Ireland, the nationalism of the United Irishmen provided an obvious alternative to a faith and fatherland ideology. Insistence upon Catholicism as a crucial test of national identity clearly leads to the exclusion of such political leaders as Wolfe Tone, Thomas Davis, and Charles Stewart Parnell. When Parnell declared, "No man has the right to fix the boundary of the march of a nation," was it a Catholic nation which he had in mind? Brendan Bradshaw's assertion that Irish identity is "a common identity based upon a common faith and a common fatherland" is thus clearly open to challenge. As with other nationalisms Bradshaw's nation is a problematic concept. To say this, however, is not to deny that those believing in a "faith and fatherland" concept have not been influential at crucial moments in Irish history, in the fields of education, gender, or sexual morality, for example.

As presented in these essays Bradshaw's main argument is to some extent a familiar one. He sees himself as restating the "received wisdom"[4] according to which Catholicism provided the basis of a nationalist ideology which united, from the 1570s onwards, what had been two hostile ethnic groups, the "old English" gentry and merchants, and the Gaelic Irish lords of the rest of Ireland. In making the case for this (an "irresistible" one, he tells us)[5] he draws upon his own work as well as that of an earlier generation of historians. However, he places this traditionalist historiography in a wider context by introducing an interesting comparative element into his analysis, contrasting Irish history with the history of Wales during the early modern period.

On the face of it, the impact of the Reformation on Wales and Ireland should not have been markedly different. Both were societies in which a Celtic language and culture were important, both had experienced the impact of Anglo-Norman colonization during the middle ages, and both were societies in which feudal lordships, not monarchy, had set the tone of governance for long periods of time. Why then did the Reformation take root in Wales but not in Ireland? Bradshaw argues that the Tudors, themselves of Welsh origin, appeared in Wales in the guise of liberators. The public image of the Reformation in Wales thus seemed, or was made to seem, a restoration of the ancient "British" church. Moreover the Welsh gentry, or many of them, were rewarded for their loyalty to Henry VIII with a rich "bonanza" of monastic lands. Equally important was the acceptance by the Tudors of the argument that the Welsh language be recognized as the medium of ritual and religious instruction. Thus the Bible, translated into Welsh from 1567 onward, became an important symbol of Welsh identity, linking nationhood with the Reformation. (This is a persuasively argued thesis, though open to the criticism that it does not allow enough for local variation or for political change.)

In Ireland, by contrast, the "old English" gentry did not benefit to anything like the same extent from the dissolution of the monasteries. Rather, much of the bonanza went to "new English" settlers. In addition, religious change in Ireland coincided with the large-scale political, economic and legal changes, in particular the overthrow of the "marcher lordships." Most significantly, in Bradshaw's view, successive administrations set their sights upon a policy of anglicization accompanied by military repression. In his view, the English control of Ireland, from the 1570s onward, rested upon an English "garrison mentality" which survived unchallenged until its overthrow in 1922. Against it was ranged an ideology of nationhood which from the promulgation of "Regnans in Excelsis" (1570) rested upon an appeal to "faith and fatherland" ("sinne ag cosnamh ár g-creidimh agus ár nduthaighe").[6]

There is clearly considerable validity in Bradshaw's stress upon the role of the Reformation and Counter-Reformation in shaping Irish history and upon the repressive aspect of English government policy. However, to see a clear-cut, unchanging pattern over four centuries is a vast claim for any historian to make. As suggested earlier, it clearly runs into difficulties if we consider the influence of the French Revolution in Ireland. But even for the period that Bradshaw is concerned with, 1533 to 1607, it is far from clear that an appeal to "faith and fatherland" overrode all other considerations or that government policy was unremittingly concerned with military repression. In the 1590s, O'Neill and O'Donnell issued a call to arms in the name of "faith and fatherland," but their appeal went largely unheard among the old English elite, led in Leinster by the earl of Ormond and in Connacht by the earl of Clanricarde.

Half a century later, in 1644, the then earl of Clanricarde, Richard Burke, himself a Catholic, looking back to the 1590s referred to the Nine Years War as being "raised only upon the private discontents of one (the earl of Tyrone) or very few particular persons and in conclusion not determined but by the extraordinary assistance, valour and fidelity of the natives themselves." There is no reason to believe that his views were untypical among the old English.[7]

Throughout his analysis, Bradshaw stresses the unity of Catholic Ireland and underplays any sense of division between "old English" and "old Irish." He argues, for example, that Geoffrey Keating in his "Foras Feasa ar Eirinn" provided a history of Ireland which served to unite both ethnic groups. However, we know from the Confederation of Kilkenny in the 1640s and the period of exile which followed its defeat, that divisions between "old English" and "old Irish" ran very deep indeed, not least because of the Plantation of Ulster which deprived many of the "old Irish" in the North of their ancestral lands. In the volumes under review there is next to no discussion of such matters. The name of archbishop Rinuccini, the Papal Nuncio, who excommunicated those who supported the compromise peace of 1646 (the First Ormond Peace) does not appear.

This omission is symptomatic of a general flaw in Bradshaw's approach in that his insistence upon the creation of a sense of national identity leads him to play down political and cultural divisions within Ireland. Cultural differences between north and south in Ireland existed in the seventeenth century as they do today, and were parallelled by the great divide in Scotland between Highlands and Lowlands. For example, Clanricarde in February 1644 urged Taaffe to suppress and destroy "those rude barbarous people (the northern men wandering in multitudes) that have done so much mischief in the county of Sligo."[8] Later, in 1645, he hoped that they would be encouraged to join Montrose in Scotland, "which would ease the country of so many, unprofitable loose men."[9] Later in the year,[10] he told Ormond that he had persuaded the Confederation Council of Connacht to petition their superiors at Kilkenny to send reinforcements to Scotland and thus get rid of "such a multitude of northern people as now do nearly oppress it." In October 1646, the old English commander Thomas Preston complained about "the distracted condition our poor kingdom is in, groaning under the intolerable pressures of an unbridled and unlimited multitude of licentious caterpillars (the Ulster forces) void of rule or reason to square their actions by."[11] In 1647, Donagh MacCarthy, Viscount Muskerry wrote from Munster to Clanricarde, confiding his suspicions of the old Irish commander, Owen Roe O'Neill:

> Being necessitated for the preservation of my own security and the safety of the lives and fortunes of my friends in particular, and all honest men in this province in general, deemed to be at the mercy and disposal of Owen Roe O'Neill if the designs on his behalf might but receive success, I took upon me a resolution to withdraw myself from the danger of men so forward and active in my destruction.[12]

In July 1647 there was open conflict in Connacht between Ulstermen and the local inhabitants. Clanricarde, writing to Ormond, referred to "a late encounter between some of the inhabitants of this county and a party of Ulstermen, wherein a 100 of the Ultrachts and many of their women were killed and drowned."[13] Clearly, Bradshaw's claim that ethnic differences were subsumed within a common Irish Catholic identity from the 1570s onward is open to question.

These ethnic differences were compounded by differences of principle among the Catholic gentry about "our religion, King and country" (words used by the old English general Thomas Preston). Bradshaw's use of the term "faith and fatherland" leads us to oversimplify the issues involved. The introduction of a third element "King" introduced the problems faced by Catholic subjects living under a Protestant monarch within a composite state. One possible solution was suggested by the Edict of Nantes. Clanricarde indeed referred to

> The last King of France, having wholly subdued his protestant subjects and taken and dismantled their principle [*sic*] towns and forts, observing their number and quality of them, he not only gave them the free exercise of their religion but trusted them in great employments and made them generals of his armies in several parts of the Christendom and these favours are still continued to them.[14]

Other Irish Catholics, however, did not contemplate such compromises. James Fitzmaurice had not done so in the 1570s when he promised that those following the banner of faith and fatherland would be guaranteed their reward in heaven.[15] The Fitzmaurice model was followed in the 1640s when the Dominican, Oliver Burke, issued an indulgence to Irish soldiers fighting heretics and other enemies of the Catholic faith. Clanricarde complained to Ormond that this was "of so dangerous consequence to all his majesty's protestant subjects, such a fomenting of the dissensions and enmities between both nations and professors of either religions."[16]

Brendan Bradshaw is right to remind us that the Irish problem should be seen as part of the wars of religion. This should not imply, however, that there were only two ideologies, Catholic and Protestant. Within each camp there were differing groups. Clanricarde, writing to Charles I's Secretary of State in 1645, distinguished two groups within the pro-English in Ireland, those who were "for the King" and those who were "covenantors" [*sic*] whose marks were "insolence and disobedience." Among the Confederates he likewise "observed two sorts: one that aim at high matters scarce within any limitation and others whom I confidently presume would really return to their obedience and faithfully serve his majesty."[17] Within the Confederate camp such conflict reached a high point in August 1646 over a compromise peace reached with the king (the First Ormond peace), the aim of which was to free confederate troops for service in England at what was obviously a crucial point. A substantial group of old English gentry, including Preston, accepted this only to withdraw under pressure of excommunication from the Papal Nuncio's party, backed by Owen Roe O'Neill. However, by June 1647 the situation had taken yet another turn and Muskerry at the head of an army in Munster called for the removal of the Nuncioist party, who he saw as "ambitious usurpers, whose vexations and tyrannies are already too much felt." Muskerry saw himself as fighting for "the avail and advancement of religion, his majesty's rights and the liberty and safety of all honest subjects."[18]

This clash between these two groups of Irish Catholics may be seen as between two ideologies, one of them based on "faith and fatherland," the other on "God, King and country." The conflict reached its peak in 1646 when the king's herald was not allowed to proclaim the peace at Waterford, Kilkenny, Clonmel, and Limerick. Ormond blamed this upon O'Neill, referring to "the application of all the country to him, either for fear of him or for love to the religiousness of the cause he pretends to countenance."[19]

Both sides saw themselves as fighting in the cause of the Irish nation. The Nuncioists declared their "intentions to render Ireland Catholic and a free nation and to settle it in due obedience to his majesty."[20] They spoke of aiming only at "the advancing of the Catholic religion in this Kingdom, the preservation of his majesty's rights and to obtain for the nation the liberties of free born subjects." They claimed to be "rescuing his majesty from his present miseries and the setting of him in his royal power." In principle there was nothing here that Ormond, Clanricarde, and the pro-compromise peace party could not agree with. In practice, however, Clanricarde criticized the imprecision of the Nuncioists' demands. He defended the Ormond Peace ("that late worthily detested peace" in the eyes of the pro-Nuncioist Bishop of Clonfert) on the grounds that "I know nothing denied that rational men can expect or desire."[21] As he wrote to Patrick Darcy, "I cannot approve of those ways that will at once hazard both religion and Kingdom by an unreasonable pressure or expectation of impossibilities here from my lord lieutenant."[22] In November 1646 the Nuncioist party demanded "that the exercise of the Roman Catholic religion be in Dublin, Drogheda and all the Kingdom of Ireland as free and public as it is now in Paris in France or Brussels in the Low Countries." In contrast, the Ormondists, taking the Graces of 1628 as their model, had been working toward a settlement of practical grievances. Here lay the crux of the matter. The Nuncioists looked to a model in which the Catholics enjoyed political power as in France or the Netherlands. Ormond and Clanricarde were conscious of living in a Three Kingdom composite state in which the situation of the Irish Catholics resembled that of the French Huguenots. Both parties saw themselves as working for the good of their nation and religion. Clearly, however, there was no agreement as to how this might best be achieved.

Amid all the discussions of the 1640s there is constant reference to an "Irish nation," which would seem to bear Bradshaw's contention that the "old English" and "old Irish" saw themselves as belonging to one Irish nation. But what was meant by that term? Clanricarde accepted that most of the Irish nation was Catholic but he did not exclude Protestants. Ormond, the Protestant Lord Lieutenant, was a test case and here Clanricarde remarked that "though in religion the lord lieutenant does differ in opinion from the generality of the nation, yet certainly he is so much concerned there by all his nearest friends and kindred as must be powerful inducements to him to allow them all fit and just satisfaction and security in the free exercise of religion."[23] Of another Irish friend, Mr. Justice Donnellan, Clanricarde wrote that he was "an earnest Protestant but I am sure no Roundhead" and that "if in anything he do incline to partiality, it is in favour to the English nation."[24] For Clanricarde the all-important category was a political one, namely, to be one of "his majesty's subjects" who might be "of several nations and professions" (sc, religious professions) and who he hoped "might live happily united together."[25] He looked for the removal of "all jealousies and disturbances between both nations" by taking off those marks of subjection and distinction from themselves that did always forment and nourish discontents between them." What these remarks suggest and what the negotiations over the Ormond Peace indicate is that for many Catholic Irish gentry, Ireland was not, as Bradshaw maintains, an unassimilable entity within the Three Kingdoms. Rather they saw themselves as one of the two nations within Ireland (three, if the Scots were included) seeking to live together as his majesty's subjects. This association of the Catholic Irish gentry with the Stuart monarchy was to persist after the Restoration and the 1688 Revolution. Indeed, as Professor O. Buachalla's fascinating recent work has shown, Irish Jacobitism has been unjustifiably neglected as a political force. Irish Catholic acceptance of the Stuarts over such a long period surely implies some acceptance of a British constitutional link.

If we look ahead to the eighteenth century, it remains clear that no simple interpretation of Irish unity based upon "faith and fatherland" is adequate. By the 1750s the Irish episcopate was concerned about outmoded assumptions by which a Stuart king, James III, appointed them and in the 1760s formulated a test oath which they hoped would be accepted by the authorities. This was also submitted to Monsignor Ghilini, the internuncio at Brussels, who violently objected (à la Rinuccini) to the inclusion of a sentence stating, "I swear that I abhor, detest and deny from the bottom of my heart the pernicious and abominable doctrine that teaches we must not keep Faith with heretics or that princes excommunicated by the pope may be deposed or murdered by their subjects."[26] Clearly, the papal bull *Regnans in Excelsis* (1570) deposing Elizabeth cast a long shadow. The Irish Catholic Committee, however, had moved on and by 1774 had drawn up an oath which condemned evasion, equivocation, or mental reservation and specifically denied that the Pope or any authority of the see of Rome could dispense them from it.[27] This unfortunately led to a split between "jurors" and "nonjurors" among the episcopate and the laity. The path of faith and fatherland never did run smooth.

It is now time to turn more specifically to the volumes under review. The first of these, *The British Problem* c. *1534–1707: State Formation in the Atlantic Archipelago*, will no doubt achieve a wide circulation and deservedly so. The editors, Brendan Bradshaw and John Morrill, assembled their contributors at a conference held at Cambridge in July 1993 and this clearly helped to produce a volume which is more unified than similar collections. Bradshaw's essay, "The Tudor Revolution," discussed above, to some extent sets the tone. Bradshaw sees Ireland as being at the heart of the British problem since it emerged during this period "as the unassimilable element within the unitary British state" (p. 43). He refers to "the impact of an irresistible force" (the British state) "on an immovable object" (the Irish nation). For Bradshaw a major dynamic of early modern state formation was "the assimilation of Europe's consolidating Renaissance monarchies striving to transmute their disparate feudal patrimonies into centralised unitary realms by arrogating to themselves the absolute sovereignty vested in the Roman Emperor in the civil code of Justinian in accordance with the maxim of humanist jurisprudence rex est imperator in regno suo" (p. 42).

This is an interesting hypothesis, expounded with magisterial confidence. The other contributors in this volume, however, take a very different stance. Where Bradshaw has no doubts about "the evolutionary process" and "the political evolution of the Atlantic Archipelago," the general tone of the rest of the volume is to stress the hand-to-mouth chance-laden penny-pinching attitude of this particular "consolidating Renaissance monarchy." Hiram Morgan, for example, tells us that none of the "British" policies pursued by Elizabeth's servants were successful. In his view, money was always the key factor (p. 88). In his excellent essay Morgan clearly challenges Bradshaw's evolutionary thesis that Elizabeth's aim was the establishment of a unitary British state. In Morgan's view her underlying purpose was "to keep foreign powers out of the British periphery" (p. 67). A somewhat similar approach is adopted by Jenny Wormald in her challenging essay on James VI/James I. She argues that James gave out strong "British" signals but was "unclear what he meant by them." Such "lack of precision therefore led to a great deal of confusion." Wormald also draws attention to the introduction of Catholic settlers into Strabane by the Earl of Abercorn and Sir George Hamilton. In her view, "the creation of Protestant Ulster which is supposed to be the root of the present troubles lay in the future after 1641." In stressing the flexibility of James's religious policies here and elsewhere Wormald provides a "revisionist" tone which undermines any rigid approach to the history of the "Three Kingdoms."

A similar flexibility is demonstrated in the remaining essays. John Pocock, in a piece of characteristic bravura, juggles with the various interpretations on offer and comes to the conclusion that "no single dominant paradigm" is feasible for the mid-seventeenth century crises of the Three Kingdoms. Derek Hirst, in a fine essay on "The English Republic and the Meaning of Britain," stresses that the policy of union in the 1650s "in fact adds one more chapter to the familiar story of contingency and crises. If empire was eventually acquired in a fit of absence of mind, so too was a united Britain" (p. 194). (Like Morgan, Hirst is at odds with Bradshaw's "evolutionary process.")

The same questioning tone is reflected in the remaining essays of the volume. Mark Goldie, in his well-argued chapter on "Scotland and England" argues that "we cannot presume that there was a long term gravitational pull towards the union." Instead, he suggests, "we must look to the specific circumstances which arose after the Revolution of 1689." Jim Smyth, in his stimulating essay, "The Communities of Ireland and the British State 1660–1707," draws attention to the complexity of a situation in which the denominations concerned—Catholic, Anglican, and Presbyterian—were divided among themselves as well as from each other. He tells us that "the process of settler differentiation from the mother country was protracted, uneven and equivocal," and that Anglican dominance was "neither pre-ordained or uncontested." To all these contributions John Morrill's wide-ranging introduction provides an appropriate framework when he remarks that "the book as a whole should end in ambiguity and a sense of incompleteness." In Morrill's view "These are the early days of a historiographical quest for an explanation of a story without end." Indeed, after his fellow editor and his contributors have had their say, a powerful case has been mounted against Bradshaw's thesis about the creation of a "unitary state." Far from pronouncing an irresistible quasi-judicial verdict, Bradshaw has opened what promises to be an ongoing debate.

The second volume under review, *British Consciousness and Identity: The Making of Britain 1533–1707*, edited by Brendan Bradshaw and Peter Roberts, is more of a mixed bag, with no clear chronological structure. Here again Brendan Bradshaw's extended version of his "faith and fatherland" thesis to some extent sets the tone. There is also an introduction which is very different in character from Morrill's contribution in the earlier volume. This editorial introduction states categorically that "The issues which were to render Ireland an unassimilable element within the British state and to fuel Irish nationalism into the twentieth century were now in place: land, religion and the garrison. The curtain had come down upon the early modern phase of British history. The stage was set on which the history of modern Britain would be enacted" (p. 7). No hint of other possibilities or alternative paradigms!

Marc Caball's essay, "Faith, Culture and Sovereignty": Irish Nationalism and Its Development," provides a powerful supplement to Bradshaw's thesis, drawing upon the bardic poets as a key source. As Caball himself notes, however, they were either in exile or on the point of departure, which suggests parallels with the diaspora nationalism of a later period and thus serves to remind us that the views of the "diaspora" and the "homeland" do not always coincide. Caball also raises the question of print culture in Gaelic society, or rather its absence. He makes the ingenious argument that the oral mode of Gaelic literary activity may well have guaranteed a wider audience than printed books could ever have hoped to reach. Against this, the point may be made that bardic culture was very much the activity of an elite which despised an uncultivated wider audience. Bardic culture was very much "high culture," though here also exile may have led to changes.

Despite the appearance of the word "British" in the title, this book is largely organized in terms of distinct national categories, namely, Scotland, Ireland, and Wales. It is thus somewhat disappointing as a contribution to the new British history. Keith Brown's discussion of "Scottish Identity in the Seventeenth Century," for example, takes a traditional, unproblematic approach to his topic. He argues that in the seventeenth century, it was the church of Scotland which was "the only truly national institution." He gives short shrift to Episcopalians, Covenanters, and Catholics and to cultures outside the Lowland belt. The peerage, we are told, possessed "a strong Scottish identity" but how far this was Presbyterian is not made clear. Jane Dawson in her essay, "The Gaidhealtachad and the Emergence of the Scottish Highlands," provides a fascinating contrast to Brown's chapter. Her general theme is the transformation of Scottish Gaeldom into a marginal culture, but she finds room in her account for fascinating detail—the Gaelic enthusiasm for Mary Queen of Scots, the rise of the bagpipes, the campaigns of Alasdair Macolla (mentioned above) which brought bitter retribution in their train, and for the Northern Isles of Shetland and Orkney which Lowlanders were more sympathetic towards than they were towards the Highlands. Part of the interest of Dawson's contribution for a student of British history is her discussion of the divide which split Scottish from Irish Gaeldom. This is a fascinating chapter, but as with Brown the light which it throws upon "British Consciousness and Identity" is indirect. For a fully "British" approach it is necessary to turn to Colin Kidd's exhilarating essay, "Protestantism, Constitutionalism and British Identity under the Later Stuarts." Kidd shows an enviable familiarity with the minutiae of the various national and regional myths of the British Isles (his phraseology), including an awareness of how their political influence changed over time. His conclusion is that "Britishness" was a very milk and water commodity. In his view, "There was only a vague sense of a shared Britishness." "A British historical identity could not be composed simply by combining material from a variety of well established patriotic myths which traditionally defined the nations of England, Scotland, Ireland and Wales." Paradoxically, however, for all its stress upon a "minimal Britishness," Kidd's "British Isles" approach pays dividends in making individual national myths more intelligible. It also has the effect of undermining editorial stress upon the evolution of a British unitary state.

The remaining essays in this collection throw valuable if somewhat oblique light upon the new British history. Alan Ford in his piece, "James Ussher and the Creation of a Protestant Identity," shows Ussher grappling with the problems presented by a Protestant interpretation of Irish Church history. His conclusion is that Ussher "constitutes a challenge to historians to move out beyond exclusive definitions of national identity" and "to rethink orders of the mind and realise that several identities can be reconciled within the self." To some extent this is also the point made by Jim Smyth in his contribution, "No Remedy More Proper: Anglo-Irish Unionism before 1707," when he discusses "other possible outcomes" to the problems of the late 1690s. In Smyth's view "only by reimagining the range of possibilities open to contemporaries do figures like Cox or Maxwell or the pro-Union Irish parliaments of 1703, 1707 and 1709 make sense" (p. 320). Philip Jenkins's piece on "Seventeenth-Century Wales," argues that Welsh cultural distinctiveness was not translated into political identity. His contribution may be seen as "revisionist" in the sense that it criticizes the influence of modern nationalistic concerns upon historical interpretations. His own aim is to explain "how Welsh elites accepted as their own such emerging British institutions as the Church and monarchy and yet shaped them to fit local concerns and traditions." All three of these contributions may be seen as a challenge to the somewhat inflexible approach of the editorial introduction.

It remains to mention two pieces which deal with literature. Andrew Hadfield in his essay, "From English to British Literature," shows how Lyly's *Eupheues* texts (1578, 1580) were very much concerned with English national identity, whereas Spenser's *The Faerie Queen* deliberately replaces an English with a British context through a particular focus on Ireland. Willy Maley's, "The British Problem in Three Tracts on Ireland by Spenser, Bacon and Milton," deserves discussion at greater length than can be given here. He sees Spenser and Milton as linked by "a vehemently Protestant English nationalism," whereas Bacon argues for the foundation of

"Britishness" in the plantation of Ulster. These contributions introduce an element of "Britishness" into their approach which is lacking elsewhere in the volume. Indeed, though there are good things in it, this volume, edited by Bradshaw and Roberts, lacks the unity of "The British Problem" edited by Bradshaw and Morrill. Perhaps part of the reason for this lies in the fact that in the "Britishness" volume it is the view from the periphery which is dominant, ignoring the core apart from the two articles on literature. If the comment is not too anglocentric, it is like Hamlet without the Prince of Denmark.

Taken together, these volumes are a reminder of how intertwined the various histories of these islands have been. They also, in my view at least, provide contrasting examples of nationalist interpretations of history, and postnationalist "academic" interpretations. Nationalist history seems to require a total emotional commitment, whereas academic history is open to a variety of hypotheses which may be expected to change in response to fresh insights or new sources of evidence. Nationalist interpretations of the past seem to be very much the view from the present, backed by powerful political considerations. Jim Smyth's "postnationalist" comments in his essay on Anglo-Irish unionism are relevant here. In his view, it is only by placing history in context that we are able to reimagine the range of possibilities open to contemporaries.

NOTES

1. It is interesting to note that the term "Atlantic Archipelago" was earlier used with reference not to Ireland but to Iceland by York Powell, Regius Professor of Modern History at Oxford (Oliver Elton, *York Powell: A Life* Oxford, 1906, p. 237). Powell, a friend of Yeats with a strong interest in things Welsh and Irish, was primarily an Icelandic scholar. In the volumes under review most of the contributors in fact prefer to use the established term "the British Isles," which has the merit of familiarity, rather than "Atlantic Archipelago." (En passant, York Powell's letter to Douglas Hyde on bilingualism is well worth reading. Ibid., pp. 280–82.)

2. Brendan Bradshaw and John Morrill, eds., *The British Problem, c. 1534–1707: State Formation in the Atlantic Archipelago* (Problems in Focus Series) (London, 1996). Brendan Bradshaw and Peter Roberts, eds., *British Consciousness and Identity: The Making of Britain 1533–1707* (Cambridge, 1998).

3. Simon Barton, "The Roots of the National Question in Spain," in Mikuláš Teich and Roy Porter, eds., *The National Question in Europe in Historical Context* (Cambridge, 1993), pp. 106–27; Norman Davies, *Heart of Europe: A Short History of*

Poland (Oxford, 1984) (paperback edition, 1986), p. 143; Linda Colley, *Britons: Forging the Nation 1707–1837* (London, 1992); Ashutosh Varshney, "Contested Meanings: India's National Identity, Hindu Nationalism and the Politics of Anxiety," in *Reconstructing Nations and State, Daedalus* (Summer 1993).

4. *British Consciousness*, p. 47.

5. Ibid., p. 70.

6. Ibid., p. 133.

7. J. Lowe, ed., *Letter-Book of the Earl of Clanricarde 1643–47* (Dublin: Stationery Office, 1983), p. 46. I have made considerable use of this source in this section of my essay.

8. Ibid., p. 115.

9. Ibid., p. 138.

10. Ibid., p. 149.

11. Ibid., p. 292.

12. Ibid., p. 448.

13. Ibid.

14. Ibid., p. 50.

15. *British Consciousness*, p. 134.

16. *Clanricarde, Letters* p. 50.

17. Ibid., pp. 144–45.

18. Ibid., p. 448.

19. Ibid., pp. 277, 287.

20. Ibid., pp. 291, 300.

21. Ibid., p. 300.

22. Ibid., p. 259.

23. Ibid., p. 297.

24. Ibid., p. 38.

25. Ibid., pp. 116, 117.

26. Maureen Wall, *Catholic Ireland in the Eighteenth Century* (Dublin, 1989), p. 110.

27. Ibid., p. 112.

Chapter Four

Parnell and Beyond:

Nationalism in These Islands, 1880–1980

(1994)

There are four nations coexisting in these islands. Nationalism, while present in all, has taken a different course in each of them. Exploring why this should be so is the theme of this lecture. In these four nations, national identity was never beyond controversy. Indeed, concepts of what constituted "Irishness," "Welshness," "Scottishness," and "Englishness," changed over time, thus putting a question mark against Enoch Powell's belief that "the nation is the ultimate political reality," or Parnell's statement that "no man has the right to fix the boundary of the march of an nation." "Nation" is a term riddled with ambiguity; nonetheless the phenomenon of "nationalism" shows no signs of disappearing. Today, in the Irish Republic, nationalism may well be in decline, but it seems to be on the upsurge in the United Kingdom, with unforeseeable consequences.

I define nationalism for our purpose as referring to political movements aiming at a great measure of independence for a group of individuals who see themselves as members of a "nation."

But what is a "nation"? Benedict Anderson's definition of "Imagined communities" stresses the role of the imagination. Other commentators emphasize the problematic character of nationhood. How do nationalists recognize members of their nation? Is it language? Religion? Race? A combination of all three? Clearly there is plenty of room for disagreement and the history of nationalism contains many examples of disagreements, which led to violence. If I imagine a community, which I call a nation and define you as a member of it, can I use force to compel you to accept inclusion? What validity does the idea of "nationhood" possess? Who decides?

And how do nationalist movements come into existence? The answer seems commonly to lie in a shared sense of grievance or a feeling of being forced to defend a set of values. But here again there is plenty of room for the role of imagination. One man's grievance may be another's blessing.

The term "nation" is so riddled with ambiguities that we can only treat any nationalist movement on its individual merits. What definition of the nation did a particular nationalist party have in mind? Or were there several definitions?—a state of affairs which could lead either to internal discord or to generalized vagueness, aimed at avoiding disunity. Parnell's grandiose phrase—"no man hath the right to fix the boundary of the march of an nation"—is an example of such ambiguity. As leader of a political coalition drawing support from the catholic church as well as its declared enemy, the Fenian movement, Parnell was compelled to be vague or else to resort to silence (as was indeed the case for much of his later career). Parnell deliberately seemed to become a symbol at such times and hence all things to all men. It was only when the chips were down after the split of 1890 that he turned to court a specific constituency—the Fenians and the Dublin working class. Until then he maintained a magnificent ambiguity which was part of the reason for his success.

Was Charles Stewart Parnell himself Irish? He was of Protestant background. He was English-speaking. He was half American. He had an English university education. If his definition of Irish included himself we may assume that Irishness for him was based upon the notion of "territoriality," that is, that those born and living within this island are by definition Irish.

But what about those who were born in Ireland and now lived in England, Scotland, or Wales or in North America, Australia, or New Zealand? Are they also Irish? The territorial nationalist says "no." (This was the view of the "Klein-Deutsch"—the little Germans of Bismark's Germany.)

Little Irelanders must surely take this view. But Parnell himself was not consistent. He ordered Irish-born voters in Britain to vote Tory or Liberal, according to his wishes. He made overtures to the Irish in the United States. But since territoriality was no longer the criterion, how were the Irish to be recognized? It could not be language, since they spoke English. For many it was the Catholic religion, but Parnell could not accept a definition which excluded him. The answer seems to be that it was those who defined themselves as Irish. They saw themselves as Irish. They saw themselves as part of an imagined community, though not all of them can be termed nationalists since not all were involved in politics.

Our topic is not just Parnell—though he clearly forms part of the story—but also "these islands." What did Charles Haughey mean when he spoke of "the totality of relationships within these islands"? As with Parnell there is a studied ambiguity here. But we may take it that he is referring to the relationship between the United Kingdom and the Republic of Ireland. For us however "these islands" refers to something more than these two states which have coexisted often uneasily since 1922. Our brief involves consideration of the four nations of England, Ireland, Scotland, and Wales, and the relationships between them.

To discuss nationalism clearly raises the question of the relationship between the three smaller nations and the much larger unit accounting for 80 percent of the population. For a nationalist, this is the main historical problem. But the totality of relationships also raises the question of divisions within these nations themselves, since as we have seen the concept of "nation" itself is problematic. How do we recognize Scots, Welsh, Irish—let alone English? Perceptions of such matters vary from person to person. Our discussion may well resemble the croquet game in *Alice in Wonderland* when Alice was using a flamingo for a mallet and a hedgehog for a ball.

With these caveats we may begin our discussion. During our period, that is, from the 1880s onward our three smaller nations—Wales, Scotland, and Ireland—resembled one another in certain ways. In all three there were areas of recent and continuing industrialization. In Wales, the counties of Glamorgan and Monmouth were both heavily industrialized. This had led to a remarkable increase of population in south Wales. In 1881 Glamorgan alone accounted for one-third of the total Welsh population of 1.5 million. The population of this county alone rose by 27 percent between 1871 and 1881. In contrast the rural counties of north and west Wales (outside such industrialized pockets as Wrexham) remained static or declined in population. In Scotland a similar picture emerges. Here the population grew threefold during the nineteenth century until it was nearly 5 million by 1911. All this increase took place in the industrialized counties of the Lowlands, in particular Lanarkshire and Renfrewshire, the area of Clydeside dominated by Glasgow and its satellite towns. In contrast the rural areas, as in Wales, lost population. Worst hit were the Highlands and the Borders. The east coast was also rural but the jute industry in Dundee and mining in Fife attracted immigrants. Finally there was Ireland. Here there was an even sharper contrast between an industrial area gaining population and the rural area, which lost population from the Famine onward. Belfast, the Irish equivalent of Cardiff or Glasgow, grew from 75,000 in 1841 to 387,000 in 1911. Dublin in contrast had suffered continuous economic decline. In all three countries, industrialization had changed the balance of economic power.

It is not only the economic facts of industrialization that introduced a new element into what had hitherto been overwhelmingly agricultural societies, but the "melting pot" effect which accompanied them. Emigrants from the English midlands, from Ireland (the Rooneys, now owners of the Pittsburgh Steelers, among them), and from the rural counties of north Wales flooded into the mining valleys of Glamorgan and Monmouth. South-west Scotland was a similar magnet for emigrants from the highlands and from Ulster. The Lagan valley also attracted emigrants from England (T. W. Moody's father, for example). The problems of the "melting pots" of Glasgow, Belfast, and Cardiff were very different in character from the rural societies in which they were now established and which they were in a position to dominate. The "melting pots" faced problems of expansion and assimilation. The rural areas faced problems of depopulation and decline. In rural Wales, for example, during the period 1881–91 the population declined in eight out of the thirteen Welsh counties.[1] Montgomery was the worst hit with a fall of over 11 percent. In Ireland there was a similar story. Here the rural population declined catastrophically.[2] Rural Scotland also faced similar problems.

Of our three national units, it was the rural problems of Wales and Ireland from the mid-nineteenth century which were most similar. In both, unlike Scotland, the landlord class was perceived as belonging to an anglicized, Anglican, English-speaking, and hence largely alien ascendancy. Welsh landlords on the whole were members of the Episcopalian established church. The Church of Wales itself was seen as the church of a minority. The payment of tithes was a grievance for the Nonconformist majority. It was only in 1870 that Gladstone appointed the first Welsh-speaking bishop since the reign of Queen Anne. In Ireland, the Church of Ireland, though disestablished in 1869, still remained the church of the landlords.

As in Ireland, landlords in Wales expected their tenants to vote in accordance with their wishes. When some independent spirits refused to do so, eviction duly followed. The evictions, which followed the Merioneth election of 1859, was still remembered over thirty years later. The uncle of Tom Ellis was one of the evicted. Ellis himself, who later became member of parliament for Merioneth, testified in 1894 about the horror which the evictions aroused.

During the 1870s the Great Depression affected the rural worlds of Ireland and Wales. In both societies "landlordism," rightly or wrongly, was blamed for the economic problems which followed in the wake of falling prices and bad harvests. In Wales the election of 1880 marked a decisive shift of power away from the landlords. In Montgomeryshire, the Liberal candidate Stuart Rendell, who surprisingly was both English and Anglican, defeated the long-established Welsh landowning family of the Wynns of Wynnstay. The great majority of Welsh parliamentary seats fell to the Liberals—29 out of the 33 Welsh seats. Six years later a similar landslide occurred in Ireland when Parnell's party gained 86 out of 106 seats. At the local level, however, landlords retained a good deal of power until the passing of the Local Government Acts in each county.

Nationalist movements in Wales as well as Ireland took up such rural grievances. Ireland indeed became the model for Welsh nationalists to follow. Parnell's success in organizing an Irish parliamentary party inspired Thomas Ellis to establish a Young Wales party. Ellis, son of an evicted Merioneth farmer, was a lad of parts who made good. A graduate of Aberyswyth and Oxford, he met Cecil Rhodes on a trip to Africa and Rhodes's enthusiasm for Irish Home Rule within an Imperial Federation led him to speak out at Bala in September 1890, calling for the establishment of the Welsh parliament. Ellis had been called "the Parnell of Wales," but that title should really be accorded to David Lloyd George. Lloyd George as a young man was elected as a Liberal MP for Carnarvon borough in April 1890. There was as yet no separate Welsh party but Lloyd George formed one of a pressure group, agitating for Welsh Home Rule. Taking over Liberal party organization in Wales was the first step. The dependence of the newly Liberal government of 1892 gave Cymru Fydd (Young Wales) the opportunity to press for Welsh aims. Rosebery, Gladstone's successor as prime minister, was forced to introduce a Welsh Disestablishment Bill in April 1894. A year later Cymru Fydd took over the North Wales Liberal Federation. In 1895 Lloyd George wrote, "I maintain strongly that all our demands whether in Church, Land, Education, Temperance or otherwise ought to be concentrated in one great agitation for self government."[3] Parnell could not have put it more clearly.

Early in 1896 a crucial trial of strength took place at Newport between the nationalists of North Wales led by Lloyd George and the Liberals of South Wales. Lloyd George was badly defeated by 133 votes to 70. He blamed his defeat upon "Newport Englishmen," but the chief opposition came from fellow Welshmen. Robert Bird from Cardiff, a nonconformist businessman, declared that Liberalism was more important than Welshness. The cosmopolitan South, in his view, would never accept "the domination of Welsh ideas." A spokesman from Methyr declared that "Glamorgan and Monmouth were not to be dictated to by the isolated county of Caernarvon" (Lloyd George's county). Lloyd George's main opposition was the coalowner D. A. Thomas, later Viscount Rhondda, and the two remained on bad terms for a long time to come.

The clash at Newport proved to be decisive. The nationalists of the North came to accept the South's verdict against Home Rule. Lloyd George was still to agitate fiercely on Welsh causes, most notably against the Education Act of 1902, which appeared to favor Church of Wales schools. He was always capable of introducing a nationalist note into his speeches, as for example in 1912 when he recalled the election of 1869: "It awoke the spirit of the mountains, the genius of freedom that fought the might of the Normans. ... The political power of landlordism in Wales was shattered as efficiently as the power of the Druids." But from 1896 his political ambitions lay in the field of social reform.

Hatred of "landlordism" was one important way in which rural Wales and Ireland resembled one another. There was another significant resemblance between them. In both religion came to be accepted by many as a crucial element in defining national identity. In Wales, nonconformity was the religion of 80 percent of those who worshiped on Sundays. The largest group were Calvinist Methodists, who were most numerous in the Welsh-speaking areas of rural Wales (Anglesey, Carnarvon, Merioneth, and Cardigan). It was these nonconformists who provided the activist political majority which for a long time (though less so today) made nonconformity and Welshness synonymous. Temperance, disestablishment, the role of the Welsh language in education—all concerns of nonconformity—became inexplicably intertwined with the Welsh national image.

In Ireland, a revived Catholicism provided the counterpart of the rise of Welsh nonconformity. Under the leadership of Paul Cullen, archbishop of Dublin from 1852 to 1878, a Devotional Revolution (Professor Larkin's term) took place. Local, traditional customs gave way to a more centralized practice. The clergy grew in numbers and influence. A major victory was won with the disestablishment of the state church in 1869, something which did not happen in Wales for another half-century. It was during these years that a strongly religious sense of national identity developed, in which for the majority of the population "Irishness" was equated with Catholicism. In 1862, for example, plans to erect a statue of Daniel O'Connell played up his religious role as the emancipation of the Catholic people of this realm.

In contrast with Wales, however, there was in Ireland a rival, competing with religion. This secular identity looked back to the American and French revolutions for inspiration as well as to the nationalist movement in Europe. For the Catholic archbishop Paul Cullen, Mazzini and Garibaldi were to be denounced as enemies of the papacy and the Roman Church. For the Fenians, Mazzini and Garibaldi were nationalists whose political vision spanned sectarian differences. In Wales a nonconformist Welsh identity became dominant. In Ireland there was a constant tension between two rival national identities, which also existed in the Irish diaspora overseas in the United States. It was Parnell's achievement to bring together these rival groups with a broad coalition, something which would hardly have been possible until after Paul Cullen's death in 1878.

The political rise of Parnell began in 1879 with his sponsorship of the Land League. After the 1880 election and his assumption of the leadership of the Home Rule Party in parliament, he was a power to be reckoned with. But the church held aloof. It welcomed Gladstone's Land Act of 1881 while Parnell remained lukewarm. The church was horrified by the Phoenix Park murders of 1882. It was in this year, however, the anniversary of Grattan's parliament, that O'Connell's statue was finally unveiled. On this occasion, O'Connell's role as a Repealer was now stressed. The nationalist movement had begun to take steps to woo the church. In 1883 Parnell's party voted against a bill which would have allowed the admission of the avowed atheist Charles Bradlaugh into the House of Commons despite having supported him in 1880. In the same year he reached an accommodation with the Catholic episcopate over support for Catholic schools, a policy move at variance with the policy of Gladstone's Liberal Party. In 1885 the policy paid off. Parnell, thanks to open clerical support, was returned, leading a party of 86 members.

As long as the Irish party was led by Protestant landowners, it was possible to maintain that the nation to which Parnell referred in his famous phrase about "the march of an nation" was not a specifically Catholic nation. At the Galway election of 1886 Parnell imposed a Protestant Liberal, Captain O'Shea, upon an unwilling electorate. Parnell's nonsectarian approach placed a strain upon party unity but did not destroy it. Parnell also survived the crises of the Pigott forgeries when he was accused of allying himself with terrorism. In 1890, however, the O'Shea divorce trial split the party. The majority, in alliance with the church, were opposed to Parnell.

In December Parnell lost the North Kilkenny by-election in the face of strong clerical opposition. After the result *The Irish Catholic* declared that

> To Catholic Irishmen it seemed as if Providence which watched over our country and its Faith had again, by inscrutable decree, ordained that the gates of hell shall not prevail against them.

1890 was the year of the so called Parnell split.

A more profound split, however, had already taken place in 1886 between North and South over the introduction of the Home Rule Bill. As in Wales, the industrialized counties placed their political weight in favor of the union. In Wales the division between North and South was largely economic, though it was reinforced by a cultural divide between a teetotalist chapel culture and a beer-drinking pub culture. In Ireland the economic contrast between the rural South and the industrial North was reinforced by similar deep religious divisions. In broad sociological terms there were similarities between the two societies. Evangelicalism and fundamentalism were characteristic of Catholic Limerick and Protestant Belfast. Outsiders might see such resemblances. In practice, however, North and South were profoundly antagonistic toward one another. The fall of Parnell confirmed the worst fears of the North. But whereas in Wales the Home Rule movement collapsed in the face of the opposition of Cardiff, in Ireland neither side gave way. The outcome was civil war first between North and South and then secondly within the South itself.

Our topic is nationalism and national identity. When we compare Wales and Ireland, however, the topic of class and class identity cannot be left out of the account, since it was here that the two countries, despite their resemblances, most sharply diverged. Much of the future of Wales was to be dominated by the working-class communities of industrialized South Wales. Rural North Wales was to play a secondary role. In contrast the future of Ireland was to be divided between a largely agrarian-based Southern Ireland and a largely industrialized North. In Wales, class-based politics dominated the scene; in Ireland the politics of nationalism, Green or Orange, Catholic or Protestant.

In Wales, during the period before the First World War politics was dominated by the Liberal Party, which was a coalition drawing upon a middle-class and working-class membership. Leadership was largely middle class. Some members reacted against this and established the Independent Labour Party in 1893. In 1900 an I.L.P. candidate, Keir Hardie, was elected MP for Merthyr. Looking back this was to be seen as a turning point for Labour. In practice, however, the Liberal Party led by Lloyd George dominated the scene. Lloyd George himself was radical enough for most Welsh tastes until after the First World War.

In the years following the end of the war, the landlord system itself collapsed. The way was now open for a more sharply focused industrial working-class party. Lloyd George had compromised himself by an alliance with the Conservative Party. In 1922 South Wales turned to the Labour Party, effectively allying itself with similar groupings in England and Scotland. Labour was unionist, not nationalist, though Keir Hardy himself often played the Celtic card, wearing a kilt on occasion.

Class alliances across national boundaries were seen as more important than distinctions based on national identity. Paradoxically, however, a new Welsh identity emerged based upon the rugby-playing, choir-singing Welsh miner. In North Wales, Welsh-speaking, teetotalist nonconformity provided a contrasting identity. Here Liberalism survived to some extent as an alternative to Labour. In major industrial areas, however, Labour enjoyed an almost unchallenged dominance.

Why did Ireland not follow a similar path to Wales? Part of the answer must surely lie in the charismatic leadership of Parnell. It was he who created and held together during the 1880s a heterogenous coalition of the urban middle class, rural small farmers, small-town shopkeepers, Catholic clergy, and immigrant American Irish. Lloyd George was clearly as charismatic a figure as Parnell, but the economic structure was weighted against him. In Wales the rural North and West could not compete with the booming South in terms of wealth and population. In Ireland the balance was more evenly based. In terms of population the South was more numerous but it was hard hit by the Great Depression. The counterparts of the small southern farmer existed in the northern counties of Ireland but Parnell was unable to win them over. The price of his alliance with the Catholic Church was failure to win Protestant support in the North. Landlords formed an alliance in the North with their tenants. Parnell himself was nonsectarian but his coalition was not nonsectarian enough. In Wales the struggle for dominance between the North and the South ended in victory for the South, despite the best efforts of Lloyd George. In Ireland, the gulf between nationalist South and unionist North widened until it became unbridgeable.

A politics based on class issues, however, did raise its head in Ireland from time to time. Michael Davitt was always aware of the importance of class and but for the intervention of Parnell in 1879 the Land War might

have seen much more of a class conflict than part of a nationalist risorgi-
mento. In the eyes of its critics in Ulster and Britain, the Land League always seemed a class war against the landlords. Parnell drew back from the
rhetoric of class war but after the split of 1890 even he attempted to play
the "class card" in urban areas as well as the countryside.

But Parnell's death in 1891 prevented for the moment the further exploitation of the "class" card in Irish politics. Moreover the split worked to
the advantage of the church, which threw its power behind the anti-
Parnellite majority. The two decades which followed the fall of Parnell saw
the growth of Catholicism as a key element in Irish national identity. In
the North, the strongly sectarian Catholic Ancient Order of Hibernians
grew in numbers and influence under the leadership of Joe Devlin. In the
South, the nationalist movement known as "Irish-Ireland" placed Catholicism at the center of Irish identity.

From 1910 onward the Irish Parliamentary Party held the balance of
power in the House of Commons and Home Rule became a distinct possibility. Nationalism thus became the key issue in Irish politics, leading to
an intensification of the rift between North and South. The North chose
"the Covenant" as its symbol of identity. In the South, Catholicism continued to be of central importance in defining "Irish-Ireland" identity.
This was brought out dramatically during the Dublin strike of 1913 when a
clerical-nationalist alliance opposed the offer made by British trade
unions on humanitarian grounds, to provide temporary shelter in England for the children of strikers. This issue posed sharply the conflict between class and national identity. The verdict went decisively in favor of a
Catholic-focused nationalism.

The Dublin strike of 1913 was an example of class-based rhetoric which
failed. The Easter Rising was an example of nationalist rhetoric which succeeded despite initial failure. Despite the presence of James Connolly
among the men of 1916, the Easter Rising marked a further shift away from
"class consciousness" to a more intense nationalism. The Easter Rising of
1916 began a shift to a greater separation symbolized for some by the
proclamation of a republic and for others by a withdrawal from Westminster. A new nationalist coalition began to form, which the church joined in
1918 in opposition to conscription. The tide of nationalism was in full
flood, not least because of a reaction against the Black and Tans.

But the division between North and South remained. If Home Rule had
been a bridge too far for Ulster Unionists in 1912, the advanced nationalism which followed was even more so. The nation which took shape after

1922 took a form which had not been envisaged by Parnell. The "Irish-Ireland" of the decades following 1922 was based upon the central importance of Catholic and Gaelic identity—of these twin pillars, Catholicism being more important in practice. The equivalent in Wales would have been a Welsh-speaking, nonconformist, teetotalist polity (a state of affairs which in fact partially came about in North Wales).

So far we have not mentioned Scotland. In terms of our four-nation model, however, Scotland is clearly as important as Wales and Ireland. How strong then was nationalism in Scotland? The initial answer must be hardly at all in comparision with Ireland or even Wales. Scottish identity had been securely established since the 1688 Revolution. It was based upon some form of Presbyterianism with the General Assembly as a key institution, plus autonomy in law and education. The disruption of 1843 had divided the Church of Scotland and the Free Church but the tensions between the two did not take on a nationalist tone. There was no real parallel here to the Welsh nonconformists and the Irish Catholics, though fears of the spread of English secularism were voiced on occasion.

As in Wales and Ireland, "landlordism" was a central issue in politics. However, this did not become a nationalist issue, though Parnell and Davitt did fish in Scotland's troubled waters during the 1880s. Many landlords were educated in England and were Episcopalian, and some of the tensions common to Wales and Ireland undoubtedly existed. There is, for example, evidence that tenants belonging to the Free Church were evicted in the years following 1843. It is thus not surprising that there should have been a swing to the Liberals in 1868. As in Wales, this year marked a decisive shift. But nationalism was weak.

As in Wales and Ireland, so also in Scotland a broad distinction may be drawn between rural and industrial areas. In Wales and Ireland, this lay between North and South. In Scotland it was between the largely rural east (excluding Dundee and Edinburgh) and the heavily industrialized West with Glasgow as its core. In the east of Scotland, where landlordism was a key issue, Gladstone like Parnell and Lloyd George was the uncrowned king. Unlike Parnell or Lloyd George, however, he made no real attempt to encourage a Home Rule movement for Scotland. In Scotland landlordism could not easily be turned into a nationalist issue, like Ireland or Wales. Hence in eastern Scotland, liberalism was a class-based party of the rural middle class.

In the industrialized West, there was a more complex situation. In central Clydeside where one-third of the population was congregated, there had been substantial Irish immigration in the second half of the nineteenth century. Here the potential existed for a Scottish nationalist movement based upon "no popery," a powerful rallying cry since the Reformation. There was also much resentment against cheap immigrant labor. Even so, however, during the period from the 1880s to 1914, the Liberal Party retained its dominance for most of the time. Scotland, like Wales, was mostly Liberal until 1922, the year which saw the rise of Labour.

Indeed what nationalism there was in Scotland during these years was Irish nationalism. The United Irish League founded in 1898 stipulated that "the Irish vote should not be committed to any British party, Tory, Liberal or Labour but directed where the interests of Ireland demanded such action." Thus in 1900 the Irish vote in the Blackfriars division of Glasgow was diverted in favor of Andrew Bonar Law, who as leader of the Conservative party supported the view that "Ulster would fight and Ulster would be right." Irish nationalism in Scotland was based upon a religious perception of "Irishness" with Joe Devlin and the Ancient Order of the Hibernians attracting more support than Sinn Fein. As in Ireland, the so called Sinn Fein rebellion of 1916 was condemned, only for attitudes to change when the leaders were shot. Ethnic or religious identity counted for more than class identity among the Glasgow Irish in the years before the First World War. Surprisingly, however, there seems to have been remarkably little overt support among Glasgow Protestants for the counternationalism of Carson. Only 8,000 turned out to greet him in Glasgow in October 1912, compared with the crowd of 150,000 which had awaited him in Liverpool a few days earlier.

The situation changed dramatically in the years following 1918. With the Irish Question safely out of the way after the Troubles of 1919–21, Irish voters in Scotland turned almost en masse toward the Labour Party. This was a remarkable victory for the Catholic politician John Wheatley. The Irish-born son of a miner, Wheatley had fought a lone fight for the idea of a Catholic socialism in the years before 1914 against the opposition of his parish priest and most of his fellow Catholics. In 1909 Robert Paterson, his parish priest, declared that Wheatley "does not care for any Bishop or priest in the Country. The man has lost his faith, if he had any, and is now, by selling papers attacking the church, an enemy of the church."[4] (Gully, p. 230).

In 1912 Wheatley's effigy was burned by a crowd singing "Faith of Our Fathers." The Labour Party was also thought to be anti-Irish as well as antireligious. Wheatley survived in part thanks to the sympathetic attitude of John Maguire, archbishop of Glasgow from 1902 (but coadjutor from 1894). Maguire, son of Irish immigrants, threw his influence on the side of Irish labor. In 1908 for example at a mass meeting in the Albert Hall, he declared: "Power is passing day by day more into the hands of the working classes. It looks as if ... the working men rule the world"[5] (Gully, p. 227). Wheatley took this as a motto for a pamphlet published in 1909 entitled *The Catholic Working Man* (Ibid., p. 228).

In 1918 the Labour Party won 7 seats in the general election of that year. In 1922 it won 30 seats and in 1923, 34. There is little doubt that Labour's success was due in part to the shift in the Irish vote away from the "nationalist" to the "class" issues. In 1924 John Wheatly became minister of health in the first Labour government of 1929–31.

During the 1920s and 1930s Scottish politics as a whole revolved around class rather than nationalist issues. The decline of the Liberal Party made possible a more open conflict between middle-class Unionism and working-class labor. There was, however, an attempt to mobilize anti- immigrant feeling in ways which had all the hallmarks of nationalism, though anti-Irish rather than anti-English in outlook. The origins of this lay in the postwar recession, as far-reaching as the Great Depression of the 1880s, but this time affecting industry rather than agriculture. Immigrant labor was an obvious scapegoat to hand and was in fact seized upon in some quarters of the Church of Scotland, not least in the General Assembly, which set up a "Church and Nation" committee in which immigrants were attacked as the source of many ills.

In 1923 the General Assembly formally approved a report entitled *The Menace of Our Irish Race to Our Scottish Nationality*. Throughout the 1920s and 1930s the "Church and Nation" committee of the General Assembly reported on the threat to the "nation." In 1934, for example, statistics were quoted to show that "the population of Scotland is every year becoming less Scottish in blood, tradition and religious attachment." The Church of Scotland saw itself as the mouthpiece of the Scottish people. In 1927, for example, it was declared that "the Church of Scotland, whose interests have been in the past so intimately involved with the Scottish people, has clearly an obligation to defend Scottish nationality such as no other institution or organisation has," against a kind of peril which was "the gravest which the Scottish people have ever confronted."[6]

The Church and Nation Committee reported that "this immigrant population is not being assimilated to any great extent by the native population. Hence there is growing up a nation within a nation and this immigrant nation manifests very marked contrasts in social and moral conduct and ideals with the native Scottish population. To such extent is this the case that the danger of race hatred and strife is very real."

Attempts were made to translate anti-Irish and anti-Jewish feeling into political action. In 1933, the Scottish Fascist Democratic Party was founded, calling for the expulsion of all religious orders and the repeal of the clauses of the 1918 Education Act providing state aid for Catholic schools. Alexander Ratcliffe, who defended Hitler, referred to the Gorbals as "Jewland." In 1940 he wrote in *Vanguard* that "we are very kind to the Roman Catholics in Scotland, the reason being seemingly that we have no Hitler in our midst to eject Popery."

In 1933 John Cormack formed the Protestant Action Society, which found a good deal of support in the depressed port of Leith. But Scottish nationalism lacked a leader and throughout the 1920s and 1930s politics revolved around questions of class rather than ethnicity (though in some Glasgow constituencies Conservative candidates played the Orange card).[7]

If we move forward to the 1980s, to what extent has the situation changed? Traditional assumptions about the link between Scottishness and the Church of Scotland have lost dominance. A new Scottish identity seems to be emerging in which immigrants of Irish descent can now be included. Interethnic hostility still survives. Celtic-Rangers rivalry is an obvious example of this, but the highly charged political rhetoric of the interwar years has largely disappeared. For the Scottish National Party, the enemy of Scotland is now England. The SNP conference of September 1989 declared that the difference between Moscow under Gorbachev and London under Margaret Thatcher or Neil Kinnock was that Moscow, for the time being, was "more liberal and tolerant towards its ethnic minorities." "We want to see Scotland broken from the English mould and recant along social democratic Scandinavian lines." The aim of the SNP was independence within Europe.

However, the SNP in the 1992 election won only 3 seats out of 70. Labour with a majority of seats remained overwhelmingly the dominant party. "Class" rather than "nation" was still the key issue. However, even the Scottish Labour Party felt obliged to take part in a constitutional convention to press for a greater degree of self-government. The "Home Rule" issue had returned.

In Wales the traditional sense of Welsh identity based upon the core of nonconformity and the Welsh language has declined. In 1979 a substantial majority rejected proposals for devolution. But Plaid Cymru, the Welsh nationalist party, has survived. The new definition of Welshness owes most to Saunders Lewis, a Merseyside emigré, who emphasized the role of the Welsh language. As a Catholic convert and a political conservative who admired *Action Française*, Lewis saw no essential link between Welsh identity and nonconformity. This new Welsh identity is weak in South Wales, heartland of the Labour Party. Here class rather than ethnicity is the key, as is instanced by the revival of conservatism in such areas as Swansea and Cardiff. Nationalist feeling is strongest in depressed rural areas where the number of Welsh speakers has declined and where the language is under pressure from immigrants hailing from the English Midlands and from Merseyside.

So far I have not mentioned England or English national identity. Can we speak of English national identity? Can we speak of English nationalism or something analogous to Irish, Scots, or Welsh nationalism? There is, I think, a sense of English national identity which has its origins in the English Reformation. It was then that the English Church became "the Church of England," Protestant, established, and controlled by the laity, in the sense that lay politicians made key political appointments. When the bishops in the House of Lords voted against the Duke of Newcastle he professed to be shocked by the fact that they had forgotten "their creator." The role of England as a Protestant nation was confirmed in the Glorious Revolution of 1688 when the legitimate king, the Catholic James II, was dispossessed. This was followed by the Act of Settlement of 1701 which made a Protestant monarchy a constitutional requirement. This is still the situation today. The key symbol of England, the monarch, is crowned in Westminster Abbey according to the rites of the Church of England. Protestantism was and to some extent still is a key feature of English identity. To this was added during the nineteenth century a sense of racial superiority—the English were the prime example of the white Anglo-Saxon race.

Throughout the nineteenth and much of the twentieth century this sense of white Anglo-Saxon Protestant superiority remained largely unchallenged. In the Napoleonic and subsequent wars, the English were undefeated. The nation was not on the defensive. Within the United Kingdom English culture was dominant. It was the smaller nations which could feel threatened by the spread of Englishness in the shape of English newspapers, English sport, English administration. The term "British" was applied to the British empire and the British monarchy, but by an understandable vanity "British" and "English" were equated in the minds of the English majority.

Since the end of the Second World War, the foundations beneath this definition of Englishness have begun to shift. The empire to defend which the war was fought has largely disappeared. The influence of the Church of England has declined to such an extent that more Catholics than Anglicans attend church on Sundays in England. The arrival in large numbers in the postwar years of immigrants from India, Pakistan, Africa, and the West Indies has created a new situation. England, which had a society of immigrants, became almost overnight a host society which began to undermine the old sense of Englishness, of belonging to a white Anglo-Saxon race. Did it also create the need for a new sense of English national identity? To many looking at the English sporting scene dominated by new immigrants this was self-evident. Others, however, most notably Enoch Powell in the 1960s and Winston Churchill, grandson of the wartime leader, in the 1990s have tried to play the nationalist card in defense of traditional English values as they see them. Nationalism as a political movement, here as elsewhere, seems to require as a necessary condition the sense of being under threat. There is thus the potential in England for the growth of nationalism.

For some, including Margaret Thatcher, the European Community offers a threat as dangerous to English nationhood as black immigration. For her and those like her the European Community is seen as undermining the sovereignty of parliament, which they look upon as a key symbol of English nationhood. The decline of Britain's status as a world power has added another element of insecurity. To some extent the disparity between the United States and Britain was hidden by the fig leaf of "the special relationship." Increasingly, however, Britain's role as a second-class partner in the alliance is becoming difficult to hide and this is leading to the growth of anti-Americanism—another possible seed of nationalism. As yet, however, English nationalism remains more potential than actual. No Parnell exists as yet to organize these varied groups into a serious nationalist coalition. The Conservative Party would need to split into rival factions to make such development possible. So far subtle adjustments seem to be taking place, making possible the acceptance of a multicultural British identity rather than a monocultural sense of English identity. Class distinctions also remain of key importance in English politics, and these work against the sense of solidarity which nationalism seems to require.

In the Republic of Ireland profound changes are taking place, but toward a European identity rather than a nationalist one. The place of Catholicism at the heart of Irish identity has been subjected to challenge over such issues as contraception and abortion. Only in Northern Ireland does the situation seem largely unchanged. Here Unionism seems to provide a classic case of nationalism—in this instance of British nationalism rather than English nationalism—a community with a strong sense of religious identity, now facing economic decline and threatened with absorption into what it sees as an alien culture. This Orange nationalism has its own flag, its own distinctive "national day," its own songs, its own version of history. What more is needed to make a nation?

But such nationalism keeps in existence an equally fervent counter-nationalism, that of Sinn Fein. The history of nationalism is full of such examples. But no single national identity seems able to encompass all the individuals living within a particular territory. What is the answer? Here the United States seems to provide the appropriate example of a state which makes citizenship the basic requirement, leaving ethnic or religious identity a luxury for those who wish to maintain it for themselves or their children.

NOTES

1. K. Morgan, *Rebirth of a Nation: Wales 1880–1980* (Oxford: 1981), p. 6.
2. J. J. Lee. *Ireland 1912–1985: Politics and Society* (Cambridge: 1989).
3. Morgan, p. 162.
4. K. Lunn, ed. *Hosts, Immigrants and Minorities* (Folkestone: 1980) p. 189.
5. Ibid. p. 184.
6. *Church of Scotland: Reports to the General Assembly.* (1927, 1933).
7. Gallagher, T. *Glasgow: the Uneasy Peace. Religious Tension in Modern Scotland, 1819–1914* (Manchester 1987) p. 158

Chapter Five

Language and Politics

(2001)

When the soul of a man is born in this country, there are nets flung at it to hold it back from flight. You talk to me of nationality, language, religion. I shall try to fly by those nets. (A Portrait of the Artist as a Young Man (1916), ch. 5, James Joyce.)

The Welsh language is the curse of Wales. Its prevalence, and the ignorance of the English language, have excluded, and even now exclude the Welsh people from the civilisation of their English neighbours [and again] the sooner the Welsh language disappears as an instrument of the practical, political, social life of Wales, the better. (Matthew Arnold, quoted in Contemporary Wales, vol. 11, 1998, p. 170)

From 1911 onwards socialism and the new miners' union were becoming the new religion. The language of socialism was English. ... To abandon Welsh become not only a valuational but also a symbolic gesture of rejection and affirmation—rejection of the political philosophy and the sham combination of Lib-Labour and the affirmation of new solidarities and new idealisms based upon secular and anti-religious philosophy. Fifty years earlier the new unions of the coalfield had issued their pamphlets, transacted their business, and organized themselves politically in Welsh. The Miners Next Step was written in English and never translated into Welsh. (Ieuan Gwynedd Jones, Ibid., pp. 170–71)

The revival of the Irish language as the badge of identity, as a component part of our culture and as the filter through which it is expressed, is a central aspect of the reconquest. (Gerry Adams, Free Ireland: Toward a Lasting Peace, p. 139)

My focus in this lecture will be upon the use of language as a political symbol. Our primary interest is the "Cultures of Ireland" but I will try to set this in a European context, including of course "these islands" as part of Europe. In the history of modern Europe language has been a key symbol of political identity and remains so in many states, from Spain to Romania.

In dealing with our theme there are many possible starting points. We might begin for example with the impact of the Reformation and the translation of the Bible into the vernacular. However I prefer to begin with the impact of the French Revolution upon "Language and Politics." During the ancien regime, the French Crown seems to have had no direct interest in promoting linguistic unity in France. Thus in 1659 as part of the terms of the Treaty of the Pyrenees Louis XIV guaranteed the inhabitants of his newly acquired territories the right to use "the language they wished, whether French or Spanish, whether Flemish or others!" (Weber, 1976, p. 7). Bilingualism or mutilingualism was to be found in the larger towns. Under the impact of the French Revolution, however, matters began to change. At first the revolutionary assemblies sanctioned the translation of their laws and decrees into the minority languages of France. By 1794, however, the mood had changed. Early in that year Barere, after examining conditions in Brittany, Alsace, and Corsica argued that "Federalism and Superstition speak lower Breton, Emigration and hatred of the Republic speak German. Counter Revolution speaks Italian and fanaticism speaks Basque. Let us destroy these damaging and mistaken instruments" (Gildea, *The Past in French History*, p. 170).

The Jacobins declared, "The unity of the Republic demands the unity of speech. Speech must be one, like the Republic." Gregoire called for the abolition of "the diversity of primitive idioms that extended the infancy of reason and prolonged obsolescent prejudices." Soon the Convention ordered that children in the Republic must learn to speak, read, and write in the "French language" and that everywhere "instruction should take place only in French."

This vision of the French-speaking Republic, however, was slow to be realized and was challenged throughout the nineteenth and twentieth centuries. Thus in 1940 Petain envisaged the future of France in terms of twenty provinces (Gildea, 1994, p. 184). In the 1860s it was estimated that a quarter of the population still did not speak French. As late as 1891 there was anxiety that priests who preached in dialect might "endanger French unity." The Catholic clergy were seen as defenders of the linguistic minorities, a fact which gave rise to political problems in the 1890s when anticlerical-ism was at its height. In 1882, the archbishop of Cambrai described Flem-ish as "the language of heaven" (Gildea, 1994, p. 183). Not surprisingly, the government in 1890 banned religious instruction in Flemish, giving rise to a controversy which went on for some years, until the concordat of 1905 (Weber, 1976, p. 82).

What we may term either civic (or Jacobin) nationalism of the French Revolution was thus strongly assimilationist in its language policies and hence in education generally. Language was very much at the center of the politics of the Republic. Despite this it was not the language in itself that was seen as constituting the nation. Language merely symbolized "the freely expressed will of the inhabitants." Past conventions were irrelevant. As Florence Gauthier has put it, when the revolutionaries "did look to the past for models it was overwhelmingly to the ancient worlds of Greece and Rome whose great republicans, the revolutionaries believed, had invented the liberty which it was now France's duty to proclaim to the world" (Dann and Dinwiddy, 1988, p. 41).

Under first the Committee of Public Safety and then under Napoleon French revolutionary ideas were carried into other parts of Western Europe. Liberty, Equality, and Fraternity, however, though apparently uni-versal in their appeal also carried with them, at least for some people, an assumption of French superiority. In 1805, for example, an official French newspaper expressed the view about the French-sponsored Batavian Republic (the Netherlands) "that the Dutch language was well on the way to becoming defunct and would before long be reduced to the level of a provincial patois, fit only for sailors, peasants and domestic servants" (Schama, 1977, p. 479). It was assumed that French would become the ac-cepted language of Flemish and Dutch culture. In Italy also the smaller states were "governed" directly from Paris by French prefects.

Thus the French civic model of the nation was assimilationist in tone, and unitary in outlook, building on the foundation of a single national language and strongly centralized educational system, the aim being to create a sense of French citizenship. It was this model which provided the basis for the building of an Italian nation under the guidance of Cavour in 1860. The assumption that Italian should be the language of the new state seems self-evident. As Lyttleton tells us, however, Italian nationality was based upon a sense of common culture and language of an educated minority. The number of those who were literate and for whom Italian was their first language did not exceed 2.5 percent of the population.

(Lytletton, 1993, p. 99). In many areas such as Naples and Sicily there was a strong sense of regional identity, based upon regional dialects. The new nation thus had to be "constructed." "We have made Italy, we must now make Italians," was the famous phrase of d'Azeglio. The process took a long time and perhaps is still far from complete.

The French civic model of nationhood had also influenced political attitudes in Ireland. For example, it lay behind the manifesto of the United Irishmen published in 1791, which looked forward to brighter prospects, "to a people united in the fellowship of freedom; to a parliament the express image of the people; to a prosperity founded on civil, political and religious liberty." Like the French revolutionaries they wished to escape from the burden of the past, asking, "are we forever to walk like bids of prey over the fields which our ancestors stained with blood" (Elliott, 1982, p. 23). What language the proposed new state would use was left unclear.

There was, however, another view of nationhood represented by the German philosopher Johann Gottfried Herder (1744–1803). The French Revolution stood for universal principles, Liberty, Equality, and Fraternity. In contrast, Herder, the romantic, was a spokesman for national cultures against the universalizing tendencies of the Enlightenment. Above all Herder stressed the importance of language as the essence of cultural identity, not a language imposed by government decree, however, but the language of the people (the "Volk"). Language, religion, and culture were the basis of a God-given variety of existence centered upon individual nations. Where the French Revolution came to see its duty as bringing civilization to other peoples, Herder stressed the centrality of individual national cultures embodied in their histories and in the songs and poetry of the ordinary people. From this viewpoint, models drawn from ancient Greece and Rome were irrelevant. Nations were to turn to the spirit of their own past, Ossian for the Scots or in Libuse for the Czechs. The Romantic nationalism expounded by Herder looked backed to national pasts, whose spirit was to be recovered through the rediscovery of their history and the revival of their language.

Broadly speaking, then, we may approach our topic "Language and Politics" bearing in mind that in an ethnic nationalist tradition language is a key symbol of identity, whereas for civic nationalism, language is instrumental, merely the means, though a powerful means, of making a political community work more efficiently. If France and Italy were nation-states constructed upon a civic model in which an official language was imposed from above in the interests of political unity, Spain, the Hapsburg monarchy, and the United Kingdom were multiethnic states in which different ethnic groupings retained their own identities under the relatively loose rein (loose in comparison with France or Italy) of constitutional monarchy.

Although the Hapsburg monarchy and the United Kingdom resembled each other, the challenges facing the Hapsburgs were far more serious and lasting. The 1848 revolution was a minor incident in the history of the United Kingdom and neither the Chartist Movement under Fergus O'Connor nor the Young Irelanders under Smith O'Brien had any serious impact at the time. Within the Hapsburg monarchy, however, the crises of 1848 revealed the existence of unrest among its various subject nationalities in Northern Italy, Bohemia, and Hungary. In 1848 the monarchy was successful in containing the attempted revolution. In 1860 it met with defeat. Defeat at Solferino in 1860 led to the loss of Northern Italy. Defeat at Sadowa in 1866 at the hands of Prussia led the Imperial Government to grant "Home Rule" to Hungary. In doing so it left a small Magyar-speaking elite in control of the Slovak- and Romanian-speaking groups within Hungary who in terms of numbers formed a majority. The result of Magyar reluctance to admit non-Magyars to equal political and educational status was to fuel Slovak and Romanian nationalist movements which took language as their key symbol of national identity. The nationality law of 1868 laid down that only those non-Hungarians who learned the language could be admitted to full citizenship. Pressure toward full Magyarization intensified after 1875 under a self-styled Liberal Government and in 1879, an Education Act obliged teaching in primary schools to be in Magyar. In Hungary the Magyar language thus became a primary political issue in the process of nation building. Ethnic minorities were defined as "non-Magyar speaking Magyars" (Seton-Watson, 1977, pp. 157–69). There was thus a marked historical irony in the appeal of Arthur Griffiths as leader of Sinn Fein against the dominance of Ireland to the Hungarian model.

In many ways, however, the linguistic tensions between Germans and Czechs in the Hapsburg territories of Bohemia and Moravia provide the most illuminating example of the issues involved. In Bohemia during the first half of the nineteenth century. German was the language of the cities and Czech the language of the countryside. In the second half of the century with the onset of industrialization Czech peasants flooded into the towns and in Prague itself the German-speaking majority eventually found itself a minority. Living within a state, the Hapsburg monarchy, where German was the official language, the Czechs felt themselves discriminated against and relations between the linguistic groups deteriorated. In 1882 the University of Prague divided into German and Czech universities. The foundation of Sokol (Czech for falcon), a society for young people interested in gymnastics, provided young Czechs with the opportunity to engage in gymnastics as a symbol of Czech identity. But it was the Czech language which provided the main focus of Czech nationalism.

In 1918 after the collapse of the Hapsburg monarchy the opportunity arose to meet Czech demands for self-determination. Had the Herder model been a safe guide to political reality the Czech-speaking nation would have achieved its freedom without any problems. Unfortunately, however, the new state of Czecho-Slovakia contained only a bare majority of Czech speakers (Sayer, 1998, p. 160). In a total population of around 13 million. German speakers accounted for 27 percent and Slovaks for 17 percent of the population. There were also substantial minorities of Ruthenians and Jews. Czecho-Slovakia, far from being an ethnically and linguistically unified nation on the Herder model, was a multiethnic society, a Hapsburg monarchy in microcosm. Inevitably Czech attempts to impose a dominant Czech identity based on language led to resistance, understandably among the Germans, but also among their fellow Slavs, the Slovaks. In Czech eyes, Slovaks possessed Slav identity indistinguisable from their own. In fact, however, the Slovaks who had formed part of Hungary for a millenium saw themselves as a distinct nation. The two languages may have been identical but even in 1918, it proved impossible to reach a compromise over the phrasing of the new national motto "Truth Will Conquer" (the last words of Jan Hus, the Czech national martyr who was burned at the state for heresy in 1415). No phrasing in Czecho-Slovak proved acceptable to either Czech or Slovak. The result was the anodyne Latin version "Veritas vincit" (Sayer, 1998, p. 111).

The enforcement of Czech-Slovak as the official language of the State caused tensions in Slovakia, although it was acceptable to members of a minority of Slovak Protestants. But it was in the German-speaking areas of the new state that the bitterness raised by the imposition of Czech-Slovak proved to be long-lasting. In 1918 Czech speakers engaged in triumphalist demonstrations in Prague. German actors were driven out of the State Theatre and a statue of the Virgin Mary situated opposite that of Jan Hus was destroyed. What this meant at the personal level is described in a memoir of 1918:

Monday, 28 October (1918) evening

In front of Obecni dum, now the seat of the National and Military Committee (that is, the domestic interim government). I meet a German
acquaintance. It is drizzling and he muffles himself up in his overcoat.
"How are you? What do you say to all this?"

"My sister cried bitterly when she heard that Austria had collapsed."
On this day not a word of German was to be heard. Not until Wednesday
did the Germans take their mother tongue into the streets again. We too
spoke with the Germans that we knew in Czech.

   Motorized units, scouts, Sokols sped in front of Obecni dum, soldiers
crossed and passed. An elegant limousine drew up, two generals got out and
took themselves off to the National Committee.

   How did the German take this? It looked as if he felt foreign, a sort of
hostage. I took a notion to relieve his feeling of loneliness. When we parted.
I said to him "Guten Tag und auf Wiederschen."

   "Thank you," he replied in Czech, and his eyes said that he was thanking
me for more than just the greeting. (Sayer, 1998, p. 169)

In the long run these tensions within a so-called national state led first
to the overwhelming pro-Nazi vote among the Sudeten Germans in 1936
and secondly to a pro-German stance among the Catholic Slovaks. The
second half of the twentieth century was to witness the ethnic cleansing of
the Sudeten Germans after 1945 and eventually in 1992 the vote by the Slovaks to leave the newly liberated Czechoslovakia. What had begun in such
high hopes in 1918 ended in tragedy and disillusion.

A full account should include the anti-Semitism of these years, exemplified in part in the life of Franz Kafka (a Czech surname). Kafka wrote in
German but he also spoke Czech, a language which he regarded with great
fondness. As he wrote to his future wife Milena

Of course I understand Czech. I've meant to ask you several times already
why you never write in Czech. ... I wanted to read you in Czech because,
after all, you do belong to that language, because only there can Milena be
found in her entirety ... whereas here there is only Milena from Vienna. ...
So Czech, please. (Sayer, 1998, p. 116)

As a member of a linguistic group which was not regarded as fully
Czech and of a religious grouping viewed with suspicion by German-
speakers, Kafka found himself in a no man's land. To the outside world he
is above all a Czech writer. Within prewar Czecho-Slovakia he was not

seen as Czech, a fate analogous to that of Irish writers who wrote in English in Daniel Corkery's Ireland.

What this brief account of language issues in central Europe suggests is that Herder's vision of a single language being the soul of a nation created serious problems when it was imposed upon what were in reality bilingual or multilingual societies such as Czecho-Slovakia, Hungary, or Romania. Elsewhere in Europe similar problems arose. In Belgium, for example, bitter rivalry between the French-speaking Walloons and the Dutch-speaking Flemish threaten to undermine the state. In Spain, Catalan and Basque nationalist movements oppose what they see as the policies of Castilianization backed by the Madrid government. Even France, the civic nation par excellence, has been forced to make concessions to Corsican nationalism. Such concerns are rarely seen as relevant to British history. In fact, however, resemblances between the Hapsburg monarchy and the United Kingdom during the nineteenth and twentieth centuries are not difficult to find.

It may seem paradoxical to suggest this. The British after all were "an island race," rulers of a worldwide empire whereas the Hapsburgs were merely masters, or would be masters, of the Danube valley. In one crucial respect, however, they did resemble each other. Both were multiethnic states which during the nineteenth century faced the challenge of powerful movements of cultural nationalism. Czech and Hungarian in the case of the Hapsburg monarchy, Irish and Welsh in the case of the United Kingdom. In 1918, the Hapsburg monarchy dissolved into three independent states. In 1922 the United Kingdom after three years of civil war was forced to grant independence to much of Ireland. Almost a century later "the Irish problem" remains unsolved. The heartland of the dominant culture in the United Kingdom was much stronger than was the case in the Hapsburg monarchy, but parliament itself was an ethnically diverse body in which "the Celtic Fringe" could not be ignored. In both states the army reflected the ethnic diversity of the state, more so at the level of troops and noncommissioned officers than in the case of the officer class. Irish nationalists were well aware of parallels in central Europe for their own situation, in particular Arthur Griffith who envisaged a British-Irish dual monarchy, with Ireland playing the role of Hungary. The fact that James Joyce lived happily in multiethnic Trieste and that Leopold Bloom in *Ulysses* is Hungarian is also worth mentioning. In 1898 the Gaelic League periodical *Fainne an Lae* expressed the hope that:

Mr Yeats ... might do for us what Kollar with his patriotic poems full of sorrow and passion and hope did for the Czech movement. (O'Leary, 1994, p. 81)

Within the United Kingdom. Wales and Ireland provide examples of significant movements of cultural nationalism, comparable to those within the Hapsburg monarchy. In Wales, the publication of the Blue Books of 1847, blaming the Welsh language and nonconformity for what was seen as the depraved condition of Welsh-speaking people, led to a backlash against English culture in Wales. The established Church of Wales in particular came under attack, and the demands for its disestablishment intensified. The result was a political movement in which language, nonconformity, and temperance were fused in a new ideal of "Welshness." This was an identity for which English-speakers, members of the Church of Wales, or the great majority in South Wales who frequented pubs did not qualify. When the University of Wales was established in 1893 on the basis of the existing university colleges, St. David's College, Lampeter, linked with the Church of Wales, was excluded and remained so, until recently. In contrast, University College, Aberyswyth, founded on the basis of the Sunday collections from the Nonconformist chapels, was included within the new national university. The National Library of Wales was established in Aberyswyth, in the heartland of Welsh-speaking Wales, although Cardiff seemed a more appropriate site to many.

What may be seen as the Irish equivalent of the Blue Books incident was the controversy which blew up over the comments made by Dr. Mahaffy of Trinity College, Dublin, in a government report (1899) on the Irish Intermediate examination. Mahaffy said that he had been told that "it is almost impossible to get hold of a text in Irish which is not religious or which is not silly or indecent" (O'Tuama, 1972, p. 67). Mahaffy's affront to the Gaelic League undoubtedly played a considerable part in arousing popular support in Ireland for the cause of the Irish language. Such support at the popular level rather than among members of the intelligentsia, however, was of recent growth. The Great Famine (1846–49) had devastated Ireland but its most catastrophic effects were felt in the poorer west and south, precisely those parts which were Gaelic-speaking. In post-Famine Ireland Gaelic language speakers declined drastically in numbers. However, the loss of language as such was not a political issue even for John Mitchel, who blamed the Famine upon the deliberate policy of the British government. The rise of Home Rule nationalism in the 1870s and 1880s did not involve the language as a symbol of national identity.

Indeed, its success in the early 1870s was associated with the political symbolism of the "Manchester Martyrs" and the imprisonment of Fenian activists. In the late 1870s the land issue came to dominate nationalist politics, along with the associated symbolism of "the boycott." Parnell himself—leader of the movement from 1878—was uninterested in the Irish language or indeed in Irish history. It was only with the establishment of the Gaelic Athletic Association by Michael Cusack that conscious support for Gaelic popular culture began to emerge. In a famous letter addressed to the GAA in 1884 he criticized the pursuit of English sports on the grounds that

> If we continue travelling for the next score years in the same direction that we have been going for some time past, condemning the sports that were practised by our forefathers, effacing our national features as though we were ashamed of them and putting on with England's stuffs and broadcloths, her masher helmets and such other effeminate follies—we had better at once, and publicly, abjure our nationality, clap our hands for joy at the sight of the Union Jack and place "England's bloody red exultantly above the green." (quoted in O'Driscoll, 2001)

Here was the Irish equivalent of Sokol. Language entered the scene after Douglas Hyde delivered his famous address. "The Necessity for De-Anglicising the Irish People" criticizing Irish dependence upon the English language. But it was not until after the foundation of the Gaelic League in 1893, at the suggestion of Eoin MacNeill, that the cause of the language began to take off. Hyde himself of Church of Ireland background, hoped to keep the Gaelic League free of political and sectarian overtones, but it was not long before Catholic clergy and Sinn Fein were heavily involved. With the rise of the Irish-Ireland movement. Catholicism the Irish language, and Gaelic games formed a heady mixture.

As we have seen, in Wales during the second half of the nineteenth century, Welsh nonconformity in alliance with advocates of temperance and Welsh language enthusiasts had created an appealing image of Welsh identity. In similar fashion the Irish-Ireland movement fashioned a model of Irishness in which the Irish language was linked with Catholicism and anti-Englishness (also including to some extent temperance). The English language and the connection with England generally was associated by Irish-Irelanders with immorality. Vigilante movements were set up to destroy shipments of English Sunday newspapers. In reaction against Mahaffy, Irish-Ireland stressed the link between the Irish language and Catholic values. Such figures as Fr. Dineen—who was later to be the compiler of a famous Irish dictionary (1927)—and Fr. Peadar Ua Laoghaire tirelessly proclaimed the message of Faith and Fatherland. Irish history was frequently put to political use for such purposes. In Fr. Peader's version of eleventh-century Ireland, Brian Boru welcomed a (totally fictitious) papal legate to Kincora as follows:

> He asked the company to drink to the health of the Pope. He praised the faith and the visible head of the faith and promised, for himself and on behalf of all who were present of the nobles of the Gael, of the race of the Gael, that, with the help of God, the Gaelic race would be loyal to the faith as long as there would be a sun in the sky and people on earth. (O'Leary, 1994, p. 215). In the pages of *The Leader*, D. P. Moran argued that "the Irish nation is de facto a Catholic nation." (Ibid.).

In all of this endeavor the idea that the nation might possess two languages and more than one church was lost sight of. In this, Irish nationalism resembled Welsh nationalism. But in concentrating upon the success of both it is easy to lose sight of the fact that both were very much minority movements. In Wales during the mid-1890s it looked as if the Young Wales League (Cymru Fydd) under the leadership of Lloyd George would come to dominate Welsh politics. In the event, however, the anglicized counties and parts of south Wales refused to submit to what they termed "the domination of Welsh ideas!" Alfred Edmunds of Merthyr asserted that "Glamorgan and Monmouth were not to be dictated to by the isolated county of Caernarvon." Earlier, a Cymru Fydd spokesman denounced Swansea as "howling Wilderness of Philistinism." In his eyes Barry was "intent on nothing but money-making," while Cardiff was "already lost to Welsh nationalism" (Morgan, *Wales*, p. 118).

The divide in Wales between North and South was parallelled in Ireland where the heavily rural South confronted the industrialized north. Even in the South it is easy to exaggerate the importance of the Irish-Ireland movement. When the crunch came in 1914 John Redmond, leader of the Irish Parliamentary Party, was able to win over the great majority of the National Volunteers to the cause of England. It was only a relatively small remnant, the Irish Volunteers, who stood out against the call to arms. Redmond's move ultimately misfired but during the early war years the Dublin administration under Birrell and Nathan continued to prepare for a takeover by Redmond's party. As the work of Leon O Broin and Senia Paseta has shown, the cause of those whom Moran called "West Britons" was by no means lost.

It was the Rising of 1916, or perhaps even more the relentless execution of the leaders by the British administration, which began an extraordinary shift of sympathy to Irish-Ireland. In 1918, an assemblage of varied Irish-Ireland political groupings under the umbrella term "Sinn Fein," won a majority of seats. In the North, however, a solid bloc of unionist seats told a different story. Here the counterpart of "Sinn Fein" was "No Surrender." The result in 1920 was partition followed in 1922 by the establishment of the Irish Free State.

Nationalist historians looking back on this period have seen the period 1916–22 as one in which the Irish people threw off the shackles of imperialism. If we bear the wider history of nationalism in mind, however, the concept of "the Irish people" is a problematic one. How was it to be defined? Who were the "we" of Sinn Fein? Did it include English and Ulster Scots-speaking Protestants, north and south, who in terms of numbers amounted to a quarter of the population of Ireland and from whose ranks many of the United Irishmen had been drawn? Only a civic, secular definition of "the Irish Nation" could include them. In defining the Irish nation, however, the revolutionaries laid great stress upon the significance of the Irish language, despite the fact that at least two signatories to the Proclamation of 1916 spoke no Irish. In 1918 De Valera declared that the Irish language was "the most distinctive symbol of their nationality." Others declared "our frontier is twofold: the language and the sea." For Sinn Fein, English was now "the language of the enemy" (p. 237). In 1918 members of Sinn Fein were urged to write to each other "in Irish rather than the language of the enemy." At the 1917 party convention it was proposed that Irish should be the language of the party executive (Laffan, 1999, p. 23). In 1921 De Valera went to great pains in having his letters to Lloyd George translated into Irish by J. J. O'Kelly and then having the English original version labeled "official translation" (Laffan, 1999, p. 239). This gap between symbolism and practice also characterized the ceremonies in honor of the memory of Archbishop Croke at Thurles in 1920. There, as Mary O'Driscoll has shown, there was great stress upon "Irish education, Irish language, Irish games" but in fact the only words in Irish were three sentences—the symbolic "copla focal" (O'Driscoll, 2001).

"The Irish people" (or most of them), in fact did not speak Irish. The Irish revolutionaries were thus confronted with the same challenge as Italian nationalists. As De Valera might have said, "We have created Irish-Ireland, now we must create Irishmen." De Valera's nation was an ethnic one on Herder's model, not a civic one. The founders of the Czecho-Slovak state faced a similar challenge in that Czech speakers constituted only 51 percent of the population. In the Irish Free State the proportion of Irish-speakers was much lower. In 1891 the census figures for the 32 counties indicated that 855 in every 1,000 were unable to speak Irish (Wall, 1969, p. 80). Within the truncated 26-county state, the proportion was no doubt somewhat better but in 1920 there were only about 200,000 native speakers of Gaelic. There was also the problem that a standard version of the language did not exist. "Irish" in fact was divided into a number of competing dialects, each seeking a place in the future standardized form of the language.

The task of building an Irish nation on the basis of "the language" was thus a daunting one. The leaders of the new state, however, following the ideas of Irish-Ireland, seem to have expected that the Gaelicization of a largely English-speaking population would be completed expeditiously. Professor Timothy Corcoran claimed that the anglicization of Ireland was the consequence of the British introduction of the national school system in 1831. This situation should now be reversed.

> The task is the restoration of Irish as the main vernacular language. ... We have to restore a situation that was profoundly changed a couple of generations ago, and reverse a situation that was made fully practicable only by the profound misuse of the primary schools of Ireland. ... The popular schools can give and restore our native language. (Farren, 1995, pp. 18–19)

When De Valera came to power in 1932 this stress upon restoration of the language increased. *Notes for Teachers: History* speedily drawn up on the orders of Tom Derrig, the new minister of education, emphasized the importance of the language in the teaching of history.

> The history of Ireland is the history of the various peoples who inhabited Ireland since the first advent of men to our shores, but it is more particularly the study of the Gaelic race and Gaelic civilisation for a thousand years to foreign domination, whether Norse, Norman or English. The Irish language was perhaps the most powerful of all the influences that saved our people from defeat and absorption by alien forces in that long struggle. It is still a very powerful influence in preserving national continuity and [it is] for this if no other reason that it should be the language used in our schools to teach our history. (*Notes for Teachers: History*, 1933, pp. 13–14)

This was a powerful message which was reinforced in the Eire constitution of 1937.

Perhaps the most significant phrases were those which referred to "our people," "our schools," "our history." Fianna Fail were presenting themselves as the leaders of a nation in Herder's sense of the word, a community distinguished by its language, fulfilling its role in a providential plan. This Romantic ethnic nationalism did not sit easily with another influential political tradition, that of Enlightenment civic nationalism which was associated with Wolfe Tone and the United Irishmen and which had strong links with such English radical freethinkers as Tom Paine. Nor did references to "the language" take cognisance of the fact that in thirty-two county Ireland, two—perhaps three—languages were spoken. To characterize English as "the language of the enemy" created enormous problems. The nation-building which took place from the 1920s onward thus was very much the Herder model emphasizing language and history. Religion was also a key symbol in the new state and the cult of the apparition of the Virgin Mary at Knock attracted much more popular support than Bodenstown with its memories of Wolfe Tone. Thus in 1940 at a mass pilgrimage in honor of the Assumption of the Virgin Mary, the preacher commented warmly upon what he regarded as a sight unique in modern Europe, a minister of education clutching his rosary beads, a reference to Tom Derrig.

In the mid-1950s, however, supporters of the Irish language become conscious that a reaction had set in against it. In a series of Thomas Davis lectures given in 1966 Fr. Martin Brennan S.J. sounded a pessimistic note about its prospects. In the Herder tradition, he looked upon the diversification of language as having an important purpose in God's creation of the world and was anxious "that the peculiarly Irish note in this symphony should not be allowed to falter now and be eternally silent" (Brennan, 1969, pp. 73–74). In a similar series published in 1972 the Gaelic scholar Sean O'Tuama expressed his view that "The Gaelic League, since its foundation, has seen the restoration of the Irish language as fundamental to the preservation of our national identity." He was worried, however, about the impact of changes in state language policy and of the decision of "the people of Ireland" to join the supranational European Economic Community (O'Tuama 1972, p. 7). In contrast critics expressed reservations about state policy with regard to the use of Irish in primary schools. In 1951 a Commission on Youth Employment considered that "There is a grave need to examine the content of primary education, more particularly the content of Irish and the treatment of that language" (Farren, 1995, p. 234).

A clerical spokesman in 1956 declared that "children must not be sacrificed on the altar of any language." Fr. O'Catháin S.J. suggested that

Irish as a secondary school subject be placed "outside the examination system altogether." He spoke against "the compulsion of threats and punishment and failure" and for "the compulsion of love and esteem." What De Valera had regarded as "the most distinctive symbol of their nationality" was now being categorized negatively as "compulsory Irish." The nation-building process begun so confidently in 1922 had run into serious difficulties. The language issue had now entered the realm of party politics and played some part at least in the revival of the Fine Gael Party. In due course a Coalition Government with Fine Gael as the major partner abolished the Irish language requirement for the civil service (Fitzgerald, 1991, p. 79). One result of this was to make it possible in 1974 for non-Irish-speaking candidates from Northern Ireland to enter the Foreign Service:

> By mid-1980's the assumptions of Irish-Ireland were a matter of public debate. In 1985 a writer in the Irish Independent attacked the need to prove we're Irish by waving the three leaved shamrock of race language and Catholicism which were an imposition by nineteenth century nationalists. (Lee, 1989, p. 658)

Four years later, Professor J. J. Lee's response in his best-selling history *Ireland 1912–1985* was to declare that the three-leaved shamrock of race, language, and religion was "the defining characteristic of normal European states and normal European peoples." The key question here is what is meant by "normal." Is it the French civic model of the state with its heavy emphasis upon secular citizenship or is it the Belgian model with its division into two linguistic-based cultures? Is it Spain with its linguistic and cultural divisions into Castilian, Catalan, and Basque or the Swiss model with its unique configuration of four linguistic communities, contradicting at every turn the Herder model of a nation-state? And is "normality" impervious to change?

Perhaps we should look no further than Wales for a comparison with Ireland. In Wales the traditional model of "Welshness" based upon nonconformity, temperance, and language survived in North Wales until the 1960s. Here also as in Ireland there was a marked shift in values, as the number of chapelgoers, observers of temperance, and speakers of Welsh declined. However, in the face of the anglicizing policy of the Thatcher years, with their assumption that the United Kingdom was a unitary state, a reaction in favor of Welsh began to take place, the turning point being Gwynfor Evans's threat to go on hunger strike if Wales did not get its own Welsh language TV Channel. The language issue once more became a key

issue in politics and in 1993 the Welsh Language Act was passed "to promote and facilitate the use of the Welsh language in Wales" (Davies, 1993,
p. 98). In terms of politics, however, the great majority in Wales voted for
the Labour Party and still votes for it. Plaid Cymru's commitment to the
Welsh language as a key symbol of Welsh identity restricted its influence
in the main to the Welsh-speaking heartland of North and West. What
changed the situation was the party's decision to move beyond its commitment to the language in the direction of more bread-and-butter issues.
It was this "new departure" which brought it success in the 1999 elections
for the newly created Welsh Assembly. The Rhondda valley, hitherto an
impregnable Labour stronghold, fell to Plaid Cymru along with other
Labour seats in South Wales, including Islwyn, Neil Kinnock's former seat,
where there was a swing of 35 percent to Plaid Cymru. The implications of
this for Professor Lee's three-leaved shamrock model of race, language,
and religion is perhaps that there is no permanent state of "normalcy." The
symbol of language may pay dividends in one political situation but not in
another. Plaid Cymru had changed tack toward a less cultural, more economic state and its gamble had paid off.

At this point I feel that I should be trying to express the "keynote" of
what is intended to be a "keynote lecture." What I have tried to do is to set
our topic in a comparative perspective involving Western Europe and to
some extent the United Kingdom. Our primary concern is of course "Language and Politics" in the Republic of Ireland and Northern Ireland. In the
former we have seen how, during the heyday of the Irish-Ireland movement, the symbolism of the Irish language exercised extraordinary influence.
We have also seen a shift in the second half of the century to widespread
acceptance of the fact that the Republic is a bilingual state and that there
were there indeed "two native languages," as Catholic bishops informed
the Pope in the late eighteenth century (Wall, 1969, p. 83).

North of the border it may well be that the situation is made more
complicated by the existence of three languages. English, Irish, and Ulster
Scots, the latter being the counterpart in Northern Ireland of the Scots of
Burns, Hugh McDiarmid, and Irvine Welsh. Here we may ask ourselves
which of the models available in Western Europe and the United Kingdom
we should turn to? Should it be Wales with its compromise between Eng-
lish- and Welsh-speakers? Should it be Switzerland with its emphasis upon
decentralization into distinct linguistic cantons? Should it be Irish-Ireland
itself as some members of Sinn Fein seem to suggest? It may well be, however, that the symbolism of language should take second place to the

priority of jobs and economic well-being, with the implication that Sean Lemass is a safer guide to the future than De Valera.

The future envisaged by Sinn Fein's policy is a relevant factor here. In his book *Free Ireland: Toward a Lasting Peace*, Gerry Adams seemed to be speaking the language of Pearse and of Irish-Ireland. He quoted Martin O. Cadhain at length:

> Not only should Irish speakers be participant in this war for the reconquest of Ireland—it is the only thing worth being part of in Ireland—but it is our duty to be its leaders and guides. If Irish is the steering force of the revolution, in this way Irish will be one of the most progressive forces in Ireland: that is the same as reviving Irish. The Irish language is the reconquest of Ireland, and the reconquest of Ireland is the Irish language. The language of the people shall revive the people. (Adams, 1986, reprinted 1994, p. 146)

Another spokesman declared:

> Our traditional Gaelic culture held values of human dignity, of cooperation, of socialism which are directly opposed to the materialism, consumerism, individualism, competitivism which predominate in the Anglo-American culture of today. (Padraig O Maolchraibhe, quoted in Wills, 1991, 33)

But Sinn Fein also has political ambitions south of the border and it may well be that it will trim its sails in the manner of Plaid Cymru if it is to make gains at the expense of Fianna Fail. As in Wales, language issues may move down in the scale of political rhetoric toward class-based issues.

Is the experience of England at all relevant? It is here that "normality" has been subjected to extraordinary changes. In England, the second-largest linguistic group after English-speakers are speakers of Urdu. In contemporary England we are witnessing a context between traditional images of Englishness as expounded by Norman Tebbit and others and those of multiculturalism. Ethnic issues associated with illegal immigrants have entered politics.

One final question may be raised. How far is the experience of Scotland relevant to our topic "Language and Politics?" In nineteenth-century Scotland, issues of national identity were not linked to language issues. For the great majority. Scotland's role in the British empire was of paramount importance and such figures as David Livingstone, the missionary of empire, were an essential part of the national myth. After the Second World War and the decline of empire, this image of Scottishness began to fade, leaving the way open for change. The Scottish National Party became a force to be reckoned with both in the Westminster Parliament and in the Scottish Parliament which was set up in 1999. Unlike Wales and Ireland, however, issues of language did not occupy a central place in politics. For the great majority it was unclear whether "Scots" was a language in itself or a dialect of English. If a language is defined as a dialect with a state behind it, Scots was still a dialect or a group of dialects, raising the question how the situation might be changed. In the case of Irish and Welsh the shift from dialect to language has been successfully negotiated. So far as Scots is concerned, its future status is unclear, as indeed is the future of Scots Gaelic. Language as such has a low priority for Scottish political parties, even the S N P. perhaps, because the dominant image of Scottish identity is at present "civic" rather than "ethnic."

BIBLIOGRAPHY

Adams, Gerry. 1994. *Free Ireland: Towards a Lasting Peace*. Niwot: Roberts Rinehart Publishers.

Brennan, Martin S.J. 1969. "Language Personality and Nation" in O'Cuiv, pp. 70–80.

Davies, Janet. 1993. *The Welsh Language*. Cardiff: University of Wales Press.

Dann, Otto and John Dinwiddy. 1988. *Nationalism in the Age of the French Revolution*. London: The Hambledon Press.

Elliott, Marianne. 1982. *Partners in Revolution: The United Irishmen and France*. New Haven: Yale University Press.

Farren, Sean. 1995. *The Politics of Irish Education 1920–1965*. Belfast: Queen's University of Belfast, Institute of Irish Studies.

Fitzgerald, Garret. 1991. *All in a Life: An Autobiography*. Dublin: Gill and Macmillan.

Gildea, R. 1994. *The Past in French History*. New Haven: Yale University Press.

Laffan, Michael. 1999. *The Resurrection of Ireland: The Sinn Fein Party, 1916–1923*. Cambridge: Cambridge University Press.

Lee, J.J. 1989. *Ireland 1912–1985: Politics and Society*. Cambridge: Cambridge University Press.

Lyttelton, Adrian. 1993. "The National Question in Italy," in *The National Question in Europe in a Historical Context*, edited by Mikulas Teich and Roy Porter. Cambridge: Cambridge University Press.

Mack Smith, Denis. 1985. *Cavour and Garibaldi 1860: A Study in Political Conflict*. Cambridge: Cambridge University Press.

Morgan, K. 1981. *Rebirth of a Nation: Wales 1880–1980*. Oxford: Oxford University Press.

Ó Broin, Leon. 1966. *Dublin Castle and the 1916 Rising: The Story of Sir Matthew Nathan*. Dublin: Helicon.

O' Cuiv, Brian. 1969. *A View of the Irish Language*. Dublin: Stationary Office.

O'Driscoll, Mary. 2001. "Commemorating Croke: Ethnic Nationalism as a Spectacle" (unpublished paper).

O'Leary, Philip. 1994. *The Prose Literature of the Gaelic Revival 1881–1921: Ideology and Innovation*. University Park: Pennsylvania State University Press.

O'Tuama, Seán. 1972. *The Gaelic League Idea*. Cork: Mercier Press.

Paseta, Senia. 1999. *Before the Revolution: Nationalism, Social Change and Ireland's Catholic Elite, 1879–1922*. Cork: Cork University Press.

Sayer, Derek. 1998. *The Coasts of Bohemia: A Czech History*. Princeton: Princeton University Press.

Schama, Simon. 1977. *Patriots and Liberators: Revolution in the Netherlands, 1780–1813*. New York: Knopf.

Seton-Watson, Hugh. 1977. *Nations and States: An Inquiry into the Origins of Nations and the Politics of Nationalism*. Boulder: Westview Press.

Trevor-Roper, H.R. 1969. *The Romantic Movement and the Study of History*. London: Athlone Press.

Wall, Maureen. 1969. "The Decline of the Irish Language," in O'Cuiv, pp. 81–90.

Weber, Eugen. 1976. *Peasants into Frenchmen: The Modernization of Rural France, 1870–1914*. Stanford: Stanford University Press.

Wills, Clair. 1991. "Language Politics, Narrative, Political Violence." *Oxford Literary Review* 13, pp. 1–2.

Chapter Six

Thatcher's Britain

Four Nations or One?

(1991)

Most of this audience, I take it, live in a political unit termed "the United Kingdom." We all agree that our schoolchildren should learn something about its history. But how are we to characterize this unit? Some historians seem to see it as a single nation. They refer to "the story of our nation." "In my opinion," states Norman Stone, "it is essential for school children to know the elements of our national past." Jonathan Clark tells us that "history is national property and the decisions to be taken on the history curriculum will be intimately connected with our national self-image, sense of heritage and purpose."

But what is this nation to which they refer? It is here that we begin to run into difficulties. Mrs. Thatcher declared that "children should know the great landmarks of British history." But, is there a British nation? And if there is one today, does it have a history stretching back beyond the early twentieth century?

Perhaps we do not have a single national history. Historians have taught us to see the rise of the nation-state as one of the signs of modernity. But suppose that the United Kingdom is not a nation-state like, say, France, but a multinational state like Belgium, Switzerland, Yugoslavia, the Soviet Union—in fact like the great majority, perhaps, of so-called "nation-states." In that case we will be distorting the complexity of our history if we speak of a single "national past" and a single "national image." The "we" and "our" of all this are rather a mixed bunch.

The notion that we have several national pasts has been obscured by the understandable dominance of England, particularly since the Industrial

Revolution and the concomitant urbanization and population rise. In terms of current population, England, with 46.3 million, is by far the largest segment of the U.K., Wales having 2.7 million, Scotland 5.1 million, and N. Ireland 1.5 million. (In 1801 English preponderance was much less marked.) As a result it became convenient for many in dealing with the history of the United Kingdom to equate it with the history of England. Thus the prime minister stated that "it was absolutely right" for the new national curriculum to concentrate on the kings and queens of England, while almost in the same breath declaring that "children should know the great landmarks of British history." British history, it would appear, is in essence English history. "We" look back to the Tudors, for example, and forget that Scotland had no Tudor dynasty.

Does it matter? After all, the Oxford History School, our leading nursery of historians, got along quite well for a century unrepentantly teaching English history. If, like Stubbs, we concentrate our attention upon political and constitutional history, perhaps the distortion is less marked. The view from Buckingham Palace, Westminster, and the Home Counties easily leads to the assumption that Britain can be safely equated with England and that the histories of Wales, Scotland, and Ireland can be dismissed, more or less, under the heading of the "Celtic Fringe." Unfortunately, the further one moves away from W.1., the more of a straitjacket a merely anglocentric history becomes. The British empire was more than an expansion of England. It was also, even in the colonial period, an expansion of the multinational British Isles.

If we accept that we live in a multinational state, we are able to make sense of many phenomena which are otherwise unintelligible. Concentration on political or constitutional history (whose importance I do not wish to downplay) may lead to an emphasis upon the unity of our historical development as exemplified in the Acts of Union of 1536–43 (Wales), 1707 (Scotland), and 1800 (Ireland). Crown and parliament symbolize the political unity of the United Kingdom. Outside this political framework, however, we immediately encounter diversity. Unlike any other state we have no national team in any sport apart for the fiction of the "British Lions" in rugby, which allows "southern Irish" to count as "British" (or, alternatively, permits Irish citizens to accept an affront to their republicanism for the sake of the oval ball). We have an established church in England but none in Wales, Scotland, or Ireland. We have differences between the common law of England and Wales (and Ireland) and Scots Law. We have a British Army which includes English, Welsh, Scottish, and Irish regiments. We have linguistic divisions between English, Scots Gaelic, and Welsh (Scots Gaelic being derived from Irish). We have distinctive educational systems, with Scotland and Northern Ireland and perhaps Wales being markedly different from that of England.

It might have seemed in the twentieth century that these national differences were moving toward a common "British" denominator. Ireland apart, the experiences of two world wars led toward a common national "British" identity. The rise of the Labour Party led to the playing down of national differences. Aneurin Bevan was not alone in setting his face against what he regarded as separatism. A process of "nation-building" seemed to be underway. The concept of "Brit" appeared.

In the neighboring island the Republic was forging a new largely Catholic national identity while in Northern Ireland, attempts were made to introduce the concept of "province of Ulster" into regular usage. All three trends toward "Britishness," "Irishness," and "Ulsterness" were reflections of current political realities. They provide a poor guide, however, to our history before the twentieth century.

Where does all this leave us? One senses a certain nostalgia for traditional English history. Why can't we return to the basic verities of "1066 and all that," as the present government seems to want? "England" is undoubtedly the most powerful national grouping within the United Kingdom and the history of the kings and queens of England should form part of a sound education in history. But England is part of a wider story. For better or worse the history of England became involved with that of the rest of the British Isles. As Norman Stone remarks, "Great swaths of a country's literature and architecture are incomprehensible without a knowledge of it" (that is, history). But "English" literature includes Scott and Burns, Swift, Burke and Yeats, Joyce and O'Casey, Gerard Manley Hopkins, and Dylan Thomas as well as Shakespeare and Milton. We simply cannot understand "our" literature if we confine ourselves to a narrow view of "Englishness." We have a multinational history.

However, I myself am not wholly happy with the term "nation." The concept of a "nation" has powerful emotional overtones which make detachment difficult. Questions of loyalty quickly arise. How are we to recognize fellow members of our nation? Are they blonde and blue-eyed? Are they Christian? Do they support the national cricket team (if the M.C.C. is a national cricket team)? I prefer to lower the emotional temperature of our concepts and see our history as "multicultural" rather than "multinational." The question, "Four nations or one?" need not then arise. Since

1920 there have been as a matter of historical fact two sovereign states within the British Isles but there are many urban cultures—Brummagem, Geordie, Glaswegian, Cockney, Scouse ("quorum pars magna fui"). Class, gender, and religion form part of our cultures. There are cultural antagonisms (hence ethnic jokes). Since the end of World War II, new ethnic cultures have made their appearance within the United Kingdom, not always without controversy. In this, our experience is not unique. France, Germany, and the Soviet Union are all affected by similar changes. To see our history in narrowly English (or Scottish, Welsh, or Irish) terms is to surrender ourselves to nationalist mythology. It is time to move on to a nearer approximation to the truth about our history.

To describe the United Kingdom as a "multinational" state makes a good deal of sense both of past and present. It is, however, not a complete description since it ignores the unifying factor of "Britishness." All but a small proportion of the inhabitants of the United Kingdom accept the term "British" when applied to them even if they do not apply it to themselves without some thought. "British" is thus a convenient shorthand to apply to the inhabitants of Great Britain and Northern Ireland. There has been a "British" history over and above our "multinational" history. We speak of "the Battle of Britain," the British army, the British navy, the British empire, the British parliament, the British constitution. Americans and others regularly refer to "the Brits" as we might refer to "the Yanks," a term of amused tolerance rather than condescension. To outsiders the term "British" means "us" or most of us, even if we have not totally internalized the description ourselves. It may be that "Britain" is a national equivalent of "Oxford University" which, famously, does not exist apart from the colleges. Visitors to Oxford, asking, "Where is the University?" are mystified when they cannot be directed to it. But "Oxford University," as in gaining an Oxford degree or an Oxford blue clearly has some kind of existence over and above the colleges. In much the same way Britain seems to exist over and above our multinational structure. The answer to our original question, "Four Nations or One?" should be perhaps "Four Nations and One."

For most of the inhabitants of these islands their primary self-description, which first comes to their lips, will be English, Irish (or Northern Irish), Welsh, or Scottish rather than British. But a majority of the inhabitants of Northern Ireland would describe themselves first as "British" and only secondarily as from "Ulster." This is true also of the children of recent immigrants from Asia, Africa, or the West Indies. Mr. Peregrine Worsthorne, the son of a recent immigrant, is perhaps an exception in describing himself as "English," not "British."

Scots, irritated at being called "English," seize upon the description "British" with relief, as do the Welsh. It is the English, or the most self-consciously WASP inhabitants of England, who gibe at the term "British" and accept it with some reluctance. If they do use it they do so as a short-hand for "English." Such are the complexities of national self-descriptions within the United Kingdom.

The "So what?" question cannot be avoided now. Does all this matter? I think it does if we are looking to the future of the United Kingdom. Since we are now a multicultural as well as a multinational society, it is impor-tant to make assimilation toward a generally accepted national identity as easy as possible for those who wish to do so. It is for this reason that we should aim at teaching a wider "British" history in our schools, which has some reference to the history of the British empire. The Irish-oriented inhabitants of Kilburn should also be able to see themselves as having a place in "our" history, if they wish to do so.

Of equal importance are the political and constitutional implications of a multinational approach. As it stands at present, the United Kingdom is a unitary state administered from Westminster with some gesture toward local interests in the form of secretaries of state for Wales, Scotland, and Northern Ireland. The resurgence of nationalist or quasi-nationalist senti-ment in Scotland, however, suggests that the establishment of a "Home Rule" Scottish Assembly may only be a matter of time. We now seem to be returning to the political pattern of the 1880s when "Home Rule all round" was a political possibility. As someone who has lived many years in the United States I do not look upon federalism as some exotic growth. To me, the United States federal constitution seems to strike a nice balance be-tween national interests and local interests. Federalism is not of course a political utopia. Corruption can exist in Harrisburg, Pennsylvania, as well as in Washington. But federalism is clearly workable and where national feelings are as strong as they seem to be in Scotland it seems desirable. Clearly also a federal solution seems equally desirable in Northern Ireland, at least in the long run. Wales is perhaps a special case. It may be that Wales is so closely integrated with England that the present solution is re-garded as satisfactory by most of its inhabitants.

In the United States constitution, the House of Representatives may be seen as the equivalent of the House of Commons. But there is also a Sen-ate, the equivalent of the British House of Lords. If we are intending to provide a federal dimension to the British constitution it may be that the House of Lords provides the best opportunity of bringing this about. As a second chamber elected according to a time frame different from the Commons, every ten years for example, the Lords could provide appropriate representation for Wales, Scotland, and Northern Ireland as well as for various ethnic groups including the "Southern Irish" (more peers like, or unlike, the earl of Longford.) Membership of the Lords would have symbolic resonance as well as political influence.

There remains the Crown, a symbol of great national significance but one which occupies a paradoxical position in a society which aims, in John Major's words, to be "classless" and "meritocratic." The Crown seems to symbolize a vanished imperial era. David Cannadine has shown how the myth of monarchy was built up in Britain during the late nineteenth and twentieth centuries. It may be that a move in the opposite direction would now be appropriate, on the lines of the Swedish, Dutch, and Danish monarchies which seem more in the nature of presidencies. A move away from Buckingham Palace to a more modest establishment would better reflect the reduced status and power of the United Kingdom. Buckingham Palace could then be opened to the public as is the case with Holywood Palace (or Dublin Castle), save when state occasions make this impossible. The "Home Counties" tone of monarchy might also be changed in some way.

What then remains of the question with which we began, "Four Nations or One?" If we accept Benedict Anderson's view that nations are "imagined communities," the concept of "nation" itself is problematic. Of the nations we have been discussing, however, it is the British nation which is most problematic since it seems to be made up of four other nations. A prime minister appealing to "the British people" is appealing to a sense of national identity which may have been stronger in the heyday of the British empire than it is today. A government centered upon Westminster which aims at preserving the United Kingdom needs to think long and hard about the nature of "British identity." That there is confusion in high places emerged in Mrs. Thatcher's speeches when she happily intermingled "British" and "English" history. There was also uncertainty in the setting up of a national history curriculum, which turned out to be not "National" in the sense of "British" but more narrowly national in the sense of Welsh, English, and "Northern Ireland." Scotland was not even included. Small wonder if immigrants from Pakistan or Bangladesh are confused about their identity if the British people have not yet made up their minds.

Chapter Seven

Four Nations History in Perspective

(2004)

I begin with a quotation which helps, I believe, to set the tone for a discussion of "Four Nations" history.

Bernard Crick in a well-known essay, "An Englishman Considers His Passport," wrote

> I am a citizen of a state with no agreed colloquial name. Our passports call us citizens of the United Kingdom of Great Britain and Northern Ireland. But what does one reply when faced by that common existential question of civilised life, which is neither precisely legal nor precisely philosophical, found in foreign hotel registers, "Nationality"?
>
> (Crick, *Political Thoughts and Polemics*, p. 94)

Crick's comment may serve as a reminder that the U.K. is a union of peoples. The nature of that union has changed over time, however, and while "Four Nations" may have been an accurate enough label for the period 1801–1921, the century or more from the Act of Union from the recognition of the Irish Free State, it is less satisfactory as a description of the situation from 1921 until now. The United Kingdom continues to exist, however, albeit subject to change, often radical in character. Histories organized on "Four Nations" lines involve taking as their starting point "The British Isles" (a term always to be used with quotation marks) rather than "Britain" if we are to do justice to the United Kingdom.

British history of course would be easier for the historian if the history of the larger island of Great Britain had been self-contained. In that event, Ireland could be ignored. But in 1169 the Normans did invade Ireland, with fateful consequences. As I write this, however, I realize that I am looking at history from an anglocentric point of view. Ireland was already involved in the history of the larger island and had been since the fourth or fifth centuries A.D. when Gaelic invaders began to make their mark upon the west and north of Scotland. No doubt the history of the larger island would have been even simpler had Hengist and Horsa remained at home. These are large questions. The fact remains that these islands are home to several peoples, whose histories are inextricably intertwined.

If it makes sense to conceptualize our common history in terms of four nations, another factor intervenes to complicate the picture. All nations are no doubt equal but some are more equal than others. And for the past millenium at least, it also makes sense for us to think in terms of "core and periphery," or "peripheries" (that is, the various societies over which the core attempted to establish a political, religious, cultural, and economic hegemony). Like all models this is open to criticism. The peripheries sometimes interacted between themselves to counter the tactics of the hegemonic power. On other occasions they were rivals. Nevertheless a model of core-peripheries remains a useful tool for the historian of "Four Nations."

As we are well aware, however, Four Nations History is a flower (or is it a weed?) of recent growth. David Cannadine in his introduction to *Uniting the Kingdom: The Making of British History* quoted Rees Davies's comment in 1988 that British history "had not really arrived." This conference ten years or so later is a sign that the situation has changed. I myself, however, would point to the existence of "four-nation history" or something very much like it in the nineteenth century in the work of such historians as Carlyle in his *Letters of Oliver Cromwell*; Macoulay in his *History of England*, Lecky in his *History of England*, and even Froude in his *The English in Ireland*. Above all there is Halevy's *History of the English People in 1815*. A four Nations historian looking for precursors could well turn to these masters with profit.

A historian such as Halevy writing *c.* 1900 was well aware of this multinational dimension to what he called "English history." In the aftermath of World War I, however, the situation changed. Ireland and the Irish question were no longer center stage. There was no longer a substantial Irish presence in the House of Commons. The Irish Problem itself seemed to have been solved and it was almost possible to forget that Ireland had ever been part of British history. Even Northern Ireland, a statelet which had been granted Home Rule, albeit against its will, could be ignored. It was in this world, the world of Baldwin and Neville Chamberlain, that anglocentric history became the norm, centerd upon a version of the past in which orderly progression was the theme of English history. Herbert Butterfield criticized this in *The Whig Interpretation of History* and his criticisms passed into general circulation. Nevertheless, the Whig interpretation itself, exemplified in the writings of George Macaulay Trevelyan, remained dominant until after the end of World War II, its influence to some extent reinforced by Winston Churchill's *History of the English Speaking Peoples*. And as print culture has come to be dominated by TV culture, Whiggish interpretations of English history have remained in full vigor as the popularity of David Starkey, Simon Schama, and others has demonstrated.

In the decades following World War II, however, a socialist interpretation influenced often by Marxism, challenged the supremacy of the Whig interpretation. To an overwhelming extent this was as anglocentric as the Whig interpretation itself. Thus Christopher Hill and others stressed the significance of an English Revolution. Edward Thompson's classic work was entitled *The Making of the English Working Class*. Thompson himself was well aware of the impact of the Irish Revolution of 1798 but there is no doubt that his attention was concentrated upon the English working class. His polemical essay, *The Peculiarities of the English* (1965), also graphically illustrated Thompson's Englishness.

During the years after the 1950s (Thompson's book was published in 1963) the Whig interpretation was very much on the defensive. With the advent of Mrs. Thatcher, the defeat of Arthur Scargill, the disarray and defeat of the Labour Party, and not least the fall of the Berlin Wall, the tide turned against the dominance of the social interpretation. Among some historians this situation took the form of an approach based upon high politics in the spirit of Sir Lewis Namier, but the most explicit attack on the social interpretation of English history came from a young Cambridge historian, Jonathan Clark, in his two books *English Society (1985)* and *English Social History*. He argued that religion rather than class conflict was the key to understanding English history in contrast with Edward Thompson who in his eloquent chapter, "The Transforming Power of the Cross," dismissed Methodism as a class ideology. Clark's scholarly work, though influential in academe (it has been reprinted several times) did not reach a wide audience. It was left to Linda Colley in her brilliant book *Britons* to achieve popular success, in a work which can also be seen as a riposte to Thompson's *Making of the English Working Class*. As she states in one revealing passage with reference to Thompson,

The urban artisan, because he had been acculturated, because he was more easily reached by propaganda and recruiting parties, and because crucially, he was not tied to the land, could be a more useful citizen in time of war than the solitary ploughman. In this respect, far from making Great Britain susceptible to revolution, precocious industrialisation and urbanisation may well have helped to keep the forces of the French Revolution at bay. (*Britons*, p. 300)

Colley's thesis argued for the significance of the rise of a British national consciousness from the mid-eighteenth century. Historians had always been aware that George III gloried in the name of "Britain" but Colley argued that this sense of Britishness permeated all classes and both sexes from the Seven Years War onward. Like Clark, she saw herself as restoring religion to a central place in this new nationality, although where he placed Anglicanism at the center, Colley argued the case for a wider, anti-Catholic, Protestantism as a key feature of "Britishness." Protestantism, in her view, was the cement which bound together the various classes of society, leading them to sing the praises of George III. Colley's thesis thus implied a radical reversal of Edward Thompson's approach and Thompson in the last review of his life showed his disquiet at this. Thompson's concept of the "Free born Englishman" was now challenged by Colley's "Briton," with the implication that patriotism was more central than class consciousness in what for her was now British rather than English history.

However, Colley's emphasis upon Britain leads her to play down the significance of the Act of Union of 1801, which created the United Kingdom of Great Britain and Ireland. There was now a new state, the United Kingdom of Great Britain and Ireland, which included what had been the kingdom of Ireland. The tone of Colley's narrative is *neo-Whig*, giving the impression that political progress was being made on all fronts in what she terms "Britain." The rise of a British consciousness is seen as an unmixed blessing. *So it might have been if Britain had been a state.* In the context of the United Kingdom, however, the Protestantism of George III led to the postponement of Catholic Emancipation for another thirty years. Catholic Emancipation, that is, the admission of Catholic MPs to the U.K. parliament, had been agreed upon by William Pitt as the price of persuading Irish Catholics to accept the Union. George III's refusal to go against the obligation of his coronation oath led to Pitt's resignation and even more importantly inaugurated the Union in terms of recrimination and bitterness. Colley's stress upon British history this leads her to ignore the Irish nature of Catholic Emancipation in a U.K. context. Continued into her treatment of the nineteenth century her emphasis upon "Britain" causes her continually to underplay the role of Irish affairs in parliament and the part played by such figures as Fergus O'Connor and Bronterre O'Brien in the Chartist Movement.

In my view the multiethnic character of the United Kingdom strikes the historian at almost every point in the nineteenth century. In Scotland, for example, the Disruption of 1843 overshadowed many aspects of Scottish social life. In Wales hostility toward the Anglican Church was a key feature of Welsh political and social life. In Ireland after many decades of pressure the Anglican Church of Ireland was finally disestablished in 1869. Thus, beneath Colley's veneer of Britishness lay bitter ethno-religious antagonisms.

There also remains the inescapable fact that the core of "Britain" was England. Colley uses British-orientated material which supports her case, but this leads her to ignore evidence for the strength of an English identity within the core, a fact which clearly led to problems with the periphery. Edmund Burke's *Reflections on the Revolution in France* is a case in point. In this work, Burke, though of Irish ethnic origin, repeatedly refers to "the people of England" and "the example of England." Part of his rhetorical style involves appealing to his audience as linked together in common cause by using the term "we." Throughout, this "we" refers to the English and "the people of England" among whom Burke ranks himself. The posthumous influence of Burke was considerable during the nineteenth century and on the basis of this evidence can scarcely be considered as contributing to a wider sense of "Britishness."

Another criticism of *Britons* must surely be that it plays down the role of class conflict. Edward Thompson's powerful article on "The Moral Economy of the Eighteenth Century" suggests that an appeal to patriotism was not enough to keep under control crowds which were moved to riot by a keen sense of social injustice. However, we perhaps should regard both Thompson and Colley as relevant for a fuller understanding of the eighteenth and nineteenth centuries. Both are classic works which have radically reshaped the perspective in which we see this important period and we need to retain the insights of both.

How a "Four Nations" historian might treat this period can only be imagined. He or she might examine the role of Ireland in the 1790s when the prospect of the admission of Irish Catholics to membership of parliament raised expectations to fever pitch and when its denial created a revolutionary situation. Colley wrote of keeping the French Revolution at bay but though this may have been true of "Britain" it was far from true in the sister kingdom. "1798" clearly indicated that Colley's "Protestantism" was an insufficient basis for creating political unity between Anglican Protestants and Dissenting Protestants. "1798" indeed was based upon an extraordinary alliance of Dissenter and Catholic under the common banner of "United Irishmen." Edward Thompson was well aware of this Irish dimension and it to some extent formed a minor theme in his discussion of English radicalism. Colley's emphasis on "Britain," however, excludes consideration of such matters and the names of Wolfe Tone or Robert Emmet do not appear in her index.

Unfortunately there is no modern Elie Halevy to produce a "Four Nation" treatment of these years. Our nearest equivalent so far is Jonathan Clark, who in his *Language of Liberty 1660–1832*, has attempted a wide-ranging analysis of political thinking in Great Britain, Ireland, and the American colonies. In an important review article, "English History's Forgotten Context: Scotland, Ireland, Wales" (*History Journal*, 1989), he also attempted to discuss recent work on the periphery. More recently he has also reviewed the work of Linda Colley, criticizing her for her stress upon what he sees as a relatively shallow British identity and playing down the significance of the more rooted ethnic identities of "English," "Scottish," "Welsh," and "Irish." Clark emphasizes the role of the established church rather than Protestantism as a key political factor. But he, like Colley, is open to criticism for neglecting class tensions as a force in politics. He is too prone to dismiss class-based analyses of historical change. In this respect he, like Colley, should be read with a copy of Edward Thompson in hand.

Clark offers an example of what a Four Nation approach might achieve and hence provides part of the answer to my question, "Where are we going?" He has the virtue, in my view, of being willing to consider the United Kingdom as a whole and to include the American colonies in his overall framework. However, for more compelling examples of what Four Nation analysis might achieve we have to turn, I believe, to other periods and other historians.

Professor Rees Davies's recently published (2000) study, *The First English Empire: Power and Identities in the British Isles*, is to my mind a classic work of the same caliber as Thompson or Colley but, unlike them, it takes the varying perspectives offered within these islands rather than confining them to "Britain" or "England." His theme is indeed the impact of the

English core upon the peripheries. Unlike Clark who is very much a man of the "core," Davies writes with the standpoint of the various peripheries in mind. Thus he begins with 1093, a key date in Welsh and Scottish history, rather than 1066, which would be axiomatic for English historians. As someone who was brought up on Stubbs's *Constitutional History* and Stubbs's *Charters*, I find Davies's approach enormously refreshing. Davies moves well beyond Stubbs's mono ethnic view of English history which took for granted that

> The English nation is of distinctly Teutonic or Germanic origin. ... This new race was the main stock of our forefathers, sharing the primaeval German pride of *purity of extraction*; still regarding the family tie as the basis of social organisation, ... honouring the women of their nation and strictly careful of the distinction between themselves and the tolerated remnant of their predecessors. (R. R. Davies, *Celts and Saxons*, p. 24)

In sharp contrast, Davies sees the history of these islands in terms of colonialism, involving the pressure of core upon peripheries. He is more concerned with mentalities and symbols rather than administrative practice. He shows, for example, how and why Edward I chose Nefyn, a tiny fishing village in North West Wales to hold a celebratory round table in 1284. The reason lay in the fact that it was at Nefyn that Gerald of Wales claimed to have delivered a copy of Merlin's prophecies (Davies, p. 32). Davies shows how Edward's imperial ambitions for the control of these islands were linked to the memory of Constantine and above all to that of Arthur whose body, together with that of Guinevere, was supposedly uncovered at Glastonbury in 1278 in Edward's presence. Arthur, a symbol from Welsh (sc. "British") history, was thus appropriated by the Crown as justification for its attempted overlordship of these islands.

In another chapter entitled "Sweet Civility" and "Barbarous Rudeness," Davies examines what he calls "the great socio-cultural" divide within the British Isles. The image of "Sweet Civility" (Edmnd Spenser's words) reflected, Davies tells us, the world as seen from southern and midland England. This was, in his words, "a lowland, arable, society, a relatively developed and monetised economy and a region of intensive and exacting lordship and powerfully penetrative kingship." This society despised those who did not share these values. The result, in Davies's view, was the creation of a cultural faultline within the British Isles. Davies's model thus draws upon the distinction between core and periphery, although the possible crudeness of this model is treated in his hands with great sensitivity.

The theme of colonialism is also taken up in another recent work, *Making Ireland British 1580–1650* (Oxford, 2001) by Nicholas Canny. Like Davies, Canny is concerned with the impact of the core upon the periphery, in this case the establishment of English and later Scottish and mixed "British" plantations in Ireland. As with Davies's book, Canny's work reflects the mature outlook of a lifetime of dedicated scholarship. It also looks back to David Quinn, who was the first modern scholar to place Irish history in a colonial framework. Both Canny and Quinn wish us to see the Irish plantations as part of a wider Atlantic framework. Canny also argues that English policy from Spenser through Strafford to Cromwell reflected a basic continuity of outlook.

Michael Hechter's study, *Internal Colonialism: The Celtic Fringe in British National Development 1536–1966* (1975), should also be mentioned is association with Rees Davies and Nicholas Canny. Hechter undoubtedly raised critical questions about the relationship between core and periphery but he ignored variations within the periphery both over time and from place to place. In terms of "Four Nation" history, however, his book is something of a landmark, pointing the way to critical questions.

Where then are we going? The work of Simon Schama and Linda Colley is a reminder that the Whig interpretation of history may well continue to dominate the outlook of the core. Nor is this necessarily to be deplored, provided that multiethnic histories are also available, in which the viewpoints of the various peripheries are taken into account. A wide Four Nations approach introduces, or offers the possibility of introducing, more than one dimension into what for some is still a simple "Our Island Story." It also offers the possibility of raising fruitful comparisons with other European nations struggling to reconcile their own Whiggish versions of history with the multiethnic realities. Spain in particular may be seen as raising such questions. Eugene Weber's fine study, *Peasants into Frenchmen* (1976), might be discussed in comparison with Linda Colley's *Britons*.

Today we are increasingly conscious of living in a multiethnic society. As the work of Rees Davies and Nicholas Canny suggests, however, this is far from being a novel situation. The history of these islands has been multiethnic over a long period, a fact which has been obscured by our preference for a simple narrative. English historians have been at fault here but so also have Irish, Scottish, and Welsh historians. Four Nations history not least offers the possibility of introducing comparisons between national traditions.

The postimperial Britain in which we find ourselves presents many features which should be familiar to students of Rees Davies and Nicholas Canny. They include such issues as ethnic identity, the pressure of a dominant language upon those of minorities, the tension between assimilationist policies and those defending cultural identity, the place of schooling in a multiethnic society and not least the place of an established church. Some historians have been more sensitive to these questions than others. We sadly miss the presence of Raphael Samuel who was continually alert to the problems of social and cultural change.

In conclusion I would suggest that we are not necessarily confronted as historians with a choice between monoethnic history and multiethnic history, between English or British history and a history which attempts to deal with "the British Isles." Each of these approaches carries its own benefits. A monoethnic historian may well be able to analyse his (or her) topic in greater depth than a multiethnic historian. What a multiethnic approach can offer, however, is a sense of the tension which exists between core and periphery. A monoethnic history carries with it the danger of imposing a reassuring Whig version of the past. A multiethnic approach may very well end up within a constricting neocolonialist framework in which the imperial power is always in the wrong. We thus need, a multidimensional approach involving both monoethnic and multiethnic interpretaters.

I know of no better guide to the complexities involved in a colonial-style situation than the Irish poet, Seamus Heaney. In a long sequence of poems he wrote recently about reading Shakespeare plays at school, Heaney reflected on the inadequacy of a crude colonial framework for understanding the outlook of a Catholic child in a school in rural Derry, which was putting on *Macbeth* or *The Tempest*. "On the other hand," (Heaney tells us) "you can do the reading that says you were force-fed colonial matter and you became a good little subject of the English language by acknowledging that Shakespeare was part of the cultural clinching of the power situation. That's one truth alright. But there is the second truth, which is that there's some form of transformation or radiance. ... There was an element of enlightenment, bringing light to your life. So is Shakespeare an imposition and a stealthy political infiltration or is he a resident transformer? Surely both."

Heaney went on to say that "it is quite true that the sense of being in two places at once has caused the tension and the energy" that drive his work (*Irish Times*, Oct. 30, 1997).

Heaney, of course, is not the only guide to such paradoxes and complexities. We may also refer to the work of V. S. Naipaul, Zadie Smith, Michael Longley, Salman Rushdie, and many others who have raised such issues. Work of literature may often be a better guide to the paradoxes of ethnic identity. Nor in this connection should we leave out the name of Shakespeare who in *Henry IV*, part I, takes as one of his themes the contrast between the values and perceptions of core and periphery. To see him as a national poet in the narrow sense does him, and us, grave disservice. We also need a multiethnic approach to comprehend his subtleties and ironies, even in such an apparently patriotic play as *Henry V*.

Chapter Eight

Civic/Ethnic Identities in a British Context

(2000)

In the 1980s Ernest Gellner, Eric Hobsbawm, and Benedict Anderson, among others, introduced new perspectives into the study of nationalism.[1] Since then nationalism itself has reemerged as a political force to be reckoned with and academic analysis of the phenomenon has developed at a remarkable rate. Amid the flood of new concepts the distinction between civic and ethnic nationalism seems to have taken particular hold. Rogers Brubaker, for example, demonstrated the importance of this distinction by contrasting the French model of civic national identity which derives from the universalism of the French Revolution, and the German ethnic model, which takes "blood" descent as the basis of German national identity, with its origins in the Romantic Movement.[2] As Brubaker showed, the contrast was not merely a matter for academic debate. On the contrary, it affected the life of thousands of individuals. In France, a civic approach to national identity led to a generally inclusive approach to immigrants. In Germany, however, second- and third-generation Turkish immigrants, German-speaking, found themselves unable to acquire German citizenship, whereas Russian-speaking "ethnic" Germans who had emigrated to Russia a century or more earlier and now wished to return encountered no such obstacles. This model of contrasting attitudes to national identity gains force if the United States is brought into the picture. Clearly, the U.S. constitution rests upon the notion of a civic American identity though this is not to deny that in certain periods and in particular states ethnic identities have been dominant, most notably in the case of slavery.

Looked at more closely, however, the contrast between French and German models of national identity appears less than absolute. In France discrimination on ethnic grounds lies behind the success of the National

Front in some areas. In Germany recent moves toward a more civic awareness have led to legislative changes in favor of Turkish immigrants. Perhaps we should think in terms of competing paradigms of national identity, with the balance favoring the one or the other according to the rhetorical or political power which they are able to mobilize. With this perspective in mind, how then should we classify the United Kingdom? In its approach to citizenship is it nearer to France and the United States on the one hand, or to Germany on the other; or are other models relevant?

Defining Britishness

The most recent British attempt to define the issues took place in 1981 with the passing of the Immigration Act. This allowed all those from within the United Kingdom to claim British citizenship provided they had at least one U.K.-born grandparent. Special treatment was also promised to those who could prove long-standing family connections with the U.K., termed "patriality." Looked at in the context of the previous 35 years, that is, since the end of the Second World War, this represents a shift away from a largely civic and inclusive definition of British citizenship toward a more ethnic and exclusive one. The Act was in fact the latest in a series of legislative changes designed to curtail large-scale immigration from former British-governed territories in Asia, Africa, and the Caribbean. The United Kingdom has apparently moved away from a broad definition of civic Britishness based upon membership of the Commonwealth to a more restricted definition based upon ethnic considerations.

The legislation of 1981 and its predecessors, passed under both Labour and Conservative governments, restricted the flow of overseas immigrants. Despite this the United Kingdom has become a multiethnic society. In sport, in politics, in entertainment, in cuisine, in business, in education, in medicine and in other activities, postwar immigrants and their second- or third-generation descendants are making a distinctive contribution to the life of Britain. Racial prejudice undoubtedly exists, but the grim scenario evoked by Enoch Powell in his notorious "rivers of blood" speech of 1964 has not come to pass. Clearly, however, problems involving assimilation into the host country remain. As I write, for example (1999), newspaper headlines are drawing attention to the murder in Bradford of a young Muslim woman by her relatives because she had broken the religious code of the traditional family. In such a case the problematic aspects of

"Britishness" and "being British" are clearly brought to the fore. How do the children of such a family perceive themselves? And, of equal importance, how are they perceived? Our earlier distinction between "ethnic" and "civic" approaches to national identity is obviously relevant in an analysis of postimperial Britain.

The problematic nature of "Britishness" is not a new phenomenon. It goes back at least to the union of the English and Scottish crowns in 1603 and to the unsuccessful attempt by James I (James VI of Scotland) to create a common British citizenship throughout his new realm of "Great Britain." The story took another turn with the Act of Union of 1707, linking England and Scotland in a parliamentary union. This was an event which brought the "civic" terms "Britain" and "Britons" into wider popular usage, though still leaving intact "Englishness" and "Scottishness" as core ethnic identities, drawing upon deep emotional roots. In many ways, however, the most significant shift took place in 1800 with the creation of the United Kingdom of Great Britain and Ireland, a political move designed to counter the threat of revolution in Ireland. Ireland, which had been constitutionally distinct, now became part of what was in effect a new state. The newly enlarged United Kingdom included a substantial proportion of Irish Catholics, many of them Gaelic-speaking. This was a situation which, in the view of the prime minister, William Pitt, required some degree of constitutional change, in particular the admission of Irish Catholic MPs into parliament. However, this change and others associated with it were slow to come. The result was the so-called "Irish Problem." But was it "Irish"? Or was it rather a civic problem originating in a failure of the dominant ethnic English majority to move the constitution in a more civic direction?

In modern terms, the Act of Union had created a multiethnic state, comparable to Spain, the Habsburg monarchy, Sweden, and the Netherlands. In this new United Kingdom, however, as was not unknown elsewhere, the dominant ethnic group opposed what seemed appropriate adjustments. King George III, with the support of the ruling Tory Party, refused to sanction the admittance of Catholics into the Protestant constitution, which, with its twin pillars of church and monarchy, became the central symbol of a Tory Anglican nationalism. Any move to admit Catholics into full membership of the constitution was regarded as revolutionary by such figures as Lord Eldon, Lord Chancellor under George III, and the Duke of Wellington. In 1811 Eldon asked:

Am I too rash in standing upon the Constitution of England and the principles of the Revolution which united and knitted together a Protestant
State and Constitution and a Church Establishment for the express purpose
of handing them down together with all their benefits, to our remotest
posterity.[3]

Tory nationalists saw themselves as defending the constitution of the
nation and its key institutions against the forces of sedition. However,
their nation was England, not the United Kingdom. Their movement was
based upon English rather than British nationalism, with the Church of
England as the key institution being defended. As Wellington wrote to
Croker in 1833,

The revolution is made, that is to say that power is transferred from one
class of society, the gentlemen of England, professing the faith of the
Church of England, to another class of society, the shopkeepers being Dissenters from the Church, many of them Socinians, others atheists.[4]

"English" and "England," not "British" and "Britain," were the basic concepts of this ethnic Tory nationalism. However, the passing of the Catholic
Emancipation Act in 1829 was a victory for a more inclusive civic nationalism. One of its most influential proponents was Thomas Babington
Macaulay, Member of Parliament and a regular contributor to the civic-
minded *Edinburgh Review*. His article on the "Civil Disabilities of the
Jews" (1831) may be taken as an expression of civic nationalism. In it he attempted to answer the charge that "the English Jews, we are told, are not
Englishmen but rather a separate people, living locally in this island but
living morally and politically with their brethren who are scattered all over
the world." Macaulay's view was that "the feeling of patriotism, when society is in a healthful state, springs up by a natural and inevitable association in the minds of its citizens who know that they owe all their comforts
and pleasures to the bond which unites them in one community." In contemporary prejudices against Jews he saw the parallels with the way that
"some of our politicians reasoned about the Irish Catholics." In a famous
passage Macaulay declared that on Tory principles,

millions of Catholics, millions of Protestant Dissenters, are to be excluded
from all power and honours. A great hostile fleet is on the sea; but Nelson
is not to command in the channel if in the mystery of the Trinity he
confounds the persons. An invading army had landed in Kent; but the Duke
of Wellington is not to be at the head of our forces if he divides the sub-
stance.[5]

Macaulay here and elsewhere puts forward the argument for an inclusive civic national identity. In fact it took several decades before decisive reforms were introduced. Jewish political disabilities were not removed until the midcentury. The grip of the Church of England upon the Universities of Oxford and Cambridge was not seriously weakened until Gladstone's first ministry (1868–74). The atheist Bradlaugh was admitted to the House of Commons only after a protracted political struggle.

Eldon's narrow ethnic nationalism was eventually defeated by a broader, more comprehensive nationalism with Palmerston as its most noted exponent. On the basis of Palmerston's celebrated use of the Latin tag "Civis Britannicus sum" it is tempting to see his nationalism as civic. In fact, however, as an Anglo-Irish landlord and member of the Protestant Ascendancy he included Irish Catholics as full members of the state only with some reluctance. It was felt that British policy in Ireland should favor those "Saxon and Protestant Irishmen" who were "friendly to the British connexion and not in the pursuit of claptrap liberality eternally to alienate our friends without in the slightest degree conciliating our enemies."[6]

Thus even Palmerston's nationalism remained ethnic, though more broadly based than the Tory version. It was exemplified in the life's work of Dean Stanley, the broad churchman whom Palmerston appointed Dean of Westminster in 1864. Not surprisingly, Stanley was a great admirer of Palmerston, who he considered

> was an Englishman to excess. It was England, rather than any special party in England—it was the honour and interests of England, rather than even the constitution or the State, or the Church of England that forced his imagination and stimulated his efforts and secured his fame. To England and to no lesser interest the vast length of that laborious life, with whatsoever short comings, was in all simplicity and faithfulness devoted.

The massive statue to Palmerston which stands in Westminster Abbey was a tribute instigated by Stanley, but an even more significant legacy of the Dean was the remodelling of Westminster Abbey itself. It was Stanley who refashioned the interior in order to make it "the centre of our national energies, the hearth of our national religion." In Stanley's eyes, the Abbey "is not only Reims and St Denys in one: but it is also what the Pantheon was intended to be for France and the Valhalla is to Germany, what Santa Croce is to Italy."

Stanley's editor suggested that it was seen by him as "the outward symbol of the harmonious unity in diversity which pervades the English

Commonwealth." The building certainly suggests comprehensiveness; but it was not a fully "civic" comprehensiveness. Stanley's "imagined community" had distinct limits. There was no place for the High Church heroes, Laud and Strafford. There were no Chartist leaders. There was no recognition of Scots such as Thomas Carlyle. The Irish patriot Henry Grattan was represented, but no other Irishmen. Cromwell's peculiar greatness was unrecognized. Stanley's Abbey thus bore the imprint of a top-down Protestant broad church nationalism. There was no Bentham, no Mill, no Daniel O'Connell, no George Eliot. The Abbey conveys the sense of being a comprehensive national monument; but the nation which it represented was still conceived in terms of monarchy, landed aristocracy, and established church. The England which it symbolized was rural southern England, with the industrialized north and midlands, Wales, Scotland, and Ireland left largely unrecognized. In short, Stanley's Abbey was a monument to a Whig version of English ethnic nationalism.[7]

The nationalism of Palmerston and Stanley was in the broad church Whig tradition going back to Samuel Taylor Coleridge and to Thomas Arnold, headmaster of Rugby School. A somewhat different broad church nationalism was set out in Sir John Seeley's influential book *The Expansion of England*, which originated in a series of lectures delivered by him as Regius Professor of Modern History at Cambridge in 1881. Seeley's "imagined community," unlike that of Stanley, was of a greater Britain beyond the seas. Seeley used the term "Britain" but spoke continuously of England, "the great English exodus" which he saw as "an extension of English nationality" which "broadly may be said to be English throughout." His Great Britain was "homogeneous in nationality."

> If in these islands we feel ourselves for all purposes one nation, though in Wales, Scotland and Ireland there is Celtic blood and Celtic languages utterly unintelligible to us are still spoken, so in the Empire a good many French and Dutch and a good many Caffres and Maories may be admitted without marring the ethnological unity of the whole.

For Seeley, "the chief forces which hold a community together and cause it to constitute one State are three, common nationality [sc. common ethnic descent], common religion and common interest." Seeley's Greater Britain was not "a mere empire." For him its union was "of the more vital kind." "It is united by blood and religion and though circumstances may be imagined in which these might snap, yet they are strong ties and will only give way, before some violent dissolving force."

Seeley also stressed the importance of the state. For him, "History has to do with the State." But his English ethnic and religious assumptions blinded him to the fact that the state in his case was the United Kingdom. Celtic culture and languages clearly had no value for him. He was well aware that "subject or rival nationalities cannot be perfectly assimilated and remain as a permanent cause of weakness and danger," but he did not see that the United Kingdom itself faced problems of this kind. Thus he failed to recognize parallels between the United Kingdom and Austria, "divided by the national rivalry of German, Slav and Magyar." It was the parallel with the United States which excited Seeley's enthusiasm. Of Greater Britain he wrote: "When we have accustomed ourselves to contemplate the whole Empire together and call it England, we shall add that here too is a United States. Here too is a great homogeneous people, one in blood, language, religion and laws, but dispersed over a boundless space."[8]

Seeley failed to see, however, that the United States was a state which rested primarily upon the notion of a civic identity, not, as he thought, "a great homogeneous people, one in blood, language, religion and laws." Seeley's United States, like his United Kingdom, was very much an "imagined community" which bore little resemblance to reality. And yet his views were extremely influential. Joseph Chamberlain, for example, found inspiration in Seeley in constructing his own version of English ethnic nationalism in the 1890s.[9]

The Civic Tradition

As the case of Macaulay has indicated, a rival civic tradition was not without influence in nineteenth-century England. Despite its title, Macaulay's *History of England* was a study of the three kingdoms of England, Scotland, and Ireland during the Glorious Revolution. Unlike the university-trained historians of the second half of the century who looked to German models, Macaulay wrote in the tradition of the Scottish Enlightenment. For him, environment rather than race was the key to political and economic development. The enormous success of his *History* indicates that his views found an audience. Acton, for one, was a great admirer who read it several times as a young man. Gladstone also read Macaulay's *History* when it was first published.

Another example of a historian who favored a civic approach was William Edward Hartpole Lecky, who like Macaulay never became an academic historian. Lecky particularly resented the racial approach of James Anthony Froude, who was later to become Regius Professor at Oxford, and his controversy with Froude may be seen as a classic case study of the tension which existed between civic and ethnic nationalism in the 1870s.

The most influential spokesman for a civic national identity was John Stuart Mill. Mill was well aware that "the boundaries of governments should coincide in the main with those of nationalities" [sc. ethnicity in our modern phraseology]. He then went on to qualify this gesture toward the idea of an ethnically homogeneous nation-state by pointing out that

> There are parts even of Europe in which different nationalities are so locally intermingled that it is not practicable for them to be under separate governments. The population of Hungary is composed of Magyars, Slovaks, Croats, Serbs, Roumans and in some districts Germans, so mixed up as to be incapable of local separation; and there is no course open to them but to make a virtue of necessity and reconcile themselves to living together under equal rights and laws.

Mill pointed out that even France, "the most united country in Europe," was "far from homogeneous." But, he went on,

> Nobody can suppose that it is not more beneficial to a Breton or a Basque of French Navarre to be brought into the current of the ideas and feelings of a highly cultivated and civilised people—to be a member of the French nationality admitted on equal terms to all the advantages of French protection and the dignity and *prestige* of French power—than to sulk on his own rocks, the half-savage relic of past times, revolving in his own little mental orbit, without participation or interest in the general movement of the world.[10]

Mill believed that his civic model applied to the relationship between England and Ireland. Unlike Tories, such as Salisbury, he did not look upon the Irish as an inferior race. On the contrary, he thought that until recent years, they had been "so atrociously governed" that they were understandably resentful of Saxon rule. Now, however, apart from the real grievance of the state church, there was "next to nothing, except the memory of the past, and the difference in the predominant religion, to keep apart two races, perhaps the most fitted of any two in the world to be the completing counterpart of one another." Mill stressed "the consciousness of being at last treated not only with equal justice but with equal consideration" as key factors in changing the attitudes of the Irish. In his view, they would come to see the benefits which necessarily derived from being fellow citizens of their nearest neighbors. What we have termed civic identity seemed crucial to Mill in dealing with problems raised by nationality. Understandably, it was France and the United States to which he referred most often. There was thus a clear contrast between Mill's approach and the emphasis on Teutonic racial links so characteristic of Stubbs, Freeman, and others.

One final example may serve to illustrate the importance of the tradition of civic identity within the United Kingdom. William Ewart Gladstone (1809–98) began his political career very much at the "ethnic" end of the spectrum. As we have seen earlier, Macaulay criticized his High Tory views as expounded in *The State in Its Relation with the Church* (1838). In 1844, on the key question of the funding of the Catholic seminary of Maynooth, Gladstone took the opposite side to Macaulay and actually resigned from the government over the issue—although, in a gesture which illustrates the tensions within him, he ended up voting for it. By the 1860s, however, he had moved toward a more liberal position and in 1869 sponsored the bill disestablishing the Church of Ireland. In the 1870s and 1880s he supported the atheist Charles Bradlaugh's repeated attempts to secure admission to the House of Commons. He was critical of the Tories, the "Jingo party," as he termed them, for their attempts to capitalize on popular English nationalist sentiment. Gladstone's own speeches and diary refer frequently to "the three Kingdoms" and he believed that the basis for any long-term settlement of the Irish question "ought to be perfect equality of Ireland with England and Scotland." Not least, he was well aware of the resemblances between Sweden ("that United Kingdom") as he put it and the situation nearer home, in which Ireland's situation seemed to parallel that of Norway. Gladstone also drew analogies between Austria-Hungary and the United Kingdom, and even between Turkish dominance in the Balkans and the Ascendancy in Ireland.

Perhaps not surprisingly, Gladstone's Home Rule Bill (1886) provided the occasion for what proved to be a decisive encounter between the protagonists of ethnic and civic identities. Home rule for Ireland was an issue which split the Liberal Party on ethnic-civic lines. Among those who opposed home rule was Sir John Seeley. The most significant opponent, however, was Joseph Chamberlain, who by his advocacy of secular education had once seemed committed to a more "civic" approach. The situation was made more complicated by the fact that Charles Stuart Parnell, leader of the Irish Party, though an advocate in theory of a civic Irish identity which would include Protestants as well as Catholics, had committed himself for tactical purposes to a working alliance with the Catholic episcopate in Ireland. The defeat of Gladstone's first Home Rule Bill was a turning point in the sense that it marked a decisive shift in favor of an English ethnic national identity. These were the years in which the Irish were referred to by such figures as Salisbury, the prime minister, as an inferior race. During the same period the idea of the Catholic Irish as a Celtic "race" took root in Ireland itself. It was a situation whose outcome was unclear even as late as 1914. It seemed possible at one stage that Irish home rule would come about based upon a civic view of Irish identity espoused by John Redmond, leader of the Irish Parliamentary Party. In the event, other forces took over, most notably Ulster Unionism, with its ethnic views on British identity, and a Republican nationalism with a strongly "Celtic" ethnic focus.

The First World War had as powerful an effect upon the political structure of the United Kingdom as it did upon the Habsburg monarchy. George Dangerfield wrote of "The Strange Death of Liberal England" but in fact his real topic was the Strange Death of the United Kingdom of Great Britain and Ireland. The civil wars which were fought in Ireland between British and Irish and later among the Irish themselves were as bitter as anything in eastern Europe. After a settlement was reached in 1921 Ireland and the Irish Question dropped out of the consciousness of the U.K. as rapidly as memories of empire were to do later in the century. Ireland, both North and South, was left to its own devices. The ministate of Northern Ireland organized itself on ethnic lines, with the two-thirds British (Anglican and Presbyterian) majority moving ever further away from a civic solution which would have recognized the rights of a one-third Irish (Catholic) minority. In the South, the Irish Free State also constructed itself along ethnic lines. Here the Irish language, which few spoke with any familiarity, became a central symbol of national identity, together with Catholicism. From the 1920s to the 1960s this situation remained almost unchanged, until in 1968, the Year of Revolution, the issue of civic identity was once again raised, this time in Northern Ireland.

After 1921, with the Irish Question apparently "solved," the truncated United Kingdom was less obviously multiethnic than it had been since 1800. Four years of war with Germany killed off any sense that English liberties had a Teutonic origin. The result was to consign such late-nineteenth-century historians as Edward Freeman and John Richard Green to oblivion. Stubbs's *Constitutional History* was still recognized as a key text, but the first chapters with their insistence upon Anglo-Saxon links with Germany were no longer read. Indeed, at Cambridge students were advised not to read them. At least one of the elements which had gone into the making of an ethnic English identity was changing. A shift toward a sense of civic "Britishness" was taking place. The postwar decline of religious observance among the Protestant churches also contributed to a shift in national identity. A nonsectarian Britishness came to be centered upon Armistice Day and the Cenotaph, and memories of the mass slaughter at Gallipoli, the Somme, and Passchendaele evoked a religious sense of mourning. A recent study discusses "The Great War and Remembrance" as one of the "Myths of the English." In fact, however, there is no doubt that the experiences of the First World War helped to create a common feeling of "Britishness" which was reinforced by such practices as buying a poppy or listening to the royal broadcast on Christmas Day. A British identity extended beyond the United Kingdom to the dominions of the British Commonwealth of Nations—and, as post-1945 immigrants to the United Kingdom have testified, to the West Indies.

The sense of British identity during these years (1918–45) may not unfairly be described as civic. This coexisted with a sense of Englishness. The Conservative prime minister, Stanley Baldwin, may be taken as an example of this. For him England was a vision of rural peace: "The sounds of England, the tinkle of the hammer on the anvil in the country smithy, the corncrake on a dewy morning, the sound of the scythe against the whetstone, and the sight that has been England since England was a land ... the one eternal sight of England."[11] This was a vision which ignored the industrialized areas of the North, Wales, and Scotland and which played down any sense that the United Kingdom was still a multiethnic society. It was a view which was echoed in other influential writers of the period. G. M. Trevelyan, like Baldwin, took England as his topic. In his *England under the Stuarts*, which has been reprinted over twenty times since 1904, Trevelyan contrasted the English and French revolutions.

> At the overthrow of the decayed society of France, ideals served as ensigns borne along before an army of material hungers. Hence the dark story of their savage vindication; hence too, the victory of ideals and hungers together in modern France of the equal laws. The French revolution appealed to the needs as well as the aspirations of mankind. But in England the revolutionary passions were stirred by no class in its own material interest. Our patriots were prosperous men, enamoured of liberty, or of religion, or of loyalty, each for her own sake, not as the handmaid of class greed. This was

the secret of the moral splendour of our Great Rebellion and our Civil War.[12]

In Trevelyan's use of "our" ("our mother tongue," "our Cavaliers and Roundheads," "our patriots," "our Great Rebellion," "our Civil War"), and his downplaying of class interest, the voice of an ethnic English nationalism may be heard. The book itself was written in 1904 but Trevelyan's heyday extended into the 1940s when he published his *English Social History*. It is easy to understand his appeal, like Baldwin's, to those who felt that English life was under threat from socialism and perhaps also fascism.

In contrast, a more civic note was sounded by the prolific academic, Ernest Barker, Principal of King's College, London (1920–27) and Professor of Political Science at Cambridge (1928–39). Unlike Trevelyan, Barker stressed the role of the state in creating a British identity. In discussing the rise of "British national character" Barker praised the way in which "the state in our island had managed to be simultaneously multi-national and a single nation ... teaching its citizens at the one and the same time to glory both in the name of Scotsmen or Welshmen or Englishmen and in the name of Britons."[13]

Like Baldwin and Trevelyan, Barker stressed the unity of the nation and played down class conflict. In the year following the General Strike he wrote of organized labour that "If it is founded on the basis of working-class organizations, it is not by any means wholly identified with a single class, and it is more and more drawing into its ranks the representatives of other classes."

During the 1920s and 1930s, indeed, there was as sharp a contest between paradigms of nationhood as had been the case in the nineteenth century. The balance swung in favor of ethnic English identity at first, only to move in favor of a civic identity (socialist style) in 1945. The success of Churchill's *History of the English-Speaking Peoples* during the postwar period indicates, however, that the pull of ethnic nationalism remained strong.

But class conflict was never far away. In the 1920s Harold Laski, for example, criticized Barker for his views. He wrote:

It is easier to think [this way] amid the dreaming spires of Oxford or in the loveliness of the Cambridge backs in June than if one is a blacklisted miner in a Welsh coalfield or a share-cropper trying to fix a decent price on his puny holding in Alabama. A democratic state validates its character by the level of rights that it maintains; and the weakness of Professor Barker's definition of rights is his complete indifference to the fact that the level is urgent.[14]

End of Empire

A radical and quite unexpected shift in the ethnic structure of the United Kingdom was to occur in the decades following 1948. Changes were noticeable earlier. Jewish refugees had arrived in Britain in the years before the war. Poles arrived after 1939. Irish men and women found ready employment in wartime Britain. The armed forces drew upon volunteers from the Dominions and the West Indies. Hence, by 1945 Baldwin's vision of "England" was beginning to lose its rhetorical power. But the decisive changes were yet to come. In June 1948 the *SS Empire Windrush* docked at Tilbury carrying several hundreds of West Indians, all seeking employment in Britain. The Minister of Labour, George Isaacs, had expressed his concern at their unexpected arrival but went on to say: "They are British citizens and we shall do our best for them when they arrive." In 1951 the total population of West Indians and Asians in Britain amounted to 80,000, largely concentrated in ports such as Cardiff and Liverpool. By 1971 the total of new immigrants had risen to one and a half million. By 1991 this figure had doubled, reaching a figure of over 6 percent of the population. Such figures did not include the massive influx of "new Irish" into Birmingham and Kilburn during the 1960s. England, or large areas of it, had become multiethnic.

All this was clearly significant in changing views about English or British identity. Of equal if not greater importance, however, was the decline of empire. Imperial Britain became postimperial Britain with extraordinary speed. The crucial step was the decision by the Macmillan government to apply for membership of the European Common Market. The attempt failed at first, but in 1972 the application of the United Kingdom was accepted. To be British no longer implied membership of a worldwide Commonwealth. Hitherto unasked questions were raised as to how European Britain was or wanted to be.

After the election of Margaret Thatcher in 1979, however, English ethnic nationalism once more began to emerge as a potent political force. Her political rhetoric drew increasingly upon nationalism, most noticeably in the debates over the Immigration Act of 1981, in the Falklands campaign of

1982, in her strained relationship with the European Union, and in her fight against "the enemy within" during the miners' strike of 1984–85. One unanticipated consequence of the rise of English nationalism during the Thatcher years was the reaction it provoked in Scotland over the poll tax, which ultimately led to the resurgence of Scottish nationalism and to the establishment of a Scottish parliament in 1999. Thatcherite policies in Northern Ireland also led to the unforeseen result of close involvement between the United Kingdom and the Republic of Ireland.

A historian writing about the United Kingdom (I had almost said "the condition of England" question) in 1999 can scarcely avoid discussing the future of nationalism. To an earlier generation, post-1945, "class conflict" seemed to be the main theme of English (British?) history, as illustrated by the works of R. H. Tawney, Christopher Hill, and E. P. Thompson. In the present circumstances of the United Kingdom, however, issues raised by ethnic and national identities, along with multiculturalism, clamor for serious discussion. In Northern Ireland, Scotland, Brixton, Notting Hill, and other parts of London; Bradford, Wolverhampton, and Leicester; and even in the Rhondda Valley, the United Kingdom seems to be taking on a new, hitherto unimagined shape. What I have attempted to suggest in this essay is that there was an earlier history of nationalism within the United Kingdom which may provide parallels with the situation today. Irish nationalism clearly forms part of the story. There was also, as I have indicated, an English nationalism, the significance of which is all too often ignored. In a multiethnic state such as the United Kingdom became after 1800, some individuals, such as Mill or Gladstone, seemed to be calling for a form of civic nationalism. In the event, however, an ethnic English nationalism remained a powerful force in politics, particularly within the Conservative Party.

The crucial difference between civic and ethnic nationalism within the British context still remains largely unexplored. In the days of empire, "British" implied an imperial identity. Today, however, if the terms "British" and "Britishness" are to mean anything, they should surely stand for a civic identity within the United Kingdom, that is, British citizenship. This would still leave traditional national categories such as English, Scottish, and Welsh largely intact. Even here, however, it is impossible to avoid issues of civic identity. In Scotland, for example, a substantial Catholic minority exists, which cannot claim to be ethnically Scots in a Highland or Lowland sense. Similar problems are raised by the existence of Asian Glaswegians. The rise of Scottish nationalism means that questions of civic identity can no longer be avoided. The Celtic fringe may sooner rather than later transform itself into a civic fringe. In postimperial England there are also new ethnic identities which need to achieve recognition within a wider civic polity.

But will a wider civic Britishness survive in a postimperial United Kingdom? One significant factor to be considered is the rise of an active English nationalism as a response to what some see as the threat of an ever-expanding European Union. The problem of constructing a civic identity in Northern Ireland also remains a continuing challenge. The future role of Scottish nationalism remains unclear, with the apparent rise of anti-English sentiment a cause for concern. The relationship of the Republic of Ireland with the United Kingdom raises new issues about the limits of national sovereignty. In London itself, the election of a mayor looks likely to revive ethnic politics on a scale not seen since the days of Charles Stewart Parnell.

The implications of these changes will take some time to work themselves out. In the field of education, for example, it seems clear that the project of a National History Curriculum, undertaken blithely by Kenneth Baker during the golden years of Margaret Thatcher, will present particular problems.[15] "Our Island Story" no longer seems as simple as it once did, though as yet there is nothing to replace it. If a history of the United Kingdom were to be written it would need to move beyond an ethnically driven narrative (à la *Braveheart* or *1066 and All That*) toward a comparative dimension in which "our" response to "our" problems could be judged more dispassionately. But would *Braveheart* still win out? Possibly.

NOTES

1. Ernest Gellner, *Nations and Nationalism*, Ithaca, Cornell University Press, 1983; E. J. Hobsbawm, *Nations and Nationalism since 1780*, Cambridge, Cambridge University Press, 1990); Benedict Anderson, *Imagined Communities*, rev. edn, London, Verso, 1991.

2. Rogers Brubaker, *Citizenship and Nationhood in France and Germany*, Cambridge, Mass., Harvard University Press, 1992.

3. Quoted J. C. D. Clark, *English Society 1688–1831*, Cambridge, Cambridge University Press, 1985, p. 364.

4. Ibid., p. 413.

5. T. B. Macaulay, *Critical and Historical Essays*, Everyman edn, London, Dent, 1933, vol. 2, p. 261.

6. E. D. Steele, *Palmerston and Liberalism*, Cambridge, Cambridge University Press, 1991, p. 292.

7. R. E. Prothero, *Life and Correspondence of Arthur Penrhyn Stanley D.D.*, London, 1893, p. 353.

8. John Clive, ed., *J. R. Seeley: The Expansion of England*, Chicago, University of Chicago Press, 1971, p. 126.

9. James Loughlin, "Joseph Chamberlain, English Nationalism and the Ulster Question," *History*, June 1992, p. 203.

10. John Stuart Mill, *On Liberty and Other Essays*, ed. John Gray, Oxford, Oxford University Press (World's Classics), 1991, pp. 430–33.

11. Quoted in Jeremy Paxman, *The English*, London, Penguin Books, 1998, p. 143. See also Phillip Williamson, *Stanley Baldwin*, Cambridge, Cambridge University Press, 1999.

12. G. M. Trevelyan, *England under the Stuarts*, London, Methnen & Co. 1904, pp. 187–88.

13. Julia Stapleton, *Englishness and the Study of Politics: The Social and Political Thought of Ernest Barker*, Cambridge, Cambridge University Press, 1994.

14. Ibid., p. 5.

15. For a lively discussion of these issues, see William Lamont's review of Robert Phillips, *History Teaching, Nationhood and the State: A Study in Educational Politics* (London, Cassell, 1998) in *History Workshop Journal*, 1998, pp. 300–33.

Chapter Nine

The Changing Face of English Nationalism

(2000)

Of the three books under review,[1] two deal with the identity of England, and the third, though concerned with "the identity of Britain," also inevitably has implications for England. Such interest in Englishness is now relatively commonplace, but twenty years ago it seemed bizarre. Indeed Robert Coll in the introduction to his book *Identity of England* (2000), tells us that he and his fellow editor Robert Dodd had great difficulty in finding a publisher for a collection of essays on Englishness. Raphael Samuel's *Patriotism: The Making and Unmaking of British National Identity* still provided a shock of novelty when it was published in 1989. All this has now changed. English identity, once accepted as an unquestioned assumption, is now seen as problematic and hence as an appropriate topic for debate.

The apparent solidity of English identity depended in large measure upon the general acceptance of the so-called "Whig interpretation of history" according to which the history of England, most fortunate of nations, was the story of liberty, gradually progressing over centuries. This history began with Magna Carta, continued with the English Reformation and the growth of religious tolerance, and was consolidated in 1688 with peaceful revolution. Later in the nineteenth century, England, avoiding the revolutionary perils of the French Revolution, moved peacefully via the various acts of Reform in 1832, 1867, 1884, and 1918 to the establishment of modern democracy. On the basis of this interpretation it was assumed that England was a special case, very different from Europe, but clearly influencing the United States. It was the version of English history which at the end of the nineteenth century was established in the schools and universities. It was a view to which Sir John Seeley offered an alternative in his *The Expansion of England* (1884) in which the establishment of a world empire was seen as the main theme of English history. Seeley's book was a best-seller which remained in print until the mid-twentieth century. At the level of school textbooks and examinations, however, it was the Whig interpretation which remained dominant.

Only now are we beginning to see that English history was not as unique as we once thought and that perhaps English history, inextricably intertwined as it is with that of Wales, Ireland, and Scotland, resembles that of Castile caught up in the tensions of the Iberian Peninsula. Thus, far from being unique, the Whig interpretation may be the English equivalent of the historical myths which bolster the self-image of other nations. Such critical views, however, are held by a minority. In the general rhetoric of politics and in the symbolism of the English constitution, reflected as it is in the rituals of parliament, the Whig interpretation remains a generally accepted framework.

The essential feature of the Whig interpretation was its emphasis upon "England," ignoring the varied histories of other countries within the United Kingdom. At Oxford, the history of England formed the core of the history syllabus. At Cambridge the constitutional history of England, taught through anglocentric collections of documents edited by Stubbs, Gardiner, Prothero, and Tanner, continued into our own day. The influence of Oxford and Cambridge history faculties extended throughout the United Kingdom into Manchester, Edinburgh, and elsewhere. The histories of Ireland, Scotland, and Wales were only discussed when they presented an obstacle in the way of the progress of England.

This situation began to change after the establishment of the new universities in the 1960s and the subsequent transformation of former polytechnics into universities. More important, however, was the rise of nationalism in Scotland and Wales and the resurgence of Irish nationalism in Northern Ireland. This critical shift within the United Kingdom was a response to Mrs. Thatcher's English nationalist policies, which were in themselves a reaction to the influence of the European community. An additional factor in these changes was the impact of immigration from the Commonwealth, especially Pakistan, Bangladesh, and the Caribbean. In the face of all these changes, coupled with increasing involvement with Europe, the old Whig interpretation began to fall apart at the seams. Wales and Scotland now found their own historians in such scholars as Rees Davies and Tom Devine. It was England which now faced the problem of making sense of its history.

In 1989, under the auspices of the History Workshop, Raphael Samuel edited three volumes of conference papers under the title *Patriotism: the Making and Unmaking of British National Identity*. This reference to "British national identity" was misleading. As Samuel explained in his introduction, the original focus of the contributors was with "English" identity. The introduction of "British" into the title was a late decision of the editors, and as the table of contents makes clear, "Englishness" remained the general theme of the collection. It was Englishness with a difference. Samuel's intention was to escape from the narrow restraints of Mrs. Thatcher's contemporary version of the Whig interpretation and to rescue the histories of minority groups within English society from the condescension of posterity ("minorities" here including also women). Samuel's own introductions and contributions raised key issues of multiculturalism for the first time and looking back the volume may be seen as a turning point in English historiography. The anglocentric emphasis of the Whig interpretation no longer seemed adequate. The question remained, however, as to how the history of England was to be treated. One solution was to see it as one of the "four nations" within the United Kingdom. But if Scotland, Ireland, and Wales could be seen as having histories in their own right, so also presumably could England. How then was a history of England to be constructed in this post-Whig phase?

The problem presented by the collapse of the Whig interpretation of history is faced by Roger Scruton in his eloquent study *England: An Elegy* (2001). In Scruton's view the England that he once knew is fast becoming a fading memory, as a result of the influx of "uninvited guests" (a phrase from his article in *The Spectator*, March 2003). He sees his "England" in extraordinarily idealistic terms and he offers repeated generalizations about a people he calls "the English," as if there had been no variation over time and place. This is a vision of England and the English in which almost all sense of conflict has been eliminated. The Reformation is dealt with, for example, as an unproblematic episode in the evolution of "the English." There is no hint of the tragic defeat of the Pilgrimage of Grace and the subsequent colonization of northern England although the Pilgrims' call for a northern-based Parliament was a clear indication that the North resented the domination of the South. Ket's rebellion in Norfolk and the revolt of Cornwall, both occurring in 1549, also implied the existence of deep divisions within "English" society. Throughout his book, indeed, Scruton plays down the extent to which English society was divided. There is no sense, for example, of the quasi-racial English antagonism toward the Welsh, Scots, and Irish and the extraordinary influence of the "No Popery" issue from the seventeenth century onward.

Rather, Scruton's theme is the "Anglican vision of England, as an Arcadian landscape enhanced by its law and institutions and made holy by ritual and prayer" (p. 111). Thus he sees law as furthering "the determination of the English to stand up to power wherever justice was opposed to it." Jury service embodied a perception that the law of England was perceived as "a common property of all in which each had a duty to uphold and which reached impartially into every household." As in other versions of the Whig interpretation, Scruton begins with the Anglo-Saxons, moving on to modern times via Magna Carta and the Bill of Rights of 1869. England was "the land of the free" (p. 129). In his description of English society Scruton rises to extraordinary heights of eloquence. He defends the collegiate way of life at Oxford and Cambridge and in particular the tutorial system. He also praises without irony gentlemen's clubs through which, in his view, "so many Englishmen refreshed their vision of community, exercised their sense of honour and formed those ties which sustained them in their working lives." Not surprisingly he also defends the system of public schools though he himself is a grammar school boy.

So uplifting is Scruton's view of England that to criticize it seems ungentlemanly. Nevertheless, the fact remains that access to the delights of this way of life was and is confined to a minority. The point was well put by R. H. Tawney in his comments upon the life of the brilliant economic historian George Unwin.

> The expansion of secondary and university education, which was to work a revolution in social life after 1900, had not yet begun. The road to learning wound steeply up the precipitous heights of English educational snobbery, crowned with the majestic towers of two ancient universities, and the doors did not open readily to a young man who possessed no more persuasive qualifications than unusual powers of mind and width of knowledge. (R. H. Tawney on George Unwin, in *Studies in Economic History: The Collected Papers of George Unwin* (London: 1927), p. xiii)

Scruton himself in some fascinating pages describes how his father escaped from the slums of Manchester by his own efforts, as a result enabling his son to enjoy the pleasures of upper-middle-class life. Nevertheless, the same point applies to Scruton's father as to George Unwin. Social mobility existed in England but its speed was slow and access was extraordinarily narrow. There were buses serving his road but it was necessary to be aware of their existence, to have the fare, and to know the exact timetable. The alternative was a slow trudge in bare feet.

Throughout his book, well written though it is, Scruton ignores the exclusiveness of the England he describes. Access to the law was largely confined to those who could pay. Oxford and Cambridge long remained bastions of the Anglican establishment. English institutions included the press gang, the poor house, and flogging, not to mention hanging. Discrimination between "gentlemen" and "players" cast a cloud over games of cricket until it was removed after the Second World War. Scruton's lament for an England which he thinks is dying if not yet dead is thus an uncritical one. As Herbert Butterfield pointed out many years ago, the Whig interpretation blinds us to the complexity of historical change and leads to self-delusion.

Robert Coll's *Identity of England* (2002) also takes England and the English peoples as its theme. Unlike Scruton, however, he is not moved by a nostalgia for the past "This book," he tells us, "is about how the English have thought about themselves," but his social range is much wider than Scruton's and he takes a more critical view of English history. Unlike Scruton, he welcomes the changes which occurred in postwar England. "Life in England after Porter and [Monty] Python seemed freer as indeed it was." Then he goes on to add that "the new freedom did not touch the central recesses of the state, which was another world" (p. 86).

There are some features common to both books. Coll agrees with Scruton in stressing the importance of the law in the evolution of English identity. Like Scruton he sees Edmund Burke as the unacknowledged master of English law in the House of Commons (p. 26). But then he adds, "this idea of the nation, it has to be said, was extremely convenient for those who could afford the lawyers and rely upon the antiquarians to provide the interpretations." In this connection he refers to the case which the copyholders of the parish of Whickham in County Durham brought in 1620 against the leaseholders of a coalmining area. The copyholders fought their case on "the estimable English grounds of law, custom and a complex view of free, common possession." They lost. In Coll's words, "Whickham parish was now at liberty to become the epicentre of the great northern coalfield and the eye of the industrial storm that was to come." In a revealing passage Coll tells us that Whickham was sitting on thick coal deposits down to three hundred feet. "With free drainage north, west and east, a navigable river and a freebooting lease enforced by a queen and verified by a court, there was no way Whickham's coal owners were going to be denied their English liberty to make money, even if it was at the expense of someone else's English liberty to live by law and custom" (p. 32). Having made this point, however, Coll goes on to qualify it, arguing that the popular nationalist rhetoric of "the Free Born Englishman" was not an empty myth. Here and elsewhere in his book Coll makes his readers aware of the complexities involved in discussing the nature of English identity.

There is a price to be paid for this in the sense that *Identity of England* does not present an overall thesis. Coll is too aware that any generalization he makes needs to be qualified. Perhaps indeed his book should have been entitled "Identities of England." However, as an introduction to key issues facing students of nationalism, it deserves high praise. Coll shows us repeatedly how generalizations based upon the concept of "imagined communities" need to be constantly qualified. He reminds us (p. 153) that "the simple short hand of black and white has become inadequate" in a newly multicultural England. "Indians from north and south, African Asians and sub-continental Asians, Africans, not to mention new-wave immigrants from eastern Europe and Africa, nationalist and religious parties, or the old differences of class and gender—the scope for fragmentation is enormous."

However, it may be that Coll has attempted to cover too much ground in this book. Perhaps indeed it should be read as a collection of essays or on occasions as "pensées" about "the condition of England." Coll's breadth of reading and of allusion recalls the late Raphael Samuel, but as with Samuel the range of reference may at times obscure the overall argument. What is missing in my view from Coll's book is a clear indication of change over time. The reader gets no sense of the importance of the Reformation and of the lasting religious divide in English society. The index under English refers to "Folk Cooking Association," "Folk Dance Society," and "Folk Lore Society" but not to politics or political parties. But surely political allegiance has provided an important clue to the identities of the English.

Richard Weight in his *Patriots: National Identity in Britain 1940–2000* (2002) provides an illuminating contrast to Scruton and Coll. His overall thesis, clearly argued throughout, is the unraveling of British identity from the highwater mark of the Battle of Britain (1940) through the 1960s when political nationalism emerged as a force in Northern Ireland, Wales, and Scotland to the 1990s and the rise of English nationalism. The importance of the Thatcher years (1979–91) is stressed as a period in which Mrs. Thatcher's attempt to impose the framework of a unitary state led to a resurgence of political nationalism, not least in Scotland, where the power of the Conservative Party collapsed. Weight then moves forward to the Blair years during which a Scottish Parliament was established (or reestablished) and a Welsh Assembly was set up. In Northern Ireland a power-sharing executive also introduced a measure of Home Rule. English nationalism made an appearance in the 1990s but attempts to create an English parliament dealing with English affairs failed to get off the ground.

Weight also makes his readers aware that England was one of "four nations" each of which could influence the other. At times, however, his four nations become three nations, the odd man out here being Northern Ireland, whose ambiguous status requires more comment than Weight provides. Northern Ireland surely is a territory, sovereignty over which is disputed between two nations, Great Britain and Ireland. Weight is right, however, to stress the "special relationship" which exists between these two nations.

The four-nation framework used by Weight is more complex than he allows for. International Rugby brings out some of the paradoxes. There is an Irish national team including players from all four provinces. At international matches played in Dublin the Irish national anthem is played, recently supplemented by the song "Ireland" as an unofficial nonpolitical anthem which all players can sing. To make matters more complicated players from the Irish Republic are regularly picked for the multinational team the British Lions, now called "the Lions."

Weight does not use the term "revolution" but the implication of his analysis is that British national identity underwent revolutionary change during the postwar years. "From 1961 to 1964," he tells us, "British national identity was assailed by forces more powerful than any it had undergone before, Americanization, decolonization, black and Asian immigration, Scottish and Welsh nationalism and a drive towards European integration. Despite a desperate and often successful struggle to cling on to national traditions, the period marked the beginning of the end of a relatively homogeneous Britishness mapped out during the Second World War." In this his analysis echoes that of Scruton. Unlike Scruton, however, Weight is optimistic about the future. He believes that the four nations will maintain a contemporary bond through culture and trade, both of which are oiled by a common language.

In Weight's view older symbols of Britishness are now in retreat. "By the early 1990's," Weight tells us, "monarchism was all that was left of Britishness" and even here by the time Blair came to power the monarchy was seen as an essentially English institution largely ignored in Wales and Scotland. Thus the mourning for Diana, Princess of Wales, was "nowhere near as intense or as extensive in Scotland as it was elsewhere on the island." The union flag also was now challenged by flags celebrating distinctive Welsh, Scottish, and even Northern Irish identities. As I write, however, on Day 8 of the Iraq War there seems to be a clear recognition that there is a role for the "British armed forces." In the armed service at least a sense of Britishness has survived while allowing for the existence in the army of distinctive ethnic loyalties.

Weight has some interesting pages (pp. 713–19) on the long-term impact of postwar immigration. He believes that "the clearest sign that the nation's identity was changing was its growing acceptance that to be English you did not have to be white." In particular he criticizes Norman Tebbit's use of the "cricket test" as a way of defining Englishness on the grounds that it denied that ethnic minorities could not have dual identities. In Weight's view, integration does not mean assimilation—"that is, a complete and unquestioning adoption of established notions of Englishness."

There is some confusion in Weight's mind as to whether he is dealing with "the Isles" (that is, the British Isles) or the island of Britain. He is also unclear about whether there are three nations or four. The status of the Republic of Ireland and of the Irish is clearly a problem for him. Thus he writes of the tragedy of the Protestants in Northern Ireland but not of the parallel tragedy of the Catholics. Unlike many historians of Britain, however, he is prepared to grasp the nettle of the problems of Northern Ireland and he has some illuminating pages about it (pp. 525–36). His quotation from Sir John Peck, British Ambassador to the Irish Republic *c.* 1972, is worth noting. "Despite all our kindred and affinity with the Irish, the ignorance of Ireland among the English is even more profound than their ignorance of Europe and the parish priest is a stranger and more sinister phenomenon than the frog's legs and the garlic" (p. 531).

One large question remains to be mentioned—how our authors have treated the role of women in English society. In Scruton's book women are conspicuous by their absence, apart from specific individuals like the author's mother. Scruton is concerned solely with men and more specifically with "gentlemen." He does not mention the fact that women were by and large second-class citizens. Scruton's England is more domesticated and the "elegy" of his title reflects his regret that women have moved toward a measure of equality. Coll, in contrast, discusses women as one of several groups, including "Celts" and "blacks" who were excluded from full membership in English society. In an illuminating section on sports, he reminds us how cricket, rugby, and football, key national symbols, were exclusively male preserves. It was only after female suffrage was achieved in 1918 and 1928 that the situation began to change. Before then, Coll notes, "the identity of women rested on institutions entirely defined by masculine authority—the household, the business, the church and especially the state," and he might have added, the trade unions. Coll makes his point clearly about the exclusion of women from traditional concepts of Englishness, but perhaps is open to criticism for not developing it further. Richard Weight, in contrast, makes his readers fully aware of the radical changes which have taken place in the social and economic status of women since World War II. Until 1948, for example, "a woman who married a foreigner automatically lost her British citizenship because nationality was seen to reside in the male" (p. 78). Full equality for women was still a distant prospect and their rates of pay even in the managerial world remained lower than men's. Overall, however, there were extraordinary changes. Scruton's England, outside certain privileged cases (such as my old college, Peterhouse, which only admitted women students in 1985), was in the death throes. This is not to say that among some groups in the new multicultural Britain, the fight for women's rights may not have to be refought all over again.

And now in conclusion, "the so what question." How significant is our contemporary concern with English national identity? The three books under discussion provide evidence for the fact that the meaning of English national identity has changed, is changing, and will continue to change. This has clear implications for politics, culture, and society within the United Kingdom. As Weight and Coll indicate, the challenges of multiculturalism cannot be ignored, particularly in England. Here the openness of admission into the legal profession is a crucial issue. There are clear signs, however, that this is occurring, for example in the recent appointment of a Sikh judge who will wear his turban rather than the traditional English wig. English law, that bastion of the Whig interpretation, is, it appears, making adjustments appropriate to social change.

NOTES

1. Roger Scruton, *England: An Elegy* (London: Pimlico, 2000); Robert Coll, *The Identity of England* (Oxford: Oxford University Press, 2002); Richard Weight, *Patriots: National Identity in Britain 1949–2000* (London: Macmillan, 2002).

Chapter Ten

England's Irish Enigma

(1997)

Ireland continues to provide a puzzle for the English. Irish immigrants, including would-be bombers like Edward O'Brien, are able to blend without difficulty into the London landscape. English visitors to Ireland find a people who seem to accept English culture as their own in the form of books, newspapers, periodicals, and television. The Irish soccer team was managed successfully by the Geordie, Jack Charlton, known familiarly as "Saint Jack." In Ireland there is a keen interest in English football teams, especially Liverpool and Manchester United. The Irish rugby team regularly includes London Irish expatriates along with Ulstermen. The work of Irish dramatists is enthusiastically received by London critics, most recently in the case of Martin McDonagh's *The Beauty Queen of Leenane.* The Irish are a familiar and welcome presence at English race courses. It is small wonder that the average Englishman is bemused when he reads of the I.R.A. praising the courage of one of their bombers for his dedicated work in "enemy territory." There seem to be two Irelands, one of which is a good neighbor, the other a bitter foe.

There are indeed several Irelands "out there," a Protestant anglicized Ireland, a Catholic Celtic Ireland, an Irish-American Republican Ireland all undergoing change, all seeking a voice. (In parenthesis, it may also be said that to Irish eyes there are also several "Englands," one of which came into view when English football supporters rioted recently at Lansdowne Road.) The Ireland of which the English (more specifically the London literary establishment) is most aware is "John Bull's Other Island" in which anglophile sentiments seem to predominate. It is a viewpoint presented ideally by the memory of Brendan Bracken, the Irishman who transformed himself (almost) into an English public schoolboy and who, despite his Fenian background, became confidant and adviser to Winston Churchill. The names of several latter-day Brackens come to mind, Irishmen or women, who have become more English than the English themselves. Anglophile Ireland, or at least a heavily anglicized Ireland, has deep historic roots. English influence is there to be recognized in the common law (still the basis of Irish law), in the Georgian architecture of Dublin, and to some extent in the form taken by Irish parliamentary institutions. English is still the language of preference for most Irish people.

The term "Anglo-Irish" came into usage during the late nineteenth century to describe those who wished to preserve the link with Britain against the attack of Irish nationalism. After the establishment of the Irish Free State in 1921 Yeats became the most influential spokesman for what was an increasingly powerless minority. In a speech to the Irish Senate, Yeats defended the Anglo-Irish tradition. Attacking government censorship and antidivorce legislation, he declared

> We against whom you have done this thing are no petty people. We are one
> of the great stocks of Europe. We are the people of Burke: we are the people
> of Grattan: we are the people of Swift, the people of Emmet, the people of
> Parnell.

Yeats saw the Anglo-Irish tradition as representing a bridge between two cultures. He and the names he mentions form part of any attempt to make sense of the present-day relationship between England and Ireland. It is not the whole picture, however. The great majority of the Anglo-Irish were not nationalist sympathizers like Yeats but Unionists of the Ascendancy who sought careers in the institutions of the British empire, especially the Army and the Indian Civil Service. "Rebels" were no more numerous among their ranks than Wykehamists like Gaitskell or Crossman were in the British Labour Party. More typical of the Anglo-Irish Ascendancy were the Duke of Wellington and Lord Palmerston.

The power and prestige of this tradition disappeared in the south after independence in 1921. It survived, however, north of the border, where the future Field-Marshals Dill, Brooke, Alexander, and Montgomery were born.

Indeed if we look for "John Bull's Other Island" today we should look no further than Northern Ireland. The literary relationship between England and Ireland is one thing, the political relationship is another. What survived in Northern Ireland until 1972 was a Protestant Ascendancy which once characterized the whole island. When English commentators discuss Northern Ireland, they usually do so in uncomprehending terms. How is it possible, they ask, for such tribalism to survive in the twentieth century? They fail to realize that "No Popery" was a key element in the English national identity from the sixteenth century onward. As Linda Colley has recently argued, it became the unifying factor behind a "British" national identity in the second half of the eighteenth century. What survives in Northern Ireland is thus the remnant of the once dominant political ideology of the United Kingdom. We should scarcely be surprised if it still remains strong in Ulster, within a Protestant community which sees itself threatened by the onset of "Popery."

Those attempting to make sense of modern Ireland would do worse than consider the annual ritual of the "Twelfth of July." Rituals and symbols count for a great deal in the maintenance of an identity. In the early nineteenth century the Twelfth of July was celebrated, along with William III's birthday on 4 November, in Dublin as well as in Protestant Ulster. In 1795 an observer described how, on the Twelfth of July in Rathdrum, Co. Wicklow (that is, south of Dublin) "every loyal Protestant house and even many cabins were decorated with Orange lilies." The statue of William III on College Green, Dublin, opposite Trinity College, remained a focus of such sentiment until it was finally blown up in 1929. The Twelfth of July rituals and the marching season which precedes them are the remains of an earlier "No Popery" tradition which stretches back in popular memory to the "massacre" of Protestants by Catholics in 1641 and the siege of Londonderry by the forces of James II in 1689. In England, Guy Fawkes Day has, outside Lewes, largely lost its "No Popery" overtones because Protestantism is no longer seen as defining English national identity. How could it in the multicultural society which England has become? In Northern Ireland, however, "the Twelfth" remains a powerful symbol of political-religious identity and power. As I write (in March 1996), the authorities in Northern Ireland are already seeking a way of avoiding the violent scenes which in 1995 accompanied Orange marches along the Garvaghy Road into Portadown. What is at stake is the future in Ulster of a Protestant Ascendancy which was once centered in Dublin in such institutions as Trinity College, the Cathedrals of St Patrick's and Christ Church, and the various military barracks at strong points throughout the city, and which ruled Northern Ireland from Stormont until 1972.

The Orange Order was a key institution of the Ascendancy. It came into being in 1795 as a landlord-backed response to the United Irishmen, who looked to France for political inspiration. Landlords organized their

Anglican tenants in defense of "Church and King." The Orange Order was thus in origin an Anglican institution confronting the threat of a Republican movement, which united, or hoped to unite, Scottish Presbyterians and Irish Catholics. In the course of the nineteenth century, however, as a resurgent Catholicism came to appear as the main danger to evangelicals, the Order widened its appeal to a more broadly based popular Protestantism. Not every Protestant joined, however. It is interesting to note, for example, that Dr. Ian Paisley is not a member of the Orange Order.

During the nineteenth century, this Protestant Ascendancy found itself challenged by an increasingly powerful Catholic Ascendancy in which the Catholic hierarchy and the parochial clergy exercised leadership. In England, Catholicism, though a scapegoat for "No Popery" agitators, remained politically insignificant. In Ireland, the growing power and prestige of such Catholic bishops as John MacHale, Paul Cullen, Thomas Croke, and William J. Walsh was a political fact with which successive British governments had to reckon. The cry of "Faith and Fatherland" in Catholic Ireland was as powerful as "No Popery" in Protestant circles and Catholicism came to be seen as the basis of Irish identity. The Catholic hierarchy looked to Catholic Europe rather than Protestant Britain. The attitude of the Catholic bishops on such issues as the Italian unification and Bismarck's policy in Prussian-occupied Poland was at odds with that of the British government. During the Great War the Irish Catholic hierarchy, against government wishes, supported the Pope's efforts to arrange a negotiated peace. (Who is to say they were wrong?) On the controversial issue of conscription the Church saw itself as speaking for the Irish people. Its support for Sinn Fein in the general election of 1918 was crucial.

In the new state which was created in 1921 the role of the church became increasingly important. Though never an established church, it was the church of the overwhelming majority within "the twenty-six counties." Such figures as John Charles McQuaid, archbishop of Dublin, and Michael Browne, bishop of Galway, had no doubts about their right to be seen as leaders of the Irish people. In 1951, for example, their criticism of a relatively mild reform proposal, the "Mother and Child" scheme, forced a minister to resign and helped to bring down the government. A Catholic Ascendancy was in place in the south, contrasting with a Protestant Ascendancy in the north.

From this Catholic point of view, Ireland was far from being John Bull's Other Island during the nineteenth century and became even less so during the twentieth. But how was this to be sensed by a visitor to Ireland?

The clearest indication of the importance of the Catholic Church in Ireland was provided by St. Patrick's College, Maynooth, which, founded in 1795 with the aid of a British government grant, became the national seminary for the Irish priesthood, at the center of a system of junior diocesan seminaries. The growing influence of the Catholic Church in the nineteenth century was symbolized by its impressive Victorian Gothic chapel.

A new factor emerged in the late nineteenth century with the rise of a consciousness of things Celtic. The artistic movement known as "the Celtic Renaissance" is associated with Yeats and the Abbey Theatre from the 1890s onward. At the popular level, however, the Catholic Church, which had once stressed the importance of learning English as a means of social mobility for its flock, came to see "Celtic" spiritual values (whatever they were) as a defense against the growing secularism of England. From the 1880s onward, the Church established links with the Gaelic Athletic Association and the Gaelic League.

From the clerical standpoint, Celtic consciousness was seen as contrasting with Anglo-Saxon culture. The Irish language became a symbol of identity as powerful in its own way as the English Crown was for English Protestantism. The teaching of Irish history took on its own distinctive shape. The meeting of St. Patrick and the Druids at Tara (however apocryphal) had no parallel in early English history. In Ireland, Niall of the Nine Hostages (c. 400 A.D.) was seen as the starting point of history. A Golden Age of monastic culture was associated with the monasteries of Clonmacnoise and Glendalough. These were the Irish equivalents of King Arthur, Hengist and Horsa, and the Jarrow of Bede. The coming of the Normans was seen as occurring very late in the day in 1169, long after Irish identity had begun to take shape. The Irish equivalent of dates that every schoolboy was expected to know were 432 A.D. (the arrival of St. Patrick) and 1014 A.D. (when Brian Boru defeated the Danes at Clontarf). The years 597 and 1066 made no sense in Irish history. Thus within the schools of the new Irish Free State a Celtic Irish identity was forged, indeed perhaps invented, on the basis of a history of Ireland, in which Catholicism was linked with a Celtic ideology, much as, in England, Protestantism was associated with the Anglo-Saxon race.

Stormont and Maynooth provide two keys toward an understanding of Ireland. The third, no less significant, is Bodenstown, Co. Kildare. The reputed burial place of Wolfe Tone, Bodenstown symbolizes in the eyes of the Republicans the lasting significance of the French Revolution in Ireland and of the nonsectarian vision of the United Irishmen. In 1794 Tone and his comrades took a vow "never to desist in our efforts until we have subverted the authority of England over our country." The Rebellion of 1798 which they led was marked by atrocity and counteratrocity and though suppressed, was an episode which left its mark upon Irish history much as "1745" did in Scottish history. But whereas 1745, as the last gesture of the Stuarts, passed into legend, "1798" became a political myth of great power, despite the repeated denunciations of the constitutional politician, Daniel O'Connell and of the Catholic hierarchy who consistently opposed the use of force in politics. Within the Protestant Ascendancy and its Orange Order, "1798" was a date to be remembered in fear and horror.

The Republican tradition in Ireland looks back to 1798, "the year of the French" but the real strength of Irish Republicanism from the mid-nineteenth century onward was to be found in the United States. The Great Famine of 1845–48 was a cataclysmic event which transformed the face of modern Ireland. Mass emigration to the United States during the Famine Years and the decades following led to the creation of an Irish-American community among many of whom there was a deep sense of grievance concerning what they regarded as forcible eviction from their native country. To an extent which the English still fail to realize, the Famine was and is seen by many Irish-Americans as an act of genocide. In speeches made in the United States, Gerry Adams is regularly able to use memories of the Famine effectively as part of his political rhetoric. In English and some Irish eyes, the Famine should have passed into history but it has not, and shows no sign of doing so. What is in question is the extent of British government responsibility for the Famine, about which contemporary historians—British, American, Irish, and Australian—are less inclined to give Whitehall the benefit of the doubt than was the case a generation ago. Academic detachment plays little part, however, in the Irish-American Republican tradition. John Mitchel's judgment that the British government was to blame became and remains Republican orthodoxy.

Irish-American Republicanism is clearly a form of "Diaspora Nationalism," the Irish-American equivalent of Zionism. The Rising of 1916 owed a great deal to Irish-American backing, as does the current Sinn-Fein movement in Northern Ireland. Indeed to use the term "Irish-American" is misleading, since the individuals and groups concerned see themselves as "Irish." From the standpoint of "Diaspora Nationalism" it is completely legitimate for the exiled Irish to play a role in the liberation, as they see it, of the native land.

Thus from the 1920s to the 1950s Irish history and politics may be seen as revolving around the three symbols of Stormont, Maynooth, and

Bodenstown. In Northern Ireland a Protestant majority based on Stormont maintained its dominance. However, it was a dominance full of anxiety. In general and local elections, and annually on the Twelfth of July, the ruling élite inculcated a siege mentality among the majority. The Catholic minority of half a million, one third of the population, were regarded as a threat to the state. Not surprisingly a system of apartheid developed, in which the minority found themselves treated as second-class citizens. There is little doubt that at both the official and unofficial levels, Catholics found themselves discriminated against when applying for jobs. Stormont was described as "a Protestant parliament for a Protestant People." In this situation two parallel cultures developed, each with their own symbols, rituals, and educational structures. Two distinctive approaches to history were taught in schools. Each community had its own hospitals. The majority played rugby and soccer, the minority hurling and Gaelic football. The majority looked to Britain and especially to Scotland, the minority to the South, especially Dublin. Among the minority, a nineteenth-century style political culture remained fixed in place with the clergy playing a leadership role. This Faith and Fatherland approach went largely unchallenged. An I.R.A. offensive in the mid-1950s mounted from south of the border petered out in the face of clerical condemnation.

In the South from the 1920s to the 1950s, there was a comparable situation, though here the minority, only 10 percent of the population, did not offer a threat to the regime. The Irish Free State turned in upon itself in an understandable process of nation-building. The nation which emerged from the crucible of rebellion and civil war was one in which Catholic, rural, and Celtic values were dominant. Though the state was in theory secular, in practice a Catholic Ascendancy centered upon Maynooth remained in place. Eamonn De Valera, daily communicant, fluent Irish speaker, and a man with roots in the west of Ireland, kept "Eire" out of World War II and as a result kept changes at bay.

In the 1960s, however, the Republic found itself facing unexpected challenges. Rapid urbanization took place, leading to the expansion of Dublin, Cork, Limerick, and Galway. The Church, geared largely to the needs of a rural society, now had to deal with the problems of sprawling urban estates, the world of Roddy Doyle's novels. The ecumenical approach of Pope John XXIII helped to undermine the attitudes of the Catholic hierarchy. The constitution was amended to remove the clause relating to "the special position" of the Catholic Church in Ireland. The hierarchy began to lose its influence within the universities. Contraception, especially the pill, became a live issue for an urban population. Not least, the influence of British television could not be kept at bay despite the establishment of Telefis Eireann in the early 1960s. Change was also welcomed by De Valera's pragmatic successor, the Dubliner Seán Lemass. In retrospect, however, the key event in ending the Republic's isolationist policy was its decision to enter the Common Market in 1972, a decision backed by an overwhelming majority in a referendum. In the decade which followed, Ireland found a new European role for itself. The Treaty of Rome rather than the Church of Rome now became its point of reference. The Republic also found a new confidence in dealing with its powerful neighbor, the United Kingdom.

Looking back over the past thirty years, the 1960s appear as a decisive decade in the history of the Republic. It was then that a current of liberalism began to appear which has led to the abolition of censorship, the acceptance of contraception, a rise of Irish feminism, and the passing, at a second attempt, of a constitutional referendum legalizing divorce. The dramatic election of Mary Robinson, a young woman of left-wing views, as president symbolized the changes which had taken place since the 1960s. Less obvious at first was the decline in the moral authority of the Church. The number of clerical students and would-be nuns dropped off dramatically. Entry into such religious orders as the Christian Brothers slumped. Numerous clerical scandals added to the sense of unease. Attendance at mass also declined.

What was occurring may be interpreted as a fundamental shift of identity. Since the mid-nineteenth century if not before, Catholicism had been regarded as a basic feature of Irish identity. This no longer seems to be the case. The connection between Celtic values and Catholicism also has been modified. Irish music and dancing have moved out of a parochial setting on to an international stage, as the success of the Chieftains and of Riverdance indicates. A new generation also seems to be turning to the Irish language with a fresh enthusiasm now that it is no longer compulsory in the schools.

North of the border, the 1960s also brought "winds of change." In 1963 the Unionist Party chose as its leader Terence O'Neill, who soon began to cultivate a more liberal image than his successors. Relations improved between Dublin and Stormont and in 1965 a meeting took place between O'Neill and Lemass. Expectations of substantive change arose among the Catholic minority, fueled in part by success of the civil rights movement in the United States. Within the Ascendancy, however, there were feelings of unease which were articulated by a young evangelical minister, Ian Paisley. In June 1966, for example, Paisley led a march in Belfast to protest against the "Romeward trend" of the Presbyterian General assembly. Northern Ireland, indeed, was England's equivalent of the American "Deep South," a society in which small symbolic gestures toward change aroused violent opposition, especially among the equivalent of "poor whites." 1968 proved to be the decisive year. A sense of relative deprivation grew among the minority as their hopes of improvement in such areas as housing, local government, and the siting of a new university (which went to the Unionist stronghold of Coleraine rather than nationalist Londonderry) were disappointed. A civil rights march in October 1968, which the authorities attempted to suppress with water cannon, provided the spark. Events moved rapidly from then on until August 1969 when the Labour government sent British troops to Northern Ireland to prevent further communal violence. Reforms followed—in the allocation of housing, in the political structure of Londonderry, where jerrymandering had been an obvious abuse, and in the abolition of the armed special constabulary (the B-Specials). The situation continued to be unstable, however, and the Stormont government resorted to a last ditch method in August 1971 of reasserting its authority, namely, internment without trial. The result was large-scale violence which led in 1972 to the establishment of direct rule by the British government. A short-lived attempt at a power-sharing government in 1973–74 ended in failure, in the face of fierce opposition from the majority.

In the early 1960s, it looked as if both North and South were modernizing peacefully and under their own terms. As one commentator put it (1967):

> In 1965, after more than forty years of aloofness, the two Irish premiers exchanged visits for the first time, and rational co-operation in matters of common concern may henceforth be expected, a co-operation made easier by the 1966 Free Trade agreement between Dublin and London.

In the South, the promise of the future seemed to be more important than the problems of the past. In Northern Ireland, however, the road to change was more complicated. Here a Protestant Ascendancy faced the problem of sharing power with what it saw as an alien minority. A civil war followed, more prolonged and bitter than its equivalent in southern Ireland during the 1920s. Bloody Sunday (1972) and the Bobby Sands hunger strike of 1981 passed into the popular history of the I.R.A. (and of Diaspora Nationalism). Other incidents, equally horrific, such as the bombing on Armistice

Day 1987, Enniskillen remained fresh in loyalist popular memory, which to some extent had its counterpart of Diaspora Nationalism among the Protestant communities of the Glasgow conurbation. The Twelfth of July retained its power as a symbol of the Protestant Ascendancy.

Looking at the interlocking histories of Great Britain and Ireland during the past century it is clear that profound changes have taken place. Today in both countries the question of "national identity" is under discussion. At the end of the nineteenth century "religion" and "race" were seen as key features of national identity, with "Englishness" and "Irishness" falling on different sides of the divide. Today, after the profound changes which have occurred since the 1960s, it seems clear that Great Britain and the Republic of Ireland are coming to share a common awareness of the importance of a civic as opposed to an ethno-religious national identity. Britain, though retaining a Protestant monarchy and an established Church, is in practice a secular state. The Republic of Ireland retains a commitment to "the Trinity" in its constitution but it too has moved toward a civic secular conception of "Irishness." The great exception to all this is Northern Ireland where as yet majority and minority see themselves in ethno-religious terms as Catholic or Protestant. The symbolism of Stormont and Maynooth still survives there. Republicanism promises a different future. In theory the symbol of Bodenstown represents Wolfe Tone's ideal of a secular, civic nationhood. In practice, however, Sinn Fein also seems to find it impossible to distance itself from sectarianism. Northern Ireland thus still seems to be trapped in a tangle of ethno-religious rivalries from which England (though less so, perhaps, Scotland and Wales) and the Republic of Ireland are managing to escape.

What then is to be the pattern for the future of "England's Irish Enigma"? Perhaps the greatest single change which has occurred since the signing of the Anglo-Irish Agreement in November 1985 is the establishment of regular consultation between London and Belfast. A further step was taken in December 1993 when a joint Anglo-Irish declaration acknowledged that

> the most urgent and important issue facing the people of Ireland, North and South, and the British and Irish Governments together, is to remove the causes of conflict, to overcome the legacy of history and to heal the divisions which have resulted, recognising that the absence of a lasting and satisfactory settlement of relationships between the peoples of both islands has contributed to continuing tragedy and suffering.

On the basis of the Anglo-Irish Agreement and the Joint Declaration, there now seems to be a "special relationship" between Britain and the Republic of Ireland. In many ways, as the opening paragraph of this essay suggested, this situation already exists at an informal level. As the De Valera period passes into history, the ties linking Britain and the Irish Republic may come in for greater emphasis than has hitherto been the case. The role of Irish troops in the First World War, for example, once ignored is now more generously recognized. The refurbishing of the British Army memorial at Islandbridge, Dublin, is a recent instance of such changes of attitude. It may come to be recognized on both sides of the Irish Sea that eight hundred years of interaction, however turbulent, cannot be written off as if they had never existed. Continuity as well as change is a fact of history and Edmund Burke's comment on the American colonies that ties though light as air can be as strong as steel may well apply with even greater force to Anglo-Irish relations. Seamus Heaney has written well of the British dimension in Irish history:

> I grew up in the minority in Northern Ireland and was educated within the dominant British culture. My identity was emphasised then eroded by being maintained in such circumstances. The British dimension, in other words, while it is something that will be resisted by the minority if it is felt to be coercive has nevertheless been a given of our history and even of our geography, one of the places where we all live, willy-nilly. It's in the language. And it's where the mind of many in the republic lives also. (*The Redress of Poetry: Oxford Lectures*)

The presence of a substantial Irish community in Britain also plays a part in sustaining a "special relationship."

What remains to be seen is how far these changes will affect the situation in Northern Ireland. Today, "the North" is a continual reminder of what was the former relationship between Britain and Ireland, an uneasy and unstable mix of colonialism and sectarianism. Northern Ireland indeed may be seen as the Republic's "British Enigma." Do the British really want to move forward toward an equal partnership, a "special relationship," or is the shadow of "John Bull's Other Island" to remain for yet another political generation?

Part II

Contested Ideas of National History

The rise of nationalism in nineteenth-century Europe was closely linked with the idea of national languages (see chapter 5 above). National schools, national literatures, and, not least, national histories soon came to form part of the same pattern. Thus in the United States, the concept of a "manifest destiny" became the basic assumption in the teaching of history in the publicly funded schools. In England "Our Island Story," linked with the rise of the idea of an Anglo-Saxon "race" came to provide the dominant framework of the national narrative. Similarly, within the Irish Free State an Irish version of "Our Island Story" was introduced into the national schools from 1933 onward.

As with the idea of nationhood itself, however, there were almost inevitably conflicting versions of what constituted national history. Within the United States, "the South" created its own version of the national myth. In the United Kingdom the English version of history was challenged in Scotland and Wales. In Ireland, as in France, the Catholic Church's view of the past contrasted sharply with that of the revolutionary tradition. For Catholic churchmen it was the penal period of the eighteenth century which required emphasis. For the Fianna Fail Party the rebellions of 1798, 1848, 1867, and ultimately 1916 formed the basis of the national narrative.

Before the Irish revolution of 1916–21 there was no place for formal history teaching within the national schools. History was considered too sensitive a topic to form part of the curriculum. After the accession to power of De Valera in 1932, however, the situation changed and the key role of Irish history was spelled out almost immediately in the government pamphlet *Notes for Teachers* (1933). At the university level the situation was more complicated, but here also within the National University the influence of nationalism, albeit of a somewhat different cast, was strong (Eoin MacNeill and John Marcus O'Sullivan, former government ministers, were professors at University College, Dublin.) Irish historical teaching within the newly created Irish Free State was thus strongly politicized.

It was against this background that younger historians began to make their voices heard. The leaders of this movement founded the Irish Historical Society and in 1938 the journal *Irish Historical Studies*, which provided a forum for critical articles and reviews. Initially the influence of the journal was confined to a narrow academic circle. From the 1960s, however, amid a wider pattern of intellectual and religious change critical approaches to Irish history began to influence wider circles of the public. The officially sponsored pattern of the past began to lose its clarity of outline. Even the Revolution of 1916 entered the realm of historical controversy after the publication in *Irish Historical Studies* (1961) of a revealing contemporary memorandum by Eoin MacNeill critical of his fellow volunteer leaders.

During the 1970s new history textbooks appeared, encouraging a more critical attitude to entrenched interpretations and in 1989 Roy Foster published a best-selling critical account of Irish history called *Modern Ireland 1600–1972*. It was this situation which led historians such as Desmond Fennell and Brendan Bradshaw to launch a counterattack upon what they termed "revisionism." In Fennell's eyes, the new trends in Irish historiography represented an attack upon the Irish people. Brendan Bradshaw for his part saw the "revisionists" as ignoring the essentially tragic nature of the Irish historical experience. However, as I suggest in my essay *The Irish and Their History* (1994) "revisionism" and the attacks upon it are perhaps better viewed as part of wider patterns of historical debate to be found not merely in Ireland but in the west at large.

My own essays printed here provide examples of such debate. The earliest of them, written in the 1950s, represent an attempt to criticize what I saw as orthodox versions of Irish history. Thus the two essays on mercantilism introduce elements of political complexity into what was presented normally as a straightforward story of colonial domination. The essay on "Ecclesiastical Politics and the Counter-Reformation in Ireland 1618–48" (1959) was based upon a lecture given at University College, Dublin, in memory of Luke Wadding to an audience which included Eamon De Valera and John Charles McQuaid, archbishop of Dublin. It represented a similar attempt to modify a simple narrative of "Faith and Fatherland" by introducing a political dimension.

The most sensitive of all such topics was, and remains, the Great Famine. My article "The Great Famine: Legend and Reality" (1951), though now clearly inadequate in the light of the immense amount of research since lavished on the topic, takes the side of what is now seen as a piece of revisionist history, *The Great Famine* edited by R. D. Edwards and T. D. Williams. The significance of the Great Famine remains and will continue to remain a piece of bitterly contested history as long as John Mitchel's conspiracy theory serves as political rhetoric.

The sensitivity of other episodes in Irish history was revealed clearly in connection with the second centenary of the Rebellion of 1798. Professor Tom Dunne argues in his remarkable book *Rebellions: Memoir, Memory and 1798* (2004) that heritage centers set up in connection with the bicentenary "reinforced the drive to commemorate an acceptable, that is nonviolent, version of the Rebellion, reducing it to the anodyne of 'heritage,' pre-packaged, simplistic and politically correct, fit for mass consumption" (p. 116). He also criticized attempts made by the authorities to play down the sectarian dimension of the Wexford outbreak in order to project an image of democracy and pluralism.

Historians such as Dunne are attempting to challenge an officially propagated version of the Irish past. To denounce such efforts as "revisionist" does a disservice to the critical role of historians. No doubt their voice will not win out against the weight of prevailing opinion, but it is essential that such attempts be encouraged, not denounced as a betrayal of the national cause. National histories, like national languages, are contested symbols of nationhood.

Chapter Eleven

The Irish and Their History

(1994)

In 1907 John Millington Synge met with bitter criticism from the Gaelic League for his alleged insults to Irish womanhood in *The Playboy of the Western World*. In 1926 Sean O'Casey ran into similar trouble in Dublin and New York for certain scenes in *The Plough and the Stars*. Both playwrights are now regarded as leading luminaries of the Irish literary renaissance. During their lifetime, however, their work seemed to touch a sensitive nerve in Irish nationalist circles, much as Caradoc Evans offended Welsh nonconformity during the same period.

Something of a similar sort seems to have occurred, though no doubt on a less elevated literary level, when historians from University College, Dublin lectured in London in the late 1980s. At one session, on "the Flight of the Earls," a member of the audience is said to have protested against the revisionist tone of the lecture by calling out, "For God's sake leave us our heroes." Another speaker was denounced in *The Irish Post* as a West Briton. What the native-born scholars regarded as legitimate historical criticism seemed to London-based Irish exiles to be misleading and offensive.[1] Within Ireland itself a clash between nationalist and revisionist interpretations of Irish history is also in full swing. Something of the same kind may also be discerned in the United States, where Kevin O'Neill recently criticized Roy Foster's study of Irish history for being anglocentric. It would be surprising if Irish communities in Britain remained immune from such tensions.

In recent years, revisionism, in the sense of a critical approach toward received orthodoxy, has been in the ascendant in Irish academic circles. The latest revisionist piece, Professor J. J. Lee's disenchanted look at Irish life in his successful book *Ireland 1912–1985, Politics and Society* (1989), seems to have touched a chord in the Irish public at large. As nationalist rhetoric turned sour and the early hopes of Sinn Féin failed to materialize, a certain skepticism among historians seemed appropriate. Nationalist history in the style of Mary Hayden, Dorothy McArdle, and P. S. O'Hegarty no longer was acceptable.

However, there are now signs of a reaction against what was becoming revisionist orthodoxy. Such controversy in historiography as in other matters, may be seen as a sign of health. In English history, the social interpretation of the English Revolution has been subjected to severe criticism by Conrad Russell, John Morrill, and Jonathan Clark. Among Irish historians, a champion of nationalism against revisionism has now made an appearance in the person of Dr. Brendan Bradshaw, Limerick-born, but now a lecturer at the University of Cambridge. In a recent article, "Nationalism and Historical Scholarship in Modern Ireland" (*Irish Historical Studies*, November 1989), Bradshaw took to task the revisionist school of Irish historians. He described them as having introduced a "corrosive cynicism" into Irish historiography. In his eyes, even the critical methods introduced by T. W. Moody and R. Dudley Edwards in the 1930s and hitherto much praised, served to inhibit rather than enhance the understanding of the Irish historical experience. Bradshaw resents especially the way in which the revisionists reject "the controlling conception of nationalist historiography, the notion of a 'nationalist past' of Irish history as the story of an Irish nation unfolding historically through the centuries from the settlement of the aboriginal Celts to the emergence of the national polity of modern times."

Perhaps the most surprising aspect of Bradshaw's antirevisionist critique is his use of Herbert Butterfield's argument that the English Whig interpretation, despite its being a historical myth, provided "a beneficient legacy" which enabled the English to avoid the horrors of revolutionary change on the French model. Echoing Butterfield's phraseology, Bradshaw asks the question, "Is the received [the nationalist] version of Irish history a beneficient legacy—its wrongness notwithstanding—which the revisionists with the zeal of academic puritans are seeking to drive out?" His answer is in the affirmative. For Bradshaw the function of the Irish historian is to enable "a progressively more heterogeneous national community to appropriate the rich heritage of the aboriginal Celtic civilization."

These are disturbing words coming from an academic historian and not less so for appealing to the authority of Butterfield. The voice may be the voice of Herbert but the hands are the hands of Machiavelli. Bradshaw in effect is stating that the historian's duty is to propagate a myth, despite its wrongness, for the sake of its supposedly beneficient consequences. This is surely the role of the politician or the journalist, not that of a scholar. The problem which it raises is not of course confined to Ireland. It was discussed in the pages of this journal (*HWJ* 29) by Jonathan Clark who argued that school history was "an initiation into a culture by the transmission of a heritage." For him, popular history (termed by Bradshaw "public history") is "a battlefield in a battle for cultural hegemony" between left and right. History, it would appear, should *either* be a story of achievement, advance, and enlightenment *or* a version emphasizing exploitation, suffering, and poverty, but not both. There is no room apparently for ambiguity. This is bowdlerized history of a paternalist kind, taking a pessimistic view of the capacity of pupils in their early teens to deal with complexity in history, even though they might very well be dealing with some measure of complexity, at that moment, in literature. It is to study William the Conqueror at the level of Just William. The study of literature in the schools has long since abandoned the approach of Mr. Bowdler. It would be sad if historians were to attempt to fill the gap with mythological history, however well-intentioned.

In reducing history to the level of myth, Bradshaw does not seem to have considered that what is sauce for the Irish goose is also sauce for the English gander. The Irish cannot complain in good faith about the persistence of long-standing myths about Irish history on one side of the Irish Sea if they are happily purveying the equivalent on the other. For Irish emigrants the beneficient legacy of such myths might be far from apparent.

Bradshaw's apparently innocent advocacy of traditional nationalism is thus open to serious criticism. It must be admitted, however, that his own hostile view of the revisionists, or some of them, is not unjustified. He is right to draw attention to the neglect of what he terms the catastrophic element in Irish history, exemplified in the long tale of massacre, conquest, and colonization during the sixteenth and seventeenth centuries. Revisionists have also played down the tragic dimension of the Great Famine of 1845–48 and the miseries of mass emigration which accompanied it. Bradshaw seems to go too far, however, in his wish to play down the role of the historian as critic. He seems to be calling for the restoration of a pantheon of Irish heroes from Brian Boru to Patrick Pearse. His reference to "the rich heritage of the aboriginal Celtic civilization" is comparable to an English romantic's wish to return to the glories of Anglo-Saxon England.

The truth is that despite Bradshaw's criticisms, the revisionists have made a major contribution to our understanding of the Irish past. The Institute of Advanced Studies founded by Eamonn De Valera proved to be a veritable revisionist seminary, with T. F. O'Rahilly's famous (or infamous) lecture on "The Two St Patricks" as its opening salvo. Later scholars followed his lead. Donnchadh Ó Corráin showed how the myth of Brian Boru as a nationalist hero was manufactured by official historians of the O'Briens. Fr. Paul Walsh in one of the early issues of *Irish Historical Studies* provided a historical criticism of a bardic life of Hugh Roe O'Donnell, showing in the process how new mythologies were created in early modern Ireland. Maureen Wall, a fine Gaelic-speaking historian who died prematurely, constructed a powerful revisionist interpretation of the Penal Laws. The volume of essays on the Great Famine, edited by T. D. Williams and R. D. Edwards, for all its lack of a tragic dimension, was the first serious attempt to criticize the nationalist view, as put forward by John Mitchel, that the Famine was planned by the British government. Theo Hoppen, in a detailed study of Irish elections during the nineteenth century, has drawn attention to the importance of local issues in deciding the outcome of parliamentary elections. In recent years traditional views about Protestant proselytism and "taking soup" have also come under criticism. Ruth Dudley Edwards's biography of Pearse, *The Triumph of Failure*, is criticized by Bradshaw for its revisionism. To me it seems an admirable work which treats Pearse as a human being rather than a plaster saint, and hence all the more heroic. All this work, and much else unmentioned, suggests that "revisionism" is merely a shorthand term for modern historiography.

What the revisionists have done is remind us that history should be a matter for rational debate, not a matter of dogma, whether religious or political. Bradshaw is right to draw attention to the significance of the Irish language and of the Celtic tradition. But as with all traditions there are ambiguities and contradictions. Are human sacrifice, blinding, polygamy, "cursing" to be considered part of the "rich heritage"? Are the marriage customs of Tory Island, as described by Robin Fox, part of this Celtic heritage? And what about "the wake" which the Church finally succeeded in stamping out after many centuries? (To many the healing rituals of the wake must have been welcome.) It is an open question whether very much remains of the Celtic heritage today in the Irish Republic, influenced as it is by English common law, the Roman Catholic Church, the United States, and the European Community.

Bradshaw seems to recognize that much of nationalist teaching about Irish history is mythical. However, he wishes to retain myth, or "public history" as he sometimes terms it, because of its "beneficent legacy." One obvious problem is who decides what is beneficent. (For Jonathan Clark this decision rests with the politicians.) For many the legacy of Irish nationalism is not as self-evidently beneficent as Bradshaw seems to believe. Yeats was not alone in thinking that the legacy of nationalism after 1922 was one of civil war and denominational narrowness, from which the Republic is only now beginning to emerge. When we look north of the Irish border it becomes even more difficult to speak easily of the beneficient legacy of myth. Bradshaw calls for a return to the nationalist tradition of Eoin MacNeill, but MacNeill's own words on the decision to carry out a Rising in 1916 seem "revisionist" in spirit. In February 1916 he wrote:

> We have to remember that what we call our country is not a political abstraction, as some of us, in the exercise of our highly developed capacity for figurative thought are sometimes apt to imagine—with the help of our patriotic literature. There is no such person as Caithlín Ní Uallacháin or Roisín Dubh or the Sean-Bhean Bhocht, who is calling upon us to serve her. What we call our country is the Irish nation which is a concrete and visible reality. ... I do not know at this moment whether the time and circumstances will yet justify revolutionary action but of this I am certain that the only basis for successful revolutionary action is deep and widespread popular discontent. We have only to look around us in the streets to realise that no such condition exists in Ireland. A few of us, a small proportion who think about the evils of English government in Ireland, are always discontented. We would be downright fools if we were to measure many others by the standard of our own thoughts.[2]

Bradshaw accuses the revisionists of attempting "to extrude national consciousness as a dimension of the Irish historical experience from all but the modern period." Here he raises an issue which is fundamental for all nationalist historians, namely, the question how far back in time can we trace national consciousness. As the vast historical literature concerning nationalism illustrates, we are entering an extremely problematic area. What is a nation? What is the criterion of belonging? Language? Religion? Class? Race? How many individuals can be said to be conscious of belonging to a particular nation at any one period? If 99 percent of the inhabitants of Ireland in 1014 saw themselves in terms of local feudal, tribal, or social identities, does it make historical sense to speak of "national consciousness"? Robin Dudley Edwards was fond of quoting Michael

Oakeshott's dictum, "History is what the evidence obliges us to believe." We are not obliged to believe in an extended sense of national consciousness in the age of Brian Boru.

When we come to the modern period further difficulties remain. Bradshaw speaks throughout his article of a single nationalist tradition of historical interpretation. It is clear even to an outsider that serious differences exist about the criterion of nationhood. Fr. Tom Burke said in 1872:

> Take an average Irishman—I don't care where you find him—and you will find that the very first principle in his mind is "I am not an Englishman because I am a Catholic." Take an Irishman wherever he is found all over the earth and any casual observer will at once come to the conclusion "Oh he is an Irishman, he is a Catholic." The two go together.

The beneficent legacy of such a view of Irish nationality is very much open to question in the eyes of those who admire the United Irishmen and the Young Irelanders. The role of the historian is surely to stand outside all of these traditions and to attempt to view them critically but sympathetically, to rescue them, in Edward Thompson's words, "from the enormous condescension of posterity."

It may be that some historians in an excess of zeal have erred more on the side of criticism than sympathy. However, to dismiss as Bradshaw does the modern critical tradition of Irish historical scholarship from 1938 onward, the date of the founding of *Irish Historical Studies*, seems to be extraordinarily idiosyncratic. It involves ignoring, for example, the distinctive revisionist tradition in early Irish history, unrelated to *Irish Historical Studies*. Binchy (1900–89), whom many would regard as the Irish Maitland, was an arch revisionist in this field. He was well aware that his critical articles would have little effect upon widely held myths about the "instant Christianization" of Ireland and he commented ruefully upon the way in which high Irish ecclesiastics provided a diet of myth rather than history during the papal visit. Patrician studies are surely one of the areas in which the revisionists made a definite contribution.

All this may seem remote to the readers of *History Workshop Journal*. What is at stake, however, is the status of history as a detached scholarly activity. Brendan Bradshaw, following in the wake of the late Herbert Butterfield, claims a privileged position for a particular interpretation of Irish history. He advocates a return to the nationalist tradition of Eoin MacNeill and Edmund Curtis, and a rejection of what he terms the revisionist "value-free" interpretation of modern Irish historiography. Not all revisionism is rejected. Bradshaw attempts to have it both ways in this regard by approving a short list of those historians who have shown the appropriate qualities of empathy and imagination. But suppose, as seems to be the case with Professor Lee, they are orthodox in one book and revisionist in another?

The truth is that Bradshaw's attempt to turn the clock back to the "golden oldies" like MacNeill and Curtis is seriously misleading. For they in terms of their own time were also revisionist. We should discard the concept of revisionism itself and return to the notion of historical scholarship as an endless debate, in which it is possible to discuss people and movements in a spirit of relative detachment. Two examples of such history come to mind. My friend and colleague Robin Dudley Edwards used to recommend J. F. Kenney's introduction to *The Sources for the Early History of Ireland: Ecclesiastical* to all newcomers to Irish history. It is still excellent advice. I would also add the various essays by Daniel Binchy in *Studia Hibernica*. Kenney and Binchy seem to me to be examples of historians who transcend the categories of "nationalist" and "revisionist."

We are still left with the problem with which we began, namely, how to reconcile the critical comments of Irish-born historians with the sensitivities of the emigrant Irish in Britain, the United States, and elsewhere. The answer to this is surely not to return to the violent prejudices of "the day of the rabblement." The Irish and their friends must learn to see Irish history in a multidimensional context rather than as partisan simplicities (as must of course the English).

It is also worth pointing out in conclusion that Bradshaw has raised an issue which, though relevant to Kilburn in 1991, is as old as the Renaissance and Reformation, namely, the moral role of history. Hugh Trevor-Roper in his Neale lecture on William Camden, "Queen Elizabeth's First Historian," showed how Camden was pressed by the Puritans to depict Mary Queen of Scots as an example of moral depravity rather than as a human being caught up in a tangled web of events. It was the Puritans who saw history in clear-cut terms of black and white with Foxe's *Book of Martyrs* as their favorite text. By this criterion, Bradshaw is laying himself open to the very charge of puritanism which he levels at others. History makes strange bedfellows.

NOTES

1. Quoted in Jonathan Moore, "Historical Revisionism and the Irish in Britain," *Linen Hall Review*, vol 5. no 3 (Autumn 1988), pp. 14–15. See also "Irish Dimensions in British Education." Report on 6th, National Conference, 11 Feb. 1989, published by Soar Valley College, Leicester.

2. F. X. Martin, "Select Documents: Eoin MacNeill on the 1916 Rising," *I.H.S.* xii (1960–61), pp. 239–40.

Chapter Twelve

Mercantilism and Ireland, 1620–40

(1958)

I

"MERCANTILISM" is a term which is capable of arousing much the same kind of unfruitful discussion among economic historians as the question of universals among the medieval schoolmen, and a disputation on the question "what was mercantilism?" would be out of place here. A somewhat unfashionable definition may serve as a text from which to diverge if necessary.

> The object of the mercantile system was the creation of an industrial and commercial state in which by encouragement or restraint imposed by a central authority, private and sectional interests should be made to promote national strength and independence.[1]

In many ways, this definition is open to criticism. It assumes, mistakenly in my opinion, that seventeenth-century governments were less hard-pressed by particular circumstances and more free to take the initiative, than was the case. It makes little allowance for the fact that industry and trade were frequently regulated by seventeenth-century governments for financial reasons rather than for long-term motives of national interest, in the case, for example, of monopolies. It does not take into account the variations in mercantilist theory and practice, which occurred from time to time, and from place to place. And it leaves out what many historians would regard as an essential feature of mercantilism, namely, its association with times of economic crisis. Finally, it exaggerates the systematic character of mercantilism and ignores the way in which the laws and proclamations of the mercantilist period resemble plugs inserted haphazard into a dyke in time of flood, which only assume a pattern in the minds of engineers of a later generation.

Nevertheless, despite its drawbacks, this definition of "mercantilism" is a useful historical generalization, which, for several reasons, forms a suitable background to a paper on the economic history of Ireland in the first half of the seventeenth century. In the first place, it is a reminder that the centralization and regulation, which were taking place in Ireland during these years, were also taking place in other parts of Western Europe. Ireland provides an example at home of the tensions which existed abroad, in such regions as Catalonia, the two Sicilies, the Seven United Provinces, Bohemia, the Spanish Netherlands—everywhere, in short, where a central authority and local economic interests came into conflict.

In the second place, the contrast between the theory of mercantilism and what actually happened can be seen at first hand in Irish history. This gap between the aims of a Wentworth and his actual accomplishments, may throw some indirect light upon the career of a Colbert. Thirdly, mercantilism provides a suitable point from which to approach Irish economic history during this period and one which involves only a limited amount of distortion, since there were few aspects of Irish economic life which were left untouched by decisions taken, or regulations made, by the English privy council. Wool, linen yarn, timber, iron, salt, beer, cattle, wine, and wheat—all these at one time or another came under the direction of the privy council. During the Spanish war (1626–30) all Irish trade with Spain was prohibited by its order. In addition, Ireland was regarded by the privy council as providing an outlet, however unwilling, for England's surplus population. In short, the Irish economy during this period formed part of a wider whole in which England was the chief partner, and the relationship between the two societies therefore inevitably raised issues which were mercantilist, according to our definition.

And yet this mercantilist relationship had only really come into being since 1600. The authority of the English privy council was effectively asserted over the whole country only in the years following the battle of Kinsale in 1601; and the process of centralization was demonstrated in the economic sphere for the first time in 1613 with the setting up of a general farm of the Irish customs. The main ports of Ireland which had hitherto been autonomous, so far as the collection of customs revenue was concerned, were now brought under a central authority, namely, the farmers appointed by the English privy council. Stated in terms of mercantilism, this was an example of the way in which "private and sectional interests" were forced to give way before a centralizing power. The picture was not simple, however. Imposts on certain articles like wine were collected by farmers who were independent of the main customs farm, while the licences for the export of linen yarn and wool also came under a separate administration, even though the payments made for these were the equivalent of additional customs duties. Nor were all the ports of the kingdom included in the general farm, since those of Ulster lay outside it. Thus, centralization was still far from complete and remained so for the twenty years 1613–33. Under Thomas Wentworth, however, the customs arrangements were fully centralized. The Ulster outports were incorporated within the great farm, the wine and other monopolies were brought in, and the lord deputy himself took over the customs administration from 1635 onward. The result was that an increased proportion of customs receipts went into the Irish exchequer during the years of rapidly rising revenue and not into the pockets of the customs farmers, though Wentworth himself took a percentage for his pains.

The centralization of the Irish customs which occurred during the early seventeenth century and particularly during Wentworth's deputyship, was an example of mercantilism in practice. A political price for these economic changes was to be paid, however, in 1640, when Wentworth was impeached on charges which were brought against him in part by groups of merchants, customs farmers, and planters whose "private and sectional" interests had suffered during the course of Wentworth's deputyship.

II

The establishment of the Irish customs farm may be termed an example of mercantilist administration. I turn now to a piece of mercantilist legislation which throws light upon the manner in which particular mercantilist measures came to be formulated.

In 1621, during the third parliament of James I, a bill was read twice and sent to committee "to prohibit the importation of Irish cattle into England and exporting of bullion out of England into Ireland under pain of forfeiture of ship and cattle."[2] The parliament came to an end before the bill was passed and nothing more was heard of it. Nevertheless it is worth discussion, since it belonged to a historical context which produced the classic mercantilist works of Mun, Malynes, and Misselden, and is in itself a remarkable example of English policy toward Ireland drawn up amid general mercantilist debate, and not, as is sometimes implied, in a separate "anti-Irish" compartment.

The years before and after 1621 were a time of profound economic crisis in England and the debates of the 1621 parliament were largely taken up with ways and means of escaping from the commercial depression. In May 1621 Sir Edward Coke was uttering a cliché when he said "Divide our native commodities into ten parts and nine arise from the sheeps' back."[3] And yet it was precisely the woolen cloth industry which was in the doldrums and with it, the major part of the economy. Sir Edwin Sandys wondered, "If ploughs be rested, cattle unsold, grazing decay, trade perish, what will follow but confusion?"[4]

The shortage of coin was blamed, in part, for the crisis, and suggestions naturally turned upon the way in which a more favorable balance of trade could be brought about, by which more coin would be attracted into the country. Those avenues of trade were especially criticized which resulted in bullion being exported abroad and a list of fourteen such nationally undesirable import trades was drawn up—Polish corn, Spanish tobacco, gold and silver thread, gold foil, the spice trade of the East India Company, and excessive wine imports, all branches of trade which could be carried on only by exporting bullion. "A ninth reason was assigned to be the bringing in of Irish cattle, for which they transported money and did not turn it into commodities" (that is, import English goods in exchange).[5] "A tenth reason was the bringing in of Scottish cattle in like manner."

Thus the proposed Irish cattle bill makes its first appearance not as an isolated act of economic aggression against Ireland but as one of a number of defensive and remedial measures designed to restore the English economy to some measure of health, though the diagnosis was not of course necessarily correct.

The debates which took place on the bill in the house of commons give no indication that there was any animus against Ireland as such. The arguments brought forward on both sides were, as might have been expected, economic in character, rather than political or religious. The Irish cattle trade was discussed as an economic phenomenon in much the same way as that of the East India Company, and for the same reasons—its effect on the export of bullion. Cranfield, the lord treasurer, who spoke in favor of the bill was supported by those members who sat for areas which were particularly affected by direct Irish competition—namely, the counties of the western seaboard, Lancashire, Cheshire, Wales, and Somerset. Sir Robert Phelips (Bath) was speaking for the farmers of Somerset when he said that (the Irish) "underselling of us undoes all grasiers and gentlemen in their lands."[6] Sir Richard Grosvenor (Chester) spoke in similar vein in favor of the bill on behalf of the dairy farmers of Lancashire and Cheshire.[7] Two Welsh members also spoke. Sir William Herbert (Co. Montgomery) who had been a planter in Kerry[8] said that Wales would be overthrown if Irish cattle were not prohibited[9] while Sir James Parrott (Haverfordwest, Co. Pembroke) favored the bill, though in a less downright fashion.

On the other hand, there were voices raised against the bill. Three of them were those of members who were, or had been, connected with Ireland. Sir John Jephson, who was a member of the Irish privy council and a planter in his own right in Mallow, Co. Cork, pleaded that it was only by exporting cattle that the Irish could pay for the imports from England, on which they depended.[10] The second voice was that of Sir John Davies (Newcastle-under-Lyme) who had been attorney-general in Ireland from 1606 to 1619 and who had played a prominent part in the plantation of Ulster. He put forward various reasons to show why the bill should not be passed—that "whatsoever is good or bad for Ireland is so for England also" and that Ireland was "a growing commonwealth and should not be supprest in the bud and nippt."[11] The third voice was that of William Towerson (City of London) a member of the Skinners' Company who had been involved in the Londonderry plantation. His argument, however, did not mention Ireland as such, but merely "the necessity in London of Irish beef"[12]—the growing population of the capital would be chiefly concerned about the price of its meat and not where it came from.

Not all those who spoke against the bill, however, were connected with Ireland. A member called Neale spoke on behalf of the Devon fishing fleets which were victualed by Irish beef for their annual voyage to the Newfoundland cod fisheries.[13] Sir Thomas Wentworth (Yorkshire), later lord deputy of Ireland, spoke against prohibiting the import of Irish cattle, though he did wish to prevent the export of bullion in payment. He attacked those who had supported the bill out of their own economic advantage—"though divers gentlemen in their own particular interests may have advantage by this bill yet we must remember for whom we serve, many corporations who have benefit by the cheapness of the meat."[14] Sir Dudley Digges, a prominent member of the opposition, also echoes this note—"We must remember the places we serve for as our private benefit but we must look to the public good. Our lands decay and we must not so much look to the loss of particulars but to the decay of the general good and riches of the King-

dom."[15] Both Wentworth and Digges therefore grounded their opposition to
the bill on the grounds that it was against the common good.

The pros and cons of the debate were summed up as follows:

> Pro. Ireland is our younger sister and it is fit to keep her as a younger sister.
> Our lands do fall by means thereof and theirs increase. Our beefs are noth-
> ing cheaper but store of money is carried thither. The grazier is undone etc.
> They hoard up our money there etc.

> Contra. But it will make beef and mutton dear, hurt tradesmen and all. Let
> not farmers and gentlemen aim only at their private profit: though money
> be carried from hence, yet it comes hither again. For their chief commodities
> come from hence. We have thence store of beef and tallow for our ships etc.[16]

It is clear from the debate that "England" did not speak with one voice
so far as this particular piece of economic policy was concerned. There
was no one English mercantilist outlook to justify the passing of the Cattle
Bill. Cranfield and Sandys were on one side, Digges and Wentworth were
on the other, but they all used arguments which can be described as mercantilist. If the bill had been passed, it would have been a mercantilist
measure. If it had been defeated, it would have been on mercantilist
grounds. In short, mercantilism was not one definite policy so much as a
general climate of opinion in which wide variations could exist at the
same time, even where Ireland was concerned.

III

The best-known instance of English mercantilist policy toward Ireland,
however, is that provided by the career of Thomas Wentworth, lord
deputy of Ireland from 1633 to 1640. Heckscher, the historian of mercantilism, suggested a possible comparison between Wentworth and Colbert,[17]
which, in view of Wentworth's administrative energy and ability, is not too
far-fetched. In support of his assessment, there are passages in Wentworth's
official despatches which in their decisiveness suggests that Wentworth
adopted the same type of long-term mercantilist policy which Colbert is
said to have attempted in France over thirty years later.

The three letters upon which this view of Wentworth is based in the main,
were written in 1633, 1634, and 1636, respectively. The first, written on 16
July 1633 by Wentworth to Charles I, contained the following passage:

for this is a Ground I take with me that to serve Your Majesty completely well in Ireland, we must not only endeavour to enrich *them* but make sure still to hold them dependent upon the Crown and not able to subsist without *us*; which will be effected by wholly laying aside the manufacture of Wools into Cloth or Stuff there and by furnishing them from this Kingdom, the Wools there grown and the Cloths there worn, thus paying double Duties to your Crown in both Kingdoms.[18]

It is this letter which is responsible for the view, expressed in so many textbooks of Irish history, that Wentworth destroyed the Irish cloth industry. In itself, however, the letter is not decisive. It was written at Chester before he arrived in Ireland and needs further corroboration before it can be valued as anything more than the kind of grandiose and uninformed plan which many a new lord deputy took with him to Dublin, only to forget within a few weeks.

After six months in Ireland, in fact, Wentworth did come to think differently. In January 1633–34, he wrote to Coke, the English secretary of state, asking for a warrant to enable him to grant export licences for wool, on the grounds that "they have no means here to manufacture it themselves so as the commodity would be utterly lost unto the Growers, unless this expedient be granted."[19] Two conclusions may be drawn from this letter. It shows, in the first place, how little his own master the lord deputy was in economic matters, and secondly, that Wentworth now denied the very existence of an Irish cloth industry which he had been so anxious to destroy six months before.

As I see it, neither of these letters provides a complete picture. The English port books for Bristol, Chester, and other Western English ports show that Irish friezes were imported in quantity into England. "Friezes" were a type of loosely woven cloth, which did not compete with the more finely woven fabrics, perpetuanoes, sempiternums, and the like, of Devon, Somerset, Wiltshire, and Gloucestershire; and they continued to be imported into England during Wentworth's period of office, without licence. I know no evidence which suggests that Wentworth interfered in any way with this Irish cloth industry.

On the other hand, though an Irish cloth industry did exist, it did not absorb all the raw wool which was produced in Ireland. A great quantity of raw wool was available for export and it was this which Wentworth had in mind, almost certainly under pressure from the wool growers, when he wrote to Coke early in 1634 asking for a warrant to grant licences.

The nearest market for Irish wool was via the ports of Youghal and Dublin to the Devon ports of Barnstaple, Bideford, and Minehead and so to the cloth industry of southwest England. This was what a nineteenth-century economist might have called the "natural" market for Irish wool. In the circumstances of the early seventeenth century, however, wool was not allowed to find its way there freely according to the laws of supply and demand. The wool trade was, in fact, closely regulated, and wool export licences provided both a source of revenue for the Irish exchequer and a method of ensuring that Irish wool was not exported elsewhere than England. The reason for this strict control was not far to seek. Irish wool was a marginal source of supply for the cloth industry of southwest England. In good years it was badly needed, while, in bad years, the English privy council did not allow Irish wool growers to find a market abroad, even though there might be a glut of wool in England. For example, in the bad year of 1621, the clothiers of Somerset sent a deputation to the English house of commons, blaming the decline of the cloth industry upon the illicit exportation of Irish and Scots wool to the Netherlands. "Except it please God to send wars in the low countries," they said, "they will beat us out of trade."[20] Under pressure of this kind, the English privy council did not lighten the system of control in any way. Similarly, in the good year of 1635, Coke wrote to Wentworth attacking the smuggling of Irish wool abroad "especially at this time when we are able to convert into cloth all the wools we can get."[21] He went on to suggest ways in which the licensing system could be made more effective.

In all this, the initiative lay not in Dublin Castle, but in Whitehall. Wentworth introduced no change of importance, and in view of the revenue derived from wool licences it was unlikely that he would wish to change the system. What he may have been able to do, however, was to enforce it more efficiently than his predecessors. Figures provided in 1640 show that there was a sharp rise in the amount of licensed wool exported from Ireland during Wentworth's deputyship and while the reasons for this may be partly sought in an absolute increase of trade, it is also likely that it was a reflection of Wentworth's efficient administration. So far as the regulation of the wool trade was concerned, Wentworth was certainly a mercantilist, but he brought about no new or striking departure from the policy of his predecessors or of the English privy council.

In assessing his mercantilism, however, one further avenue remains to be explored, based upon letters which he wrote in 1634 and in 1636. In 1634 he wrote to Portland, the English lord treasurer, stating that he intended to prevent the manufacture of wool in Ireland,[22] and he was still of this opinion in 1636 during his visit to England. In his report to the English privy council in that year,[23] he stated his case in unmistakable mercantilist terms:

> there was little or no manufacture amongst them, but some small beginnings towards a clothing trade which I had and so should still discourage all I could, unless otherwise directed by his Majesty and their lordships, in regard it would trench not only upon the clothing of England, being our staple commodity, so as if they should manufacture their own wools, which grew to very great quantities, we should not only lose the profit we made now by indraping their wools but his Majesty lose extremely by his customs. … Yet have I endeavoured another way to set them on work and that is by bringing in the making and trade of linen cloth.

He went on to describe how he had imported workmen, looms, and flax seed into Ireland. In short, Wentworth said that he had discouraged the manufacture of woolen cloth, but as a compensation had introduced the manufacture of linen.

It was understandable that Wentworth should not encourage the development of an Irish cloth industry,[24] in the sense of a manufacture producing a finer type of cloth than the friezes. His outlook was hardly his own, however, so much as that of the English privy council and even had he wished to encourage the manufacture of woolen cloth, it is scarcely conceivable that he would have been allowed. In 1622, a committee sent to investigate the state of Ireland had recommended the encouragement of a cloth manufacture, but nothing had come of this suggestion, in view of the industrial crisis and unemployment in the English clothing counties. It would be unprofitable to pursue the matter further, but even had Wentworth tried to set up cloth manufacture in Ireland, I find it difficult to believe that he would have been more successful than he was with his economic excursions into iron-smelting, trade with Spain, and above all, linen weaving. And those Irish historians who attack Wentworth on this score may perhaps be reminded that a cloth industry set up in Ireland to produce an English type of cloth would presumably have been no more "Irish" than Richard Boyle's ironworks. A successful cloth manufacture would have been the industrial equivalent of a "plantation."[25]

It is, however, Wentworth's attempt to found a linen industry in Ireland which provides the best commentary upon his mercantilism. Wentworth did not of course claim to have established the spinning of linen yarn. This was an old industry which, during the early seventeenth century, was concentrated in Ulster. There, the spinning of linen yarn was a domestic industry, catering not merely for the home market, but also for export to Lancashire, where mixed with cotton wool, it served to produce the fustian goods which at this period were the characteristic products of industrial Lancashire.[26] The main ports of exit were Drogheda, Dundalk, Derry, Coleraine, and Carrickfergus; the English staple ports were Chester and Liverpool, "no other place being allowed for landing the same."[27] The trade was organized as a monopoly and no yarn could be exported without a licence from John West, the patentee.

What Wentworth tried to do was to introduce a weaving industry on his own account. He took steps to ban the export of linen yarn unless it complied with certain specifications,[28] presumably hoping by this proclamation to ensure an adequate supply of cheap yarn for his own looms. The effect of the ban can be traced in the export figures for the years 1635–39,[29] which were based upon the licences granted.

	1635	1636	1637	1638	1639
Total in packs[30]	1,415	1,307	823	1,553	1,177

There was thus a sharp drop for the year 1636–37 as a result of Wentworth's policy. Nearly all the yarn for this year was exported through Drogheda, which accounted for 655 out of 823 packs. Export of linen yarn from other ports dropped in many cases to nothing.

	1635	1636	1637	1638	1639
Drogheda	829	700	655	858	666
Dundalk	282	265	000	366	164
Dublin	37	32	23	79	69
Derry	147	111	16	107	147
Coleraine	43	69	000	36	45
Carrickfergus	45	80	000	52	52
Bangor	9	8	000	000	000

These of course were official figures which take no account of smuggling. They suggest, however, that Wentworth admitted defeat in 1638, when the backlog of exports was to some extent made up. On the other hand there was a decline in 1639, which would fit in with the complaints of a "decay in trade" which was made during the Irish parliament. The statistics of seventeenth-century officials need not of course be accepted at their face value entirely. Linen yarn may well have been smuggled out of Dundalk and other ports without leaving a trace in the official records. If this was so then the extent of Wentworth's intervention shrinks even further. At their face value, the figures show an "official" picture from which it seems clear that at best Wentworth's mercantilist measures operated for one year only. At worst, these measures may not have operated at all, though some account must be taken of Wentworth's efficiency in these matters, and of the charge brought against him at his trial, that his interference in the linen trade had caused considerable distress among the Irish in Ulster.[31] Wentworth also admitted at the trial that his weaving scheme had failed, and that he had lost £3,000 in the venture.[32] In conclusion, the importance of this "linen episode" in Wentworth's economic policy has been greatly exaggerated. Certainly there seems to be no compelling evidence to show that he founded the Irish linen cloth industry.

In my opinion, Wentworth's mercantilism, and perhaps mercantilism in general, emerges from this examination as being of much less importance than is often supposed. In other words, the economic policies of seventeenth-century governments take their place as one factor, not always the most important, within a general economic situation. It would appear that governments possessed less freedom of action and less power to control events than a historian like Cunningham believed, and that the interest of a great administrator like Wentworth lies in the way in which he was compelled to work within a given economic framework, much as he tried to break out of it or enlarge it for his own purposes. Perhaps, also, it may be said that this episode in Irish history throws some indirect light on France in the second half of the seventeenth century. It may be that in their limitations and their failures, Colbert and Wentworth had most in common, and not as Heckscher suggests, in their success.

Finally, if the actions of governments were not all-important, Irish economic history is more complex than is often supposed and cannot be summed up in a list of acts of parliament. The English parliament was not exclusively preoccupied in legislating against the interests of Ireland. And yet, studies of the economic history of Ireland during the seventeenth century have tended to be dominated by this simple, almost simple-minded, conception of the economic relationship which existed between England and Ireland. For some historians, Ireland has been a Cinderella consistently denied the opportunity of trying on a golden slipper by an Ugly Sister, "England," who enjoyed all the economic advantages life could offer. "Ireland" and "England" have been seen almost as human beings, instead of complex, articulated societies in which different economic interests could create tension both internal and external. "England" is described as capable of being "roused to jealousy" or as possessing "a contemptuous hatred" of Ireland. As a consequence of this anthropomorphism, it has followed that whenever an act was passed in the English legislature which had the effect, direct or indirect, of restricting Irish trade, historians have described "England's" actions in terms of "jealousy" or "envy" or other similar human emotions. Clearly any economic measure can be explained away on these terms. The Cattle Acts, for example, of Charles II's reign, prohibiting the import of Irish cattle into England need only be seen as yet another example of a deep-rooted tradition of hatred toward Ireland. To such historians, detailed discussion of the contemporary economic and political background seems superfluous. They are content to place the Cattle Acts and similar measures into an interpretation of Anglo-Irish history which is as oversimplified as the English "Whig interpretation of history" itself.

This view of Irish economic history tacitly assumes that "English" policy was always aggressive in a crude sense—as if the Ugly Sister noted that Cinderella's economic situation had slightly improved and feeling herself threatened, took steps to reduce her unfortunate sister to her former condition. The assumption is that the Ugly Sister herself was always as much mistress of her own fate in fact, as she was in mercantilist theory, and that she was never compelled in times of economic crisis to take defensive measures, which might, directly or indirectly, affect "Ireland." Measures which may seem to later historians to be acts of economic aggression committed by a jealous England acting according to well-tried principles within a historical vacuum were perhaps more often than not the actions of a hard-pressed executive or of a legislature, within which parties debated possible remedies for a confused crisis, the causes of which were but dimly discerned. In the early seventeenth century indeed, "England" regarded herself as far from being the fortunate Ugly Sister; she resembled rather an industrial Cinderella, feeling (as Flanders had done in the thirteenth century) the pinch of large-scale industrial unemployment. The policy of the English privy council or the projected bills of the English parliament, may, therefore, on occasion be described more historically, as symptoms of uncertainty and depression rather than as part of a tradition of calculated Machiavellianism.

NOTES

1. *Palgrave's Dictionary of Political Economy* ii. 727.
2. Notestein, *Commons Debates*, 1621, iii. 35.

3. Notestein, iii. 319.

4. Ibid. iii. 345.

5. Ibid. v. 490.

6. Ibid. iii. 214.

7. Ibid. ii. 356–57.

8. *Cal. Carew MSS*, 1603–24, p. 257.

9. Notestein, iii. 290.

10. Notestein, iii. 214.

11. Ibid. iii. 289–90.

12. Ibid. iii. 214.

13. Ibid. ii. 357.

14. Ibid. iv. 157–58.

15. Ibid. iii. 215.

16. Ibid. ii. 356–57.

17. Heckscher, *Mercantilism*, i. 262. He also refers to Cecil and Laud in the same context. George Unwin in his *Industrial Organisation in the Sixteenth and Seventeenth Centuries*, p. 172, makes the same comparison.

18. Knowler, *Strafford's letters*, i. 90–91.

19. Knowler, *Strafford's letters*, i. 202.

20. Notestein, v. 505–6.

21. Knowler, *Strafford's letters*, i. 423–24.

22. Ibid. i. 193.

23. Ibid. ii. 19–20.

24. For example, the importation of Fuller's earth into Ireland was prohibited in 1636 (*Cal. S. P. Ire.*, 1633–47, p. 136) but this was not a completely new measure, since it went back to a decision of the English privy council in 1623.

25. A cloth manufacture near Dublin had been set up by Sir Thomas Roper and was in existence in 1622. *Cal. S. P., Ire.* 1615–25, p. 361.

26. Wadsworth and Mann, *Cotton Trade and Industrial Lancashire*, 1600–1780, pp. 14–25.

27. "Thomas Cave's instructions for customs officers ..." T.C.D. M.S.F. 3.1.17.

28. Steele, *Tudor and Stuart proclam.*, ii. 32, no. 310.

29. P.R.O. S.P. 63/259/f.220. They begin in 1635 because it was in that year that Wentworth took over the customs farm and began to incorporate the linen and wine monopolies into it.

30. A pack = 4 cwt.   1 cwt. = 120 lb.

31. Rushworth, *Trial*, p. 67. article xiii.

32. Ibid. p. 422.

Chapter Thirteen

Ecclesiastical Politics and the Counter-Reformation in Ireland, 1618–48

(1960)

The internal politics of the Counter-Reformation varied in accordance with the individual circumstances of each European country. Nevertheless, many of the problems raised were common to all. The reception of the Tridentine decrees, the clash of regular and secular clergy, the pressure of local, ecclesiastical, and secular interests, the influence of the Spanish monarchy, and the part played by changing conditions in the structure of the Curia itself, especially the foundation of the Congregation of Propaganda in 1622—these affected societies as disparate as the Holy Roman Empire and Ireland. Against this background, Irish ecclesiastical history is of more than parochial or diocesan interest, and its disputes during the early seventeenth century throw light, by analogy, upon wider European developments. Indeed, so far as the British Isles are concerned, the Counter-Reformation was mainly an "Irish question," much as Catholic Emancipation was to be later, although it was to throw up no figures of the same caliber as Campion or Parsons.[1]

The pattern of Irish ecclesiastical history in the early seventeenth century reflected the immense importance of local ties. Even in "normal" circumstances, local affiliations were a decisive factor in the appointment of a bishop and in missionary conditions, such as obtained between 1600 and 1650, tendencies toward localism were accentuated. Only in exceptional circumstances, as during Rinuccini's nunciature,[2] were local voices ever overridden, and though in theory the choice rested with Holy Office or Propaganda, local interests usually had the final say. Indeed, it was essential for a candidate for a bishopric to have the backing of the local gentry as well as the local clergy if his future path were to be smooth. For Killaloe,

Malachy O'Queely, in 1624, had the written support of the O'Briens;[3] for Leighlin, in 1642, Edmund O'Dempsey had the promise of Terence O'Dempsey, viscount Clanmalier to pay him an annual subsidy;[4] and in the Clanrickarde territory of Galway, it is scarcely surprising to find John Bourke, first as bishop of Clonfert (1641) and then as archbishop of Tuam (1647). In every diocese, especially in Ulster, a similar situation existed, and these enduring local pressures can hardly be stressed too much.

Such climatic conditions, local though they were, had a place in broader patterns of weather. It was not to be expected that religious movements in Ireland should be unaffected by the tensions of secular politics. Indeed, differences of political attitude were already implicit in the way in which a resident hierarchy was restored in 1618 and the following decade. This restoration had its *raison d'être* in the Tridentine policy of making episcopal authority the linchpin of Church reform.[5] Before 1618 there was no resident hierarchy in Ireland and, although metropolitans existed for the provinces of Armagh, Dublin, Cashel, and Tuam, only on rare occasions were any of them to be found in the country. Thus the decision to restore the hierarchy may be regarded as one of the most important events affecting the Counter-Reformation in Ireland during the first half of the seventeenth century. When it came to the point, however, the political divisions of Ireland between pro-English and pro-Spanish elements, going back to the days of Kinsale and before, shaped the way in which the restoration of the hierarchy was carried out. During the first phase *c.* 1618–*c.* 1624 the main say in episcopal appointments seems to have rested with the pro-English archbishop of Armagh, Peter Lombard, long resident in Rome and a man of considerable influence. Originally enthusiastic for the cause of the Ulster earls, Lombard had come round to the view that the best hope for the future lay in trying to reach some practical "modus vivendi" with the English Crown.[6] It was understandable that while power rested with him, episcopal appointments were confined to areas of Ireland still unplanted, where old English traditions were strongest. David Rothe, Lombard's viceprimate and a man of similar sentiments, was appointed bishop of Ossory in 1618 and, during the next few years, the vacant sees of Limerick, Dublin, Emly, Meath, Cork, and Cloyne and Ferns were filled. Rothe apart, the most prominent of this group were Thomas Dease of Meath, who later refused to countenance the 1641 rebellion, and John Roche of Ferns, whose family was of typical old English stock. (Fleming of Dublin, a Franciscan, was the exception, since, though he was "old English," his sympathies were seemingly pro-Spanish like those of most of his order.) This choice of candidates and of dioceses, though tinged with a political coloring, could be justified on ecclesiastical grounds. It was, after all, in unplanted areas that Catholic landowners were most numerous and that some approximation to normal episcopal administration was feasible.

Thus, politically speaking, the outlook of the Catholic hierarchy in 1624 was identical with that of Peter Lombard. It was a situation which might well have persisted for a decade and perhaps longer. There were, however, Irish ecclesiastics who looked to the Spain of Philip IV as the chief hope of the Counter-Reformation, much as their predecessors had turned to Philip II. Among them were numbered Florence Conry, absentee archbishop of Tuam, the Franciscans of St. Isidore's, Rome, and St. Anthony's, Louvain, and many, though not all, of the clergy educated in Spain and the Spanish Netherlands. In Rome they could count upon the political backing of the exiled earl of Tyrone, Séan O'Neill, whose position and influence, until his death in 1632, resembled that of the exiled Stuart, Henry, cardinal of York, in the next century. Their hopes were centered upon a reversal of the plantations in Ulster and the reestablishment of Catholic government in Ireland—a prospect which could hardly be achieved without Spanish help—and their attitude to the English Crown was naturally in marked contrast with that of the Lombard bishops, who were prepared to cut Irish losses in Ulster and to accept the political status quo, in the long-term interest of Catholicism.

Before 1624 the balance of power in Rome favored the "old English"; after that date the balance was rapidly tilted in favor of Ulster and the pro-Spanish party. A change of policy is, perhaps, discernible in June 1625 when, a month before Lombard's death, appointments were made to the three Ulster dioceses of Kilmore, Raphoe, Down and Connor (and Elphin). Ecclesiastical reasons may be found for this, but it may also be suggested that the change was due to a sudden shift in the political winds, which occurred as a result of a breach in Anglo-Spanish relations. In 1623 the Spanish Match had been the cornerstone of English foreign policy; by 1625 the two countries had drifted into war. In these circumstances Ulster, which had been a liability to Spain during the years of Anglo-Spanish friendship, now once more became useful as a strategic threat to England and the danger of Spanish invasion was taken seriously by the lord deputy in Ireland, Falkland. The powerful Spanish lobby in Rome was once more placed at the disposal of the Ulster exiles. The Anglo-Spanish war also had the result of driving a further wedge between the "English" and "Spanish" groups. Those of Lombard's way of thinking were afraid of a new wave of persecution by the English Crown, on grounds that the loyalty of Catholics was suspect. Those who followed Tyrone and Conry, however, drew fresh hope from the war. It was at this point, in 1625, that the death of Peter Lombard provided the opportunity for a trial of strength between the pro-English and the pro-Spanish groups within the Irish hierarchy.[7] The change of cardinal protector of Ireland in 1624 from cardinal Ravalli to cardinal Ludovisi may also have been important.[8]

Many letters passed to Rome from the Spanish court, from the earl of Tyrone and from various Irish bishops, all of them trying to bring influence to bear on the Roman authorities. The pro-English elements considered they had a strong case in opposing the election of any candidate likely to arouse disquiet in Dublin and London on political grounds. This, for example, was the view of John Roche, bishop of Ferns. Roche considered that no one ought to be chosen against whom the English Crown might have political objections, arguing that no rest would be given either to the primate or to those who had admitted him to the see.[9] His view was shared by Francis Nugent, leader of the Irish Capuchins, who spoke out strongly against the influence of the Ulster earls and suggested Rothe of Ossory, a most learned man, as the most suitable candidate.[10] But, working at a distance, and with only the hypothetical support of an heretical monarch, the voices of Roche, Nugent, and the "old English" went unheard at Rome. Lombard had owed his own appointment in 1601 to the support of Hugh O'Neill and Philip II: it was unlikely, in 1626, in similar circumstances of Anglo-Spanish hostility, that any candidate not approved by Tyrone and Philip IV should have any chance of success. It could also be argued that it was right and proper, in accordance with tradition, for a native of Ulster to succeed to Armagh.[11] Not surprisingly, therefore, Lombard's immediate successor was one of Tyrone's candidates, Hugh MacCaughwell, O.F.M., a native of Down-patrick, former guardian of St. Anthony's, Louvain, and now Lector in theology at Ara Coeli, Rome. Tyrone's influence was confirmed after MacCaughwell's sudden death in 1626, when another of his candidates, Hugh O'Reilly, bishop of Kilmore, was appointed to Armagh. The appointment of Thomas Walsh to Cashel in 1626 also seems to have taken place under Spanish auspices.[12] As a consequence of these political comings and goings, the Irish episcopate during the Anglo-Spanish war of 1625–30 tended to split into two political groups. On the one side, looking to Madrid and Brussels, were the four metropolitans, O'Reilly, Fleming, Walsh, and Conry, and the Ulster bishops. On the other side, facing Rome, but glancing nervously in the direction of

Whitehall, were the small group of "old English" bishops, Ossory, Meath, Cork, Ferns, and Limerick. Influence in Rome and force of numbers favored the former. In contrast, the "old English" bishops had the backing of the Catholic gentry in the richest parts of Ireland, still unplanted.

Politics, however, were not the sole cause of disunity. A further source of difference lay in the bitter conflicts which took place in the dioceses of Ossory, Cork, Meath, and Waterford between the secular bishops and the regular clergy and, in Dublin, between the regular archbishop and the secular clergy. The year 1625 had marked a change in the balance not merely between the pro-English and the pro-Spanish groups, but also between secular and regular clergy, especially the Franciscans. Peter Lombard, a secular and pro-English in policy, was succeeded by Luke Wadding, Franciscan and pro-Spanish, as adviser to the Holy Office on Irish affairs. It was no accident that a high proportion of episcopal appointments after 1625 should be either regular or proregular clergy. Fleming, archbishop of Dublin, who, in 1625, had been the only resident Franciscan among his fellow bishops, was joined within a few years by several members of his order. For a brief period, indeed, in 1626, three of the four Irish metropolitans were Franciscans, and Thomas Walsh, archbishop of Cashel, though not a regular, was a relative of Wadding and favorably disposed toward the Orders. Perhaps the bishop who symbolized most dramatically the influences at work in ecclesiastical politics after 1625 was Bonaventura Magennis, a native of Down, a Franciscan, and a nephew of the earl of Tyrone, who was appointed to Down and Connor in 1630.[13]

In ordinary circumstances, relations between the regular and secular clergy amounted to little more than healthy rivalry. In the 1620s and 1630s, however, more was at stake than a place in the ecclesiastical sun. Political differences accounted for a good deal of the hostility between the secular bishops and the Franciscans, but an additional major source of conflict, within certain dioceses, lay in the different attitudes of the bishop and the religious orders to the disciplinary decrees of the Council of Trent. The Tridentine reforms, by restoring and reinforcing episcopal authority at the expense of bodies which had secured special exemption, created the probability of clashes with regular clergy in many dioceses. In Ireland the position was complicated by the fact that the early stages of the Counter-Reformation had been carried on successfully, without much help, or opposition, from a nonresident episcopate. The Franciscans, particularly, could regard themselves as having borne the heat and burden of the day during a period of persecution. They thrived in the missionary conditions of the first decades of the century and toleration by the state, from *c.* 1620, appeared a mixed blessing when it made possible the return of an episcopate determined to enforce the Tridentine decrees. The Franciscan, Thomas Strange, complained in 1630 that "the bishops stand as neere for themselves as if they were in quiet possession, soe that they will not permit us to use any faculties and [are] forever building upon the Council of Trent."[14] On the other side, the attitude of the secular bishops was represented by David Rothe, bishop of Ossory, who complained to Wadding that "The Council of Trent, which in all the practizable parts thereof hath been full often received … is rejected by some regulars … because some would not be subject to the reformation of regular discipline established in that councell."[15]

Not all dioceses were affected by these struggles. The bishop of Ferns could write to Wadding that "nowhere in this land are we at less odds than in my charge,"[16] while the archbishop of Cashel wrote that "we live in as much peace and quiet, thanks be to God, as you live in S. Isidoro."[17] But in the dioceses of Meath, Ossory, Cork, and Waterford, relations between the bishops and the Franciscans were bad.[18] Struggles over jurisdiction were aggravated by unseemly financial wrangles, which recall for their bitterness the case of Hunne in pre-Reformation England.[19] Appeals made to the proregular metropolitans over the head of the ordinaries did not tend to improve relations within the episcopate itself; and, at a meeting of the archbishops of Dublin and Cashel and the bishops of Ossory, Cork, Ferns, and Waterford in August 1629, the suffragans made a special point of exhorting metropolitans to exercise discretion in hearing appeals against their suffragan bishops.[20] The archbishops of Cashel and Tuam both complained of their suffragans and vicars apostolic resisting visitations.[21]

Two further issues added to the existing hostility and suspicion. The first of these was a clash between the Dublin Franciscan, Strange, backed by his archbishop, and the secular priests, Harris and Cahill, who looked to Ossory and Meath for sympathy. According to Cahill, the regulars were guilty of maintaining propositions that regulars alone were truly pastors; that it was safer and more seemly to confess to a regular; and that regular superiors were higher in rank than bishops.[22] In 1631 these views were brought before the largely secular, theological faculty of the Sorbonne[23] and condemned, whereupon the regulars complained to Wadding that their views had been grossly misrepresented. Fleming of Dublin blamed the whole business upon the bishops of Meath and Ossory, especially the latter, whom he described as the "*primum mobile*, who underhand troubles all."[24] The ill-feeling was still reverberating under Wentworth in 1634.

A second reason for bitterness lay in the doubts which arose with regard to livings formerly under regular control before the dissolution of the monastic houses. The Cistercians claimed that parishes which had been impropriated to their monasteries were still canonically theirs. If this were so, their juridical position vis à vis secular bishops was substantially strengthened and they could claim a foothold in many dioceses, including the right to nominate incumbents. The attempts which bishops were making to reestablish a normal parochial system based upon their own secular clergy were impeded and it was not surprising that they should take a stand upon the issue. They, for their part, maintained that cardinal Pole's recognition of the monastic dissolution and his placing of the rights of presentation into the hands of the local bishop was as valid for Ireland as for England. But there was sufficient doubt about the whole matter for both sides to feel certain that they were in the right and to be convinced that their opponents were guilty of bad faith. Patrick Comerford, bishop of Waterford, wrote, in 1631, asking Wadding to look into the Vatican archives in order to discover the truth about the whole affair.[25] He wrote:

> I heard some learned men say that Cardinal Poole's legatine power did not extend itself to Ireland; others say that his authoritie was revoked as soon as Paul IV was made Pope; others, that he was suspected of false dealinge and schisme; others that his dispensation was recalled; others, that it tooke effect onely in the province of Canterburie; and others, many other things which were tedious to write. But I am persuaded that in the records of the Vatican a man might finde in the original letters and the intercourse betwixt the same Popes and Kinge Philip and Queene Marie and Cardinal Poole, all the veritie of this matter; wherfor, good cousin, do your countrie and friends this pleasure.

Thus the Counter-Reformation episcopate and clergy in Ireland were clearly and deeply divided among themselves in 1630 and the years following. It was a situation in which politics and religion could hardly have been more confused. To some, who may be termed "Royalist," the future of Catholicism seemed to depend on some kind of *rapprochement* with the English Crown, based upon acceptance of the status quo, unsatisfactory though it might be. Others, belonging to a "Hapsburg" party, looked still to Spain, and preferred to hope for a full Catholic restoration, in which churches would be restored and plantations reversed. Alongside this division and to some extent coincident with it, lay the split between secular bishops, as Tridentine in outlook as seemed feasible, and the regular clergy, especially the Franciscans, content with the canonical status quo until times should alter. Ecclesiastical politics reflected, with some distortion, the prevailing secular divisions within Ireland.

These cleavages among the hierarchy, so obvious in the 1630s, did not cease to exist when in 1642 the Confederation of Kilkenny came into being. But they became less obvious. Perhaps as a result of the papal bull, *Nuper pro Parte*,[26] confirming the privileges of the Franciscans, and, perhaps also, because the four metropolitans were proregular, little is heard of trouble between the regulars and the secular bishops. For this reason historians have tended to assume that during the early years of the Confederation the hierarchy acted and spoke in unison.[27] Looked at in this way, the episcopal divisions over the Inchiquin Truce in 1648, when a minority of the bishops were excommunicated, appears as a sudden explosion. It is as well to remember, however, that the personnel of the hierarchy as late as 1645 was still largely what it had been in 1630. Even in 1648 three out of the four metropolitans, O'Reilly of Armagh, Fleming of Dublin, and Walsh of Cashel were men who had been appointed before 1630. The leaders of the hierarchy, thus, all represented a point of view which opposed compromise with the English Crown. Associated with them was MacMahon, bishop of Clogher, described by Rinuccini as "entirely swayed by political rules and motives."

On the other side of the fence, the royalist outlook among the episcopate was now represented by a triumvirate: Rothe of Ossory, Dease of Meath, and Tirry of Cork. The strength of this group had been reduced by the death of Roche of Ferns in 1636 and the senility of Arthurs, bishop of Limerick, now in his nineties. It was presumably the fact that the royalist bishops were so heavily outnumbered on the episcopal bench that led Patrick Darcy, architect of the Confederate Constitution, to minimize, as far as was decently possible, the political influence of the hierarchy. Darcy's constitution, based upon a council of twenty-four members and an elected assembly of about two hundred, deliberately avoided the complication of a second chamber in which the antiroyalist episcopate would have held the balance of power. Bishops sat of right in the general assembly, where their votes might be swallowed up in the great mass of elected representatives. In the Supreme Council the bishops were entitled to three seats, but here again could be outvoted by their lay colleagues. In any separate assembly of the clergy, the voice of the "royalist" bishops of Ossory, Meath, and Cork was liable to be overwhelmed in the face of the four united metropolitans. Behind the scenes, however, they seem to have enjoyed considerable influence with the Supreme Council.

But it was not until peace negotiations began between Ormonde and the Supreme Council, in 1644, that an issue arose which recalled the bitterness of the Armagh elections of 1626–27. Here again two contrasting points of view existed.[28] On the one side Meath, Ossory, and Cork still adhered to their policy of compromise with the English Crown and were content with more or less the situation before 1641. On the other hand, the majority of the episcopate, led by the four metropolitans, O'Reilly of Armagh, Fleming of Dublin, Walsh of Cashel, and O'Queely of Tuam wished, understandably enough, to hold on to what was held in 1644, in the way of churches and church property, and to acquire from the state some measure of juridical recognition. A meeting held in May and June 1645, while the Assembly was in session, brought these views into open conflict and it was decided by a majority of the bishops that, *even at the cost of a breakdown in negotiations*, the Confederation was bound to insist upon keeping churches, abbeys, monasteries, and chapels in their hands. This declaration was signed by the four metropolitans and by seven other bishops, of whom Comerford of Waterford and Malony of Killaloe, were the only "old hands." Three other bishops, unnamed, but almost certainly Tirry of Cork, Rothe of Ossory, and Dease of Meath, refused to sign.[29] Clearly the patterns of 1630 were repeating themselves. In June 1645 the episcopal representatives on the Supreme Council, now four in number, were O'Reilly of Armagh, Walsh of Cashel, O'Queely of Tuam, and MacMahon of Clogher, all of them united in their "antiroyalist" outlook.[30] This situation also helps to explain why the Supreme Council in 1643 had taken the line that no new episcopal appointments were to be made without its permission.[31]

In the years 1645–46, however, a number of changes took place which combined to make the situation more fluid. In 1645 O'Queely (Tuam) died and in 1646 Tirry (Cork) and Arthurs (Limerick). In addition, in 1645 two new bishops were appointed, Nicholas French to Ferns and Edmund O'Dwyer as coadjutor to Limerick with the right of succession. Finally, the papal nuncio, Rinuccini, arrived in Ireland late in the year. At first sight, these changes seemed to have reduced the ageing Ossory and Meath to negligible importance and with them, the royalist point of view among the hierarchy. Later developments, however, were to show that this was by no means the case.

Rinuccini's main object in coming to Ireland was to establish the Tridentine reforms upon a firm footing[32] and, for this reason, he intended to fill up vacant bishoprics as quickly as possible.[33] His eagerness forced the hand of the Supreme Council and they also provided a list of *episcopabili*.[34] The net result of all this was the creation of ten new bishops in March 1647 and, with them, as it turned out, an increased say for the "royalists." The coming of Rinuccini tended at first to reduce them to silence, and in the stand which he took against the peace negotiations with Ormonde in mid-1646 there was no bishop found to oppose his wishes. By 1648, however, military defeats and political mistakes had undermined the nuncio's position to the extent that it was possible for the voice of compromise to be heard once more. This time Ossory and Meath were no longer isolated. They were joined by Ferns and Limerick, by Ardagh and Dromore, by Killala, and by the new archbishop of Tuam.[35] In Rinuccini's early estimate, French of Ferns and O'Dwyer of Limerick were the brightest stars of the hierarchy and he had spoken highly of them both when he arrived. French he had thought most likely of all the episcopate "to promote ardently and judiciously the cause and splendour of religion," and O'Dwyer seemed to him to be fully Roman in both practice and example.[36] Rinuccini had been responsible for pressing the claims of James Plunkett to Ardagh.[37] In this he overrode the local interests of the O'Farrells and he showed a similar disregard for local ties in backing Oliver Darcy for Dromore. The new archbishop of Tuam, John de Burgo, who had been bishop of Clonfert from 1641–47, was also a leading member of this royalist group, which was completed by the adhesion of Kirwan of Killala, a bishop since 1645, and Lynch of Kilfenora, whose name had been put forward by the Supreme Council.[38] Taken all in all, the resistance to the nuncio's excommunication was surprisingly large.[39] It was reduced in July by the death of Dease of Meath, who, in Rinuccini's words, "has just died to the great blessing of the country"![40]

In contrast, when the nuncio's majority among the bishops is closely examined, it is remarkably small. His supporters in 1648 were drawn from two main groups. In the first place came the other metropolitans, Armagh, Dublin, and Cashel.[41] Allied with them were the hard core of Ulster bishops, Kilmore, Down, and Connor, and above all, MacMahon of Clogher. The second nucleus among the nuncio's supporters was the group of bishops who owed their elevation in 1647 specifically to the intervention of the nuncio. Walter Lynch of Clonfert and Boethius MacEgan of Ross were both loyal adherents of his, while Robert Barry of Cork was put into that see specifically by Rinuccini's supporters, in the face of viscount Muskerry's opposition.[42] The bishops of Emly and Clonmacnoise were also members of this group. The two groups formed the basis of Rinuccini's majority and it was from their ranks that he drew the five who signed the decree of excommunication in May 1648.[43] Henceforth the episcopate was to be openly divided in its attitude to future political developments.

The issue over which the bishops split was whether or not the Confederation should be permitted to make a truce with Inchiquin. As time went on, this became the thin end of the wedge which was to lead to the re-opening of peace negotiations with the earl of Ormonde. And this, in its turn, raised the problem of the juridical recognition of the Church. Looked at from one point of view, the bishops who opposed the nuncio have been described as politically minded time servers.[44] If, however, the background of the previous twenty years is taken into consideration, politics and religion appear to be equally confused on either side. In essentials, the differing outlook between Ormonde's bishops and O'Neill's bishops went back to the days of Peter Lombard and Florence Conry. The religious orders also behaved in 1648 as they had done earlier. The Franciscans sided with Owen Roe O'Neill in 1648 as they had with Sean O'Neill in 1626, whereas the Capuchins maintained the outlook of Francis Nugent, backed by the Jesuits and other regulars. The new factor in 1648 was the presence of Rinuccini and it was this which accounted for Dromore, Ardagh, and Cork acting, so to say, "out of character." But if this novelty is ignored, the features of the split in 1648 were essentially what they had been before the Confederation existed, and, in some ways, before the seventeenth century began.

NOTES

1. Recent work on the Counter-Reformation in Ireland 1600–50 includes the following: P. J. Corish, "The reorganisation of the Irish church, 1603–41" in *Proc. Irish Catholic Historical Committee* (1957); Corish, "An Irish Counter-Reformation Bishop: John Roche," in *Irish Theological Quarterly*, xxv. 14–32, 101–23; xxvi. 101–16, 313–30; Corish, "Rinuccini's Censure of 27 May, 1648," ibid., xviii. 322–37; Corish, "John Callaghan and the Controversies among the Irish in Paris," ibid., xxi. 32–50; Corish, "The Crisis in Ireland in 1648," ibid., xxii. 231–57; Corish, "Two Contemporary Historians of the Confederation," in *Irish Historical Studies*, viii. 217–36; J Silke, "Primate Peter Lombard and Hugh O'Neill," and "Primate Lombard and James I," in *Irish Theol. Quart.*, xxii. 15–30, 124–49; see also T. L. Coonan, *The Irish Catholic Confederacy and the Puritan Revolution*, Dublin 1954; B. Jennings, O.F.M. (ed.), *Wadding Papers*, Dublin 1953; Franciscan Fathers, *Father Luke Wadding*, Dublin 1957.

2. Cf. A. Hutton (ed.), *The Embassy in Ireland of Rinuccini* (1873) 130.

3. *Wadding Papers*, 80–81. He did not get this see.

4. *Father Luke Wadding*, 567. This book contains valuable summaries of episcopal backgrounds, edited by C. Giblin, O.F.M., under the title "The Processus
Datariae and the Appointment of Irish Bishops in the Seventeenth Century,"
508–616.

5. Cf. H. Jedin, *A History of the Council of Trent*, (1957) i. 129–30.

6. Cf. Silke, op cit.

7. *Wadding Papers*, 121, 125. Cf. J. Orcibal, *Origines de Jansenisme* (1947), i
p. 234, 236.

8. *Father Luke Wadding*, 529, 533.

9. *Wadding Papers*, 141–43.

10. Ibid., 122.

11. Ibid., 158.

12. Ibid., 177.

13. *Father Luke Wadding*, 554–57.

14. *Wadding Papers*, 440.

15. Ibid., 554.

16. *Wadding Papers*, 543.

17. Ibid., 614. This was not Thomas Strange's view of Cashel: ibid., 441.

18. Ibid., 557.

19. Cf. K. Pickthorn, *Early Tudor Government* (1967) ii. 112–14.

20. Corish, "An Irish Counter-Reformation Bishop: John Roche," in *Irish
Theol. Quart.*, xxvi. 314–15.

21. *Wadding Papers*, 521, 611–12.

22. Ibid., 510–11.

23. Ibid., 533.

24. Ibid., 557. On the other hand, John Roche of Ferns described Rothe as "first
for doctrine and devotion among the bishops of this Kingdom." Moran, *Spic.
Ossor.*, i. 190.

25. *Wadding Papers*, 489.

26. *Annales Minorum* xxviii (1633–40), Clara Aqua 1941, 715–16. I am indebted
to Fr. Benignus Millett, O.F.M., for this reference.

27. Coonan, *Confederacy*. C. V. Wedgwood, *The King's War*, (1958) 260–61, 595,
refers to "the Irish priests" and "the clergy" without distinction of views.

28. The appointment of four new bishops in 1641 to Ardfert, Down and Connor, Clonfert, and Leighlin did not change the balance of power within the episcopate as a whole, although it did suggest Propaganda rather than the Holy Office
was now dealing with Irish affairs. Giblin, op cit., 564.

29. *Commentarius Rinuccinianus*, i. 527–29. The recusants were described as
"qui vel intra vel valde prope terminos factionis adversae rendent et nati sunt."

30. Gilbert, *Ir. Confed.*, iv. 280.

31. Ibid., ii. 119.

32. Hutton, *Embassy*, 130.

33. Ibid., 274.

34. Ibid., 105–7.

35. For a list of this group in January 1649, cf. Hynes, *The Mission of Rinuccini*, 264, n. 4.

36. Hutton, *Embassy*, 141. Later he changed his views, and charged French with duplicity. Ibid., 352.

37. Ibid., 131, 193–95.

38. Ibid., 106.

39. Of the list of twelve names submitted by the Council in December 1645, six were consecrated bishops, and of these, two, Kildare and Cork, supported the nuncio: loc. cit.

40. Hutton, *Embassy*, 402.

41. The bishops still maintained external unity as late as 2 May 1648 although dissension was rumored to exist. For a list of these bishops, cf. *Comment. Rinucc.*, iii. 140.

42. Hutton, *Embassy*, 170.

43. *Comment. Rinucc.*, iii. 206–7. Cf. Corish, "Rinuccini's Censure of 27 May 1648," in *Irish Theol. Quart.*, xviii. 332–37.

44. Coonan, *Confederacy*, 278. In essentials, Dr. Coonan adopts the outlook of the *Aphorismical Discovery*, written by a supporter of Owen Roe O'Neill and the Ulster party.

Chapter Fourteen

The Politics of Mercantilism, 1695–1700

(1959)

The Irish Woollen Act of 1699 and the linen measures which accompanied it are commonly looked upon as a classic piece of mercantilist policy. The episode is regarded as a carefully contrived piece of official policy by which the exportation of Irish woolen goods was prohibited while in compensation the Irish linen industry was to be allowed and encouraged to expand. As Sir George Clark put it:

> If the English had wished to impoverish Ireland they would not have lacked an excuse for restricting the Irish linen trade as they had restricted the Irish woollen trade. So far from doing all this they promised to encourage it by all possible means, as an equivalent for the lost opportunities for the woollen manufacture. They kept their promise.[1]

The historian of the Irish linen industry, Conrad Gill, also refers to a "bargain" between the English and Irish governments as an essential part of the story.[2] At the same time, however, it is generally recognized that the English woolen industry also played an important role in pressing for restrictive measures against Ireland, but the political background to the whole episode has never been fully investigated. This essay is an attempt to fill in the relevant political, constitutional, and religious details to a story which has hitherto been treated in purely economic terms. It may also be said to raise the general question as to how far economic history can be treated in isolation from the rest of social history. This may seem a commonplace, but as C. H. Wilson has recently pointed out, "the nature of policy has hardly anywhere been related sufficiently to the resources, geography, politics and social structure of the different states."[3] His advice is not least relevant for the last decade of the seventeenth century, most political of decades, in which nothing, not even the Bank of England, was immune from politics.

I

For practical purposes, the attack upon the woolen industry of Ireland may be said to have been launched by the Bristol economist, John Cary, in his widely read pamphlet, *Essay on Trade*, published in 1695.[4] In December of that year, when the agitation for a merchants' council of trade was being pressed, the two Bristol members of parliament were urged by Cary and others to raise the matter in debate,[5] and in 1696 Cary himself was sent to London to act as the special representative of the Bristol merchants.[6] But though Cary was acutely conscious of Irish competition, he did not make Ireland the only scapegoat for the commercial and financial crisis affecting the south-western counties. Equally objectionable in his eyes was the East India Company, which imported calicoes and silks into England to the detriment of English woolens.[7] The fact that London enjoyed a monopoly of this lucrative trade at the expense of the outposts like Bristol, was another source of grievance.[8] Cary's theoretical objections to the Company however, did not prevent him from becoming a trustee in 1698 when its monopoly was broken.[9]

Without political backing, Cary's views stood little chance of being translated into statute since neither of the two trading interests that he had attacked was politically defenseless. The East India Company was not merely a commercial monopoly with great financial reserves, it was also a powerful political lobby, which could, and had, mobilized opinion in both houses of parliament.[10] Similarly, though there was no Irish representation in the English parliament, the Irish parliament itself, in which the woolen interest was strongly represented, was a continual source of anxiety to William III and his ministers. Despite the fact that the Irish House of Commons at this date was drawn exclusively from the ranks of the English colonists, it had proved exceedingly intractable, claiming the "sole right" to initiate financial legislation and refusing to ratify the Treaty of Limerick, part of which was passed only in 1697, six years after it had been signed.[11]

Neither William III nor the Whig Junto were anxious to increase their difficulties in the Irish parliament by sponsoring restrictive measures against the Irish woolen trade and any questions involving the East India

Company or Ireland were bound to be treated by them as much on grounds of political expediency as on economic merits. It was not surprising that the first general report of the Board of Trade, made on 25 November 1696,[12] turned a blind eye toward these two difficult problems, despite the fact that John Pollexfen, a severe critic of the East India Company, was a member.

Though the obstacles in the way of Cary's policy were great, the English woolen industry was by no means ill-equipped for bringing political pressure to bear on the government. However, existing constitutional arrangements, in particular the number of boroughs, greatly favored the south-west, as compared with East Anglia, the other main center of the cloth industry. Compared with Cornwall, Devon, Dorset, and Wiltshire, the Eastern counties of Norfolk, Suffolk, Essex, and Lincoln were all seriously under-represented in parliament.[13] Divided geographically, these two main units of the English cloth industry were also divided by economic interest. To the weaving interests of the south-west, cheap Irish wool was a necessary raw material, and anything which tended to interfere with its supply was felt as an immediate danger, quite apart from the direct competition of Irish woolens exported abroad. To the weavers of East Anglia and the silk weavers of London and Canterbury, however, the threat from the silks and calicoes of the East India Company was more immediate.

This division of interest in the English cloth industry explains the fact that when the attacks upon the East India Company and the Irish woolen trade were launched late in 1696 and early in 1697, they came from different quarters. The pressure against the East India Company came largely from London and East Anglia, and during the course of December, petitions against the Company were presented from Norfolk,[14] Peterborough,[15] London, Whitechapel,[16] and Kettering.[17] By contrast, mostly during March 1696–97, complaints against the Irish woolen trade came from Bristol,[18] Crediton,[19] Bideford,[20] Barnstaple,[21] Great Torrington,[22] Exeter,[23] Minehead,[24] and Taunton.[25]

East Anglia was first in the field on 30 November 1696, when Sir Henry Hobart (Norfolk) and Thomas Blofeld (Norwich) introduced a bill to restrain the importation of East Indian calicoes and silks.[26] This manoeuver met with surprising success, despite the neutral silence observed by the Board of Trade, and passed its third reading in the Commons on 6 February 1696–97.[27] Hobart's fellow teller was Charles Paulet, a member of the Whig Junto, which may indicate that the government at this stage was benevolently disposed. But the bill had still to face the Lords and there, success was improbable. One member of the Commons remarked that "it had cost the weavers £500 to endeavour to prohibit the East India silks; and that they had no more to spend; but that he did not doubt but the Linen-drapers would find money enough to manage the Weavers and hinder the passing of the bill." This judgment proved correct. The East India Company was too tough a nut to be cracked without complete government support and in July 1698 even Montague was surprised at the resistance which he met with over the Two Millions Bill. He wrote to Shrewsbury, "I was not ignorant of what I undertook, nor insensible of the Opposition I should meet with from such a set of men as the East India Company; but really the dispute was more obstinate than I did expect."[28] It was surprising indeed that Hobart's bill should have got as far as it did between November 1696 and February 1696–97.

In contrast, the attack upon the Irish woolen trade was not launched until 27 March 1697 when Sir Joseph Tily (Exeter) and Sir William Ashurst (London) obtained leave to bring in a bill to prevent the exportation of Irish woolen manufactures into foreign parts. Tily's part is self-explanatory in the light of his Devon background, but Ashurst's role is obscure. Perhaps the explanation lies in his being a director of the East India Company, and hence only too eager to use the agitation against Irish woolens to distract attention from Indian calicoes. There was little time, however, for Ashurst's bill to get very far and it had been read only once on 5 April 1697, before parliament was prorogued on April 16. It did have the result, however, of drawing the government's attention to the matter and to possible political complications. The Privy Council therefore ordered the Board of Trade on April 20 to take into consideration the trade of England and Ireland, and to suggest how trading relations might be improved to the advantage of both nations.[29]

It is clear from these preliminary skirmishings that the initiative in the formation of economic policy lay not with the Board of Trade or even the government but with the House of Commons. Once parliament had been prorogued, however, the government was free to consider its future policy toward Ireland and the East India Company. On 23 December 1697, the Board of Trade (John Locke was a notable absentee) gave its opinion on both matters as part of a general survey of English trade.[30] Its view on the East India trade was that it might be requisite to discourage the wearing of Indian linens, unless the Company showed that reexports brought in as much bullion as was carried out.[31] As for Ireland, the Board noted that English woolen manufacture was affected by the export of Irish woolen goods and suggested as a remedy that H. M. subjects in Ireland should be diverted to linen.[32]

The fate of these two proposals was to be very different, but in each case, political rather than economic considerations played the major part in deciding the course of events.

II

Four persons were responsible for the working out of government policy toward Ireland at this date. In the English Privy Council itself, Charles Talbot, earl of Shrewsbury, confidant of William III, was secretary of state; in Ireland, his opposite numbers were the lords justices, newly appointed after lord deputy Capel's death in 1696. These were Charles Paulet, now marquis of Winchester and the Huguenot, Henry de Ruvigny, earl of Galway. To them was added as lord chancellor, early in 1697, John Methuen, member of the Board of Trade and member of parliament for the clothing town of Devizes. Methuen owed his position on the Board of Trade,[33] and as Irish lord chancellor,[34] to Shrewsbury's influence.

Their policy had been laid down for them in the royal instructions to the lords justices, dated 23 April 1697,[35] which called for a "bill to encourage the linen industry in Ireland"[36] Clearly at this date the English government had no plans for direct action against the Irish woolen industry. What Shrewsbury envisaged was a linen bill drawn up by the Irish parliament as a sop to English parliamentary criticism to show that something was being done to divert Irish attention away from wool. In August, he wrote to Galway:

> I wish that some bill that would effectually encourage the linen manufacture were in such forwardness that it might be perfected this session. It would be of great advantage to England as well as Ireland and unless something be now done to show the Parliament here that the Irish will turn their industry to what may divert them from the woollen trade, that is, what the English are so jealous of, the next session the Irish will certainly receive a mortification on the subject, what was done at the end of the last being intended as a fair warning to them.[37]

The result of Shrewsbury's pressure was the drawing up of a linen bill, under the guidance of an Ulster landowner, James Hamilton of Tullymore. After passing through the Irish parliament during September, Hamilton's bill was forwarded, in accordance with the terms of Poynings' Law, to the English privy council,[38] and from there it was sent on to the Board of Trade for further scrutiny.[39] In Ireland, it had been a stormy parliamentary session which saw the difficult ratification of part of the Treaty of Limerick, and it is perhaps a measure of the harmlessness of Hamilton's bill that it got through without much trouble. The charge was later to be made in November that whoever drew up the bill had meant it to be useless, though Galway denied this in a letter to Shrewsbury.[40]

Meanwhile, in accordance with the Privy Council instruction of April 22,[41] the Board of Trade had been proceeding with its own plans for Irish woolens and linens, but four months elapsed before a final draft was approved. It was not until August 17 that a small group met, consisting of John Pollexfen, Abraham Hill, and John Locke, to discuss the trade of England and Ireland.[42] Their discussions went on daily, presumably around the question whether Ashurst's bill to *prevent* the export of Irish woolens should be adopted or some other scheme merely to *discourage* the Irish woolen manufacture. On August 31 Locke's moderate scheme for discouragement was adopted.[43]

Locke had already, in September 1696, made enquiries concerning Irish linen from his Dublin friend William Molyneux,[44] but this had been some time before Ashurst's attack upon the Irish woolen trade had been made in the Commons. In fact Locke's interest in Irish linen in 1696 seems to have formed part of the discussions in the Board of Trade to free wartime England from excessive dependence upon Baltic linen imports.[45] His scheme of August 1697 was a response to a different set of circumstances and though it did aim at discouraging Irish woolen manufacture, it was essentially moderate compared with Ashurst's bill. He explicitly disavowed the suppression of Irish woolen exports on the ground that smuggling would be impossible to control.[46] Instead he suggested the imposition of duties upon oil, teasels, and the various utensils used in woolen manufacture, as well as a quasi-excise duty upon woolen stuffs while still on the loom. These duties were to be put into force gradually, not by parliamentary statute, but by royal proclamation. In compensation for all this, linen manufacture was to be encouraged by allowing hempseed and linen to be imported free of duty; land on which flax was grown was to be free of tithe, duties upon imported calico were to be increased, and spinning schools were to be set up to bring the use of the double wheel into fashion. It should be noted that Locke's scheme avoided the constitutional issue of a clash between the English and Irish parliaments; it was also intended to discourage Irish woolens by executive action (proclamation) and to encourage Irish linens by legislative action in Ireland (Irish parliamentary statute). P. Laslett's comment on this scheme is that it "recommended the deliberate destruction of woollen manufacture there. ... This is not easy to reconcile with Locke's political principles."[47] Seen against the immediate background, however, Locke's plan was essentially more moderate than any other. Discouragement over a period of time and immediate suppression by the English parliament were two distinct methods, and the Irish parliament itself in 1698 came round to adopting a plan similar to Locke's.

In October 1697, then, Hamilton's linen bill and Locke's "Representation" were both under consideration as a basis for future policy. On October 30 and each succeeding day until November 11, Hamilton's bill was discussed, line by line.[48] There were considerable differences of opinion within the Board of Trade, in the course of which it emerged that Locke was in a minority of one.[49] Sir Francis Brewster, a member of the Irish parliament, was summoned before the Board to give his opinion of Hamilton's bill, which he criticized on the grounds of being too coercive and impracticable. Brewster considered that "people will not be brought to apply themselves to any manufacture by Terror but by rewards and profit." "He thought that it was very necessary that a Bill should be sent over such as their Lordships should think proper. That though it were rejected yet it would do much good. Because they are afraid of some severe Law from England against their Woollen Manufacture and rather than incur that danger, they would apply their thoughts some way or other to promote this of Linnen."[50] The Board of Trade then drew up an amended scheme, "but Mr Locke excused himself from signing the Representation." Clearly this was one occasion on which Locke did not carry the Board with him.

Though there were disagreements within the Board, there had been no support for Ashurst's bill. The general opinion of the Board of Trade seemed to be that encouraging the Irish linen trade might well be enough. Such moderate plans were possible while the English parliament was not sitting, but on December 3, it met and within a fortnight, Ashurst's bill to suppress Irish woolen manufactures had been reintroduced, this time under more powerful opposition auspices.

III

On 14 December 1697 the attack upon Irish woolen manufactures was taken up again by one of the most prominent members of the Tory opposition, Sir Edward Seymour. Seymour controlled a group of members referred to by Defoe as "Tsar Seymskie's Western Empire"[51] which normally worked in conjunction with the Hyde-Granville faction and also had close relations with Harley.[52] In this session the Irish woolen trade was to become a major opposition issue, and if Harley's agitation for the resumption of William III's Irish grants is also taken into consideration, Irish affairs formed a great source of embarrassment for William and the Whig Junto. The accusation that William was favoring Ireland and Holland at the expense of England was ground well chosen by the Tories, and the introduction of Seymour's Irish woolen bill was part of the campaign. The King's government was eventually to be placed in the awkward position of having to choose between its interests in England and Ireland, a choice which during 1697 and 1698 it tried hard to avoid.

But though Seymour's plan was part of a parliamentary campaign, it was also grounded in local political and economic attitudes. Seymour's usual seat was Exeter and only after he had lost the election there in 1695, did he sit for his pocket borough of Totnes. All his links were with the south-west counties, and it was natural that he should attempt eventually to recover lost ground by making the most of the Irish woolen issue. When the next general election took place in the summer of 1698, Seymour and his fellow Tory Sir Bartholomew Shower again contested the Exeter election, and the major theme of their campaign was the danger from Irish woolens. On 19 August 1698, Shower spoke at the Guildhall, Exeter, in the following vein: "that it is the interest of this Kingdom in general, as well as of this country, that Ireland should be humbled. Not that the country should be drowned or the people massacred but that a check be put to their bold attempts for turning the woollen manufacture out of its old channel by removing it from hence thither. It must impoverish us and I wonder our gentry are not more sensible of the danger for it will lessen the value of their lands."[53] The result of the election was victory for Seymour and Shower.[54]

Thus when Seymour introduced his Irish woolen bill on 14 December 1697, an economic question became caught up into national politics, to be decided not upon grounds of common good but upon trial of political strength. In view of government influence in the Commons, Seymour's bill did surprisingly well and on 21 March 1697–98 passed its third reading. In contrast, however, Hobart's attack upon the East India Company, which had been so successful in the previous session, petered out with a defeat on the second reading on January 24. The explanation for this defeat lay in Montague's plans for raising a loan of several million pounds by opening up the East India trade to all who subscribed to a large government loan. Hobart's bill, had it been allowed to progress further, might well have prejudiced Montague's financial policy.[55]

The parliamentary situation during the first six months of 1698 rested on the fact that the government had decided to use the East India Company for its own financial purposes. In addition, the Junto showed no enthusiasm for Seymour's bill which was held up in the Lords from March to July, when parliament was dissolved.[56] The pressure for a mercantilist policy derived not from the government but from parliamentary opposition. However, William III's government was much weaker where Ireland was concerned than it was on East Indian affairs. There was no Irish group in Parliament as there was an East Indian group, on which the government could rely to cover its flank against the attacks of the opposition. Moreover, the government's position over Ireland was gravely weakened with the publication of William Molyneux's pamphlet, *The Case of Ireland*. Molyneux wrote this early in 1698 to refute the supposition that the English parliament could legislate for Ireland, basing his arguments in the main upon John Locke and the *Modus Tenendi Parliamentum*. The timing of its publication was unfortunate since it played into the hands of the Tory opposition. Bishop William King of Derry was no friend of Seymour's woolen bill, but he saw that Molyneux's pamphlet was likely to have a boomerang effect. In April he wrote to Francis Annesley in London, concerning the *Case of Ireland*, that he feared whether "anything of this nature may be seasonable at this time and whether it will not exasperate rather than prevent the mischief that is coming on us."[57] King was right. Seymour's party raised the question on June 22,[58] and several full-scale debates were held. On June 27 Molyneux's book was ordered to be burned by the common hangman, and in order to placate the opposition, William III's speech at the dissolution contained a definite promise that something would be done to discourage the Irish woolen trade.[59]

Meanwhile, Montague had been successful in "tacking" his "Two Millions" bill. On July 2 it passed the Commons for the third time, and as soon as it had passed the Lords, parliament was dissolved. So far from East Indian imports being banned or limited, as Sir Henry Hobart and the East

Anglian woolen interest had demanded, the trade was being thrown open to a wider circle of merchants. But if for the moment, the East Indian issue had been settled as the government wished, the future for its Irish policy was extremely uncertain. A good deal depended upon support for the Whig Junto in the forthcoming general election and upon the success of the lords justices in persuading the Irish parliament to pass measures to placate the opposition in England.

IV

For the moment, attention shifted to Ireland, where the government was faced with the task of summoning the Irish parliament and persuading it to pass measures agreeable to Seymour and the Tory opposition. The first steps were taken by the Irish lord chancellor, John Methuen. On July 29 he produced a compromise solution which he placed before the Board of Trade.[60] As an official of the Irish administration he was naturally opposed to any policy of suppressing the export of Irish woolens but he suggested as an alternative that a high duty should be imposed upon Irish draperies in order to remove the advantage of cheapness which they held at the moment. He also suggested that experienced people should be brought into Ireland from abroad in order to improve linen manufacture. He mentioned in particular a family of refugees, named Crommelin, who had been, and would be, useful in these matters. Methuen's compromise solution was adopted, and during the remaining months of the year, he and the lords justices attempted to have a bill incorporating these suggestions passed by the Irish parliament.

Methuen's compromise appears reasonable to the detached mind, and it is not clear at first sight why the Irish parliament did not accept it immediately. The Irish parliament were being asked to impose duties upon Irish woolens in order to subsidize Irish linens. What was there to object to in this proposal, which was intended to forestall a complete prohibition by the English parliament? The answer lies in the fact that this economic change carried with it political and religious implications. The so-called "Irish" parliament was at this date the constitutional organ of the English Protestant interest. It was they who were "the flock masters and woollen manufacturers of the Kingdom,"[61] and it was they who stood to lose if the Irish woolen manufacture declined. In contrast, linen manufacture was at this date largely, though not completely, concentrated in Ulster,[62] where the majority of linen workers were Scots dissenters.[63] In 1698 the English "interest" in Ireland, which compared to the Irish and the Scots was a minority of a minority, was being asked to sacrifice its own economic position in order to improve that of the Ulster Scots. It was for this reason that similar plans to encourage the linen industry had failed in 1692 and 1695.[64]

But there was also religion to be considered. During the 1690s the Irish parliament resisted every attempt made under English Whig auspices to introduce toleration for the Ulster Scots dissenters. From this point of view the Irish parliament was the constitutional organ of the Church of Ireland, and Bishop King boasted in 1696 that "the dissenters' interest in this Kingdom is really in itself very weak and low, as sufficiently appeared in the last session of our parliament when all their interest combined with the lord deputy's, the speaker of the House of Commons and all his adherents could not carry anything we had not a mind to."[65] The political and religious concessions which lord deputy Capel had pressed for in 1696, were now being asked for in the economic sphere by Methuen. This was quite clear to someone like Bishop King who, as bishop of Derry in the heart of the Presbyterian North, was acquainted at first hand with the economic strength of the Dissenters and the dangers to the Church of Ireland if the linen industry were encouraged. On 10 March 1697–98 he wrote to Annesley opposing Seymour's bill on the grounds that the North would be gainers by it, and that the Catholics were overjoyed at the prospect.[66] On April 2 he wrote to a correspondent in Coleraine of the mischief which the woolen bill would create in both Kingdoms "and particularly in the protestant English interest of Ireland."[67] King's attitude over this general question was also affected by a legal struggle, in which he was engaged at that moment, with the Irish Society over their leasing of certain episcopal lands to Presbyterians.[68]

The economic point was put most clearly in a pamphlet, Tisdal's *Conduct of Dissenters*, published in 1712, a few years after the Woollen Act had been passed. Tisdal argued that "the failure of our Woollen Manufactory sunk the Church interest of Ireland in the same proportion that the encouragement of the Linen manufactory did raise the interest of the Presbytery. The weavers of the former being generally conformists who were obliged to return for England or disperse themselves in the Low Countries, as those of the latter were generally Dissenters who came from Scotland since the Revolution Tis evident the Dissenters seem at present to be almost in full possession of that considerable Branch of our trade." He then went on to criticize Crommelin's linen colony at Lisburn "in the center of the Northern Presbyterians."

In the face of these religious and economic complications, the passing of Methuen's woolen and linen bills through the Irish parliament was a matter involving considerable political dexterity. The question was all the more difficult because of the administration's need for supply. William III hoped that the Irish parliament would agree to find the £138,000 necessary to keep five of his regiments in existence. There was no question therefore of forcing the woolen and linen bills through. If the lords justices were to be successful in obtaining supply, their treatment of the woolen and linen bills would have to be delicate; and in fact their correspondence with Shrewsbury over these issues revealed great anxiety.[69]

As a compromise solution, Methuen's plan had a good chance of success but it had still to surmount two hurdles—the English Board of Trade and the Irish parliament. On 5 October 1698 at a meeting of the Board, attended by Meadows, Pollexfen, Locke, and Hill, Methuen's woolen and linen bills were considered, but it was not until 13 October, after several days' discussion that a decision was reached. The Board's view, expressed in a formal "representation," was that the additional duties of 20 percent on Irish broadcloth and 10 percent on the new draperies were insufficient. They suggested an alternative figure of the order of 43 percent to bring Irish cloth to a "par" with that of England.[70]

There was little chance, however, that these amendments would be accepted by the Irish parliament. Methuen had already felt himself compelled in the interests of harmony to allow the Irish House of Commons to draw up their own woolen bill.[71] To Secretary Vernon in London, the situation in Ireland looked bleak, and on October 25, in one of his regular weekly reports to William, he expressed the view that even though the Irish parliament passed a woolen bill imposing duties upon themselves, these would not be sufficient to meet English objections, especially as the Commissioners of Trade had just reported that an additional duty of 40 percent was necessary to bring the price of Irish woolens on a par with English.[72]

At this date, there was no doubt that the official attitude in English government circles was based on the hope that an acceptable compromise would be reached in Ireland before the English parliament met. In fact, however, there was no sense of urgency in Dublin. No discussion took place on the woolen bill during the months of November and December, and it was not until early in January that it was read for the first time. It passed both houses very quickly before parliament was prorogued on

January 26. In its final form, the Act imposed duties of 20 percent on broadcloth and 10 percent on new draperies.[73] No concession was made to the Board of Trade view that 40 percent would be necessary to bring Irish woolens to par. News from England presumably acted as a spur, for by then the English parliament had already met, and Seymour's bill had been introduced once more.

But if the Irish woolen interest had agreed to impose duties upon itself, there was no willingness to subsidize the linen industry. The lords justices had expected their linen bill to pass and the woolen bill to fail,[74] and for this reason did not mention the woolen bill in their address to Parliament. In fact, however, exactly the reverse occurred. The main opposition occurred in the House of Lords,[75] where Bishop King of Derry was among the leaders. He was opposed to both woolen and linen bills,[76] but though the linen bill was rejected, the woolen bill got through.

In view of subsequent events, however, all the political energy expended in Ireland appeared misplaced. The real decisions were to be taken in the English parliament which met in December.

V

It is conceivable that the Irish Additional Duties Act might well have been an acceptable compromise a year earlier. But by January 1698–99 the political situation in England had changed to such an extent that the Whig Junto were no longer in control of the House of Commons. The opposition, led by Sir Edward Seymour, whose name was noted particularly by Hermitage,[77] pressed hard for the disbanding of William's army and the government was unable to resist this pressure. In these circumstances, Seymour's Irish woolen bill, which he introduced on 20 December 1698, went through three readings in the Commons without difficulty. The government, even if it had wished, would have been unable to prevent its passage, but there was no sign of any officially inspired resistance. It passed the Commons for the third reading on 6 March 1698–99, and then went to the Lords. There, some attempt was made by Irish interests to delay the bill on the grounds that it was framed entirely in the interests of Exeter.[78] But opinion in the Lords was against this or any plea on constitutional grounds. The bill became law in 1699. It forbade the exportation of Irish cloth abroad, including the colonies. Irish woolen manufacture was henceforth to be confined to the domestic market.

All this had been unforeseeable in September when Methuen had drawn up his compromise. The elections had given no ground for pessimism, and Vernon, on writing to Portland,[79] had remarked that "we have a new Parliament and nobody can make a fixed judgement what temper they will be of. It is certain the Animositys they have one against another will be strong and I don't know but little accidents and emergencys may turn the balance either way." Even when parliament had met, Seymour's candidate was not elected Speaker, which appeared to Hermitage as a good sign.[80] But it soon became clear that for the moment the opposition was in control. Indeed, as is well known, William III threatened to leave the country in anger at the success of Seymour's disbanding measures.

If from the Dublin point of view, the parliamentary situation had grown worse, it was also the same within both the government and the Board of Trade. Somers had been very critical of Methuen in October,[81] and may well have been glad to see his discomfiture in January.[82] The Board of Trade, by January 13, had come round to the view that the exportation of wool and woolen manufactures from Ireland or the English plantations in America "ought to be prohibited or discouraged, by the most coercive and proper means."[83] It is worth noting that Locke did not sign this document.

If the suppression of Irish woolen manufactures was undertaken without the consent of the Irish parliament, the encouragement of Irish linen had to be also. The scheme adhered to was that which Methuen had suggested in mid-1696 with the essential difference that it was now to be financed by England. Crommelin, the Huguenot refugee, was to be the official agent of the English Treasury in its scheme for encouraging the manufacture of fine linens in Ireland.[84] Crommelin agreed to supply capital to the value of £10,000 in the form of machinery and raw material and to instruct in the manufacture of fine linens. As its share of the bargain, the English Treasury was to pay him eight percent on his money, a personal salary of £300 a year, and a further sum to pay three assistants.[85] Thus in the interests of a section of the English woolen industry, linen was to be encouraged in Ireland while at the same time the export of Irish woolen manufacture was forbidden. The turn of the East India Company, politically a much harder nut to crack, came in 1701 when its silks and calicoes were forbidden to be imported into England, save for reexport.[86]

By way of conclusion, it may be suggested that if the Irish Woollen Act was mercantilist, it was mercantilist with a difference. Sir George Clark, in a recent discussion of the topic of mercantilism, has stated that "there was always a tussle between the interests of trade as the traders understood them and the desire of the statesmen to control and direct economic affairs [but] whenever it came to a sharp opposition between them ... economic considerations gave way before political considerations."[87] This may well have been the case with much economic legislation, but exactly the opposite occurred with the Irish Woollen episode from 1696 onward. The final statute of 1699 was a victory for unofficial lobbying: the Irish Woollen Act was a "country" not a "court" proposal; it was most unwelcome to the English government and so far from being an example of the way in which the state controlled commerce it showed how commercial interests controlled state policy. Constitutional forms in this instance, and perhaps also in others, could give a misleading impression by exaggerating the role played by the state. The constitutional procedure leading to acts of parliament was one and the same, although the backgrounds in which they took their rise might be vastly different. It was always the state which acted in legislation but the tail might very well wag the dog without the constitutional story alone giving any impression to the contrary. In this way mercantilism can seem to be the process by which the state regulated commerce when the process was exactly the opposite.

If constitutional language can be misleading, the same criticism may also be leveled at the use of national categories, in this instance "England" and "Ireland." It is usual to describe economic policies in this way. Thus to many Irish historians the Woollen Act has appeared to be "the beginning of a systematic war waged by England on Irish industrial prosperity." English historians for their part have continued to use this terminology, though in a somewhat different vein. In fact, however, these terms are irrelevant to the main issues. If Bishop King's evidence is to be accepted, the majority in Ireland welcomed this "systematic war" against the woolen trade: it was the English interest in Ireland, not the Catholic Irish or the Ulster Scots, which felt itself threatened by the Act. Enclosure for sheep farming was no more popular with the peasantry of seventeenth-century Ireland than it had been with that of sixteenth-century England. To tell the story in terms of national differences is to introduce extraneous considerations which bring darkness, not light. This point is perhaps not irrelevant when economic relations between England and other countries in the seventeenth century comes up for discussion. The truth is that such language is far too cumbersome for the purposes for which it is used.

As a postscript, the question may be raised whether or not the Act did fulfil the purpose for which it was designed. It will be recalled that John

Locke[88] had opposed complete prohibition on the grounds that it would be impossible to prevent smuggling, and this view seems to have been justified by the later course of events. In 1734 the merchants of Cork admitted openly that they were exporting woolen goods to Lisbon.[89] So far from having been destroyed the Irish woolen industry was still sufficiently interested in exports to press for the repeal of the Woollen Act as late as 1780, when Lord North, under the threats of the Irish Volunteers, agreed to its repeal.[90] The dissolution of this piece of mercantilism, however, no more than its inception, was a completely economic story.

NOTES

1. G. N. Clark, *The Later Stuarts* (1934), p. 305.

2. C. Gill, *Rise of the Irish Linen Industry* (1925), p. 17.

3. C. Wilson, "Mercantilism: Some Vicissitudes of an Idea," *Economic History Review*, 2nd ser. X (1958), 187.

4. Criticisms, however, had already been made in 1680 by the author of *Britannia Languens*. See *Early Tracts on Commerce*, ed. J. R. McCulloch (Cambridge, 1952), p. 402.

5. P. McGrath, *Merchants and Merchandise in Seventeenth Century Bristol* (Bristol Record Soc., 1955), pp. 165–67.

6. *Ibid.* p. 164. n.

7. This section of the pamphlet was published separately in 1696 under the title, "A Discourse concerning the East India Trade, Shewing It to Be Unprofitable to the Kingdom of England." The Company was subjected to parliamentary criticism early in 1696. D. Ogg, *England in the Reigns of James II and William III* (Oxford, 1955), p. 309.

8. It was "against common justice and the birthright of Englishmen to exclude any of them from so great a part of the trade of the Nation and that Bristol, Exeter, Plymouth and Hull should not trade to the East Indies as well as London." Quoted in S. A. Khan, *The East India Trade in the Seventeenth Century* (Oxford, 1923), p. 208.

9. *Cal. S. P. Dom. 1698*, p. 370.

10. R. Walcott, "The East India Interest in the General Election of 1700–1701," *English Historical Review*, LXXI (1956), 223–39.

11. William was forced to give way on the notorious question of the "omitted clause." Cf. J. G. Simms, *The Williamite Confiscation in Ireland* (1956), pp. 61–63.

12. *H. of C. Journals*, XI (1742), 593 ff.

13. This fact is well brought out pictorially in A. Browning, *English Historical Documents, 1660–1714* (1953), p. 221.

14. *H. of C. Journals*, XI (1742), 623. These petitions were not necessarily "spontaneous" and their inspiration may well have come from Westminster.

15. *Ibid.* 633.

16. *Ibid.*

17. *Ibid.* 635.

18. *Ibid.* 621.

19. *Ibid.* 747.

20. *Ibid.* 621.

21. *Ibid.* 754.

22. *Ibid.* 759.

23. *Ibid.* 751.

24. *Ibid.* 750.

25. *Ibid.* 751.

26. *Ibid.* 601.

27. *Ibid.* 695.

28. *Correspondence of Charles Talbot, Duke of Shrewsbury*, ed. W. Coxe (1821), p. 543.

29. P.R.O. Co/391/10. fol. 81.

30. B.M. Hoane 2902 (Hill MSS.) fols. 171–80. Abraham Hill was a member of the Board and several official documents relating to the Board are to be found among his private papers.

31. *Ibid.* fol. 173. v.

32. *Ibid.* fol. 177. v.

33. *Hist. MSS. Com. MSS. of the Duke of Portland*, iii. 576.

34. Shrewsbury to Somers, 24 December 1696, *Correspondence of Charles Talbot, Duke of Shrewsbury*, ed. W. Coxe, p. 451.

35. *Cal. S. P. Dom. 1697*, p. 134; P.R.O. CO/391/10, fol. 81.

36. There was nothing new in this. Capel had been given similar instructions in 1695. *Cal. S. P. Dom. 1694–95*, p. 457; cf. also *ibid. 1691–92*, p. 174.

37. *Hist. MSS. Com. MSS. of the Duke of Buccleuch*, ii. 543.

38. *Ibid.* p. 564.

39. P.R.O. CO/391/10, fol. 331.

40. *Hist. MSS. Com. MSS. of the Duke of Buccleuch*, ii. 582.

41. P.R.O. CO/391/10, fol. 262.

42. *Ibid.* fol. 201.

43. P.R.O. CO/319/10. fol. 226.

44. Locke to Molyneux, 12 September 1696. *Locke's Works* (1812), ix. 387.

45. P.R.O. CO/391/9. fols. 16, 20, 37, 51.

46. B.M. Harleian MSS. 1324, fols. 22–31.

47. *William and Mary Quarterly*, 3rd ser. XIV (1957), 397.

48. P R O CO/391/10, fol. 331.

49. *Ibid.* fol. 343.

50. P.R.O. CO/391/10, fol. 343.

51. R. Walcott, *English Politics in the Early Eighteenth Century* (Oxford 1956), p. 63.

52. B. M. Portland MSS. (S) Seymour to Harley, 13 November 1695.

53. *Cal. S. P. Dom. 1698*, pp. 378–79.

54. *Ibid.* p. 381.

55. "If the subscribers be debarred from [bringing Indian silks in] ... they may ask where their profit lies; to go to India and come back again with pepper?" Vernon to Shrewsbury, 10 May 1698. *Letters Illustrative of the Reign of William III*, ed. G. P. R. James (1841), II, 76.

56. In April Sir Miles Cook expected a great debate in the Lords and "a hard tug when it comes to the question." *Cal. S. P. Dom. 1698*, p. 173.

57. T.C.D. MSS. N. 3.1. fol. 212. 16 April 1698. This was also Sir Richard Cox's view. *Hist. MSS. Com. MSS. of the Duke of Portland*, iii., 609.

58. *H. of C. Journals*, XII (1742), 324.

59. *Cal. S. P. Dom. 1698*, p. 339.

60. He had ceased to be a member of the Board in September, when his place had been taken by a nominee of Blaythwayt and Montague, George Stepney. This was a blow to Locke's influence, since he and Blaythwayt were strongly opposed.

61. The lords justices report 8 July 1699 (P.R.O. TI/62/fol. 228). *Cal. Treasury Papers, 1697–1701/2* (1871), p. 316.

62. C. Gill, *The Irish Linen Industry* (Oxford, 1925), p. 21.

63. P.R.O. TI/62/fol. 230.

64. See above. p. 487. n.

65. Quoted in J. C. Beckett. *Protestant Dissent in Ireland* (1948), p. 34.

66. T.C.D. MSS. N. 3.1. fol. 192. King said that the Catholic Irish "always looked upon good flocks as hurtful to their interest and therefore the first thing the rabble did in '88 was to destroy them." *Ibid. loc. cit.*

67. *Ibid.* fol. 205.

68. This struggle raised the constitutional issue of the Irish House of Lords. King wished his cause to be heard in Ireland; the Irish Society appealed to the English House of Lords. The question was whether the Irish House was the highest court of appeal for a legal issue raised in Ireland. In the event, the decision went against King.

69. *Hist. MSS. Com. MSS. of the Duke of Buccleuch*, II, 617, 620.

70. B.M. Harleian MSS. 1324, fol. 67; also available in *H. of C. Journals*, XII (1742), 439–40.

71. *Hist. MSS. Com. MSS. of the Duke of Buccleuch*, II, 600.

72. B.M. Add. MSS. 40772 (Vernon MSS.) fol. 235.

73. *Irish Statutes (1765)*, III, 472–73.

74. *Hist. MSS. Com. MSS of the Duke of Buccleuch*, II, 615; *ibid.* 616.

75. *Ibid.* 599, 617.

76. T.C.D. MSS. N. 3. 2. fol. 68. King to Annesley, 3 February 1698–99.

77. B.M. Add. MSS 17677 (SS) (Hermitage) fol. 420. v.

78. *Hist. MSS Com. House of Lords MSS*, III, 107.

79. 13 Sept. 1698 B.M. Add. MSS. 40772 (Vernon MSS.) fol. 100.

80. B.M. Add. MSS. 17677 (SS) (Hermitage) fol. 420.

81. *Correspondence of Charles Talbot, Duke of Shrewsbury*, ed. W. Coxe (1821), p. 557.

82. Somers regarded Methuen as "equally the aversion of the Whigs and the Tories both here and in Ireland." W. Coxe, *op. cit.* p. 558. According to Vernon, Methuen was "marked out for ruin." *Letters Illustrative of the Reign of William III* (1841), II, 218.

83. *H. of C. Journals*, XII (1742), 427.

84. *Cal. Treasury Papers, 1691–1701/2* (1871), pp. 372–73.

85. W. R. Scott, *Joint Stock Companies* (Cambridge, 1912), III, 102.

86. 11 & 12 William III, c. iii.

87. Sir George Clark, *War and Society in the Seventeenth Century* (1958), pp. 71–72.

88. *En passant*, it seems clear that John Locke's role in the formation of economic policy was somewhat less decisive than recent commentators have maintained. See M. Cranston, *John Locke* (1957), p. 406.

89. *Hist. MSS. Com. MSS. of the Earl of Egmont*, II, 27.

90. W. E. H. Lecky, *History of Ireland in the Eighteenth Century* (1892), II, 242.

Chapter Fifteen

Fr. Mathew: Apostle of Modernization

(1979)

Father Theobald Mathew is one of the most neglected figures in nineteenth-century Irish historiography. To his contemporaries he appeared to be leading a "moral revolution"[1] in its own way as important as the campaigns of O'Connell, but whereas O'Connell has continued to attract the attention of historians (including Professor R. Dudley Edwards), Father Mathew's reputation remains embalmed within the tradition of the Irish Capuchins and remote from the concerns of Irish historians.[2] Those scholars who have commented upon his role in Irish history have in general confined themselves to his association with Daniel O'Connell and the Repeal Movement.[3] It is the intention of this essay to take another look at the career of Father Mathew and the Temperance Crusade in the belief that there must be something amiss with our interpretation of the pre-Famine period when a man and a movement highly regarded by contemporaries slip through the historians' nets so easily.

This neglect of Fr. Mathew may be attributed to several factors, among which may be included a long-standing tendency among Irish historians to interpret nineteenth-century Irish history in terms of political nationalism. From this point of view, it is hard to make sense of, or even be interested in, the Teetotal Crusade. In fact, the crusade only becomes intelligible in terms of social history, and in a transatlantic context at that. It was in New England in the 1820s that the teetotal movement first took off and it was impulses from the United States which led to the formation of powerful teetotal movements in Britain and in Ireland. Expressions of gratitude to the United States for its moral leadership were regularly made in pamphlet literature of the period and it was not surprising that Fr. Mathew himself should have visited the United States. The American evangelist

Asenath Nicholson came to Ireland in 1845 to visit Fr. Mathew and in her book *Ireland's Welcome to the Stranger*, she paid glowing tributes to him. William Lloyd Garrison and Frederick Douglass saw him as a significant figure. From the point of view of social history, therefore, Fr. Mathew and the Mathewite Crusade form part of a wide transatlantic movement of attempted reform, which was linked with other reform movements of the period, most notably the campaign against slavery.[4]

Another reason for neglect may be sought in an understandable tendency to see Fr. Mathew in specifically Catholic terms. This has had the effect of making him less comprehensible historically by isolating him and his movement from the largely non-conformist context in which teetotalism had its origins. But the difficulty is more apparent than real. A way for overcoming it is suggested by the work of John Bossy, *The English Catholic Community, 1570–1850*, in which he argued that the position in which the English Catholics found themselves was essentially that of a "sect," excluded from the mainstream of public life. In the first half of the nineteenth century, the Irish Catholics, who later formed a major component of Gladstone's grand ethnic, nonconformist, coalition, may be seen as occupying an analogous position, though later in the century their clergy undoubtedly assumed many of the attitudes of an established church. If this was the case, it is not surprising that an Irish Capuchin should make common cause, with the Quakers and with American evangelicals like Mrs. Nicholson.[5] Late in the 1840s, Fr. Mathew was to regret the way in which "*other sects*" had withdrawn support from his crusade, which seems to imply that he thought of himself as belonging to a sect. Mrs. Nicholson looked upon Fr. Mathew as an ally in the same godly cause. She praised his use of the scriptures to defend temperance and she in her turn handed round copies of the Douai Bible. The boundaries between the sects had become fluid. Thus the Capuchin no less than the American missionary may be seen as part of the great evangelical movement which G. M. Young regarded as one of the two dominating influences of the Victorian period.

In the third place, there has been a tendency to see Fr. Mathew too exclusively in terms of drink and abstinence. The teetotal crusade was not however an end in itself; rather, Fr. Mathew saw it as a means to social improvement. A contemporary observer described him as ...

> avoiding all political questions, no man seems more eager than he for the practical improvement of this country. Leases and rents, farming implements, reading societies, music societies, he was full of these and his schemes of temperance above all.[6]

Of his visit to Passage West Co. Cork, it was said:

> his object in establishing the temperance rooms was to afford the teetotals a place of meeting for the purpose of weaning them from a public house, supplying them with good books and in a short time, lecturers who would instruct them in mechanism, husbandry and every other science that would tend to improve their condition, enlarge their understanding, and fit them for the enjoyment of those blessings with which the present time was so pregnant. His object was such and it had been accomplished in many parts of the country that had at this moment libraries in which were to be found the Sacred Bible, historical and geographical works and works of all kinds for the improvement of the operative.[7]

This notion that Fr. Mathew saw his mission as one of "improvement" carries more conviction today perhaps than a decade or so ago, when, under the influence of the late Kenneth Connell, pre-Famine Ireland was seen as a radically diseased society plunging inevitably to disaster.[8] In 1960, however, John Vaizey and Patrick Lynch suggested interpreting Irish society in terms of a "Dual Economy"—a Modernizing East and a Traditional West. Their views have undergone criticism at the hands of several scholars but their overall distinction seems to have survived.[9] If we do accept it, albeit in a modified form, it undoubtedly explains the attitudes of those contemporaries who while recognizing the serious problems which Ireland faced, did not think that "improvement" was impossible. Among them, we may place Fr. Mathew along with other reformers of the period, such as Thomas Drummond and William Blacker. The "Apostle of Temperance" may be seen, without undue paradox, as the "Apostle of Modernisation."

Recent work among British social historians has also been helpful in making sense of teetotalism in Ireland. In particular, Dr. Brian Harrison's fine study, *Drink and the Victorians*[10] provides us with a model of teetotal activity within these islands which we may use to assess the nature of the Mathewite movement. Dr. Harrison emphasizes the social gap which existed between the "moderate" antispirits movement of the 1820s and the more "extreme" teetotal movement of the 1830s. He sees this difference as reflecting a social and religious division in English society between the aristocratic establishment and the dissenting middle and working classes. In support of his thesis he notes the importance of Methodists, Quakers, and Congregationalists in the leadership of the teetotal movement and the extent to which they were involved with other radical causes such as the anti-Corn Law League and criticism of absentee landlords. Even where a conscious political motivation was absent, Dr. Harrison sees teetotalism as providing the "lower classes" with an effective weapon of moral criticism to use against their social superiors. Thus Teetotalism and Chartism may be seen as running parallel to one another, even overlapping as in the case of the Temperance Chartist Henry Vincent. The mass meeting and the reading room were common to both movements.

If we accept Dr. Harrison's thesis about the social and political overtones of the teetotal movement, it helps to explain how the Irish teetotal movement was absorbed so successfully into O'Connell's Repeal Movement despite the reluctance of Fr. Mathew himself. We may detect radicalism, for example, in Mrs. Nicholson's account of her stay in Ireland. She joined the causes of teetotalism and republicanism and was very critical of the members of the establishment with whom she came into contact. In particular, she charged the Reverend Nagle of the Achill mission with treating his converts like freed slaves. Nagle himself suspected that she was the emissary of "some democratic and revolutionary society." In the light of this, it is interesting to note how the statement of principles made by the Repeal Movement sounded the notes of "moral improvement," before political reform.

> Our first principle is to preserve and increase the VIRTUE of the people. The man who is drunken, quarrelsome, idle or selfish may shout for Repeal but he brings disgrace on our cause and is not worthy to be a free citizen of an Irish nation. The murderer, the intimidator and the Ribbonman are foes to Ireland. It should be the boast of a Repealer that having his mind fixed on the holy and glorious object of his country's regeneration, he had conformed his self to a virtuous and manly life.[11]

In the light of these general remarks we may now examine the implications of more detailed comments relating to the Mathew Crusade in the year 1840. In March of that year the Inspector General of the Royal Irish Constabulary addressed the following circular letter to about twenty police barracks in the south of Ireland.[12]

12th March, 1840.

Constabulary Office,
Dublin Castle,

strictly confidential:

With a view to receive as much information as possible on the subject of the present movement of masses of the people in certain parts of the Country, in favor of Temperance, as encouraged by the Rev. Mr. Mathew, I request you will send me, at your earliest convenience, detailed and unreserved answers to the following Queries—on the understanding that whatever use may be made of the information itself, the sources from whence it proceeds shall not be made public.

1. State the period of the Rev. Mr. Mathew's visit to your District.

2. The probable proportion of Protestants to Roman Catholics in your District.

3. The total number of Persons who have taken the Temperance pledge, and what proportion of this number are Protestants.

4. Whether any, and what number of Women, or of Men above those of the Working Class have taken the pledge.

5. Whether the Society is supposed to have any particular Religious or Political object or bearing, and what it is.

6. Whether any who have taken the pledge have since violated it, and in what numbers.

7. Whether those in general who have taken the pledge were formerly of sober or intemperate habits, and what is the feeling of those who have refused the pledge towards those who have taken it.

8. Is it true or false, that numbers of the People take the pledge in a state of intoxication, or at least get drunk after determining to take it?

9. Does the taking of the pledge appear to be associated with superstitious feelings, in many instances;—such as the expectation of immediate manifestations of the Divine judgement, in the event of violating it &c.?

10. What influence has the pledge had on the general conduct of the People, especially at Fairs, Races, and on similar occasions?

11. How many Public Houses have been closed since the introduction of the Temperance pledge, or have the applications for Publicans' Licences been sensibly diminished?

12. State the effect which the Temperance Society has produced upon crime, by enumerating the crimes commited during the six months preceding, and the corresponding period immediately after Mr. MATHEW's visit, confining your attention exclusively to crimes that have their origin in drunkeness, as homicides and other acts of violence.

13. Are those who take the pledge bound by any rules beyond the pledge itself—are they united as a Society in which there are any thing like office bearers, who exercise a control over the members, &c., or have they any regular places or times of meeting, or do they wear any badge except the medal, and when is that worn?

14. State the number of Protestant and Roman Catholic members of the Force in your District, and the number of each persuasion who have taken the pledge.

You will see the importance of weighing well the foregoing Queries, and of carefully concealing from *every* individual the object you have in collecting the information that will enable you to answer them satisfactorily. I am aware of the difficulty of specifying, in several of the cases, the exact numbers, but still you may be able to approximate to the truth.

I need scarcely add, that I shall be glad to receive from you such further observations as the subject referred to may suggest.

D. McGREGOR.

Inspector General

Though the questions are not phrased according to the interests of modern scholars, the answers to them enable us to go some way toward building up a picture, impressionistic though it may be, about the impact of the
Mathewite movement upon these parts of Ireland and by implication to
suggest some conclusions about Irish society.

What then was the reaction to Fr. Mathew's Crusade? Several historians,
among them Dr. Norman and Professor Larkin, have stressed the revivalist
atmosphere of the temperance meetings.[13] This aspect of the movement
undoubtedly emerges from the police reports. Police observers noted, for
example, the habit of getting drunk before taking the pledge "in order, as
they express it, to take their leave of drinking." It was also believed by
many that if the pledge was violated in any way, an immediate manifesta-
tion of divine judgment would bring punishment to bear on the head of
the transgressor. At Loughrea (Co. Galway), a police witness was assured
that Fr. Mathew could cure blindness. Police also noted the "engineering"
of apparent miracles by little boys who pretended to be incapable of walk-
ing and then, after receiving Fr. Mathew's blessing, threw away their
crutches. In Co. Limerick the police reported meeting an old man, unable
to speak English, who told them that "he would not venture out at night,
being afraid of ghosts, but that since he got the medal he would not be
afraid to travel any distance at night." In Abbeyleix (Co. Laois), many of
those with whom the police spoke believed that if they violated the pledge
in the slightest degree, God's wrath would fall upon them by causing mad-
ness or some other grievous malady. Some also believed that if they wore
the medal they could not be shot by policemen or soldiers. At Enniscorthy
(Co. Wexford), it was believed by some that receiving the pledge would
avert any kind of misfortune. Crowds on the steamer carrying would-be
pledgers from Arthurstown (Co. Wexford) to Waterford City included
many invalids who anticipated a cure at the hands of Fr. Mathew. On the
return journey, however, the police witness heard many expressions of disappointment.

Clearly this type of evidence confirms the view that some aspects of the
temperance crusade were far removed from any hint of "modernization."
Yet to see the crusade entirely in these terms is misleading. In fact, the

police reports enable us to be more precise about several types of reaction. We may make, in the first place, a broad distinction between urban and rural reactions. In the urban environment of Limerick City, for example, a teetotal society was founded in 1839, the full title of which was "St. Mary's Temperance and Mortality Society." "Mortality" here referred to payments made by the society toward the funeral expenses of its members. Financial help was also given to paid up members who had fallen ill. The weekly subscriptions of two pence per week were placed in a savings bank. In these features, provision against illness and death and the emphasis upon self-help, St. Mary's temperance society resembled other benevolent societies of the early Victorian period. Where it differed from them was in its emphasis upon the total avoidance of drink. The rule of the society stipulated that:

> it is to be the duty of every member who shall discover another member violating his pledge, to proceed forthwith to the Society's room and have it entered in the book specifying the name, time, place and in what way violated.

The role of the clergy indicated another difference. Rule 12 stated that:

> The Reverend President requires that every Roman Catholic member of the society will go to confession at least within the period of six months and that a book be kept in the society of St. Mary's Chapel in which each member complying with the request will insert his name. This book is to be examined every six months by the Reverend President and in the event of any member being found to neglect this duty that he shall be obliged to assign the cause of his neglect.

What is interesting about this rule, perhaps, is not so much the assumption about the authority of the clergy, as the manner in which that authority is being exercised. We are far removed here from the rural world of ghosts, medals with magical properties, and fears of direct divine intervention. (Perhaps fear of the retribution of the president, Rev. John P. Nolan took its place.) This is clearly an environment which took literacy and keeping records for granted and which contrasted sharply with the ethos of the countryside. It also seems clear that the face-to-face relationship which existed between priest and people in such rural institutions as "The Station" is being replaced here by something much more formal.

The gap between new urban and traditional rural approaches may also be seen in the eighth rule of the society, dealing with funerals. It was laid down that a sum of money be made available for the purchase of scarves which would be worn only at funerals of members or their wives. Here we may see a deliberate attempt being made to break away from the drinking patterns traditionally associated in Ireland with death. The wake and the funeral were occasions on which drink was regarded as a symbol of kinship, solidarity, and neighborliness.[14] The teetotal society, linked by ties based on ideology, was setting itself up against the powerful pressures of custom. Thus the medal presented by Fr. Mathew in an urban context carried with it the obligation to observe a new social code linked with the virtues of thrift and self-help. It is also clear from this book of rules that there was an administrative substructure to the Mathewite crusade. It was not merely, as has often been suggested, a charismatic movement based upon Fr. Mathew's miracle working.

Limerick was not the only town involved. In addition to Limerick and to Cork, "the Mecca of Mathewism" (84,000) many other towns in the south became focal points of the teetotal endeavor. Towns like Clonmel (20,000), Waterford (28,800), Galway (33,100), and Kilkenny (23,700) possessed strong Mathewite groups. Smaller market towns such as Ennis (9,700), Tralee (11,000), Listowel (5,000), and Skibbereen (4,400) were also involved. At Ennis, for example, the "Ennis Total Abstinence Society" met regularly on Sunday evenings. Subscriptions were made to provide medicine for the sick poor and to provide for the families of members who had died without leaving sufficient means of support. Members of the society wore medals openly along with scarves and hatbands at funerals of their fellows. The police report also stated that at their procession on St. Patrick's Day, traditionally a time for "drowning the shamrock" in hard liquor, the Ennis society displayed the flags and banners of their trades and emblems of plenty such as "the Plough" and "a loaf of Bread."

At Ennis, the Mathewite movement was aiming at economic and social as well as moral improvement. Similar comments were made about other towns. At Skibbereen, which Lewis described in his *Topographical Dictionary* as "much improved" and "a very flourishing place," the police saw no sectarian or political object to the movement.[15] "The motive seems to me," the inspector reported, "to be a sincere desire to overcome the great cause which has long obstructed their improvement and moral and physical advancement." The same inspector made an interesting comment in answer to the official query about the influence of superstition:

> I cannot discern any superstitious feeling associated with the taking of the Temperance Pledge.—It is a voluntary act—a solemn vow made before God and the world—and the solemnity of that vow resembles the solemnity of

an oath with the feeling that public opinion, that is the opinion of the man's neighbours rather than the imminent manifestations of Divine Judgement attaches to him who violates it, a stain not to be disregarded by an Irish peasant.

A similar type of reaction occurred in the report about Clonmel where the inspector saw the movement as working for good. He expected that it would lead a poor people "to increase their comforts, peace and happiness and elevate materially their national character." He also noted "an increase of small deposits to the Savings Bank, principally from a class of trading people who were not in the habit of making any deposits heretofore, a very great increase of application on the Loan funds and punctuality in keeping up with the weekly proportions of the loan!" He added that "many of those who heretofore could not get security, do not find difficulty at present in procuring it owing to their improved habits of life!"

Reports about other towns make the same point. At Waterford the inspector saw "a permanent determination in the minds of the working classes to abstain from the use of intoxicating liquors with *a hope to improve the condition of the community.*" In Co. Galway, it was reported that many took the pledge from a motive of economy as well as of morality. At Limerick, members of the Temperance Society planned to carry banners and scarves belonging to the trade unions as well as their medals on St. Patrick's Day.

We are accustomed to think of pre-Famine Ireland as an overwhelmingly rural society, but as the picture emerges piecemeal from the inspectors' reports we become aware of the importance of towns. It was from the towns, small though they were in proportion to the rural population, that the Mathewite movement, like the Repeal Movement, and like the teetotal movements in Britain, emerged.[16] The Mathewites were urban-based, with a small activist group in each town acting as a central focus of activity. In Connell's presentation of Ireland as a "peasant society" this would have been largely incomprehensible. Against the background of the Lynch-Vaizey model of a dual economy, however, we may see it in terms of a "modernizing" cash sector influencing the rest of its rural hinterland though still, it is true, leaving large areas untouched. All in all, however, the temperance tea party and the savings bank went together.

Leadership of the movement seems to have come from a middle class, if we accept the repeated comments of the police. At Tulla (Co. Clare), they noted that "the most respectable appeared to regulate the movement of others" at the regular Sunday meetings. At Charleville, they commented on a considerable number of respectable farmers, shopkeepers, and even higher classes. At Dingle, it was reported that a dozen "of the better sort of shopkeepers" joined the society. It was noted that 150 comfortable farmers and shopkeepers joined at Rathkeale, about 300 "respectable" at Enniscorthy, at Cahir "a great many above the working class," at Cappoquin 15–20 shopkeepers, at Parsonstown 100, at Philipstown 60, at Tralee 100. At Kilkenny, however, though a few respectable mechanics and shopkeepers took the pledge, the inspector was informed "that this type of person do not appear to feel any interest in the progress of temperance." At other towns, Loughrea, Listowel, and Mountmellick, for example, there were apparently very few above the working class. While it is difficult to be precise about the type of person who took an active part in the Mathewite movement, we would not perhaps be wrong in speaking of a middle-class core, which included of course the clergy. These "respectable" members of society were those whose patronage lay behind the establishment of reading rooms in the various towns and in the purchase of newspapers. Literacy— in English—was one of the methods through which the aims of the movement were to be achieved. In this, as in other aspects, the movement resembled other "improving" movements in Britain and the United States.

Dr. Harrison noted that there seemed to be "an inverse relation between radical political agitation and teetotal moral crusading."[17] The more teetotalers there were, the fewer radicals. This judgment largely holds good of the early history of the Mathewite crusade when, as we have noted, there was a great deal of revivalism and of zeal for "improvement." But even as early as 1840 the police noted political agitation among the teetotalers of certain areas. At Corofin (Co. Clare), the inspector reported that the parish priest made a political harangue to the effect that a Clare was the first county in Ireland to achieve a victory in 1828 in returning O'Connell to Parliament, "a victory gained by sobriety," it should continue to be in the vanguard. He strongly backed O'Connell against the conservatives over the Irish Corporations Bill, "the passing of which would be of such advantage." At Oughterard (Co. Galway), the inspector noted that some were tempted to use the society to bring their own religious or political object in view. Here, as with economic improvement, we seem to be some way from the traditional rural world.

The police at Charleville reported that the society there had decidedly political-religious objects in view. A number of workmen were overheard saying, "we lost the battle of Vinegar Hill and Ross by Drunkenness but we are more secure and united now when the Battle comes. No Whiskey, no Tatters." Another Protestant witness was told, "Father Mathew will soon pull down your churches and put you under one fut [*sic*]." On Saint Patrick's Day, it was reported that an inflammatory speech had been made to the effect that "they should prepare for war against their enemies and that they would have to wade up to their necks in Protestant blood and the Poor Houses now preparing would be made prisons for them and that they would have no English laws here." If these remarks were correctly reported, the incorporation of the Teetotal Crusade into the radicalization of the Repeal Movement was an understandable progression for many.

Indeed, at Kenmare, links between teetotalers and radicals seemed already to exist. The police considered that the Temperance Society had become "a sort of organisation" for "the radical party." Inspector O'Malley Burke reported that the commonalty thought that "what they call the cause of the people is the object of the society and [that] anxious for aggrandisement, the lowest classes eagerly joined an institution in harmony with their prejudices." The inspector complained of what he called "the worst characters" talking politics until the late hours. "The consequence is," he complained, "that they are self-sufficient and insolent, and hence respectable members of property are led to look upon the society as an instrument of Revolution." He felt that medals and processions occupied "the exclusive motive of the vulgar in whose minds they are associated with scenes of triumph and excitement."

In Tipperary, one inspector suspected that newspapers of "violent politics" were supplied for temperance reading rooms. At Newport (Co. Tipperary), it was said that the temperance processions were beginning to display "something like a political appearance." At Roscrea and at Enniscorthy, Ribbonmen were suspected of joining in the movement. At Arthurstown (Co. Wexford), the police inspector felt that, if temperance was the chief object, he did not see:

> the use of parading with Flags, Banners, and Musick three deep with medals and other badges with death heads and cross bones forming the most prominent devices but ingeniously set forth as emblematical of the victims of intemperance and by which it is remarked the late rebellion was lost and it is whispered that if the battle was to be fought over again it would not be lost in consequence of intemperance as before.

But in other areas the radicals do not seem to have had it all their own way. Not everyone approved of processions. At Rathkeale (Co. Limerick),

respectable Roman Catholics were said to have considered them quite unnecessary for the furtherance of the Temperance cause. There was also
controversy about the color of ribbons—black, white, or green—to be
worn with medals during processions. Green was proposed at Bruff (Co.
Limerick), but the Rev. M. Cussen P.P., described by the police as "a most
excellent man," objected to this and succeeded in having black substituted.
Even so, to the three cheers for the Temperance Movement and for Fr.
Mathew, three cheers were added for Daniel O'Connell. At Newport (Co.
Tipperary), on St. Patrick's Day, several thousand Mathewites walked in
procession wearing medals suspended from black or green ribbons, which
may have indicated a division within the local movement. At Belmullet,
the organizer of the St. Patrick's Day procession, a certain Robert Carey,
merchant, informed the police that there would be "no exhibition of Party
feeling," and "No flags—banners—or Party tunes calculated to give of-
fense to any of her majesty's subjects." The Band, he stated, intended to
play "the National Airs" of "Patrick's Day" and "Garryowen."

Does all this amount to something which we can call modernization?
At the very least it shows that the Mathewite movement owed its success
to something more than the charismatic appeal of a particular individual,
though there were undoubtedly those who sought salvation by touching
the hem of Fr. Mathew's garment. But the urban thrust of the crusade, its
emphasis upon such values as literacy, thrift, and insurance against illness
and its involvement in politics in some areas link it with other movements
which were attempting to cope with the new problems of a changing
world. In this respect, the Mathewite movement and the Repeal movement, for all their differences at the local level, may be regarded as spring-
ing from the same impulses. O'Connell, despite the emphasis currently
laid upon his Gaelic background, was as much a man of the modern world
as Fr. Mathew. Each represented a shift from "local" to "cosmopolitan"
values,[18] an attempt by urban men to control and reform rural society. To
say this does not mean we have to adopt the attitude of the reformers
themselves and to condemn the old world in creating the new, nor is it to
say that the worldview of the repealer and the teetotaler was in itself more
rational than that of the Ribbonmen and of the poitin maker. But the
world which was coming into existence favored the one rather than the
other—or at least seemed to.[19]

I am grateful to Professor Maureen Murphy of Hofstra University, to Jim
Barrett and Vic Walsh of the University of Pittsburgh, and to Brendan
McGiolla Choille of the State Paper Office in Dublin for their help.

NOTES

1. The phrase is J. G: Kohl's. See J. G. Kohl, *Travels in Ireland* (London, 1844), p.98. On Fr. Mathew generally, see pp. 93–113.

2. Such works of official history contain useful material. See especially Fr. Augustine, *Footprints of Fr. Mathew* (Dublin, 1947); J. F. Maguire, *Fr. Mathew: A Biography* (London, 1863). (My copy was sold by the Belfast Friends Institute Library in 1973.); P. Rogers, *Father Theobald Mathew: Apostle of Temperance* (Dublin, 1943). See review on *I.H.S* by T. P. O'Neill, IV. 372–4.

3. L. J. McCaffrey, *Daniel O'Connell and the Repeal Year* (University of Kentucky, 1966), pp. 21–23; E. Norman, *A History of Modern Ireland* (London, 1972), pp. 74–75; P. O'Farrell, *Ireland's English Question* (London, 1971), pp. 105–106; E. Larkin, "The Devotional Revolution in Ireland, 1850–1870," *American Historical Review* (June 1972), pp. 635–52.

4. A. Nicholson, *Ireland's Welcome to the Stranger* (London, 1847). For other references to Fr. Mathew in an American context see W. T. Garrison, *William Lloyd Garrison, the Story of His Life* (New York, 1889) vol. iii, and F. M. Holland, *Frederick Douglass: The Colored Orator* (New York, 1969) pp. 116–17. I am indebted to my colleague Richard Blackett for these references.

5. On the role of Quakers in the teetotal movement see E. Isichei, *Victorian Quakers* (Oxford, 1970), pp. 235–43.

6. Fr. Augustine, *Footprints* (Dublin, 1947), p. 242.

7. Ibid. p. 252.

8. K. H. Connell, *The Population of Ireland, 1750–1845* (Oxford, 1950), p. 117.

9. P. Lynch and John Vaizey, *Guinness's Brewery in the Irish Economy, 1759–1876* (Cambridge, 1960). For the main criticisms, see J. H. Johnson, "The Two Irelands at the Beginning of the Nineteenth Century," in *Irish Geographical Studies* (Belfast, 1970), pp. 224–43; J. Lee, "The Dual Economy in Ireland 1800–1850" in T. D. Williams, ed., *Historical Studies VIII* (Dublin, 1971) pp. 191–201.

10. B. Harrison, *Drink and the Victorians: The Temperance Question in England, 1815–1872* (London, 1971); B. Harrison and B. Trinder, *Drink and Sobriety in an Early Victorian Country Town: Banbury 1830–1860* (London, 1969). See also J. R. Barrett, "Why Paddy Drank: The Social Importance of Whiskey in Pre-Famine Ireland," in *Journal of Popular Culture* (1977) pp. 155–66; R. Stivers, *A Hair of the Dog: Irish Drinking and American Stereotype* (London, 1976); R. F. Bales, "Attitudes Towards Drinking in the Irish Culture," in D. J. Pittman and C. R. Snyder (ed.), *Society, Culture and Drinking Patterns* (New York, 1962); R. F. Bales, "Cultural Differences in the Rates of Alcoholism" *Quarterly Journal of Studies on Alcohol*, v. 6 (1945–56).

11. Enrollment in the Repeal Movement by Mr. Thomas Byrne, 19 September 1843. In the possession of Mrs. H. F. Kearney.

12. S. P. O. Dublin, O.P. (MA) 1840, 131/10.

13. Cited above, no. 3.

14. S. O'Suilleabháin, *Irish Wake Amusements* (Cork, 1947); K. Danaher, *The Year in Ireland* (Cork, 1972); N. Z. Davis, "Some Tasks and Themes in the Study of Popular Religion," in C. Trinkaus (ed.), *The Pursuit of Holiness* (Michigan, 1974).

15. S. Lewis, *A Topographical Dictionary of Ireland* (London, 1837).

16. The towns were also the support of the Repeal Association. See T. N. Brown, "Nationalism and the Irish Peasant 1800–1848," in *Review of Politics* (October 1953), vol. xv, p. 435.

17. Harrison, op. cit.

18. On modernization there is an interesting article by Professor S. P. Hays in *Peasant Studies*, vol. v (April 1977), pp. 68–79. See also E. A. Wrigley, "The Process of Modernisation and the Industrial Revolution in England," in *Journal of Interdisciplinary History*, vol. iii (1972–73), pp. 225–59.

19. At a personal level, the writer regrets the impact of modernization upon the drinking habits of Dublin's intellectuals exemplified in the destruction (1970) of Hartigan's "snug" and the rise of the "lounge bar."

Chapter Sixteen

The Great Famine

Legend and Reality

(1957)

The course taken by Irish nationalism during the nineteenth century was largely determined by men and circumstances peculiar to Ireland; its general direction, however, was profoundly affected by wider European influences. Like other nationalisms of the period, Irish nationalism owed to the Romantic Movement its eagerness in seeking out history as an indispensable ally; and during the second half of the century it came to be conceived in historical terms, taking as its intellectual basis an interpretation of Irish history. Most nationalists sought, and found, in Irish history the justification and inspiration of their political opinions, Mitchel and Pearse, Davitt and Connolly being the most prominent and providing the most lasting contribution.

In doing so, they reflected a general shift of emphasis in European thought. History, which for the *philosophes* was an irrelevant absurdity, became for nineteenth-century thinkers the essence of political philosophy, a change the extent of which can be measured by comparing the American Declaration of Independence of 1776 with the Proclamation of the Irish Republic in 1916. Both Americans and Irish rejected the authority of the British Crown and established a republic; but whereas, in 1776, the appeal of the colonists was to the Rights of Man (life, liberty, and the pursuit of happiness), in 1916 it was the "historic rights of the Irish people, which in every generation ... have asserted their right to national freedom" that provided much of the intellectual basis for the Rising. Thomas Jefferson assumed the self-evident truth of John Locke's political philosophy when drawing up the Declaration of American Independence; the men of 1916 turned to history for their justification. In doing so, Pearse, no less than Connolly, was a child of the nineteenth century, during the course of which the related historicisms of Hegel and Marx had supplanted the rationalism of Locke and Bentham.

The eventual success of the Irish revolution inevitably brought with it the enshrinement of the successful interpretation of Irish history. In popular textbooks, in some newspapers, and in many schools this view of Irish history came to be accepted almost without criticism and any departure from it seemed to betray the actions of 1916. Meanwhile, in the Six Counties of Northern Ireland, the government was at some pains to create a history of its own. The Six Counties sought their reflection in the past, and a historical monster called "The Province" made its appearance, not merely in the sixteenth century, but also in the second millenium B.C.[1] The results were as bizarre as those of Marxists who attempted to canonize Sir Thomas More and Sir William Petty in a calendar of Marxist forerunners. All this and similar attempts to use history for political purposes may cause alarm but certainly not surprise. What is surprising indeed is for a government to sponsor a work of free historical research, leaving the authors at liberty, if the facts warrant, to strike at the most strategic point of the "official" interpretation. When this happens, there is cause for congratulation.

It is difficult to believe that before the publication of *The Great Famine*,[2] in 1957, there had been no detached treatment of this central episode in Irish history. Yet such was the case. No significant addition had been made since almost the time of the Famine itself, when circumstances did not favor detachment. The main lines which the history books were to follow for over a century were in fact laid down in 1847 by John Mitchel's friends, Father John Kenyon and Devin Reilly. It was Father Kenyon who categorically claimed that "the plentiful harvests of golden grain [were] more than sufficient—ever since the potato blight—to support, and to support well, our entire population," while, a month or so later, Devin Reilly's letter to the *Nation* declared that the Irish people were being "coolly and gradually murdered" by the British government.

The definitive expression of this view was given by John Mitchel in his writings, notably *The Last Conquest of Ireland* (1860), *An Apology for the British Government in Ireland* (1860), and *History of Ireland* (1869). Arthur Griffith in his introduction to Mitchel's *Jail Journal* (1913) accepted this interpretation of the Famine, and it received its latest expression in 1952 in P. S. O'Hegarty's *History of Ireland under the Union*, from which the following quotation is taken (p. 328):

In the known facts of the business there is justification for the view that
the Government policy under which over a million died, and over a million emigrated in five years, was a deliberate policy of extermination in
pursuance of English political advantage, so as to ensure Ireland remaining indefinitely and powerlessly under England's control. ... The
whole course of Government measures right through the crisis, deliberately or automatically it matters not, was inspired and directed towards
starvation.

This is almost identical with Mitchel's view, which may now be elabo-
rated in a little more detail.

According to Mitchel, "the Almighty indeed sent the potato blight, but
the English created the famine." Even before the Famine, the Devon Commission, set up by Sir Robert Peel, had recommended some measure of
depopulation in the interest of the landlords. But Peel found it difficult
until the Famine to carry out any large-scale changes. Then came 1845, and
"how the famine helped Sir Robert Peel and how Sir Robert Peel helped
the famine forms the whole history of the island for the next five years."
Peel, not Russell, is the villain of the story, and in this may be detected the
influence of the long feud which had gone on between Peel and O'Connell's
Repeal Movement. Peel "could wait but he knew that hunger could not
wait." His policy was therefore one of complete inaction. His government
did not take the obvious step of closing the ports, with the result that
"abundant and magnificent" crops of grain and herds of cattle were
shipped to England, while the Irish starved. But for this, Smith O'Brien
pointed out, Irish resources would have been "abundantly adequate."
Indeed the 1847 census of agricultural produce showed that the harvest
"would have amply sustained *double* the entire population of the island,"
that is, sixteen million people. It is true that Indian corn was imported by
the government, but "a government ship sailing into any harbour with Indian corn, was sure to meet half a dozen sailing out with Irish wheat and
cattle." The failure to close the ports provides the explanation why, though
potato crops failed elsewhere in Europe, there was no famine save in Ireland. It is thus no exaggeration to say that a "million and a half of men,
women and children were carefully, prudently and peacefully slain by the
English government." The Famine was "artificial"; it was a deliberate conspiracy of the British government in the interests of the landlords. Ireland,
so far from being a poor country, was a "rich and fertile" land, which produced every year "abundance and superabundance to sustain her own
people and many more."

This was Mitchel's version of the Famine, which in its essentials became an integral part of the nationalist interpretation of Irish history. The British government became, for nationalists, the equivalent of the papacy in Orange mythology—not an institution capable of honest mistakes, but a gigantic conspiracy against the Irish people. This view of the Famine remained unchanged between 1847 and 1957. But it was not entirely without competitors. In Father O'Rourke's *History of the Famine*, Sir Charles Trevelyan's *The Irish Crisis* and James Connolly's *Labour in Irish History*, the Famine was regarded as a social disaster, not a political conspiracy; where Mitchel blamed the British government, Connolly blamed the social system. All these accounts, however, like Mitchel's, are open to criticism on the grounds either that their sources of evidence were insufficient or else that they had a political axe to grind. The time was indeed ripe for a history of the Famine, which would use material and methods not available to writers of earlier generations.

The Great Famine consists of seven chapters by different contributors, each a specialist in the aspect of the Famine with which he is concerned. The question must now be asked, how far does modern historical research confirm or modify the view of the Famine which Mitchel first popularized, and which has left such an enduring mark upon Irish nationalism?

The picture provided by the writers of this present volume is very different from Mitchel's, both in its general emphasis and in detail. Mitchel's story of the ships sailing into the harbor, for example, is exploded once and for all by Mr. T. P. O'Neill. During the year 1846–47, imports of wheat and flour into Ireland were five times greater than exports. Three times as much barley entered Ireland as left it, and four times the quantity of Indian corn was imported as oats exported. Thus even though the ports were not closed, the balance of food imports over exports was substantial. Mr. O'Neill has examined elsewhere the exact difference it would have made had the ports been closed, and he gives figures very different from Mitchel's. So far from there being enough to feed sixteen million people amply, the food which was exported would have provided the three million destitute of 1847 with a daily ration of 1⅓ ozs. of wheat and 9 ozs. of oats. This diet would have compared unfavorably with the contemporary workhouse diet. The English government's decision not to close the ports still remains open to criticism, but the realities of the situation were very different from what Mitchel would have his readers believe. Many more ships carrying food sailed into Irish harbors than out of them.

Ireland was in fact incapable of feeding its population without imports, once the potato failed. This indeed was the fundamental difference between Ireland and other countries of western Europe.

The British government also emerges from this volume much better than might have been anticipated. It may have lacked foresight and generosity, and have been guilty of grossly underestimating the human problems involved, but it was not guilty of either criminal negligence or of deliberate heartlessness. Surprisingly, in view of Mitchel's strictures, the verdict on Peel is more favorable than that on Russell. Dr. K. B. Nowlan considers that Peel showed "reasonable promptness" and some degree of foresight. Mr. O'Neill believes that "if success is the yardstick of judgment in this matter, Peel's measures certainly merit praise. He showed an initiative unusual in that era of laissez-faire and undertook tasks at variance with current economic theory." Peel's policy was in fact more imaginative than Russell's. Even though he did not close the ports, he was responsible for importing Indian corn in 1845 which was sold at less than cost price to private individuals, but not to commercial buyers. It was this action which prevented the exploitation of scarcity in the spring and summer of 1846, and even the *Nation* admitted the extent of Peel's success.

By comparison, Russell was much more the slave of current economic fashion. Yet the appointment of Russell as prime minister in mid-1846 was welcomed by O'Connell, who had predicted that a conservative government would mean famine. Russell's doctrinaire economic views committed him to a policy of nonintervention in 1846, when the potato crop suffered a complete failure. The solution for the Famine was now to be found in the inauguration of public works, by which the destitute would earn sufficient money to feed themselves. The government was not to intervene in the buying and distribution of food, and the field was to be left open to private traders. This scheme sounded well on paper, and it passed through parliament in 1846 without criticism from the Irish members. O'Connell was still too enamored of the Whig connection to sacrifice future political benefits by untimely criticism. What O'Connell gained on the political swings by Peel's fall, however, Ireland lost on the economic roundabouts, as O'Connell himself saw later in the year. In mid-1846, however, main attention was focused upon the controversy between Old and Young Ireland, and it was not until the Famine had begun that serious attention was given to it.

Russell's miscalculation was to treat the Famine by an extension of normal methods, and his mistake was to have disastrous consequences. The price of food rose sharply and the government did nothing to keep down prices. The ports remained open. Finally, the government put as much financial responsibility as possible on the local landowners, and when things went wrong with the public works scheme it blamed the landlords. Even so, at the height of the Famine in 1847, the Repeal Party showed no united opposition to Russell. They were given the opportunity to vote with the opposition in favor of Bentinck's Railway Bill, to invest sixteen million pounds in Ireland. When they came to vote, however, only seventeen Repealers favored the bill, five abstained, and the remaining six openly supported the government.

At length even Russell was forced to give way before the realities of the Famine. In the spring of 1847, the free distribution of food began, and by the middle of the year more than three million destitute people were receiving a daily food ration. Russell's earlier policy of public works had completely failed, and he found himself committed to a policy of government assistance far more radical than that of Peel in 1845.

For all this catalog of errors and rigidity, the tale is not one of deliberate extermination. Dr. Nowlan assures us that Russell, though unimaginative and parsimonious, was moved by no hatred or even ill-will toward the Irish people. The failure to close the ports was capable of being defended on economic grounds and even his policy of public works was not as farcical as is often made out. In insisting that public money should be devoted to public works, the government adopted a high-minded but unrealistic attitude. The Irish landlords pressed for productive works such as drainage, and had the government been as devoted to their interests as Mitchel maintained, it would have given way. There was indeed a strong party in the British cabinet which opposed Russell on this matter, but though they won over the lord lieutenant to their views, they could make no headway in the face of the refusal of the civil service to take part in commercial activities. Though the machinery of public works broke down eventually under the strain of finding employment for the starving millions, Mr. O'Neill's verdict is still comparatively favorable. "The board of works," he writes, "deserves great credit for the manner in which it dealt with the tasks imposed upon it. These were impossible, but it is doubtful if any department of state could have done more." The daily feeding of over three million people was a remarkable achievement by the standards of any nineteenth-century administration.

Finally, Sir William MacArthur disposes of Mitchel's statement that the British government deliberately concealed the number of famine deaths in the census of 1851. Mitchel's view has a superficial plausibility in that the number of deaths by starvation was recorded officially as only twenty thousand. To these, however, must be added deaths by dropsy, fever, and dysentery, which bring the total to about 350,000. Sir William MacArthur regards this as a gross underestimate: the total was probably well in excess of half a million, and for the famine years as a whole may not be much less than a million. It was not conspiracy, however, which made the official figures so low. Sir William states categorically that his observations "are not intended as a criticism of the compilers of that great work, the census of 1851. They faced many difficulties in gathering their figures of death and disease, and sorted and analysed them with scrupulous care and infinite patience. They themselves were well aware of the unreliability of many of the returns they dealt with, and were careful to point out some of the possible sources of error."

If this book may be said to have a lesson, it is that the Famine was a national disaster above and beyond politics. Political interests and decisions form part of the story, but, as a whole, the story is not the exclusively political one which Mitchel and others would have us accept. Against the background of starvation, fever, panic-stricken emigration, and widespread eviction, the political mistakes and mismanagement fade almost into insignificance. To use Dr. Oliver MacDonagh's words, "Granted the existing agrarian framework, the Ireland of the early 1840's was grossly overpopulated." The excess population was concentrated in the relatively infertile west. Improving agriculture was at a discount. The rapid growth of the population was encouraged by the swing toward tillage since the 1780s, and, in its turn, encouraged more and more subdivision of land. "Ireland," as Dr. McDowell remarks, "was a nation of landlords." The picture often given in textbooks of two classes in Irish society, landlord and peasant, is misleading in this respect. In many cases the Irish Catholic tenant of a great Protestant landowner was the de facto landlord to a host of lesser tenants, holding their land from him on one-year leases. And it was normally the middleman who made the profit.

Pressure of population forced rents up. But the population continued to increase, albeit at a diminishing rate which was lower in the 'forties than in the earlier decades of the century. Because of high rents the ubiquitous potato provided an accepted standard of living. Potatoes could be grown on land which was too poor for grain and of little use for grazing, and it was mainly for this reason that the poor land in the west could support so many.[3] The complete dependence on the one crop of so many who farmed for subsistence and without reserves provided the elements of a most dangerous situation. The signs were there to be read in the partial famines of 1822, 1831, 1835, 1836, 1837, 1839, and 1842 (and also in the virtual absence of famine between 1741 and 1817); but even at this date it is difficult to see what could have been done to prevent disaster. Improving agriculture implied larger holdings and therefore evictions. Security of tenure in the existing situation was of little use unless production per acre rose. High rents would continue as long as the population increased. Land reclamation and drainage demanded the expenditure of capital which was not available in Ireland. The most prosperous farmers in Ireland were indeed the graziers of Limerick, Tipperary, Roscommon, and Meath who, in Dr. E. R. R. Green's words, "would not have deigned to turn a sod with the plough." For such a problem, mass emigration was perhaps the only solution.

Only one part of the Irish economy was in a healthy state, the industrial area centered on Belfast, which had benefited from the technological changes of the late eighteenth and early nineteenth centuries. Elsewhere in Ireland, the effects on Irish industry of the Industrial revolution had been disastrous, though the Union had indeed created an open market for Irish agriculture. In eastern Ulster there was no famine as such and deaths here were largely due to fever brought in by fugitives from other parts of Ireland.

The Ireland of 1845 as described in this work was a "ramshackle" and "ill-balanced" society. Mitchel's "abundance and super-abundance" simply did not exist. Humanly speaking, the Famine was inevitable. Even if the remedial measures of 1846–48 had been wholly successful, the only practical solution would have been mass emigration. The Famine did what no government could have done, to force two million people to leave Ireland during the years 1845–50 and so create conditions in which a balanced society was possible once more.

If it is naïve to blame the British government for the disaster of the Famine, nevertheless there were cases in which government action could have prevented unnecessary suffering. Many evictions were carried out in a heartless manner, and the amendment to the 1847 Poor Law, at the suggestion of William Gregory, M.P., and known as the "quarter acre clause" needlessly increased the rate of evictions. Often houses were leveled while the occupants were receiving indoor relief within the workhouse. Emigration was often forced on tenants by landlords' pressure. In this connection, Dr. MacDonagh describes an estate in Roscommon where, in 1848, 2,400 people were occupying 2,100 acres which produced only one-third of the food necessary to feed them. The Union workhouses of the district were full, and the total expense of subsidized emigration was considerably less than the cost of a year's food. It was thus decided to offer "emigration or eviction." One's sympathy is naturally with the tenants, but even so Dr. MacDonagh's general conclusion is that "there is no general moral judgment to be passed. Landlords stand condemned for specific acts of inhumanity, dishonesty and irresponsibility; but not, in justice, for a point of view and tangle of economic difficulty which, in nine cases out of ten, they merely had the misfortune to inherit."

Taken all in all, the general impression conveyed by this book is one of "inevitability" unless a radical change in the social system took place. The reliance upon the potato as the basic food of the population was a risk which carried the possibility of famine along with it. The wonder perhaps is not that the Famine came in 1845, but that it did not come before, and not that a million died, but that so many were saved. One thing does emerge from a reading of this volume: there was no simple solution for a problem of such complexity. "Repeal" was one answer, but there was no way out without a great deal of human suffering.

Despite its omission of a section dealing with population problems, *The Great Famine* is a striking example of social history at its best. The contributors to the volume were faced with the difficult task of analysing in a scholarly but imaginative way the life of Irish society at a critical moment in its existence. Their problems were not made easier by an immediate environment in which the Famine was still a live emotional and political issue. Nevertheless, they achieved success, and one would be hard put indeed to name a work of similar breadth and originality in nineteenth-century Irish history. In a sense, the Famine has now, thanks to their labors, become part of Irish history. Before, it was part of the present; now, it has been laid to rest.

It remains to wonder what effect *The Great Famine* will have upon the teaching of nineteenth-century Irish history. The time lag between the publication of research and its effect upon the writers of textbooks can often be half a century or more. Perhaps in the case of the Famine the time lag will be shorter. So much valuable work deserves a better fate than to be ignored. Until its conclusions are incorporated into the textbooks, Irish history in the nineteenth century will remain present politics. If war is too important a subject to be left to generals, political history is too important to be left to the politicians.

NOTES

1. *Ancient Monuments Not in State Charge* (Belfast, 1952), pp. 9, 41.

2. *The Great Famine*, edited by R. Dudley Edwards and T. Desmond Williams, Browne & Nolan, Dublin, 1956, 30s.

3. Other causes must also be taken into consideration, such as fishing and seasonal migration.

Chapter Seventeen

Colonizing Irish History
Canny Sets the Agenda

(2002)

"The period 1534–1691 in Irish history, though an age of economic advance and intellectual activity, was above all an age of disruption. Prolonged and fundamental conflict over sovereignty, land, religion and culture produced changes more catastrophic and far-reaching than anything Ireland had experienced since the Anglo-Norman invasion of the twelfth century, or was to experience again till the great famine, the land war, and the struggle for national independence." Such are the concluding words of the late T. W. Moody in his introduction to volume III of *A New History of Ireland* (1976). In his brilliant new book, *Making Ireland British*, Nicholas Canny provides his own interpretation of this revolutionary period, but whereas Moody was able to call upon the services of nearly a score of specialists, in the tradition of the *Cambridge Modern History*, Canny has worked as an individual scholar over three decades and more. The publication of this book thus provides the occasion to contrast the approach of an individual scholar with that of a well-organized team. It also gives us the opportunity to compare two generations of Irish historians.

Moody's judgment about the significance of the period 1534–91 does not include the concept "revolution" but it is implied in his overall tone. Canny is in full agreement about the revolutionary character of the changes involved but his emphasis is different. Canny's theme, following upon the approach of his mentor, David Quinn, is to stress the deliberate conquest and colonization of Ireland. Canny's argument in fact is that Spenser set the agenda for this policy, which was followed up by others, including Thomas Wentworth, Earl of Strafford, and later carried to completion by

Oliver Cromwell. Radical changes would have come to Ireland without doubt in the wake of the invention of gunpowder and the printing press. Nor could Ireland have expected to remain immune from the impact of the Reformation and Counter-Reformation. In Canny's view, however, what differentiated the history of Ireland from other areas of these islands was its exposure to systematic colonization. It was this experience which distinguishes Irish history from that of Wales and Scotland, though it perhaps links it with that of Bohemia and Andalusia.

Colonization was not the only option available. The Crown often preferred to proceed upon the basis of agreement with such magnates as Ormond, Thomond, and even, at one phase of his career, with Hugh O'Neill. What marked a distinct shift was the publication of the papal bull *Regnans in Excelsis* (1570), followed by the rise of a Puritan faction led by Robert Dudley, earl of Leicester, at Elizabeth's court. Mary Queen of Scots, now living in exile in England, became the focal point of plots against Elizabeth. It was these years which witnessed Leicester's expedition to the Netherlands (1585), the execution of Mary (1587), the defeat of the Spanish Armada (1588) and in Ireland the revolt of the earl of Desmond (1579–83) which was crushed by the lord deputy Grey with the utmost severity. In an unforgettable passage of his *view* Edmund Spenser described the impact of Grey's scorched-earth policy on the local inhabitants:

> Out of every corner of the woods and glens they came creeping forth upon their hands, for their legs could not bear them. They looked anatomies of death, they spake like ghosts crying out of their graves, they did eat of the dead carrion, happy were they could find them, yea and one another soon after in so much as the very carcasses they spared not to scrape out of their graves, and if they could find a plot of watercress or shamrocks, there they flocked as to a feast for the time, yet not able long to continue therewithal, that in short space there was none almost left and a most populous country suddenly left void of man or beast.

Canny wants us to believe that the policy of conquest and colonization adumbrated in Spenser's *View of the State of Ireland*, and also implied, he believes, in *The Faerie Queen*, represent the main thrust of English policy. This is Canny's judgment in the conclusion to his book but in earlier chapters he himself provides material which indicates that other options were available. Thus he shows how Gaelic Irish lords such as the earl of Clancar (MacCarthy Mór) successfully opposed in the law courts the administration's attempts to seize their lands. Even after Mountjoy's victory at Kinsale a policy of moderation toward the defeated O'Neill prevailed, backed by the English general Mountjoy. O'Neill was received at court and the plantation of his lands and those of O'Donnell ceased to be part of the government agenda. The aim of Ormond "to govern by lenity and to qualify the Irish by polity" was as much in the running as Grey's militant option of the "reducing of this country into civility." Canny's insistence that "Spenser set the agenda" thus needs to be qualified. "Did Spenser set the agenda?" might be more appropriate. No doubt the hard-line views expressed by Spenser and others were influential but the views of the pamphleteer Robert Payne, writing in 1590, that "the better sort [of the Irish were] very civil and honestly given," deserve due consideration. Spenser was one voice among many. Another voice was that of Robert Devereux, earl of Essex, who famously met Hugh O'Neill in a private encounter.

Without denying the significance of the Spenserian viewpoint it can be argued that the real revolutionary years did not begin until the accession of James VI to the throne of England. Hitherto, the Scots as "the postern gate" had been viewed as a major threat to English power in Ireland. Now, as fellow subjects of James they were allies, a factor which as much as any other helped to undermine the position of O'Neill and O'Donnell. Henceforward Ulster was not a "march" protecting the northern frontier of Ireland, but another province of James I's multikingdom state. Even so it was not James's accession in itself which was decisive as the aftermath of the Gunpowder Plot (1605), a doomed enterprise which might be termed "terrorist" from our own contemporary viewpoint and which led to an understandable reaction.

The main flood of Scottish settlers into Antrim and Down, where their descendants still live, was unrelated to the Flight of the Earls, but was the consequence of the sale of the estates of Con O'Neill. It would hardly have occurred unless James had become king. In itself, however, it was unrelated to the Spenserian agenda in which the Scots had no role to play. As is well known, James as king of Scotland pressed for a "forward" policy in relation to the Highlands and the Borders. We need to know more about this Scottish dimension to Irish history, though major contributions have been made in recent years by such scholars as Jane Ohlmeyer, Jane Dawson, and Allen McInnes.

The informal plantation of Antrim and Down, crucial though it is for the later history of Ulster, has left far less in the way of evidence than the formal plantation of the six counties of Ulster. Understandably, therefore, Canny's main focus is with these. He provides a marvelously clear account of the decision making involved, bringing out the crucial role of the lord deputy, Sir Arthur Chichester in bringing in the Scots. Perhaps Spenser had an influence but it is difficult to avoid the conclusion that Sir John Davies played a much more central role than Spenser. As attorney general and later as speaker in the Irish parliament, Davies was at the center of decision making and one of the revolutionary aspects of his period in office was the introduction of the English common law, something which in itself was not opposed by the old English gentry. The old English of the Pale did not oppose the plantation of the lands of their former enemies, O'Neill and O'Donnell, and in fact felt aggrieved that they were not given a prominent role in its implementation.

In the aftermath of the Flight of the Earls in 1607, Chichester and Davies argued the case of those who had served in the Crown forces (the servitors) as against a policy which pressed for the introduction of private capital (the undertakers). Ultimately a compromise was arrived at in which servitors such as Chichester himself found a role, while a prominent place was also secured for undertakers, chief of which were the London companies. Individual "native proprietors" also were allocated lands. But the overall aim, encouraged by James himself, of creating a "British" presence proved more difficult to achieve. As Canny shows, the English often, perhaps usually, preferred the Irish as tenants to the Scots, on the ground that they were likely to pay their rents. The Scots for their part showed themselves to be remarkably "clannish" and were unenthusiastic about close contact with the English, a tradition which survives today in contemporary Ulster. In areas controlled by the London companies, the Ironmongers successfully created a "British" plantation whereas the Haberdashers ended up with a Scottish one. What Canny makes clear is the contrast between the Ulster plantation and the Munster plantation. English settlers much preferred to go to the rich lands and relatively urban environment of the river valleys in Munster. Ulster, in contrast, always remained the bleaker option.

Some of this story is familiar but Canny brings a freshness to the telling and a citing of detail which carries us with him. He has also made excellent use of the recent work of John McCavitt and Victor Treadwell. The latter in particular has brought into the picture the figure of George Villiers, duke of Buckingham and favorite of James I, England's "gay" monarch. Buckingham's influence with the king introduced a wholly unpredictable element into the process of plantation, and parts of Ireland, hitherto unplanted, became the target of courtiers "on the make." The political scene became more complicated, however, from 1618 when James attempted to bring influence to bear on Spain in favor of his son-in-law, the Elector Palatine. Political events once again began to play a key role in increasing the influence of Irish Catholics. The attitude of Catholic clergy such as Peter Lombard began to shift in favor of the Stuart monarchy. As Canny himself repeatedly shows, "alternative futures" continually emerged.

Thus the simplicity of his Spenserian model requires modification. Not the least important factor affecting Ireland was the economic crisis of 1620 which forced the Crown to summon parliament and to set up a commission to investigate the state of the plantations in 1622. It goes without saying that Ireland was not necessarily the most central concern of James's chief minister, Lionel Cranfield, but as the cause of financial loss it demanded his attention. The records of the 1622 commission uncovered by Victor Treadwell are thus an important new source hitherto ignored by historians.

Treadwell shows that Buckingham erected a vast system of patronage in Ireland, using the policy of plantation for his own benefit and those of his clients. The 1622 commission backed by Cranfield uncovered abuses which showed the extent to which planters preferred to draw rents from Irish tenants rather than expend their own capital in attracting Protestant English or Scottish tenants as specified in their plantation articles. The policy of continued plantation seemed in jeopardy, but the fall of Cranfield in 1624 strengthened the position of the established planter interest brought about by Buckingham. Canny shows how Kilkenny and Tipperary, the territories associated with the earl of Ormond, became a prime target for planters such as Sir William Parsons. The position of the "old English" was now in jeopardy and it was not surprising that they should press for reassurance from the Crown. The outbreak of war with France and Spain strengthened their hand and they were able to bring the Crown to consider the remedy of their grievances in the document known as "The Graces" in return for the grant of subsidies. Once again an alternative future emerged. Canny shows us how the president of Connacht tried to keep the danger of plantation at arm's length by referring to the threat posed by Connacht men, an "active people [who] in numbers of idle swordmen [were] the worst and most dangerous in Ireland."

The appointment of a new lord deputy Thomas Wentworth in 1633 marked, in Canny's view, a return to the full-blooded policy of plantation drawing upon the records of the 1622 commission for factual guidance. The theme of "conquest" was aired once more, though linking Wentworth with Sir John Davies rather than Spenser. A new factor was the political alliance of Wentworth with William Laud, archbishop of Canterbury. Laud was no Puritan. On the contrary he was determined to root out Puritanism which he regarded as a main cause of political unrest. Thus Wentworth's plantation policy, though having religious implications, had a different tone from that of his predecessors. There was no room, for example, for the presence of Scots in a planned plantation of Connacht. Why Wentworth was appointed in the first place still requires explanation but Canny does provide a fresh view of his deputyship which stresses the anxieties which the policy of plantation aroused among the hitherto loyal "old English." Another key factor in creating unrest was the impact of the Court of Wards and Liveries, a financial instrument in principle but one which, by imposing the oath of supremacy upon those taking "livery" of their lands, aroused fear among the Catholic gentry. Canny's view of Wentworth's deputyship brings a fresh viewpoint which invites further investigation of this key episode.

So far in his book, Canny's approach has been "top down" in its emphasis. In his later chapters, however, his perspective shifts and the reader is provided with the view from the "bottom up," in the sense that we now are made aware of the responses of those who saw themselves as victims of plantation policy. It is here that Canny's knowledge of the Irish language comes into play, providing a marked contrast with the monolingual approach of most earlier historians of the period. Canny invites us to analyse the reaction of the Irish community to the policy of the plantations. But who were "the Irish"? In answering this question Canny makes a distinction between those who remained in Ireland and those who were forced to leave for the European continent, in particular the Spanish Netherlands. It is among the latter that Canny finds the greatest emotional involvement with the crisis of "the Irish nation." For many of these exiles, among them Florence Conry (Flaithrí Ó Maol Chonaire) and Geoffrey Keating (Seathrún Céitinn), their Catholic faith was the main symbol of their Irish nationhood, overriding historical distinctions between "Gael" and "old English." Even the common experience of exile did not always bring unity, as the bitter divisions of the 1650s were to demonstrate. Within Ireland itself the position was even more complicated. Canny shows, for example, how some Gaelic poets were pro-English even to the extent of imitating the verse of Sir John Davies who was an unusual combination of poet and attorney general. Another complication was that in some areas the introduction of commercial criteria into what had been a largely feudal society benefited those who had hitherto been outside the golden circle of the established families. As Canny shows, satirical references to the social mobility of "churls" indicate that profound changes were taking place.

But perhaps Canny's main achievement in his book is his analysis of the rising of 1641. His main source for this are the Depositions which have remained largely unexamined for over three centuries in Trinity College, Dublin. Historians have regarded the accounts of those who were dispossessed in the rising as so emotionally biased as to be unusable. Canny, however, shows that by reading "between the lines" and asking the "right" questions it is possible to construct a convincing picture of the reactions of those involved. Using this evidence he suggests, for example, that there were significant differences between the various provinces, with Ulster understandably the most involved and Munster the least. He also shows convincingly how protoindustrial developments such as the ironworks at Castlecoote or Castlecomer, key centers of plantation, became prime targets for the insurgents. Not least, Canny draws parallels with similar happenings in Europe, most notably the Massacre of St. Bartholomew's Day and other tragic episodes in the French wars of religion. Here he is able to draw upon the approaches of French historians of those episodes in making a distinction between those insurgents who attacked their victims physically and those, mainly the priests, who were largely interested in the destruction of objects such as Bibles. Canny makes clear that if we are to consider the reaction of "the Irish" to plantation policy, the rising of 1641 must be our primary concern. It is his considerable achievement, I believe, to bring "1641" out of the distortions of propaganda and into the (relatively) detached environment of history. Even so, there is more to do, not least to investigate what contemporary Catholic reaction was to those events. "1641," of course, had an immense and long-lasting effect upon Protestant attitudes to the Catholic Irish both in England and Scotland. Canny suggests, however, that it was not a long-considered plot but the result of short-term thinking.

Nicholas Canny's book is a magnificent achievement which deserves widespread recognition. It represents the culmination of over three decades of scholarly endeavor during which he has constantly reworked his chosen theme of colonization. As a graduate student he benefited greatly from a thorough grounding in colonial history at the University of Pennsylvania. He also had the advantage of knowing Irish well and he has clearly put this to good use. David Quinn and G. Hayes McCoy were among his predecessors in this particular field but it is no disparagement of their work to say that this book marks a new departure. This work will no doubt become the classical statement of the colonial interpretation of Irish history. It is also an outstanding contribution to "Three Kingdoms" history, drawing as it does on Canny's research into the interaction of all three. He also demonstrates clearly how decisions taken almost casually at court could determine the future of the inhabitants of this island.

But, to return to his primary argument, was Ireland a colony tout court? Thanks to the work of such scholars as Edward Said and Stephen Greenblatt, such an interpretation today may be seen to be in the ascendant. It provides the central thrust of much work in Irish studies, following the lead of Field Day and such critics as Seamus Deane. In politics colonization also serves as a basic theme of Sinn Fein rhetoric. Thus in December 2001 Gerry Adams addressed an audience in Cuba:

> The Irish people, like the peoples of Latin America, [have] been subject to colonisation which has left and continues to leave an indelible mark on our society. We have suffered the expropriation of our resources, the exploitation of our labour, division and conflict among our people, and the attempted eradication of our cultures and traditions.

In stressing the importance of colonization Nicholas Canny's work thus forms part of a wider picture. Indeed, it may well have been the influence Edward Said exercised indirectly through the work of such younger scholars as Andrew Hadfield and Willy Maley which led him to highlight Edmund Spenser, whose *View of the State of Ireland* is a key text for anticolonialist critics (Said, *Culture and Imperialism*, p. 5). I for one do not wish to deny the importance of this "colonial" approach. Indeed in my book *Strafford in Ireland*, (1959), the epigraph is taken from Joseph Conrad's *Heart of Darkness*:

> The conquest of the earth which mostly means the taking it away from those who have a different complexion or slightly flatter nose than ourselves is not a pretty thing when you look into it too much.

This said, however, other aspects of Irish history require mention. There is a strong case, I believe, for conceptualizing events in Ireland during this period as a chapter in the Europeanwide "wars of religion." The concept "Early Modern Ireland" which the editors applied to volume III of *A New History of Ireland* is surely much too anodyne. The title "The Irish Wars of Religion" would have drawn attention to the way in which this relatively remote country was drawn into the mainstream of European history. In the mid-sixteenth century, as the work of Kenneth Nicholls has shown, the loyalties of most Irish were "clan" based. In 1554, for example, the earl of Kildare levied a fine of 340 cows upon the MacCoghlans. The call of "Desmond Abu" was the rallying cry for the followers of the earls of Desmond. Fifty years later religious issues were central. Hugh O'Neill attempted to rally Ireland against the Crown in the cause of religion. In England itself and among Crown supporters in Ireland, religion—often in the form of "Puritanism"—was a powerful force. The climax came in 1641 with an event, the rising of 1641, which Canny himself, as we have seen, compares with the massacre of St. Bartholomew's Day. The arrival of Archbishop Rinucinni in Ireland in 1645 reinforced this religious dimension, which was to be confirmed in Cromwell's campaigns.

Religion was thus clearly a key issue. Indeed, Nicholas Canny himself repeatedly refers to the religious aspect as a motive force behind plantations, even in the case of Thomas Wentworth. However, it would be unfortunate if we were compelled by historians to choose between either colonization or religion as the main feature of Irish history in these years. If we stress colonization we are led to seek parallels with the English colonies in the New World. In contrast, an emphasis upon religion draws us in the direction of the Europe of the Reformation and Counter-Reformation, and highlighting events such as the massacre of the Spanish garrison at Smerwick in 1584 and the aftermath of the 1641 rising against a European background. We need to keep both interpretations in view if we are to avoid distortion.

It is also worth reminding ourselves that the involvement of his daughter and son-in-law in Bohemia preoccupied James I in his later years. The defeat of the Czech nobility at the battle of the White Mountain in 1620 was followed by atrocities which parallel those of Cromwell in Ireland thirty years later. In Prague, six months after the battle, over twenty Czech leaders were executed in the Old Town Square. The rector of Prague University was treated with great cruelty and his tongue was cut out and nailed to the block before he was beheaded. Three-quarters of the kingdom, Derek Sayers tells us, changed hands in the 1620s, Church and Crown estates excepted. In 1624 Catholicism was proclaimed the only permitted religion. As a consequence, a fifth of the nobility and almost a quarter of the burghers left the country. It is difficult to avoid the parallel with Ireland.

In history, as in literature, we need to avoid adopting single-minded monocausal interpretations. At moments Nicholas Canny seems to be arguing for the view that there was a simple progression of plantation policy from Spenser via Strafford to Cromwell. At other times he reminds his readers of the paradoxes of the Irish situation. There is thus a rich underlying complexity about Canny's book, like Irish history itself. He deserves widespread recognition for his achievement.

Chapter Eighteen

Visions and Revisions
Views of Irish History

(2001)

This is a fuller version of an after-dinner speech given at the conference of "Irish Historians in Britain" held at the University of Sussex on 14–16 April 2000. Hugh Kearney taught at U.C.D. and at Sussex in the 1950s and 1960s.

Our conference, I note, is held under the rubric of "Irish Historians in Britain." On looking at the program, however, I note that several speakers include a literary dimension to their talks. Clearly we are interpreting Irish history in an interdisciplinary spirit appropriate to Sussex, my alma mater (or one of them). In the year 2000, such an approach has become almost unavoidable. Literary critics, such as Declan Kiberd, Seamus Deane, and Terry Eagleton see "Irish History" as very much their turf and are more than willing to comment upon the misconceptions of historians. In my view we should welcome such commentaries in the hope that we will learn from them. In my own university career I have welcomed opportunities to work with literary critics in running joint seminars, including one with Denis Donoghue in 1961.

When I first came to University College, Dublin, in 1950, Irish historians took as their model the value-free "scientific" approach of the Institute of Historical Research in London and hence kept literature at arms' length. Robin Dudley Edwards and Theo Moody, both graduates of the Institute, founded *Irish Historical Studies* in 1938 with this aim in mind. Once praised as the founders of modern Irish historiography, they have since come under criticism for constructing a bloodless model for Irish history lacking any tragic sense. In assessing their achievement, however, it is necessary to contextualize the intellectual environment in which they found themselves. They saw their role as creating conditions in which a relatively detached Irish history, acceptable north and south of the border, might be produced. In the south, the Catholic Church was a powerful force. University College, Dublin, though in principle a secular institution, had a clerical presence in certain key departments such as ethics, politics, philosophy, and psychology, where appointments were made with the advice of John Charles McQuaid, archbishop of Dublin. Clerical students from the diocesan seminary at Clontarf and the seminary of the Holy Ghost Fathers at Kimmage, together with the nuns drawn from several religious orders, formed a conspicuous section of the student body. Apart from *The Bell* there was no secular publication other than *Irish Historical Studies*. Thus, in my view, Edwards and Moody did remarkably well to maintain what they saw as a critical approach to an entrenched establishment view. Thus, under their auspices Fr. Paul Walshe produced a reassessment of Luaigh O Clerigh's *Life of Hugh Roe O'Donnell*. Three decades later this would have been termed "revisionist."

Nor were they entirely without thoughts about the historian's craft. At the Irish Conference of Historians in 1955 Michael Oakeshott, at that time external examiner to the N.U.I., read a paper entitled "The Activity of being a Historian," in which he argued the case for studying the past for its own sake without consideration of its contemporary, "practical" implications. In language which seems today extraordinarily "sexist," he declared that the world in general wishes only to learn from the past:

> It deals with the past as with a man expecting it to talk sense and to have something apposite to say. But for "the historian" for whom the past is dead and irreproachable the past is feminine. He loves it as a mistress of whom he never tires and whom he never expects to talk sense.

(At this point Fr. John Ryan S.J., professor of early Irish history, walked out.) Oakeshott's words were somewhat oracular, but Moody and Edwards may well have felt that he sympathized with the aims of *Irish Historical Studies*.

The dangers of a "practical" approach to history was all too clear to them. What the political establishment viewed as the role of history was set out in *Notes for Teachers: History*, issued in 1933 by Tom Derrig, minister for education in the newly arrived De Valera government. Teachers were warned that "Irish history has been much distorted by those who wrote from the enemy's standpoint." In a seminal passage the *Notes* stated:

> The history of Ireland is the history of the various peoples who inhabited Ireland ever since the first advent of men to our shores, but it is more particularly the study of the *Gaelic race and Gaelic civilisation* and of the resistance of that race and civilisation for a thousand years to foreign domination, whether Norse, Norman or English. *The Irish language* was perhaps the most powerful of all the influence in preserving national continuity and for this, if for no other reason, it is most fitting that it should be the language used in our schools to teach our history. (Emphasis added.)

Such advice was offered to teachers in the national (primary) schools. Secondary schools run by various religious orders followed their own traditions, but the Christian brothers offered an approach to Irish history close to that of *Notes for Teachers*. In such quarters we are far from the "dear, dead past" of Oakeshott's paper. At Synge Street and elsewhere history was very much alive.

I spent twelve generally happy years within the History Department at University College, Dublin, and was in fact reluctant to leave when in 1962 I was offered a post at the newly established University of Sussex. In Dublin I had taught mainly British history. At Sussex I found myself involved in a new interdisciplinary environment. Courses in "History and literature" were encouraged and I eventually suggested a course entitled "Politics and Literature in the Age of Yeats and Joyce" to be taught by myself and Matthew Hodgart, a literary critic and an expert on Joyce (among much else). By the standards of 2000 we were no doubt very unsophisticated. Our method was to choose a short story such as "Ivy Day in the Committee Room" or "The Dead" and discuss it from our own particular angle, literary or historical. As a historian I learned from Hodgart what a critic might look for in a text. Hodgart himself stated that the course had taught him that events such as the Fall of Parnell had actually occurred with real consequences. Our other readings were taken from Yeats, Somerville, and Ross, George Moore, Synge, and O'Casey. We also invited visiting speakers, among them F. S. L. Lyons from the nearby University of Kent, Leon O Broin, Kenneth Connell, Rosemary Harris, Theo Moody, and a youthful Joe Lee who startled us with his revisionist views on Irish conditions in the 1880s. Leon O Broin's fine study *Dublin Castle and the Rising of 1916* put forward the vision of an alternative Home Rule future. Looking back it is salutary to realize that the only general book available to us was Tim Pat Coogan's *Ireland since the Rising* (1966). Since then there has been an extraordinary efflorescence of Irish historiography and literary criticism on both sides of the Atlantic.

At Sussex Hodgart and myself seemed to be dealing with what Oakeshott calls a "dead" past, although for Marxists on the faculty the past was very much alive. (The anniversary of Peterloo was celebrated in 1969, for example). This was the heyday of the brilliant Marxist trio, Christopher Hill, Eric Hobsbawm, and Edward Thompson. Literary critics such as Arnold Kettle were also attempting to promote a Marxist approach to literature. So far as Ireland was concerned, however, there was a general feeling that North and South were moving toward mutual accommodation and tolerance. The meetings of Terence O'Neill and Sean Lemass promised better things. The blowing up of Nelson's Pillar in 1966 was seen as an empty gesture by a few hotheads rather than a portent for the future. In 1968, however, the situation changed radically. Student rioting exploded in Paris. At Sussex, as elsewhere, students staged demonstrations and occupied administrative buildings. In Northern Ireland a civil rights movement raised political expectations, which were dashed by the strong-arm tactics of William Craig, minister of home affairs at Stormont. In France and England the unrest soon blew over. In Northern Ireland, however, the crisis expanded ever further. British troops arrived in August 1969. In August 1971 internment without trial was introduced. On 30 January 1972 thirteen men "apparently armed" were shot dead and seventeen wounded by British paratroopers. On 24 March 1972 Stormont was suspended and a few days later Direct Rule was introduced. Nearly thirty years later, despite several attempts to introduce devolved government, the situation remains unresolved. It was a future quite unforeseen in the 1960s. In the year 2000 "The Great Divide" between North and South seems even more marked than ever. Northern Ireland has moved to a sharper sense of religious and ethnic awareness, while in the South there has been a shift away from Catholic nationalism toward a more secular class-based society.

So far as historians are concerned small-scale revision of nationalist orthodoxy had long been the order of the day. In 1957, however, the publication of *The Great Famine* edited by Edwards and Williams, professors at U.C.D., marked what was seen by many as a major step forward in critical historical analysis of a major episode, perhaps the crucial episode, in modern Irish history. In the 1960s historians began to look at the Rising of 1916 in a more critical vein. A reaction against the orthodoxy of *Notes for Teachers* was well under way, assisted by a shift to social history under the influence of the French *Annales* school. However, after the outbreak of violence in Northern Ireland, nationalism once more emerged as a powerful force, particularly among Northern Catholics. The result has been to sharpen the tensions between revisionist and traditionalist approaches to Irish history. In particular *The Great Famine* came in for severe criticism.

Professor Roy Foster's masterly survey *Modern Ireland 1600–1972* (1988) became and remained a battleground. In it he spoke out against the certainties of the nationalist story, arguing that Irish history was very far from being "a linear narrative" or "an apostolic succession." In making his argument Foster could point to the support of such historians as Oliver McDonagh and Michael Laffan. Perhaps his chief inspiration, however, was his mentor F. S. Lyons, provost of Trinity. Lyons, a Northerner by background, had been shattered by the collapse of his liberal expectations for Northern Ireland. His response was to call for "a clearer view of our history and a vision for the future which stressed the importance of cultural unity and cultural diversity." Drawing upon the liberal Presbyterian tradition, Lyons seemed to be calling for a "civic identity" for Ireland. Overall there seems little doubt that the Troubles in the North influenced the direction taken by him in his book *Culture and Anarchy* (1979).

The revisionist response to "the Troubles," however, did not go unchallenged. In particular it came under criticism at the hands of Desmond Fennell, an able and prolific journalist, and of Brendan Bradshaw, a distinguished Cambridge historian. The most formidable attack, however, came from the North in the writings of the Derry-born literary critic Seamus Deane, in particular his contribution to *Revisiting the Rising* (1991), his introduction to the three-volume anthology of Irish literature *The Field Day Anthology* (Derry 1991), for which he was the general editor, and in his Clarendon lectures at Oxford, published as *Strange Country* (1997).

For Deane the story of Ireland is relatively simple, since its history (and literature) reflect a basic division between colonists and colonized. The task of historians and literary critics is to illustrate how profoundly Irish history and literature have been influenced by this fact. He believes that all writing is "profoundly political." He has also derived a good deal of inspiration from the work of Edward Said, whose *Culture and Imperialism* was published in 1993. The cultural critic Hayden White, for whom history is a form of rhetoric, has also influenced Deane. In *Strange Country* he dismissed the work of both Lyons and Foster, declaring "the rhetoric of revisionism obviously derives from the rhetoric of colonialism and imperialism."

In my view it would be unfortunate if Irish history became polarized between the competing paradigms of Foster and Deane. Both represent two possible interpretations of Irish history. Both are attempting, in Edward Thompson's words, to rescue certain groups from "the condescension of posterity." As a Southern Protestant of Trinity College background, Foster is understandably sympathetic to the Anglo-Irish, now a submerged community in the South, though this does not prevent him from being alert to the value of Gaelic poetry. He is critical of Patrick Pearse, but he is not alone in this. In contrast, Deane comes from a Derry background and must surely feel that Foster does not appreciate fully the colonial-style situation in which Catholics in Northern Ireland found themselves for fifty years and more after 1920.

How far Irish history should be interpreted in colonial terms is an issue in its own right irrespective of Seamus Deane's personal experiences. It is difficult to deny the colonial aspect of Irish history.[1] The work of such prominent Irish historians as David Quinn and Nicholas Canny has provided clear evidence for the validity of a colonial approach.[2] Literary critics such as David Lloyd, Edward Said, Declan Kiberd, and Seamus Deane himself have argued for the centrality of Ireland's colonial and postcolonial experience in making sense of Irish history and literature. The contribution of such critics would have been welcome in the Sussex of the 1960s. To interpret all Irish history and literature solely in terms of a colonial or postcolonial paradigm, however, is to run the danger of reductionism. This was the charge which Marxist critics of the 1930s and later laid themselves open to. Placing the work of, say, Joyce in a colonial context undoubtedly reveals neglected aspects of his work, but to see Joyce solely as a postcolonial writer is to reduce the multidimensional character of his art. It also runs the danger of ignoring the literary qualities of such stories as "The Dead," leaving the critic unable to explain why this story is superior as a work of art to earlier stories in *The Dubliners*. Above all, such critics may become predictable in their responses, as we have seen, for example, in approaches to *The Tempest* or to *Mansfield Park*.

Postcolonial Ireland is not the only Ireland. There are indeed many Irelands. We may think, for example, of Frank McCourt's Limerick and Roddy Doyle's Dublin, together with Brian Friel's Ballybeg and Glen Patterson's Belfast. Another Ireland is that of the London-born John Walshe, whose *The Falling Angels* (1999) provides a marvelous evocation of the mind of a boy born to Irish parents in London and henceforth caught between two worlds. Seamus Deane himself has shown in a recent memoir how different his urban Derry was from the rural Co. Derry of Seamus Heaney. In this memoir he also shows his awareness of the Protestant working-class Ireland of East Belfast:

> I would cross its most notorious street, Sandy Row, and hear Saturday night Evangelists screaming through loudspeakers about Popery and repentance, and pass by the clamorous shops and smell the sweet aromas of the Erinmore tobacco factory, above the railway bridge, and then return to my rented room in a nearby Catholic neighborhood, to read Milton and Dickens—whose seventeenth and nineteenth-century works were suddenly coexistent with my own.

In a striking sentence which moves beyond a merely colonized perspective, he declares:

> I knew the bitterness of Protestantism and its philistine pride but for the first time I began to sense its magnificence.[3]

What of the future? The tension between Foster's "revisionist" view of Irish history and Seamus Deane's approach will no doubt remain, reflecting the contrast between a postnationalist South and a North still bitterly divided on ethnic and religious grounds. What is more disturbing is the prospect that certain groups within the American Diaspora should back a politically based historical orthodoxy. In the State of New York, for example, the view that the Great Famine was a form of genocide has received official recognition. To my mind there are clear parallels between these kind of pressures and those of fundamentalist groups within the Jewish Diaspora or in the American Bible Belt. A return to the world of *Notes for Teachers*, in which a particular interpretation of history or science receives official backing and henceforward is beyond criticism, seems possible. It may well be that something tantamount to genocide occurred during the Famine perhaps in certain forces or at particular times, but critical history implies that such a conclusion should be based upon testable hypotheses, not certainties based upon dogma. To their credit, historians such as James Donnelly are standing out against attempts to turn the writings of John Mitchel into Holy Writ, but clearly the future of a postnationalist, pluralist approach to Irish history is not without problems. However, the recent publication of Senia Paseta's recent book, *Before the Revolution: Nationalism, Social Change and Ireland's Catholic Ente 1879–1922* (Cork 1999), is a reminder of the rewards which still await those who attempt to break away from the constraints of an overfamiliar story. Her book foreshadows a shift to a more class-based history of a kind unfamiliar to nationalist historians.

NOTES

1. I write as a historian who quoted Conrad's *Heart of Darkness* as the epigraph to *Strafford in Ireland* (1959).

2. Perhaps this is the place to mention that Raphael Samuel described me as a postcolonial historian in *History Workshop* (1998). On postcolonialism, see also Colin Graham's excellent article, "Liminal Spaces": "Post-Colonial Theories and Irish Culture," in the *Irish Review*, No. 16 Autumn/Winter 1994.

3. *The New Yorker*, 14 April 2000.

Index

About the Author

Hugh F. Kearney was Amundson Professor of History at the University of Pittsburgh from 1975 to 1999. Born in Liverpool and educated at the University of Cambridge, he has taught at universities in Dublin and Sussex and at Edinburgh, where he was Richard Pares Professor of History from 1970 to 1975. He is the author of *Strafford in Ireland, 1633–1641, Scholars and Gentlemen: Universities and Society, 1500–1700, Science and Change, 1500–1700,* and *The British Isles: A History of Four Nations.*